Lecture Notes in Computer Science 16335

Founding Editors

Gerhard Goos
Juris Hartmanis

Editorial Board Members

Elisa Bertino, *Purdue University, West Lafayette, IN, USA*
Wen Gao, *Peking University, Beijing, China*
Bernhard Steffen, *TU Dortmund University, Dortmund, Germany*
Moti Yung, *Columbia University, New York, NY, USA*

The series Lecture Notes in Computer Science (LNCS), including its subseries Lecture Notes in Artificial Intelligence (LNAI) and Lecture Notes in Bioinformatics (LNBI), has established itself as a medium for the publication of new developments in computer science and information technology research, teaching, and education.

LNCS enjoys close cooperation with the computer science R & D community, the series counts many renowned academics among its volume editors and paper authors, and collaborates with prestigious societies. Its mission is to serve this international community by providing an invaluable service, mainly focused on the publication of conference and workshop proceedings and postproceedings. LNCS commenced publication in 1973.

Margherita Antona · Constantine Stephanidis
Editors

HCI International 2025 – Late Breaking Papers

27th International Conference on
Human-Computer Interaction, HCII 2025
Gothenburg, Sweden, June 22–27, 2025
Proceedings, Part V

 Springer

Editors
Margherita Antona
Foundation for Research and Technology -
Hellas (FORTH)
Heraklion, Crete, Greece

Constantine Stephanidis
University of Crete, and Foundation for
Research and Technology - Hellas (FORTH)
Heraklion, Crete, Greece

ISSN 0302-9743
ISSN 1611-3349 (electronic)
Lecture Notes in Computer Science
ISBN 978-3-032-12780-8
ISBN 978-3-032-12781-5 (eBook)
https://doi.org/10.1007/978-3-032-12781-5

© The Editor(s) (if applicable) and The Author(s), under exclusive license
to Springer Nature Switzerland AG 2026

This work is subject to copyright. All rights are solely and exclusively licensed by the Publisher, whether the whole or part of the material is concerned, specifically the rights of translation, reprinting, reuse of illustrations, recitation, broadcasting, reproduction on microfilms or in any other physical way, and transmission or information storage and retrieval, electronic adaptation, computer software, or by similar or dissimilar methodology now known or hereafter developed.
The use of general descriptive names, registered names, trademarks, service marks, etc. in this publication does not imply, even in the absence of a specific statement, that such names are exempt from the relevant protective laws and regulations and therefore free for general use.
The publisher, the authors and the editors are safe to assume that the advice and information in this book are believed to be true and accurate at the date of publication. Neither the publisher nor the authors or the editors give a warranty, expressed or implied, with respect to the material contained herein or for any errors or omissions that may have been made. The publisher remains neutral with regard to jurisdictional claims in published maps and institutional affiliations.

This Springer imprint is published by the registered company Springer Nature Switzerland AG
The registered company address is: Gewerbestrasse 11, 6330 Cham, Switzerland

If disposing of this product, please recycle the paper.

Foreword

The HCI International (HCII) conference was founded in 1984 by Gavriel Salvendy (Purdue University, USA, Tsinghua University, P.R. China, and University of Central Florida, USA) and the first event of the series, "1st USA-Japan Conference on Human-Computer Interaction", was held in Honolulu, Hawaii, USA, on 18–20 August. Since then, HCI International has been held jointly with several Thematic Areas and Affiliated Conferences, with each one under the auspices of a distinguished international Program Board and under one management and one registration. Twenty-seven HCI International Conferences have been organized so far (every two years until 2013, and annually thereafter).

Last year, we celebrated 40 years since the establishment of the HCII conference, which has been a hub for presenting groundbreaking research and novel ideas and collaboration for people from all over the world. Over the years, this conference has served as a platform for scholars, researchers, industry experts, and students to exchange ideas, connect, and address challenges in the ever-evolving HCI field. The conference has evolved itself, adapting to new technologies and emerging trends, while staying committed to its core mission of advancing knowledge and driving change.

The 27th International Conference on Human-Computer Interaction, HCI International 2025 (HCII 2025), was held as an 'on-site' conference at the Gothia Towers Hotel and Swedish Exhibition & Congress Centre, in Gothenburg, Sweden, on June 22–27, 2025, with the additional option for 'on-line' participation. It incorporated the 21 thematic areas and affiliated conferences listed below.

A total of 7972 individuals from academia, research institutes, industry, and government agencies from 92 countries submitted contributions. 1430 papers and 355 posters (as short research papers) were included in the volumes of the proceedings published just before the start of the conference. Additionally, 439 papers and 104 posters were included in the volumes of the proceedings published after the conference, as "Late Breaking Work". The contributions thoroughly cover the entire field of human-computer interaction, highlight the evolving role of computers in diverse contexts, and demonstrate how HCI research is shaping and improving user experiences across a wide range of domains, influencing technological progress and its effective integration into various sectors. The volumes constituting the full set of the HCII 2025 conference proceedings are listed on the following pages.

I would like to thank the Program Board Chairs and the members of the Program Boards of all thematic areas and affiliated conferences for their contribution towards the high scientific quality and overall success of the HCI International 2025 conference. Their manifold support including paper reviews (via a single-blind review process, with a minimum of two reviews per submission), session organization, and their willingness to act as goodwill ambassadors for the conference is most highly appreciated.

This conference would not have been possible without the continuous and unwavering support and advice of Gavriel Salvendy, founder, General Chair Emeritus, and Scientific Advisor. For his outstanding efforts, I would like to express my sincere appreciation to Abbas Moallem, Communications Chair and Editor of HCI International News.

September 2025   Constantine Stephanidis

HCI International 2025 Thematic Areas and Affiliated Conferences

- HCI: Human-Computer Interaction Thematic Area
- HIMI: Human Interface and the Management of Information Thematic Area
- EPCE: 22nd International Conference on Engineering Psychology and Cognitive Ergonomics
- AC: 19th International Conference on Augmented Cognition
- UAHCI: 19th International Conference on Universal Access in Human-Computer Interaction
- CCD: 17th International Conference on Cross-Cultural Design
- SCSM: 17th International Conference on Social Computing and Social Media
- VAMR: 17th International Conference on Virtual, Augmented and Mixed Reality
- DHM: 16th International Conference on Digital Human Modeling & Applications in Health, Safety, Ergonomics & Risk Management
- DUXU: 14th International Conference on Design, User Experience and Usability
- C&C: 13th International Conference on Culture and Computing
- DAPI: 13th International Conference on Distributed, Ambient and Pervasive Interactions
- HCIBGO: 12th International Conference on HCI in Business, Government and Organizations
- LCT: 12th International Conference on Learning and Collaboration Technologies
- ITAP: 11th International Conference on Human Aspects of IT for the Aged Population
- AIS: 7th International Conference on Adaptive Instructional Systems
- HCI-CPT: 7th International Conference on HCI for Cybersecurity, Privacy and Trust
- HCI-Games: 7th International Conference on HCI in Games
- MobiTAS: 7th International Conference on HCI in Mobility, Transport and Automotive Systems
- AI-HCI: 6th International Conference on Artificial Intelligence in HCI
- MOBILE: 6th International Conference on Human-Centered Design, Operation and Evaluation of Mobile Communications

Conference Proceedings – Full List of Volumes

1. LNCS 15766, Human-Computer Interaction — Part I, edited by Masaaki Kurosu and Ayako Hashizume
2. LNCS 15767, Human-Computer Interaction — Part II, edited by Masaaki Kurosu and Ayako Hashizume
3. LNCS 15768, Human-Computer Interaction — Part III, edited by Masaaki Kurosu and Ayako Hashizume
4. LNCS 15769, Human-Computer Interaction — Part IV, edited by Masaaki Kurosu and Ayako Hashizume
5. LNCS 15770, Human-Computer Interaction — Part V, edited by Masaaki Kurosu and Ayako Hashizume
6. LNCS 15771, Human-Computer Interaction — Part VI, edited by Masaaki Kurosu and Ayako Hashizume
7. LNCS 15772, Human-Computer Interaction — Part VII, edited by Masaaki Kurosu and Ayako Hashizume
8. LNCS 15773, Human Interface and the Management of Information: Part I, edited by Hirohiko Mori and Yumi Asahi
9. LNCS 15774, Human Interface and the Management of Information: Part II, edited by Hirohiko Mori and Yumi Asahi
10. LNCS 15773, Human Interface and the Management of Information: Part III, edited by Hirohiko Mori and Yumi Asahi
11. LNAI 15776, Engineering Psychology and Cognitive Ergonomics: Part I, edited by Don Harris and Wen-Chin Li
12. LNAI 15777, Engineering Psychology and Cognitive Ergonomics: Part II, edited by Don Harris and Wen-Chin Li
13. LNAI 15778, Augmented Cognition, Part I, edited by Dylan D. Schmorrow and Cali M. Fidopiastis
14. LNAI 15779, Augmented Cognition, Part II, edited by Dylan D. Schmorrow and Cali M. Fidopiastis
15. LNCS 15780, Universal Access in Human-Computer Interaction: Part I, edited by Margherita Antona and Constantine Stephanidis
16. LNCS 15781, Universal Access in Human-Computer Interaction: Part II, edited by Margherita Antona and Constantine Stephanidis
17. LNCS 15782, Cross-Cultural Design: Part I, edited by Pei-Luen Patrick Rau
18. LNCS 15783, Cross-Cultural Design: Part II, edited by Pei-Luen Patrick Rau
19. LNCS 15784, Cross-Cultural Design: Part III, edited by Pei-Luen Patrick Rau
20. LNCS 15785, Cross-Cultural Design: Part IV, edited by Pei-Luen Patrick Rau
21. LNCS 15786, Social Computing and Social Media: Part I, edited by Adela Coman and Simona Vasilache

85. CCIS 2772, HCI International 2025 — Late Breaking Posters: Part II, edited by Constantine Stephanidis, Margherita Antona, Stavroula Ntoa, George Margetis and Gavriel Salvendy
86. CCIS 2773, HCI International 2025 — Late Breaking Posters: Part III, edited by Constantine Stephanidis, Margherita Antona, Stavroula Ntoa, George Margetis and Gavriel Salvendy

https://2025.hci.international/proceedings

27th International Conference on Human-Computer Interaction (HCII 2025)

The full list with the Program Board Chairs and the members of the Program Boards of all thematic areas and affiliated conferences of HCII 2025 is available online at:

http://www.hci.international/board-members-2025.php

HCI International 2026 Conference

The 28th International Conference on Human-Computer Interaction, HCI International 2026, will be held jointly with the affiliated conferences at the Montréal Convention Centre (Palais des congrès de Montréal), in Montreal, Canada, 26–31 July 2026. It will cover a broad spectrum of themes related to Human-Computer Interaction, including theoretical issues, methods, tools, processes, and case studies in HCI design, as well as novel interaction techniques, interfaces, and applications. The proceedings will be published by Springer (part of Springer Nature) in a multi-volume set. More information will become available on the conference website: https://2026.hci.international/.

General Chair
Constantine Stephanidis
University of Crete and ICS-FORTH
Heraklion, Crete, Greece
Email: general_chair@2026.hci.international

https://2026.hci.international/

Contents

Accessibility and Innovations in Intelligent Environments

Human-Centered Technologies for Autism and Neurodiverse Populations

Accessibility and Inclusive Interaction Design

Towards Inclusive Data Visualization: Investigating Accessibility in Scientific and Technical Charts

Haifa Alshehri[(⊠)], Stephanie Ludi, and Wajdi Aljedaani

Department of Computer Science, University of North Texas, Denton, USA
`{Haifaalshehri,WajdiAljedaani}@my.unt.edu,`
`Stephanie.Ludi@unt.edu`

Abstract. Scientific and technical charts are widely used in online resources; however, they often present significant accessibility barriers for individuals who are blind or have low vision (BLV). This study examines the challenges and concerns that BLV users encounter when interacting with online scientific and technical charts. Through a qualitative study, we identified several accessibility issues that prevent effective interaction with charts. A key finding is that many screen reader applications are unable to detect or interpret online charts. This indicates that the image was inaccessible without a text description and labels, rendering the screen reader useless. Furthermore, the study's results highlight the need for careful investigation into various types of charts to develop more inclusive accessibility solutions. Additionally, large language models demonstrate significant potential in generating chart descriptions and facilitating interactive conversations with BLV users. Future research will focus on creating adaptive solutions to further enhance chart accessibility.

Keywords: Accessibility · Visualization · Charts · Challenges · Blind · Low Vision

1 Introduction

Modern life is increasingly driven by data, with visual representations such as charts and graphs playing a crucial role in helping people understand complex information. These visualizations reveal patterns and trends that are often hidden in raw data, enabling effective communication and informed decision-making across various domains, including education, healthcare, business, and government [22, 27]. However, these benefits are not equitably shared with visual impairments, especially those who are blind or have low vision (BLV), often face significant barriers to accessing visual content online.

This issue is especially critical in STEM fields, where understanding scientific and technical charts is essential for developing deep subject knowledge. BLV students often require alternative formats such as tactile graphics or auditory descriptions to interpret visual material, but current solutions remain limited and inconsistent [8, 10, 15, 19, 43]. Given that over 314 million people worldwide live with visual impairments, including

© The Author(s), under exclusive license to Springer Nature Switzerland AG 2026

M. Antona and C. Stephanidis (Eds.): HCII 2025, LNCS 16335, pp. 3–17, 2026.
https://doi.org/10.1007/978-3-032-12781-5_1

45 million who are blind [14], improving access to visual data is not a niche concern but a global necessity.

Despite the availability of accessibility standards like WCAG, many digital platforms still fail to support screen reader functionality effectively, especially for graphical content [2–4, 31]. Screen readers alone cannot interpret charts or diagrams without meaningful alternative text or structured descriptions, yet these resources are often missing. Automated image description methods remain unreliable for complex visuals [29, 33], underscoring a pressing need for more robust solutions.

Recently, Large Language Models (LLMs) have emerged as promising tools for generating dynamic, context-aware descriptions of complex visual content [34, 39]. Tools like Be My Eyes, now powered by GPT-4, allow users to receive real-time AI-driven assistance, including video interpretation and chart explanation [9, 35]. These developments raise new opportunities for enhancing accessibility through intelligent, conversational interfaces.

In this study, we define BLV users as individuals with visual impairments who use assistive technologies (e.g., JAWS, NVDA, VoiceOver) to navigate digital environments. We investigate the challenges they face in accessing scientific and technical charts and examine the potential role of AI in improving chart accessibility. In this study, we investigate the following research question:

(RQ) What are the barriers and concerns that blind and low vision individuals currently have with online scientific and technical charts?

This research question (RQ) guides our investigation by examining the barriers and concerns of BLV individuals. We address this question by examining the perspectives of BLV users through a quantitative study that investigates the accessibility issues associated with scientific and technical charts. The contributions of this paper are as follows:

- To explore the challenges faced by BLV individuals when accessing and interpreting scientific and technical charts.
- To identify potential solutions and design considerations that address these challenges, aiming to improve the accessibility of charts for BLV users.

2 Related Work

2.1 Current Technology for Accessibility

There have been numerous studies investigating the accessibility of charts for Blind and Low Vision users. The existing studies have used a variety of techniques including adding alternative text for visualization elements as in [1, 16, 25] and sonification [5, 23, 37, 45] techniques that convert data into sound, pitch, rhythm, and volume to represent different data points. Tactile representations are used to convey information by allowing exploration through touch [17, 28, 32], providing summarization through text [13, 43], and using question-answering systems [26, 43]. Automatic text description generation has been provided using natural language processing techniques [11, 30, 46]. Lastly, advanced large language models (LLMs), such as GPT-4 and Google Gemini, have been utilized to generate automatic text descriptions in a few studies [39]. Choosing one of these methods is a crucial design decision [27].

2.2 Barriers and Accessibility

Previous studies in this area, such as Seo et al. [40], have reported significant challenges when teaching STEM subjects such as data science to BLV students, highlighting difficulties in effectively accessing visualization data tools. Traditional accessibility methods, such as braille and tactile graphics, are often effective alternatives but costly, time-consuming to produce, and challenging to scale for classroom settings. Consequently, Seo et al. have developed an MAIDR library to enhance the accessibility for BLV learners. The MAIDR system provides customization modes (braille, text, and sonification) to BLV learners [41]. Similarly, Joyner et al. [24] have also emphasized the complexity of handling modern data visualizations, noting that advanced visualization types often exceed the capabilities of traditional accessibility techniques. Complementing these observations, Sharif et al. [42] empirically show that screen reader users interacting with online charts are 61% less accurate and require 211% more time than sighted users. Even before task performance begins, one-third of sampled visualizations are entirely undiscovered, and those that are detectable often present only a "blank graphic" role without a semantic structure. Users must navigate linearly, making it difficult to identify overall patterns. The same authors later created the VoxLens accessibility library [43], which reduces interaction time and enhances the accuracy of information extraction. Our study further highlights the challenges faced by individuals with BLV. The participants in our study were already active in the computing field and had substantial experience with computers, software, and mathematics. Despite their expertise, they continue to face significant barriers when interacting with charts. This highlights the importance of designing alternative sensory modalities and exploring large language model (LLM) technology to enhance accessibility [6, 7].

Consistent with Keilers et al. [18], our study confirms that data visualizations remain largely inaccessible, forcing blind and low-vision users to rely on sighted assistance. Participants in both studies expressed a strong desire for independent access and frequently encountered barriers, such as missing alt text and poor structure. Unlike Keilers et al.'s focus on recommendations, our research explicitly identifies the challenges across visualization and asks about the favorite visualization types to make them more accessible and context-specific.

2.3 Accessibility in Chart-Type

Other challenges faced by BLV users, such as the variety of chart types and the complexity of data, have not been sufficiently addressed in existing research. Studies primarily focus on simpler charts, such as bar and line charts with few datasets [24]. N. W. Kim [27] conducted a comprehensive review of data visualization papers from 1999 to 2020, noting that approximately 80% of the 65 examined papers primarily addressed basic chart types, thus limiting the scope of accessibility solutions. Additionally, their findings indicated that advanced visualizations, including statistical maps (in 6 out of 56 studies) and network graphs (in 4 out of 56 studies), were less commonly explored. In our study, we focused on a variety of chart types that have received little attention in previous research, asking participants about their familiarity with specific charts, particularly stacked charts, circuit diagrams, and class diagrams.

3 Methodology

This section presents the methodology of our study, details about participants, the data collection procedure, and an analysis of the data required to answer the research question. We focused on the following research question:

RQ: What are the barriers and concerns that blind and low vision individuals currently have with online scientific and technical charts?

3.1 Data Collection

To address the research question, we conducted an online survey with nine participants who are blind or have low vision (BLV), all of whom were aged 18 or older and enrolled in STEM courses. The survey aimed to explore how frequently BLV users engage with charts and how assistive technologies support their interpretation and understanding of visual data. With approval from the Institutional Review Board (IRB) at the University of North Texas, participants were recruited through online mailing lists targeting BLV students in STEM and IT-related fields. Informed consent was obtained from each participant at the beginning of the survey.

3.2 Design

Visualization studies commonly adopt structured methodologies that involve stages such as pre-surveys, participant screening, training, and post-surveys. Choi et al. [12] analyzed 141 visualization experiments and reported that 29% included pre-surveys and 32% incorporated post-surveys, highlighting the importance of robust data collection practices in generating meaningful insights.

In this study, we began with a pre-survey designed to identify the specific barriers that blind and low-vision (BLV) individuals encounter when interacting with charts. This exploratory phase was intended to inform the design of a follow-up investigation.

The survey focused on the challenges encountered during interactions with charts and graphs. It comprised ten questions: seven multiple-choice items and three open-ended questions designed to elicit detailed, qualitative responses. The instrument was developed using the Qualtrics online platform [36], which offers built-in accessibility features and tools for data collection and analysis. All responses were anonymized to protect participant confidentiality.

3.3 Participants

The survey was distributed using the snowball sampling technique via two targeted email mailing lists: one for students in STEM fields and another for students and practitioners in the IT sector. This method helped preserve participants' privacy while reaching a relevant audience. Participants were informed of the estimated time required to complete the survey. A total of nine individuals who are blind or have low vision participated. Among them, two had low vision and used screen magnification systems, while the remaining seven were blind. Seven participants held academic backgrounds in computer science or information technology, and the others majored in business. One participant brought valuable experience as a computer science instructor for blind students, emphasizing that the ability to create and interpret charts and diagrams is a critical skill in programming and data science education.

4 Study Results

This section presents the study's findings in response to the research question. A survey involving nine participants with blindness or low vision (BLV) was conducted to gather both quantitative and qualitative data through multiple choice and open-ended questions. As illustrated in Fig. 1, the results highlight the primary challenges BLV users face when interacting with online scientific charts.

The most frequently reported issue, identified by 8 out of 9 participants, was the inability of screen readers to provide meaningful information. In many cases, charts lacked text descriptions and proper labeling, rendering them incomprehensible to assistive technologies. As a result, screen readers failed to convey the visual content effectively. The only participant who did not report difficulties attributed their success to their extensive experience as a data science instructor and familiarity with tools designed to create accessible charts.

The second major challenge was the reliance on sighted individuals, such as teachers or colleagues, to verbally describe or explain chart content. This dependence limited participants' autonomy in accessing scientific data. Additional barriers included difficulty distinguishing data points or interpreting unlabeled axes. Even when screen readers could detect the presence of a chart, missing or unclear axis labels often led to confusion.

While tabular data was seen as a more accessible alternative, several participants noted that navigating large tables using a screen reader could be cognitively demanding and time-consuming [42].

The survey also explored the extent to which blind and low-vision (BLV) individuals need to engage with charts in their academic or professional contexts. As illustrated in Fig. 2, eight out of nine participants (89%) reported that interacting with graphical content is necessary for their work or studies. Only one participant indicated that they do not need to access any form of graphics. These findings underscore the critical importance of ensuring chart accessibility, as the majority of BLV users regularly encounter visual data in educational or occupational settings.

Participants were asked to identify the assistive technologies available on their devices. The survey allowed multiple selections to reflect the possibility that participants may use a combination of tools when interpreting charts. Two participants reported frequent use of magnification software, two used tactile displays, and three selected refreshable Braille displays. All participants indicated that a screen reader was an essential and regularly used tool for accessing content.

While most accessibility research has focused on basic chart types such as bar and line charts, relatively few studies have investigated the accessibility of more complex visualizations, including node-link diagrams [45], Venn diagrams [11], heat maps, and box plots [41]. To explore the practical relevance of various chart types, participants in our study were asked to indicate the visualizations they regularly engage with in

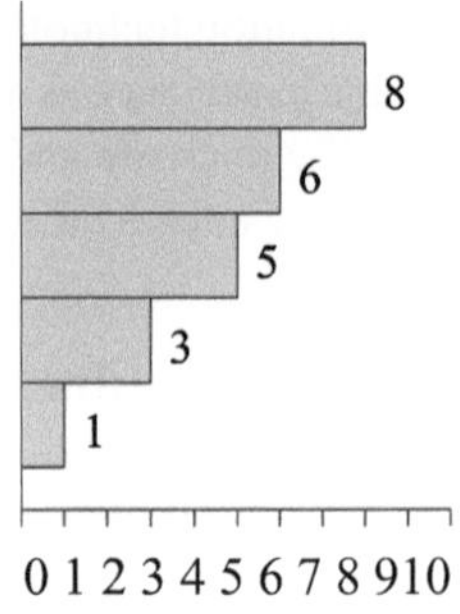

Fig. 1. Top challenges faced by blind and low vision users.

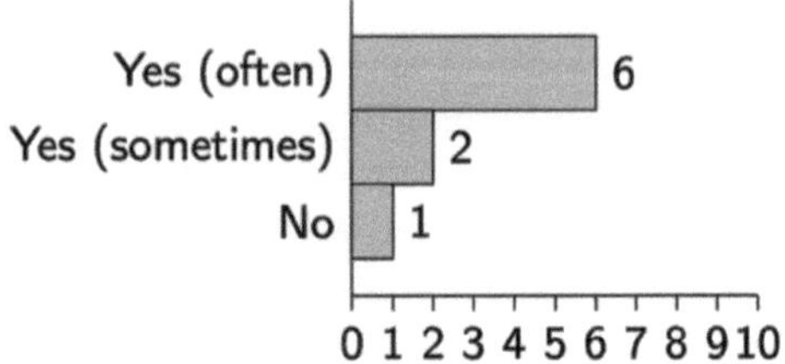

Fig. 2. Do BLV need to interact with charts?

academic, professional, or everyday contexts. The survey included a predefined list of common chart types, along with an open-ended field for specifying additional ones.

As shown in Fig. 3, the most frequently mentioned chart types were bar charts (78%), line charts (78%), pie charts (78%), and stacked charts (66%). Several participants also cited domain-specific diagrams such as circuit diagrams, class diagrams, and flowcharts, particularly those working in fields like software engineering and programming. When asked to identify the chart types most critical to improve for accessibility purposes, participants again highlighted bar charts (78%), line charts (78%), and stacked charts (78%) as the most relevant. Additionally, one expert participant noted other meaningful visualizations, including heat maps, histograms, and box plots.

4.1 Participants Feedback

We conducted a thematic analysis using a structured and iterative process to examine participants' responses to the open-ended survey questions. Initial open coding was used to assign descriptive labels to meaningful segments of text. These codes were then refined and grouped into higher-level categories using axial coding. Through this process, five major themes emerged, reflecting participants' lived experiences and specific needs related to chart accessibility. To ensure authenticity, the analysis remained grounded in the participants' own language and perspectives.

Dependence on Human Assistance A prominent theme was the continued reliance on sighted individuals for interpreting charts, even when assistive technologies were

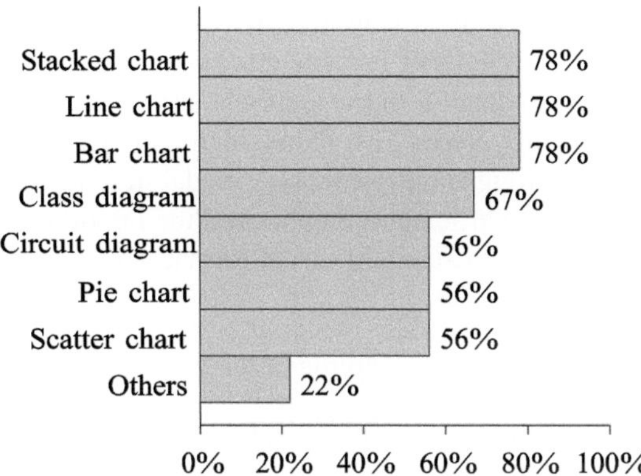

Fig. 3. Accessibility and Chart Types.

available. Many participants expressed frustration with this dependence, highlighting how it limits autonomy and privacy. As P1 shared:

"I dislike having to ask colleagues for descriptions. Some are very good about itsome are clearly annoyed."

Also, P5 noted

"I usually ask for sighted assistance in trying to figure them out, or else use GPT4-powered Be my Eyes on Windows. They could be made more intuitive and accessible."

Lack of Standardization and Navigability Participants identified several accessibility barriers stemming from the lack of standardized practices in presenting and supporting charts across platforms. These included inconsistent or missing alternative text, limited screen reader compatibility, and significant challenges in interpreting complex visualizations, particularly those that rely on spatial relationships, such as scatter plots. Unlike bar or line charts, these chart types require enhanced accessibility mechanisms, including comprehensive alternative text or interactive exploration features, to be usable by blind and low-vision (BLV) users.

The absence of such accommodations often led participants to feel excluded from key content or disengaged from tasks involving data analysis. As P8 explained:

"I generally don't interact with them at all because they're not in Braille with tactile lines on paper, and my screen reader doesn't make them navigable."

Similarly, P9 shared:

"Some types of charts are easy, but others especially scatter plots, can be difficult to interpret the shape."

These insights underscore the urgent need for consistent and standardized design practices, as well as accessible chart formats that support multimodal interaction and promote equitable access to data for individuals who are blind or have low vision.

Multimodal Accessibility Needs This theme highlights participants' strong preference for accessing charts through multiple sensory modalities, including tactile, auditory, and textual formats. Several participants emphasized the importance of alternative representations that extend beyond standard visual formats to support diverse perceptual needs. For example, P2 expressed:

"fully tactile, auditory, and AI description of the graph"

While P4 emphasized the importance of audio representations and screen reader–compatible chart labeling, P8 described a desire for spatial audio feedback combined with keyboard navigation to better understand directionality within charts. These comments collectively reveal a clear demand for multimodal support, enabling users to interpret complex visual data through sensory channels that align with their individual abilities and preferences. This highlights the necessity of designing flexible, inclusive visualization systems that accommodate a range of perceptual strategies beyond sight alone.

Strategies for Engaging with Charts This theme discusses the diverse and often personalized strategies employed by blind and low-vision (BLV) participants to engage with charts in both academic and professional contexts. Participants reported leveraging a range of assistive technologies, including screen readers, magnification tools, and code-based solutions such as LaTeX, SVG, or Excel, to either access or generate visual content.

"Usually, I am looking at charts in research papers. I usually will listen to a paper without reference to the charts. If the charts are necessary to understand, I will bring them up separately using a magnifier and try to interpret them."

Others, for example, P6, emphasized the cognitive benefit of visualizations, stating:

"Charts can help me understand material better."

In more active roles, participants such as P4 described chart production workflows:

"I need to make charts for presentation or in the case of copying them from other sources I need to get description of the content of the chart. I am using screen reader capabilities, Excel, sometimes SVG code to make a picture or LaTeX to create simple picture."

These responses highlight not only the challenges participants face but also their notable technological adaptability. Many exhibits a high degree of digital literacy, actively experimenting with and integrating multiple tools and strategies to navigate accessibility barriers and meet their informational needs.

Integration of AI and Assistive Tools Participants reported using a variety of AI-powered and assistive technologies to enhance their understanding of visual data. Tools such as JAWS Picture Smart AI [21], SAS Graphics Accelerator [38], Be My Eyes [9], and ChatGPT [35] were mentioned as instrumental in interpreting charts. These tools offer descriptive outputs in multiple formats. JAWS provides both concise and detailed textual descriptions, while SAS Graphics Accelerator enables access through text, tables, and sonification. The integration of AI into assistive technologies reflects the active engagement of BLV users with emerging solutions to improve accessibility.

In addition to leveraging existing tools, participants proposed forward-thinking ideas for advancing chart accessibility. For example, P4 recommended the creation or adaptation of a structured language specifically designed to describe charts. This language would utilize a standardized vocabulary to convey key elements, such as axes, data points, patterns, and trends, thereby facilitating the automatic generation of accessible charts. These responses demonstrate participants' strong technical literacy and proactive stance, not only in utilizing current tools but also in envisioning future solutions to promote inclusive data access.

5   Study Discussion

This section presents the key findings and implications of our study. We highlight four primary takeaways:

5.1   Takeaway 1: Accessibility Improvements Are Critically Needed

Charts play an essential role in education, professional settings, and everyday decision-making. However, our findings reveal that accessibility remains a significant barrier, often rendering crucial information inaccessible to individuals with blindness or low vision (BLV). This disconnect limits their ability to engage fully with scientific and technical content, hindering their participation in academic and professional environments.

To address this issue, we emphasize the need to raise awareness about accessibility among designers, developers, educators, content creators, and researchers. Increasing awareness can drive the adoption of accessible practices such as consistently including alternative text for charts and images. Effective alternative text should concisely describe chart content in a way that supports meaningful interpretation [30]. In addition to alt text, inclusive design can incorporate other modalities such as tactile graphics, large-print visuals, sonification, 3D-printed models, and haptic feedback, all of which offer enhanced pathways for access.

5.2   Takeaway 2: Leverage LLMs for Chart Descriptions—with Caution

Our study highlights the growing use of large language models (LLMs) to support chart interpretation among BLV users. Participants (e.g., P1, P2, P3, and P5) reported using tools like ChatGPT and the AI-powered Be My Eyes app to assist with chart descriptions. These tools offer the potential to reduce reliance on manually authored alt text and can help scale accessibility efforts across platforms.

However, critical concerns persist. LLMs may misinterpret visual data, omit important details, or simplify complex relationships in ways that reduce the accuracy or utility of the description. To ensure reliable accessibility, further research is needed to systematically evaluate LLM-generated descriptions across different chart types and complexity levels. Comparing LLM outputs with traditional methods will be essential for advancing these tools into more trustworthy and effective solutions for BLV users [39].

5.3   Takeaway 3: Support for Multi-Sensory Modalities is Essential

Our findings reveal that most BLV participants prefer interacting with charts through multiple sensory modalities. Tools that combine auditory, tactile, and textual formats were viewed more favorably than those relying on a single modality. For example, some systems generated charts with both audio feedback and tactile representations, while others provided descriptive text augmented by sonification. These multimodal approaches provide users with flexibility in accessing complex data and support a more comprehensive understanding across diverse perceptual preferences.

5.4   Takeaway 4: Accessibility Must Extend Across Diverse Chart Types

A key challenge identified in this study is the lack of universal standards for accessible chart design, which complicates efforts to generalize best practices across visualization types. While prior research has focused primarily on basic chart forms, such as bar and line charts, our findings emphasize the need to broaden accessibility efforts to include more complex visualizations.

For instance, stacked charts present significantly greater accessibility challenges compared to standard bar charts, due to their segmented and cumulative data representations. Designing accessible versions of such charts—whether tactile, auditory, or sonified—requires thoughtful consideration of how to convey both individual segments and their relationships. Future research must expand to encompass a broader range of chart types and interaction models, with tailored strategies that reflect the structural and cognitive demands of each format.

5.5   Limitations and Future Work

This study has several limitations that should be acknowledged. The sample size was relatively small, with only nine participants who identified as blind or low vision (BLV). While their responses offered rich and meaningful insights, the limited number of participants restricts the generalizability of the findings. Future studies should aim to include a larger and more diverse sample to capture a broader range of experiences and preferences.

All participants were affiliated with STEM-related fields, which may have influenced their familiarity with data visualization practices and tools. The findings may not fully reflect the experiences of BLV individuals in non-STEM domains. For example, chart interpretation is also essential in public-facing contexts, such as during health emergencies like the COVID-19 pandemic. Including participants from non-STEM backgrounds in future work would help explore how accessibility needs vary across different domains.

6   Conclusion

This study identified several key barriers that prevent blind and low vision (BLV) users from effectively interpreting scientific charts, including the absence of alternative text, undetectable charts, and limited support from screen readers. Despite these challenges, many participants demonstrate strong digital literacy, leveraging tools such as AI and machine learning to extract data and generate textual descriptions. These findings are crucial for developing more inclusive tools and visual designs. Future solutions should guarantee semantically rich alternative text, full keyboard control, and robust screen reader navigation, enabling BLV users to explore individual data points with equal ease. Moving forward, research should investigate a broader range of chart types, including stacked charts and class diagrams, as more frequently selected by participants, and integrate usability testing to evaluate the effectiveness of alternative design solutions for BLV users.

Appendix

Chart Accessibility Survey Questions

- Q1) What best describes your most recent job or area of study? If you are employed, you only need to consider your work, not schooling, unless you feel it is relevant.

  - Business (Management, Administration, Finance, etc.)
  - Electronics or Electrical Engineering
  - Engineering (e.g., Mechanical, Civil, Materials, Industrial)
  - Computer Science / Information Technology
  - Math
  - Science (Biology, Chemistry, Physics, etc.)

- Q2) As part of your education or job, do you need to interact with, access and/or interpret information in charts?

  - Yes, often
  - Yes, sometimes
  - No

- Q3) What assistive technology do you use when using your computer?

  - Magnification software or settings
  - Screen reader
  - Refreshable Braille display
  - Tactile graphics display
  - Nothing

- Q4) What types of charts do you interact with or need to access? Select all that apply

  - Bar chart
  - Line chart
  - Scatter plot
  - Pie chart
  - Stacked chart
  - Class diagrams

- Circuit diagram
- Others [free text box]

– Q5) What types of charts are you most interested in having increased accessibility to help you in school or on the job? Select all that apply.

  - Bar chart
  - Line chart
  - Scatter plot
  - Pie chart
  - Stacked chart
  - Class diagrams
  - Circuit diagram
  - Others [free text box]

– Q6) Please describe how you typically need to interact with the charts you selected above. If you have any tools, workarounds, or obstacles, please share them with us.
– Q7) What challenges do you face when you need to access specific information in charts that contain numbers and labels (such as a bar or line chart)?

  - Trouble recognizing the chart axes.
  - Trouble recognizing or distinguishing data points or bars.
  - The screen reader cannot provide any useful information.
  - Access is only possible through a written or verbal description from a sighted person (e.g., teacher, co-worker)
  - Others [free text box]

– Q8) Which of the following features or supports would you find useful in your use of charts?

  - Written description of the chart to provide an overview, that would be compatible with a screen reader or refreshable Braille display.
  - The ability to ask questions about the chart and get answers about it at a high or low level of granularity.
  - The ability to navigate the chart, with output by screen reader.
  - The ability to search for parts of a chart to get specific information.
  - Getting an audio indication of the patterns and trends within a chart using sonification or sound cues.
  - Better on-the-fly tactile support.
  - Other [free text box]

– Q9) What features would you like to have to help in your understanding and navigation of the charts that you use? (Open Question)
– Q10) Please tell us anything else that you feel would be good to share about your use of, need for, challenges with, or strategies to interact with charts. (Open Question)

  End of Questions

References

1. Alam, M.Z.I., Islam, S., Hoque, E.: Seechart: enabling accessible visualizations through interactive natural language interface for people with visual impairments. In: Proceedings of the 28th International Conference on Intelligent User Interfaces (2023)
2. Alghamdi, A.M., Aljedaani, W., Eler, M.M., Ludi, S.: Accessibility guidelines and standards: analyzing stack overflow posts. In: Proceedings of the 21st International Web for All Conference, pp. 118–122 (2024)
3. Alghamdi, M., Aljedaani, W., Jalali, H., Ludi, S., Eler, M.M.: Understanding developer challenges and trends in web accessibility: a stack overflow analysis. In: Universal Access in the Information Society, pp. 1–17 (2024)
4. Alghamdi, M., Aljedaani, W., Ludi, S., Javed, Y.: Automating accessibility compliance: Leveraging machine learning to analyze developer challenges with wcag guidelines. In: 2025 8th International Conference on Data Science and Machine Learning Applications (CDMA), pp. 61–66. IEEE (2025)
5. Aljedaani, W., Chimpiri, U.K., Gaddam, D., Shaik, V.A., Karasala, Y., Eler, M.M.: Beyond sight: Empowering visually impaired users with audible graphs. In: Proceedings of the 21st International Web for All Conference, pp. 39–41 (2024)
6. Aljedaani, W., Eler, M.M., Parthasarathy, P.: Enhancing accessibility in software engineering projects with large language models (LLMS). In: Proceedings of the 56th ACM Technical Symposium on Computer Science Education, vol. 1, pp. 25–31 (2025)
7. Aljedaani, W., Habib, A., Aljohani, A., Eler, M., Feng, Y.: Does chatGPT generate accessible code? Investigating accessibility challenges in LLM-generated source code. In: Proceedings of the 21st International Web for All Conference, pp. 165–176 (2024)
8. Austin, D., Sorge, V.: Authoring web-accessible mathematical diagrams. In: Proceedings of the 20th International Web for All Conference, pp. 148–152 (2023)
9. Be My Eyes. Be my eyes: Bringing Sight to Blind and Low-Vision People (2023). Accessed 25 February 2025
10. Beck-Winchatz, Riccobono, M.A.: Advancing participation of blind students in science, technology, engineering, and math. Adv. Space Res. **42**(11), 1855–1858 (2008)
11. Brown, J.R., Doore, S.A., Dimmel, J.K., Giudice, N., Giudice, N.A.. Comparing natural language and vibro-audio modalities for inclusive stem learning with blind and low vision users. In: Proceedings of the 25th International ACM SIGACCESS Conference on Computers and Accessibility, pp. 1–17 (2023)
12. Choi, J., Oh, C., Suh, B., Kim, N.W.: Vislab: crowdsourcing visualization experiments in the wild. In: Extended Abstracts of the 2021 CHI Conference on Human Factors in Computing Systems, pp. 1–7 (2021)
13. Demir, S., Oliver, D., Schwartz, E., Elzer, S., Carberry, S., McCoy, K.F.: Interactive sight into information graphics. In: Proceedings of the 2010 International Cross Disciplinary Conference on Web Accessibility (W4A), pp. 1–10 (2010)
14. Dineen, Bourne, R., Ali, S., Huq, D.N., Johnson, G.: Prevalence and causes of blindness and visual impairment in Bangladeshi adults: results of the national blindness and low vision survey of Bangladesh. Br. J. Ophthalmol. **87**(7), 820–828 (2003)
15. Duijzer, C., Van den Heuvel-Panhuizen, M., Veldhuis, M., Doorman, M.: Supporting primary school students' reasoning about motion graphs through physical experiences. Zdm **51**(6), 899–913 (2019)
16. Eler, M.M., Aljedaani, W.: Investigating user perceptions of epilepsy-related seizure triggers in mobile apps: an analysis of user reviews. In: Proceedings of the 2025 CHI Conference on Human Factors in Computing Systems, pp. 1–19 (2025)

17. Engel, C., Weber, G.: Improve the accessibility of tactile charts. In: Human Computer Interaction-INTERACT 2017: 16th IFIP TC 13 International Conference, Mumbai, India, September 25–29, 2017, Proceedings, Part I 16, pp. 187–195. Springer (2017)
18. Keilers, C., Tigwell, G.W., Peiris, R.L. Data visualization accessibility for blind and low-vision audiences. In: International Conference on Human–Computer Interaction. Springer, pp. 399–413 (2023)
19. Fitzpatrick, D., Godfrey, J.R., Sorge, V.: Producing accessible statistics diagrams in R. In: Proceedings of the 14th Web for All Conference on The Future of Accessible Work (2017)
20. Freedom Scientific. JAWS® Picture Smart AI: Transforming Accessibility with AI-Powered Image Descriptions (2024). Accessed 25 February 2025
21. Ghoneim, R., Aljedaani, W., Bryce, R., Javed, Y., Khan, Z.I.: Why are other teachers more inclusive in online learning than us? exploring challenges faced by teachers of blind and visually impaired students: a literature review. Computers (2073–431X) **13**(10) (2024)
22. Holloway, L.M., Goncu, C., Ilsar, A., Butler, M., Marriott, K.: Infosonics: accessible infographics for people who are blind using sonification and voice. In: Proceedings of the 2022 CHI Conference on Human Factors in Computing Systems, pp. 1–13 (2022)
23. Joyner, S.C.S., Riegelhuth, A., Garrity, K., Kim, Y.-S., Kim, N.W.: Visualization accessibility in the wild: Challenges faced by visualization designers. In: Proceedings of the 2022 CHI Conference on Human Factors in Computing Systems (2022)
24. Jung, C., Mehta, S., Kulkarni, A., Zhao, Y., Kim, Y.-S.: Communicating visualizations without visuals: investigation of visualization alternative text for people with visual impairments. IEEE Trans. Visual Comput. Graph. **28**(1), 1095–1105 (2021)
25. Kim, J., Srinivasan, A., Kim, N.W., Kim, Y.-S.: Exploring chart question answering for blind and low vision users. In: Proceedings of the 2023 CHI Conference on Human Factors in Computing Systems, pp. 1–15 (2023)
26. Kim, N.W., Joyner, S.C., Riegelhuth, A., Kim, Y.: Accessible visualization: Design space, opportunities, and challenges. In: Computer Graphics Forum, vol. 40, pp. 173–188. Wiley Online Library (2021)
27. Landau, S., Gourgey, K.: Development of a talking tactile tablet. Inf. Technol. Disabil. **7**(2) (2001)
28. Leotta, M., Ribaudo, M.: Evaluating the effectiveness of stem images captioning. In: Proceedings of the 21st International Web for All Conference, pp. 150–159 (2024)
29. Lundgard, A., Satyanarayan, A.: Accessible visualization via natural language descriptions: a four-level model of semantic content. In: IEEE Transactions on Visualization & Computer Graphics (Proceedings of IEEE VIS) (2022)
30. Mack, K., McDonnell, E., Jain, D., Lu Wang, L., Froehlich, J.E., Findlater, L.: What do we mean by "accessibility research"? A literature survey of accessibility papers in chi and assets from 1994 to 2019. In: Proceedings of the 2021 CHI Conference on Human Factors in Computing Systems, pp. 1–18 (2021)
31. Moured, O., Baumgarten-Egemole, M., Müller, K., Roitberg, A., Schwarz, T., Stiefelhagen, R.: Chart4blind: an intelligent interface for chart accessibility conversion. In: Proceedings of the 29th International Conference on Intelligent User Interfaces, pp. 504–514 (2024)
32. Murillo-Morales, T., Miesenberger, K.: Audial: a natural language interface to make statistical charts accessible to blind persons. In: Computers Helping People with Special Needs, pp. 373–384. Springer-Verlag, Berlin, Heidelberg (2020)
33. Nylund, K., Mankoff, J., Potluri, V.: Matplotalt: a python library for adding alt text to matplotlib figures in computational notebooks. In: Computer Graphics Forum, p. e70119. Wiley Online Library (2025)
34. OpenAI. Gpt-4: Openai's Large Multimodal Model (2023). Accessed 25 February 2025
35. Qualtrics. Qualtrics Research Core (2017). Accessed 30 April 2025

36. Riedel, B.: Browsing modes for exploring sonified line graphs. In: Proceedings of BCS HCI, 2 (2002)
37. SAS Institute Inc. SAS® Graphics Accelerator: User's Guide (2017). Accessed 25 February 2025
38. Seo, J., Kamath, S.S., Zeidieh, A., Venkatesh, S., McCurry, S.: Maidr meets AI: Exploring multimodal LLM-based data visualization interpretation by and with blind and low-vision users. In: Proceedings of the 26th International ACM SIGACCESS Conference on Computers and Accessibility, pp. 1–31 (2024)
39. Seo, J., O'Modhrain, S., Xia, Y., Kamath, S., Lee, B., Coughlan, J.M.: Designing born-accessible courses in data science and visualization: challenges and opportunities of a remote curriculum taught by blind instructors to blind students. In: Eurographics/IEEE VGTC Symposium on Visualization, vol. 2024, pp. 2403-02568 (2024)
40. Seo, J., Xia, Y., Lee, B., Mccurry, S., Yam, Y.J.: Maidr: making statistical visualizations accessible with multimodal data representation. In: Proceedings of the 2024 CHI Conference on Human Factors in Computing Systems, pp. 1–22. ACM (2024)
41. Sharif, A., Chintalapati, S.S., Wobbrock, J.O., Reinecke, K.: Understanding screen-reader users' experiences with online data visualizations. In: Proceedings of the 23rd International ACM SIGACCESS Conference on Computers and Accessibility, pp. 1–16 (2021)
42. Sharif, Wang, O.H., Muongchan, A.T., Reinecke, K., Wobbrock, J.O.: Voxlens: making online data visualizations accessible with an interactive javascript plug-in. In: Proceedings of the 2022 CHI Conference on Human Factors in Computing Systems, pp. 1–19 (2022)
43. Sorge, V., Lee, M.G., Wilkinson, S.: End-to-end solution for accessible chemical diagrams. In: Proceedings of the 12th International Web for All Conference (2015)
44. Wang, R., Jung, C., Kim, Y.: Seeing through sounds: mapping auditory dimensions to data and charts for people with visual impairments. In: Computer Graphics Forum, vol. 41, pp. 71–83. Wiley Online Library (2022)
45. Wu, S., Wieland, J., Farivar, O., Schiller, J.: Automatic alt-text: Computer generated image descriptions for blind users on a social network service. In: Proceedings of the 2017 ACM Conference on Computer Supported Cooperative Work and Social Computing, pp. 1180–1192 (2017)
46. Zhao, Y., Nacenta, M.A., Sukhai, A., Somanath, S.: Tada: Making nodelink diagrams accessible to blind and low-vision people. In: Proceedings of the CHI Conference on Human Factors in Computing Systems, pp. 1–20 (2024)

Emotional Engagement and Accessibility in Game-Based Education: A Case Study with Elementary School Teachers

Sheisa Bittencourt[1]([✉]) [iD], Regina Heidrich[1] [iD], Elisângela Vilar[2] [iD], and Jacinta Renner[1] [iD]

[1] Postgraduate Program in Cultural Diversity and Social Inclusion, Feevale University, Novo Hamburgo, Brazil
`sheisa.court@gmail.com, {rheidrich,jacinta}@feevale.br`
[2] Research Centre for Architecture, Urbanism and Design, CIAUD, Lisbon School of Architecture, Universidade de Lisboa, Lisboa, Portugal
`ebpvilar@edu.ulisboa.pt`

Abstract. This paper explores the perceptions of elementary school teachers regarding the accessible educational game *Planeta ODS*, designed to engage both students and educators in classroom discussions about the United Nations Sustainable Development Goals (SDGs). Grounded in Brazil's National Common Curricular Base (BNCC), which promotes equitable and inclusive education, the study adopts a qualitative case study methodology based on semi-structured interviews. To assess teachers' emotional responses to the game, the Geneva Emotion Wheel (GEW) was employed, enabling deeper insights into the emotional and motivational impact of the game. Findings indicate that the game was positively received in terms of clarity, pedagogical relevance, and visual appeal, suggesting alignment with teachers' expectations and curricular goals. The results reinforce the potential of inclusive game-based learning to support accessible education practices in public schools.

Keywords: Accessible Digital Game · Sustainable Development Goals · Human-Centered Design · Inclusive Design · Inclusive Education · Game-based Learning

1 Introduction

Accessibility in digital games extends far beyond technical adaptations; it is fundamentally a pedagogical and social concern. Despite increasing awareness, the integration of accessible games into formal educational settings remains limited, due to barriers such as the absence of specific regulations, outdated school infrastructure, and insufficient teacher training. These challenges hinder the full potential of inclusive educational technologies.

A strategic approach to promoting accessibility is the development of standardized guidelines and toolkits. In computing and related technological fields, such frameworks

© The Author(s), under exclusive license to Springer Nature Switzerland AG 2026
M. Antona and C. Stephanidis (Eds.): HCII 2025, LNCS 16335, pp. 18–29, 2026.
https://doi.org/10.1007/978-3-032-12781-5_2

are well-established and describe essential design features to ensure usability across diverse user profiles [1] For example, Britto and Pizzolato, as cited by Perkoski and Orlando [1], propose web development guidelines tailored to users with autism, emphasizing predictability, consistency in layout, and clarity of information—principles that are equally applicable to game design.

In this context, accessibility in educational games refers to adapting both hardware and software to meet the needs of users with disabilities, thereby enabling full and autonomous participation. These adaptations are crucial in education, where digital games can serve as powerful pedagogical tools that promote engagement, personalization, and interactive learning. Ensuring that all students—regardless of ability—can access these resources contributes to a more equitable and inclusive educational environment.

While accessibility is increasingly recognized as a core component of software development [2], the gaming industry has been slow to adopt inclusive practices, often excluding significant portions of the population [3] Accessibility in games should not be limited to assistive technologies; it also involves including marginalized users in design and development processes. Authors such as Fontoura Junior [4] and Bierre et al. (2005) advocate for the direct involvement of users with disabilities to ensure meaningful inclusion.

In response to these challenges, a case study was conducted during the development of *Planeta ODS*—an inclusive educational game designed in alignment with Brazil's National Common Curricular Base (BNCC) and centered on the 17 United Nations Sustainable Development Goals [5]. The game integrates features such as text narration, high-contrast visuals, and customizable controls to support students with visual, auditory, and motor disabilities, who also participated in its development alongside educators.

This article, part of a broader research initiative, presents the case study conducted with elementary school teachers who evaluated the game's pedagogical and emotional impact. The findings contribute to ongoing discussions in Human-Computer Interaction (HCI), Inclusive Design, and Technology-Enhanced Learning, demonstrating how inclusive game-based tools can enhance classroom practices and support the implementation of inclusive educational policies such as the BNCC.

2 Methodology

This study employed a qualitative case study approach [6] to investigate elementary school teachers' perceptions and emotional engagement with *Planeta ODS*, an inclusive educational game designed to support classroom discussions on the United Nations Sustainable Development Goals (SDGs). The research design was approved by the Feevale University Research Ethics Committee (protocol no. 17566519.4.0000.5348) and adhered to ethical guidelines for human-subject research in educational contexts.

The COVID-19 pandemic exacerbated long-standing educational challenges in Brazil, including school dropout, learning gaps, and disparities in student performance. Although Brazil has officially achieved universal enrollment in elementary education, learning poverty—defined by the World Bank as the percentage of 10-year-olds unable to read and understand a simple text—has increased dramatically. In Latin America, this figure rose from 55% to 71% following approximately 10 months of school closures [7].

In response to this urgent context, the Laboratory of Inclusion and Ergonomics (LABIE) at Feevale University was tasked with developing a digital educational game on the 17 SDGs, specifically tailored to the needs of school-aged children. The goal was to ensure that accessibility features in the game would remove barriers to participation without reducing the cognitive challenge or gameplay quality. Thus, *Planeta ODS* was designed to support students with various types of disabilities—visual, auditory, motor— while maintaining a dynamic and inclusive learning experience.

The game incorporates a variety of accessibility features, including customizable controls for students with reduced mobility, subtitles and audio descriptions for those with visual or auditory impairments, adjustable interfaces, and compatibility with assistive devices such as adaptive keyboards and controllers. For example, the customizable control system allows users to reconfigure key bindings to match their physical capabilities, while audiovisual aids ensure full comprehension of narrative elements and instructions.

Planeta ODS follows a point-and-click adventure format, emphasizing problem-solving, strategic thinking, and scenario exploration. Players navigate a dystopian future in which humanity faces extinction. The main character travels through time, assisting citizens, solving challenges, and introducing humanitarian and ecological knowledge. Each game level features **dual scenarios—past and future—**with distinct visual color schemes optimized for students with visual impairments. Players progress through structured missions, identifying a core problem related to the SDGs, gathering suggestions from non-playable characters (NPCs), collecting items, and confirming whether the problem has been solved in the future timeline.

To assist teachers in integrating the game into their lesson plans, the videos embedded in *Planeta ODS* include expert commentary on each SDG, providing pedagogical scaffolding aligned with the BNCC. These features also enable the game to be used as an educational tool even in low-resource environments.

Data were collected through semi-structured interviews and the Geneva Emotion Wheel – GEW [8], allowing for the triangulation of thematic perceptions and affective responses. While this article focuses on the evaluation phase, the broader project employed a participatory design methodology, involving both educators and students with disabilities throughout the game's development. This inclusive approach ensured that accessibility features were not only technically effective but contextually relevant for users in Brazilian public schools.

2.1 Participants

The participant group consisted of five female elementary school teachers (aged from 30 to 55 years old) from municipal public schools in the state of Rio Grande do Sul, Brazil. Selection criteria included:

(i) a minimum of 5 years and up to 35 years of teaching experience in basic education.
(ii) demonstrated familiarity with the National Common Curricular Base (BNCC).
(iii) interest in integrating digital technologies into pedagogical practice, even in settings with limited technological infrastructure.

The participants varied in terms of subject area (science, arts, physical education, mathematics), prior experience with digital tools, and working environments (urban and peri-urban schools). This diversity enriched the data and offered a comprehensive picture of the challenges and opportunities for implementing accessible educational games across Brazil's heterogeneous school system.

2.2 Data Collection Procedures

Two primary instruments were used to gather data:

- Semi-structured interviews, guided by a protocol organized around thematic axes:

  - Initial impressions and alignment with BNCC.
  - Content clarity and pedagogical relevance.
  - Visual design and engagement.
  - Accessibility features.
  - Suggestions for improvement.

- Geneva Emotion Wheel – GEW [8], adapted to assess teachers' emotional responses to the game, including categories such as "Relief," "Satisfaction," "Interest," "Pride," "Hope," "Joy," "Surprise," "Anger," "Uncertainty," and "Other," each with four levels of intensity.

The semi-structured interview is a data collection technique that combines predefined questions with the flexibility to explore emerging topics during the conversation. It follows a basic script but allows the interviewer to adapt the questions or delve deeper into specific issues based on the participant's responses. This approach balances the structure required for comparisons across interviews with the openness needed to capture detailed and contextual information, making it particularly well-suited for qualitative research [9].

The semi-structured interview consisted of ten questions, each aligned with specific thematic axes, as shown in Table 1.

In addition, we considered the teachers' satisfaction with using the game as a pedagogical tool. To assess this satisfaction more deeply, we employed the Geneva Emotion Wheel (GEW), a validated instrument for measuring emotional responses, which allowed participants to express their feelings during the planning and implementation of the *Planeta ODS* game.

Based on neuroscience-informed definitions of perception, the GEW is a self-report instrument designed to capture emotional experiences by estimating emotional triggers and reactions. Unlike tools that require respondents to choose from a predefined list of emotion words, the GEW organizes these terms within a theoretically grounded two-dimensional structure defined by orthogonal axes [8].

Operationally, the GEW is structured as a Cartesian circle with "x" and "y" axes, where various emotions are positioned around a central point within concentric circles. Participants mark the intensity of each emotion felt in relation to a given object or experience. Smaller circles near the center indicate lower emotional intensity, while larger, more distant circles indicate higher intensity [8]. In addition to labeled emotions

Table 1. Semi-structured interview thematic axes and questions.

Thematic Axis	Question
1) General First Impression	What was your first impression after watching the video, playing the game, and analyzing the BNCC competencies related to alternative agriculture?
2) Clarity and Content Relevance	How would you assess the clarity and relevance of the information presented in the video and in the demonstration of the game? Did the content manage to stimulate your interest regarding the theme of alternative agriculture and its integration with the BNCC competencies?
3) Stimulation of Interest	— (Covered in previous question.)
4) Suitability for the Target Audience	Do you believe the content is suitable for the target audience (teachers and students) in the context of competencies addressed by the BNCC?
5) Visual and Graphic Impact	How would you rate the visual impact and graphic design of the video and the game?
6) Use of Practical Examples	Were the practical examples presented in the video and game sufficient to support the understanding and application of alternative agriculture and BNCC competencies?
7) Accessibility Features	How would you assess the accessibility of the video and game for students with disabilities?
8) Emotional Experience	Choose the aspect of the video or game you wish to evaluate first, and then select the emotion that best describes your experience.
9) Suggestions for Improvement	Do you have any suggestions to improve the content or the format of presenting the video or game?
10) Final Comments	Please share any final remarks about your experience.

at varying intensity levels, the wheel includes the options "None" (for when no emotion is experienced) and "Other" (for emotions not listed on the wheel). As described by Sacharin, Schlegel, and Scherer [8], '*If none of the emotions are experienced, respondents may indicate "None" in the center of the circle. If the emotion felt is not listed, they may write it under "Other".*' During application, participants indicate emotional intensity by marking positions increasingly distant from the center as intensity rises.

The data collection steps described in this study were crucial for capturing teachers' perceptions and lived experiences with the inclusive educational game in the school environment. This process combined direct observation during the presentation with follow-up semi-structured interviews, allowing for a comprehensive understanding of how accessibility features may be integrated into pedagogical practice.

For this study, the GEW was adapted to include the following emotional categories: "Relief," "Satisfaction," "Interest," "Pride," "Hope," "Joy," "Surprise," "Anger," "Uncertain," and "Other," each represented with four levels of intensity. Figure 1 illustrates how the GEW was customized for this research.

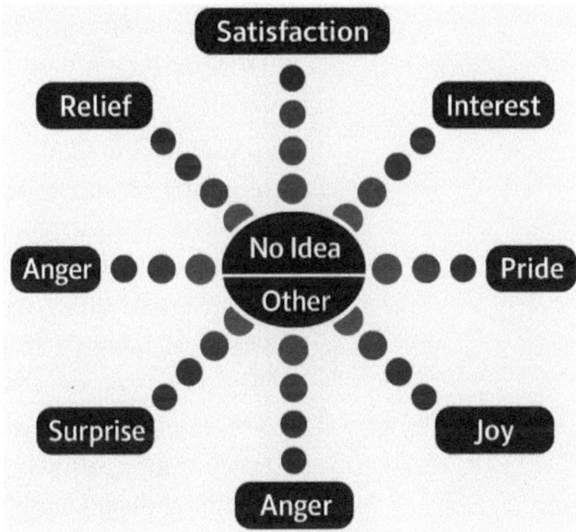

Fig. 1. Geneva Emotion Wheel adapted from (Sacharin et al., 2012), for this specific study.

The GEW served as a complementary instrument to the interviews, enabling a more nuanced understanding of the affective dimension of participants' engagement with the game. This mixed-methods strategy provided a richer interpretation of the data by combining verbal reflection with emotional self-assessment.

2.3 Application Protocol

Data collection followed a five-step protocol, during individual online sessions lasting approximately one hour. Each session included: i) a briefing and informed consent process; ii) a demonstration of the *Planeta ODS* game and video content; iii) the semi-structured interview; and iv) the application of the GEW.

At the beginning of each session, participants were briefed on the study's objectives, data privacy protocols, and asked to sign an informed consent form, including authorization for audio and video recording.

The demonstration of the *Planeta ODS* game and video content was organized in sections as outlined in Table 2, each designed to explore teachers' perceptions of the game's accessibility features and its applicability in accordance with the BNCC.

After the presentation of the *Planeta ODS* game and the SDG-themed video materials, participants completed the semi-structured interview followed by the GEW assessment. Then, after responding to questions 1 through 8 of the semi-structured interviews, the teachers were invited to indicate on the wheel the emotion they felt and its intensity for each question. Questions 9 and 10, which required open-ended responses, were not included in the GEW model.

To ensure consistency and methodological rigor, the GEW application followed five structured steps:

Table 2. Stages for presentation the *Planet ODS* game and video content.

Stage	Description
1) Contextualization	We clarified that the game is still under development. Therefore, we presented only the menu. We emphasized the importance of introducing the *Planeta ODS* game from its initial stages
2) Menu Demonstration	We presented the main menu of *Planeta ODS*, highlighting its simple and navigable interface. We showed how the game is designed to facilitate navigation for all students, including those with disabilities. We highlighted accessibility features and implementations in the menu
3) Integrated Accessibility Features in the Menu	Text Narration: the menu includes a text narration option, allowing the activity to be conducted independently. High Contrast Mode: the color scheme can be adjusted for better visual comfort, aiding reading and navigation for users with low vision. Adjustable Font Size: the font size can be modified to suit individual needs. Keyboard Navigation: controls can be operated via the keyboard or adaptive devices. These options are described and highlighted during the game introduction, demonstrating how they were planned to meet the needs of students with visual, motor, or cognitive disabilities
4) Expert Videos	We presented videos recorded by specialists who explain specific concepts related to SDGs. These videos were selected to support teachers in introducing SDG-related topics in the classroom
5) Potential for Exploration	We demonstrated how, even without the complete game, the menu alone offers a clear vision of how the game will allow students with disabilities to participate autonomously

1. *Introduction and Orientation:* Each teacher was welcomed individually and introduced to the GEW as a tool for evaluating their emotional responses to the game experience.
2. *Explanation of the Instrument:* The GEW was presented as a Cartesian wheel, with concentric circles representing emotional intensity and labeled categories positioned radially. Participants were instructed on how to mark their emotional responses, with "None" and "Other" options available.

3. *Emotion Mapping*: After responding to the first eight interview questions, each teacher reflected on her experience with the game and marked the relevant emotions and their intensity on the wheel.
4. *Data Registration:* All markings were documented systematically. This enabled quantitative aggregation of emotional intensities to complement qualitative insights from the interviews.
5. *Debriefing Discussion:* Finally, a brief follow-up conversation was held to allow participants to elaborate on their emotional reactions. Teachers were also invited to complete a short self-report titled *Emotional Evaluation of the Game in Development*, further enriching the dataset.

This process was repeated with all five participants, enabling a detailed and personalized understanding of their emotional engagement. Overall, the use of the GEW provided valuable insight into how each teacher experienced the game, revealing moments of excitement, frustration, pride, and areas in need of additional support.

The emotional data obtained through the GEW offered a multifaceted assessment of *Planeta ODS*, highlighting not only its effectiveness as an educational tool but also the emotional landscape involved in the adoption of new technologies by educators.

The last two interview questions were excluded from the GEW, as they elicited narrative and contextual responses. To strengthen analytical validity, triangulation between interview content and GEW data was employed to identify patterns of engagement, satisfaction, frustration, and perceived usability.

To enhance the validity and credibility of findings, the study followed principles of thematic saturation, cross-checked interview themes with emotional data from the GEW, and ensured anonymity and data protection throughout the research process. The convergence of verbal and emotional indicators supported the reliability of emerging patterns and added depth to the interpretation of participants' experiences.

3 Results and Discussion

Thematic analysis was conducted on the interview transcripts, and emotional data collected via the GEW was triangulated to enhance interpretive depth. Quantitative summaries (e.g., percentage agreement) were used to highlight trends and consensus.

Following the semi-structured interviews and application of the Geneva Emotion Wheel (GEW), it was possible to identify clear patterns—referred to here as thematic axes—in the teachers' perceptions regarding the application of the Planeta ODS educational game in school settings. These are summarized in Table 3 below.

The data suggest a high degree of acceptance across most dimensions evaluated. Below, we explore the six axes in greater depth, beginning with content clarity.

The evaluation of the questionnaires revealed that the teachers identified the game as applicable, clear, and relevant. Most expressed positive first impressions, with emotions such as interest, pride, and satisfaction, typically scored between levels 3 and 4 on the GEW scale.

Teachers in subject areas like Biology showed enthusiasm for applying the game in their lessons, while those in less directly related areas (e.g., Arts and Physical Education)

Table 3. Summary of Participants' Perceptions.

Axis	Description
1) Clarity and Relevance of Content	– 80% of the teachers considered the game's content to be clear and relevant to their subject areas. – 20% noted that although the content was clear, it could be more specific for subjects such as Arts and Physical Education.⇒ Most teachers expressed satisfaction with the pedagogical structure and clarity, but pointed out the need for more tailored examples beyond Biology and Science.
2) Suitability for the Target Audience	– 100% of participants found the content appropriate for students in general. – Some, however, noted that specific adjustments may be needed for better application in disciplines not directly linked to the SDGs.⇒ The results reinforce the general adequacy of the game but highlight the opportunity to broaden its interdisciplinary reach.
3) Stimulation of Interest and Visual Impact	– 60% reported that the game successfully engaged both themselves and their students, particularly highlighting its visual appeal. – 40% wished for more interactivity, suggesting that although the visual design is strong, additional dynamic elements could improve engagement. ⇒ Indicates a solid base but room for enhancing interactivity.
4) Accessibility	– 100% praised the inclusion of accessibility features such as text narration and high-contrast mode. – 40% suggested adding more features to support students with motor or auditory impairments. ⇒ Strong accessibility foundation, with potential for expansion to accommodate more specific needs.
5) Technological Limitations	– 60% expressed frustration regarding the lack of infrastructure (e.g., no computer labs), which limits in-class application. ⇒ Highlights the need for offline or low-tech alternatives (e.g., videos, printable materials).
6) Suggestions for Improvement	– 80% recommended the inclusion of more practical examples adapted to various school subjects, particularly Arts and Physical Education. ⇒ Reinforces the demand for broader curricular applicability.

expressed uncertainty about how to adapt the content. This suggests that while the content is strong, interdisciplinary integration remains a challenge.

The content's information architecture and narrative clarity were generally well-rated, with 80% of participants assigning levels 3 or 4 in the GEW assessment. However, teachers from non-STEM areas suggested a lack of curricular alignment, indicating that discipline-specific adaptation could increase pedagogical reach. This reinforces the importance of modular content design for broader curricular integration.

Interest stimulation was also rated positively, with teachers indicating they were motivated to use the tools to make their lessons more dynamic. However, one teacher expressed frustration, particularly with the technological limitations of her school, which hinder the full implementation of digital resources.

Regarding audience appropriateness, teachers found the material suitable for their students and again indicated satisfaction at the highest levels (4). Nonetheless, they advocated for the inclusion of diversified examples to ensure alignment with various curricular areas.

Visual and graphic design elements were also highly rated (level 4 on the GEW), with the game's aesthetics being recognized as essential to sustaining student attention.

Similar to findings by Petrie and Bevan [2], teachers in this study emphasized that accessibility should not be seen as a secondary feature, but as an essential design principle. Accessibility was praised, with participants expressing surprise and interest in levels 3 to 4 on the GEW. The availability of subtitles and contrast options was noted positively, although further suggestions were made to enhance accessibility for students with more severe impairments.

From an emotional perspective, teachers had an overall positive experience, with 80% expressing pride and satisfaction in engaging with an inclusive educational resource. Still, one teacher exhibited mixed feelings—pride in the resource and frustration with the logistical barriers in her school, located in a socioeconomically disadvantaged area.

Suggestions for improvement included:

- Producing longer videos featuring additional expert voices for more comprehensive and multidisciplinary perspectives.
- Incorporating more practical examples tailored to a variety of subjects.
- Expanding the game's accessibility features.

Final comments highlighted the alignment of the game with BNCC competencies and its potential to support inclusive classroom practices. However, some teachers noted that rigid adherence to BNCC guidelines may sometimes constrain innovation and creativity. While tools like the game and the videos were viewed as highly valuable, technological constraints—particularly the absence of computer labs—were seen as significant barriers to implementation. This underscores the need for scalable, flexible solutions.

In summary, the game demonstrated strong potential to generate teacher engagement and align with BNCC goals of making learning more dynamic and appealing. The content's clarity, visual integration, and accessibility contribute to meaningful and contextually relevant learning experiences, essential to students' formation.

Based on this analysis, we conclude that although *Planeta ODS* was well received overall, there are key areas for refinement to enhance its pedagogical versatility and inclusivity. Expanding interactivity, improving discipline-specific relevance, and offering solutions for low-resource settings are critical for broader adoption.

4 Conclusion

This study demonstrates that inclusive digital games—such as Planeta ODS—hold significant promise as pedagogical tools capable of promoting engagement, accessibility, and curricular alignment in basic education. By integrating Universal Design principles and human-centered approaches, the game offers a model for the effective application of educational technology in alignment with Brazil's National Common Curricular Base (BNCC).

The findings reveal that teachers perceived the game as pedagogically relevant, emotionally engaging, and accessible to a broad student population. 80% of participants reported high levels of satisfaction with the clarity and relevance of the content, particularly in science-related subjects. However, the perceived lack of curricular specificity for areas such as arts and physical education suggests the need for greater interdisciplinary customization in future iterations.

Accessibility features—including text narration, high-contrast modes, and keyboard navigation—were well received, but 40% of participants recommended the addition of further features, particularly for motor and auditory impairments. These insights underscore the importance of iterative co-design processes and inclusive validation, especially when aiming to serve diverse educational contexts.

A major limitation identified was the lack of technological infrastructure in public schools, with 60% of teachers reporting that insufficient access to devices or internet connectivity hinders the integration of digital games in their practice. This reinforces the need to design resilient educational technologies that function in low-resource environments, including offline content and analog-compatible materials.

The emotional responses, collected using the Geneva Emotion Wheel (GEW), revealed high levels of interest, pride, and satisfaction, confirming that teachers not only recognized the game's pedagogical value but also felt motivated to experiment with inclusive digital tools. These affective outcomes are crucial in promoting the adoption of innovation within school cultures, especially when technological change is accompanied by uncertainty or resistance.

In conclusion, Planeta ODS represents a viable example of how accessible and inclusive digital tools can support the goals of equity and innovation in education. The study contributes to the field of Human-Computer Interaction in Education by demonstrating that emotionally meaningful and contextually adaptable designs are essential for ensuring real-world impact. Future work should explore longitudinal assessments of student learning outcomes, as well as the development of modular content libraries for broader disciplinary integration.

Acknowledgments. This work was supported by Feevale University, Novo Hamburgo, RS, Brazil, FAPERGS – Research Support Foundation of the State of Rio Grande do Sul, Brazil and CNPq – National Council for Scientific and Technological Development, Brazil.

Disclosure of Interests. The authors have no competing interests.

References

1. Perkoski, I., Orlando, R.: Acessibilidade em jogos digitais para uso em sala de aula: recomendações para professores de turmas inclusivas. Educação e Cultura Contemporânea. **17**, 418–437 (2020)
2. Petrie, H., Bevan, N.: The evaluation of accessibility, usability and user experience. In: Stephanidis, C. (ed.) The Universal Access Handbook, pp. 1–30. CRC Press (2009). https://doi.org/10.1201/9781420064995-c20
3. Bittencourt, S.A.d.C., Heidrich, R.d.O., Amaral, F., Bassani, P.S.: The use of assistive technologies for blind students in virtual museums as a possibility in teaching: case study – the presence in absence exhibition. In: Dhamdhere, S., Andres, F. (eds.) Assistive Technologies for Differently Abled Students, pp. 212–238. IGI Global (2022). https://doi.org/10.4018/978-1-7998-4736-6.CH011
4. Fontoura, P.H.F. Jr.: Recomendações para o desenvolvimento de jogos educacionais: aspectos para a inclusão de pessoas com deficiência visual (2018). https://repositorio.ufscar.br/handle/20.500.14289/11477
5. United Nations. Objetivos de Desenvolvimento Sustentável | As Nações Unidas no Brasil. https://brasil.un.org/pt-br/sdgs. Accessed 05 June 2025
6. Yin, R.: Estudo de Caso: Planejamento e métodos. Bookman, Porto Alegre (2001)
7. Almeida, A.O.: Educação não é privilégio. Revista Pesquisa 303 (2021)
8. Sacharin, V., Schlegel, K., Scherer, K.R.: Geneva Emotion Wheel Rating Study, Geneva (2012)
9. Gil, A.C.: Métodos e Técnicas de Pesquisa Social. Editora Atlas, São Paulo (2008)

On the Potential of Co-making Hacks to Improve the Accessibility of Makerspaces

Koray Canlar[1]([envelope]) [iD], Julia Miriam Andrea Jacoby[1] [iD], and Frode Eika Sandnes[2] [iD]

[1] Department Product Design, Oslo Metropolitan University, Oslo, Norway
`{koray.canlar,juljac}@oslomet.no`
[2] Department Computer Science, Oslo Metropolitan University, Oslo, Norway
`frodes@oslomet.no`

Abstract. Makerspaces are collaborative environments that provide local production capabilities to various maker groups. As the makerspaces aim to democratize production for as many people as possible, the accessibility of these spaces is getting increased research attention. This study investigates the potential of makerspaces to make themselves and their tools more accessible through their own means of local production. We applied a research-through-making approach in participatory co-making sessions with participants from a rehabilitation hospital and a university makerspace. Then, the 3D printing experience is analyzed with the use of the harmonised European Standard (EN 301 549) accessibility requirements for Information and Communication Technology (ICT) products and services. The findings from co-making sessions revealed three possible levels for 'hacking' and improving the accessibility of the (1) maker, (2) interface, and (3) space. On the maker level, hacks focus on aiding the maker personally while they navigate and interact with the makerspace and tools. The interface level would provide the user a connecting and guiding interface in-between different webpages, software, and hardware interfaces. The spatial level for possible hacks would provide the accessibility improvements related to clearances, reach and approach distances when the makers interact with 3D printers inside the makerspace. We argue that the goal of these hacks is to improve the agency and independence of people with disabilities and reduced physical functions, as well as assisting product users by increasing their access to making.

Keywords: Makerspace · Accessibility · Participatory Design · Co-Design · 3D Printing · Making · Accessibility Hacking

1 Introduction

The maker culture and acts of making promote access to learning-by-doing in transdisciplinary collaborative makerspaces where people with similar interests interact (Bosse et al., 2018). These places allow for students, organizations, and the public to learn from each other (Kohtala, 2017). To make the most of such collaborative making environments for as many people as possible, the accessibility of makerspaces and their tools

© The Author(s), under exclusive license to Springer Nature Switzerland AG 2026
M. Antona and C. Stephanidis (Eds.): HCII 2025, LNCS 16335, pp. 30–49, 2026.
https://doi.org/10.1007/978-3-032-12781-5_3

for several user groups becomes crucial. The accessibility and the technology democratization of makerspaces and maker activities such as do-it-yourself (DIY) are a relatively newly emerging area of research that's getting increasing attention (Sarwar and Wilson, 2022). This study asks the research question: How can maker approach/mindset/tools allow makerspaces to *make* themselves more accessible and inclusive? with the aim of investigating the potential of makerspaces to better their accessibility through their own means.

The study first analysed the maker tools and interfaces in a makerspace according to their accessibility to users with varying abilities, and then explored the potential of hacking these tools and interfaces to improve their accessibility for specific use cases. The term *hacking* in this paper will refer to acts of adapting, modifying, customizing the participant's tools, the makerspace tools and interfaces such as 3D printers and the makerspace environment. We argue that this potential of makerspaces can lead to the improvement of the *agency* of makers and their independence in making. The act of hacking the tools and the makerspace is the focus of the study's exploration, as the means of conducting these hacks and modifications are sourced from the context of the makerspace itself.

The outcome of specific cases of accessibility hacks may inspire and lead to improvements for other challenging issues related to makerspace tools for users with reduced functioning who rely on assistive technologies. Furthermore, the dissemination of how these accessibility hacks are made in makerspaces in-house can be utilised by all makerspaces as an example to follow for *making* their makerspace accessible. The concept of a makerspace tinkering itself is recently gaining attention in human computer interaction (HCI) research, such as being mentioned as *makerspacing the makerspace* (Allen et al., 2023). Consequently, the improved accessibility of makerspace tools, or even just the emphasis that it is possible to modify inaccessible tools into being accessible, can arguably render the context of makerspaces less daunting and more approachable for individuals with various types of reduced functioning.

The makerspace addressed in this study is inside the Sunnaas Rehabilitation Hospital in Norway. The hospital has a long history of having a workshop space to produce and adapt individualized assistive tools for their patients. The makerspace is a recent initiative by the hospital to integrate rapid prototyping technologies in their already existing workshop practices (see Fig. 1). While there have already been initial prototypes made by the hospital staff in the makerspace, our study enabled the patients participating in *making* to gain knowledge and access to the 3D printers within the makerspace for the first time.

This activity of hacking the makerspace tools can also be seen as an effective onboarding method for newcomer makerspace members with varying abilities. Adopting from product design literature, Terzioglu (2017) discusses the case of product repair and care, it can enable people to interact with products on a more meaningful level because of the act of problem-solving needing detailed investigation into the functions and the materials of products. A similar way of thinking can be applied to the context of makerspaces, in the sense that the new member forms the required bond and the sense of belonging to the makerspace by spending time understanding it's functions, making it more accessible and personalising the space to their need. Thus, the goal of makerspaces *making* themselves accessible through in-house modifications to their tools can be highly beneficial. Both for them to become more approachable and inclusive, but also for providing suitable grounds for people with varying abilities to empower themselves with maker skills and tools.

Our study employed a research method derived from research-through-design that we call *research-through-making* into the makerspace context, which involved co-making sessions with participants from the rehabilitation hospital and a university makerspace. Our findings during the research through making process regarding the accessibility barriers led us to go through analysis of the interfaces and the overall process of 3D printing using *Accessibility requirements for ICT products and services* standard (ETSI, 2021), which also incorporates the Web Content Accessibility Guidelines (WCAG). The addition of the guidelines for the analysis allowed us to identify some of the key accessibility barriers for novice users. The analysis showed that the barriers were not the interfaces in the 3D printing tools but were the lack of interface continuation between different software and hardware elements involved. Afterwards, we discuss our findings gathered from the user journey throughout the co-making process including the interfaces used while producing the 3D printed objects together. Lastly, we propose ways and further directions to connect the currently fragmented interfaces in 3D printing stages.

1.1 Makerspace and Accessibility

This accessibility study is intentionally conducted in collaboration with a rehabilitation hospital. There are several factors which make the context of the recent makerspace initiative inside the Sunnaas Rehabilitation Hospital compelling for investigating the accessibility of makerspaces and maker tools.

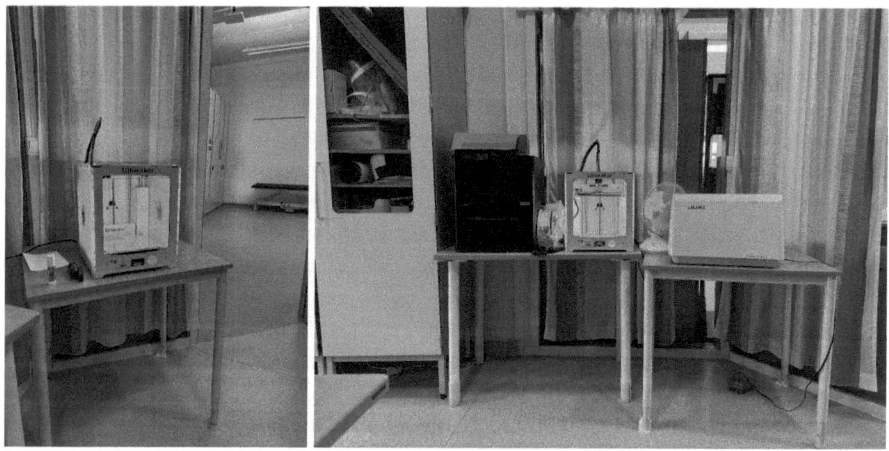

Fig. 1 The developing *makerspace* in Sunnaas Rehabilitation Hospital (left), with the newer 3D printer (right)

The first factor is the location of the makerspace (see Fig. 1), which makes it possible for it to attract users with accessibility needs from various rehabilitation departments within the hospital. The makerspace is located next to the recreational space for physical rehabilitation, where the patients regularly engage in recreational activities such as painting to help with the recovery of their ability to do daily tasks. This 3D printer initiative is very recent, and until the initiative, the hospital produced custom-made aids for their patients with a low-tech workshop operated by an experienced carpenter. This study was the first trial where patients were invited to participate in the making process for themselves. Thus, with the aim of patient participation, the makerspace in this context must be accessible for varying abilities. Co-design with individuals in target cohorts is a trend that is gaining momentum. For example, the authors' have previously explored co-design of customized prosthetics (da Silva, et al., 2019) or customized toys for hospitalized terminally ill children (Usó, et al., 2020).

In continuation of the first factor of patient participation, the accessibility of the makerspace is also connected to the long-rehabilitation times and the patients' agency. Many of the hospital's patients have long-recovery times that requires them to spend hours or accommodate in the hospital. Between the long times, tight rehabilitation schedules, and the reduced physical functions, the patients can have trouble regaining their agency and self-dependence, which is a primary motivation to seek rehabilitation in the first place (Kawano et al., 2023). Accessibility of makerspace and maker tools can help tackle this agency problem by empowering the patients to participate in 3D printing and making activities with minimal help from and dependence on the hospital/makerspace staff.

The last factor is that the overall hospital experience and tools that the patients use during their long rehabilitation stays have many opportunities for developing and making accessibility hacks. In other words, the context makes it possible to hack beyond the makerspace and into the hospital context as well, personalizing mass-produced hospital products such as the hospital bed. However, it should be noted that, while patients would use the hospital makerspace for hacking the hospital's accessibility, there are medical procedures that the hospital must adhere to when making modifications or customizations to their equipment (Lipschultz, 2012).

1.2 Background for Approach – Research Through Design

Defining *research through design* in terms of scientific research theories is somewhat difficult. A simple, working definition from Stappers and Giaccardi (2017) can be summarized as actions of design which have a formative role in the knowledge generation. For our case, it is about understanding a complex problem and answering it through iterative prototyping. Furthermore, Gaver (2012) argues that there is a clash between the expectations from the traditional science that a research methodology should be falsifiable, and the unfalsifiable outputs that research through design can provide as an approach. To be clearer about this, research through design by its nature, takes the basic principles of design thinking, where multiple possibilities of solutions are generated to answer complex, wicked problems. Consequently, as Gaver (2012) explains, it can't, and doesn't aim to, provide a concrete answer that can be tested and found false or true. Instead, this generative approach tells that the findings might solve the problem, which is a statement that can't be falsified with any number of disproving attempts. However, this flexibility of solutions is what makes research through design a fitting approach for complex real-world problems which can't be met with singular concrete solutions and requires creative problem solving. This is also complemented by the transdisciplinary nature of the study which can "grasp the complexity of problems and take into account the diversity of life-world" (Pohl & Hirsch Hadorn, 2007).

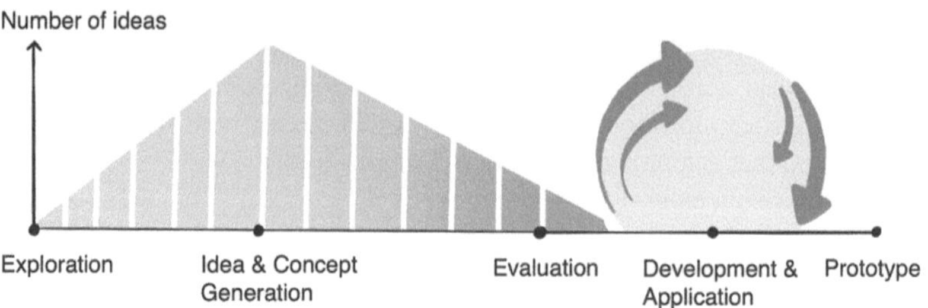

Fig. 2 The stages of research through design (RtD)

The research through design method for this study will also, ideally, contribute to a multitude of tangible solutions to each specific user case. As it can be understood from the name research through design, the research data will be generated from every step of the design processes of various assistive products, solutions, and modifications. The main stakeholder and the focus of this study is the assistive product users who have different physical disabilities. And together with other stakeholders (designers, makers with engineering and other backgrounds, design researchers), they will be able to provide varying inputs to the research at different stages of the study. Consequently, it can be helpful to think of the research process in the traditional design thinking steps (Keitsch & Vermeulen, 2020) to better understand and discuss the stakeholders' roles and participation in the research (see Fig. 2).

2 Methodology

2.1 Research Through Making

To achieve the analysis and consequent exploration, the study utilizes a research-through-design (RtD) method, or in this case we can refer to it as research-through-making. The authors would like to clarify that we do not propose research-through-making as a novel method, as the term has been used in various meanings within design, architecture and learning science literatures previously (Correa & Holbert, 2023; Sivtseva, 2020; Candy, 2019; Wherry, 2015). The research-through-making approach we present is simply an application of RtD method to the specific context of makerspaces and makers with a focus on accessibility. This approach involves going through a full process of analysing user needs specific to a use case of a makerspace tool or interface and producing relevant accessibility *hacks* with the help of rapid prototyping opportunities which are present inside the makerspace.

The whole making process and the produced physical and/or digital artifacts (hacks) are the sources of data for investigating the potential of makerspaces *making* themselves and their tools to be more accessible. Participatory workshops were conducted together with assistive product users and makers to identify accessibility barriers for makerspace tools and interfaces, which were then tackled through hacks and modifications produced inside the makerspace. Following this approach, the study endeavoured to illustrate the inherent production flexibility of the makerspace context, which utilizes the local materials with the products being made on the spot, even by the users themselves (Gershenfeld, 2017).

The workshops included the first author and the participants discussing and co-creating to make an accessibility solution specific to the participant's needs. The main goal of the workshop was to hack the 3D printing process and related interfaces to gain an understanding of and alleviate barriers for accessibility in 3D printing technologies for novice users. The workshop was facilitated by the researchers in collaboration with a rehabilitation hospital which houses production workshop facilities that can make assistive solutions for their patients in-house and recently added a 3D printer to their production capabilities. The collaboration was supported by the hospital whose strategy is to develop their current abilities to produce assistive solutions for specific needs of their patients. Then, the second workshop with a single co-making session was conducted in collaboration with the researchers' university (OsloMet) makerspace.

The recruitment of participants was done through the connections from the Sunnaas rehabilitation hospital and from OsloMet's university makerspace. Potential participants from the hospital who were willing to learn more about 3D printing were reached by invitation of the hospital employees to their patients with different types of physical accessibility needs. The interested patient was further informed about the study through a text explaining the steps of the workshop and the expected study outcome. The participants from the university makerspace were recruited by invitation from the first author. This was followed by a providing the participants information letters and consent forms. After the information and consent processes were completed, the workshop followed the steps below in two separate sessions to allow time for 3D printing (see Fig. 3).

During both workshop sessions with the participants, only the produced objects and the interfaces of maker tools and software were recorded to be analyzed by the researchers. The necessary data management and ethics approvals for this level of recordings have been received before the conduct of the workshop sessions. Norwegian Agency for Shared Services in Education and Research (SIKT) approval reference number is 409194.

Thus, to reach our findings, we have utilized (1) the objects and hacks that were produced during the sessions and (2) the participants' learning and the interaction with the 3D printer as data, and no health-related sensitive information were collected from the participants.

The research-through-making approach (see Fig. 3) involved two consequent co-making sessions each lasting one hour. First co-making session included the steps of (1) introducing the workflow of the 3D printer and warming up with a printing of a small model from Thingiverse, (2) discussing on the participant's accessibility needs, (3) deciding on specific problems to produce accessibility hacks for the makerspace, (4) and the researcher and the participant developing the hacks for production. The second co-making session included (1) user testing the produced accessibility hacks in the makerspace with the participant, (2) utilizing the hacks to produce an object for

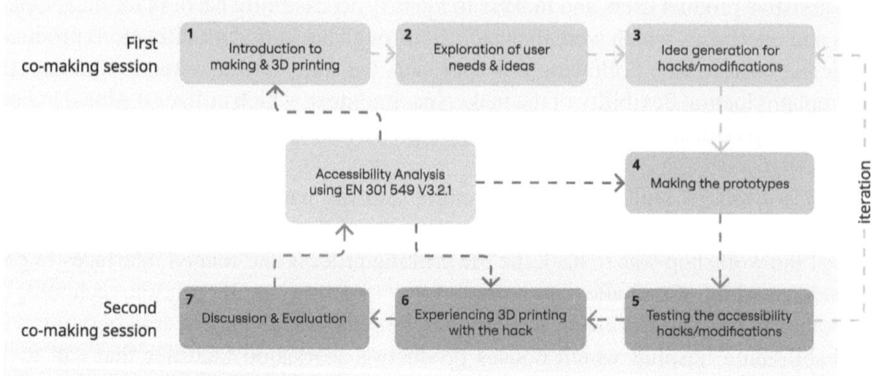

Fig. 3 The stages of research through making approach

participant's preference, and (3) discussing on the hack, the process, and the prototype with the participant.

In total one participant with physical limitations from the hospital and three participants from the university makerspace joined the study. The participant from the hospital was a patient in the Spinal Cord Injury Department of Sunnaas Rehabilitation Hospital who was a wheelchair user and had back pains limiting their movement and ability to reach. The other three participants were makers from the university makerspace. Their maker knowledge and skills varied with one being an experienced staff engineer and two being student mentors at the makerspace.

2.2 Accessibility Analysis Criteria

Our investigation into the accessibility barriers in the 3D printing experience of the participant, a novice 3D printer user, will go through the steps of the research-through-making approach and involves two focuses. Both focuses make use of the 'Accessibility requirements for ICT products and services' Harmonised European Standard (EN) 301 549 V3.2.1 (2021–03) (ETSI, 2021). The EN accessibility requirements was chosen because it covers accessibility of web and application interfaces, physical products and physical environments. This wide coverage of guidelines provided a suitable framework for investigating makerspaces in multiple levels. First, we briefly looked into the accessibility of the webpages where the participant browsed, found, and acquired the ready-made 3D-modelled files for printing. The guidelines regarding these webpages in EN accessibility requirements are adopted from the Web Content Accessibility Guidelines (WCAG) (ETSI, 2021).

Manual expert accessibility evaluations of the webpages done by the first author and our observations of the participant's experience in the workshops were used to look at one of the four WCAG principles and its guidelines. These principles were included and excluded based on their applicability to the participant's physical limitations. As the first participant was a wheelchair user with limited reach but had no noteworthy reduced sensory functions, the guidelines addressing *perceivable* (sensory-focused), *understandable* (cognition-focused), and *robustness* (assistive device-focused) were considered less relevant in the study context. The guideline of *operable*, with its focus on navigation and interaction, was the applicable principle for the participant's physical limitations and discussed in this analysis with several sub-guidelines. The investigated webpages were initially put through automatic WCAG checkers that provide scores and flag the elements with accessibility problems. Although there were many elements flagged in the HTML codes by the automatic checkers to be improved to reach the accessibility standards fully, many of the flagged problems were unrelated to the principle of *operable* and were not in the scope of this study.

Then, more focus is given to the analysis of the whole 3D printing experience through the frame of several applicable guideline clauses of EN. The EN requirements have an exhaustive list of accessibility clauses which are not fully applicable to investigated cases in this research. Therefore, our study selected clauses from the EN guideline by taking the physical limitations of the participant and the barriers they faced with the investigated interfaces in consideration, excluding the ones that are outside the scope. The EN guidelines referring to *operable* principle were included both for the website and printing preparation software interfaces, excluding non-applicable ones such as *keyboard accessible*, as the participant only interacted through a pointer. The guidelines for the physical interface of the 3D printer were included from the *8. Hardware* heading, focusing on the guidelines for *8.3. Stationary ICT* and *8.4. Mechanically operable parts*. The inclusion and exclusion of the guidelines and principles were assessed and agreed upon among the authors as part of research quality assurance.

2.3 Author's Positionality Statement

The first author who conducted the workshops will be mentioned as 'the researcher' in this section. The researcher in the research through making approach can be argued to have several roles and identities that should be acknowledged. The researcher has no reduced functioning, with a background in design research and is a maker with sufficient technical knowledge to use rapid prototyping tools and software in makerspaces.

During the introduction stage, the researcher mainly acted as a facilitator, where the participant was briefed and introduced to how rapid prototyping (mainly focusing on 3D printing) works and what can the maker approach offer them to produce accessibility hacks. During the exploration and idea generation stage, the researcher took the role of initiator of the discussions and then the mediator between the participant's problem space and the solution space of alternative hack ideas. During the co-making and 3D printing stages, the role of the researcher started with guiding the participant through the digital interfaces, which then turned into the role of a co-maker shared with the participant (dividing tasks such as setting up the 3D printer and cleaning the excess support filaments from the final printed object etc.). During analysis of the making process and interfaces in terms of accessibility, the researcher utilized accessibility assessment guidelines to analyze interfaces of webpages, software and hardware used in the overall 3D printing experience.

3 Findings

The co-making sessions with four (one patient + a group session with three makers) participants concluded with the production of: introductory printing of 3D object models (chosen together with the participant from Thingiverse), the hacks printed with the 3D printer for improving the accessibility of the 3D printing experience for the participant, and a final object or assistive part that the participant wanted for their own daily use. The production of the final objects was aimed both as a motivation for the participants to join the study and to test out the accessibility hacks that were 3D-printed in the first sessions. The research-through-making approach with co-making sessions reached several findings that are related to the act of producing the hacks with the 3D printer, the accessibility analysis of the whole 3D printing experience for the novice user, and the participation of the patient in the co-making process. The findings are presented in the order of the steps of the research-through-making approach (see Fig. 3) by connecting each step to the related EN accessibility guidelines shown in the table below.

Our observations suggest the webpages of Thingiverse are one part of the user journey and not the source of the problem for user navigation. The pressing accessibility problem observed in the workshop was that the whole 3D printing process was a fragmented experience between different interfaces of webpages, 3D printing preparation/slicing software, analog data transfer (computer-to-SD card-to-printer) and the interface of the 3D printer itself. This was especially noted when the participant was asked at the end of the second co-making session about their dependency for guidance with 3D printing process. The participant stated that even after the introduction activities for 3D printing in the first co-making session, they required explicit directions of the next step after they were done with an interface (such as transferring 3D files from computer to the 3D printer). This lack of interface continuity between the steps results in the inexperienced user requiring guidance and pointers in every step/change of the process, impacting their agency and their ability to access and use 3D printing (see Fig. 4).

3.1 First Co-Making Session

Introduction to 3D Printing. The first sessions were important to illustrate the motivation and ability of inexperienced users to learn and complete simple production tasks using maker tools, in particular 3D printers in this case. The resulting products/objects for the participant focused more on introducing the 3D printing skills and knowledge to the novice user (see Fig. 5), exploring accessibility barriers, modifying the user's wheelchair and hospital bed and the user's makerspace experience more accessible more than focusing on the maker tool itself. The barriers observed in the first co-making session showed the possibility of achieving the improved accessibility to the experience by a small number of well-targeted hacks and modifications informed by the accessibility guidelines.

Browsing and Acquiring 3D Model Files From Thingiverse. The participant used a trackpad to operate the website interface with a pointer successfully, as the website interactions did not require or provided alternatives for complex pointer actions (9.2.5.1 Pointer gestures), and allowed the user to cancel out on touches by mistake (9.2.5.2

Table 1. Overview of 3D printing interactions and their connection to accessibility guidelines

Interaction in the 3D printing process	Related guidelines from EN accessibility requirements
Browsing and acquiring 3D model files from Thingiverse	9.2 Operable, 9.2.4 Navigable, 9.2.4.2 Page titled, 9.2.4.4 Link purpose (in context), 9.2.4.5 Multiple ways, 9.2.5.1 Pointer gestures, 9.2.5.2 Pointer cancellation
Preparing the files for printing	11.2 Operable, 11.2.2 Enough time, 11.2.2.1 Timing adjustable, 11.2.5.1 Pointer gestures, 11.2.5.2 Pointer cancellation, 11.7 User preferences
Using the SD card for file transfer	8.4.3 Keys, tickets and fare cards, 11.2.4.5 Void (Multiple Ways)
Moving around and approaching the 3D printer	8.3.2.3 Obstructed forward reach, 8.3.2.3.1 Clear space, 8.3.2.4 Knee and toe clearance width, 8.3.4.3.2 Forward approach
Powering-up and shutting down the printer	4.2.8 Usage with limited reach, 8.3.2 Forward reach
Reading the digital screen of the 3D printer	4.2.8 Usage with limited reach, 8.3.5 Visibility
One-button knob interaction with the 3d printer	4.2.7 Usage with limited manipulation or strength, 4.2.8 Usage with limited reach, 5.5.1 Means of operation, 5.7 Key repeat, 8.3.2 Forward reach, 8.4.2.1 Means of operation of mechanical parts
Glass panel install and removal	4.2.8 Usage with limited reach, 5.9 Simultaneous user actions, 8.3.2 Forward reach
Removing the print and excess support filament materials	4.2.8 Usage with limited reach, 5.9 Simultaneous user actions

Pointer cancellation). The participant navigated through pages with different types of 3D objects premade by other users. This navigation was supported by the page's inclusion of relevant titles and explanations for links inside them (9.2.4.2 Page titled, 9.2.4.4 Link purpose in context). Once the participant chose objects, which were a shoehorn to use in hospital, and a picture frame for personal use, there were multiple ways to acquire and export 3D files onto the next step, but it was not communicative enough for the participant (9.2.4.5 Multiple ways). For the purposes of this step of the co-making session, the webpages were operable (9.2) and navigable (9.2.4).

Preparing Files for Printing. The interface of UltiMaker Cura preparation software allowed the participant to operate with the pointer in all interactions. Some shortcuts were required to be instructed to the participant to navigate the 3D space in the software (11.2 Operable). Alternatives for not requiring these shortcuts were provided as one-click buttons (11.2.5.1 Pointer gestures) and allowed the user to cancel out on touches by mistake (11.2.5.2 Pointer cancellation). The observations from consequent sessions

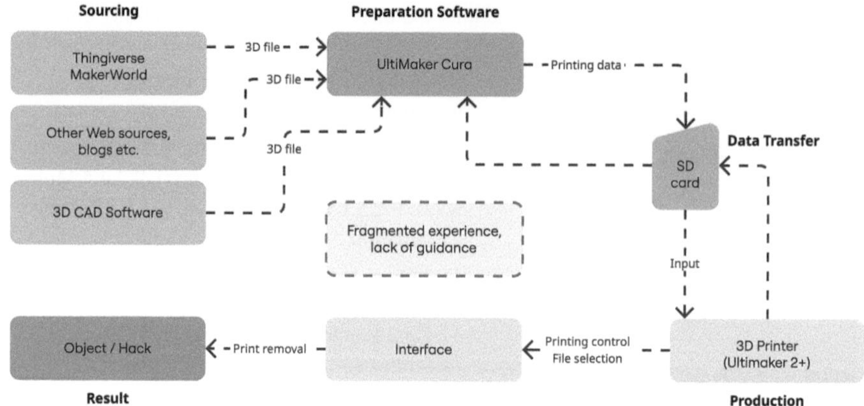

Fig. 4 Fragmented steps and interfaces of the 3D printing experience

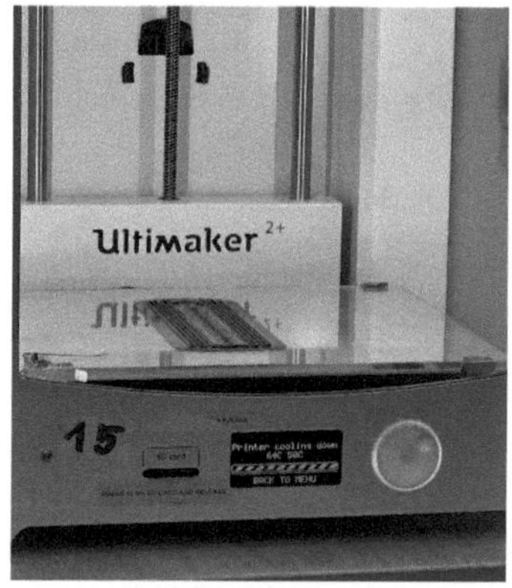

Fig. 5 Introductory printing the model of participant's choice (a shoehorn) from Thingiverse

revealed that preparation interface for 3D printing provided enough flexibility for the participant's choices and fine tuning the preferences (see Fig. 6), which stayed as preset for the second co-making session (11.7 User preferences). The pace of the process was also suitable (11.2.2 Enough time) and in the participant's control (11.2.2.1 Timing adjustable). The 3D printing after the startup process did not require a time-critical action from the participant.

The apparent accessibility barrier from our observations here is the lack of continuation between the consequent steps and changing interfaces. Each interface of the experience such as the preparation software interface (e.g. UltiMaker Cura) and the webpages of Thingiverse and MakerWorld in themselves are not overly complicated and act accordingly to the expectations. However, when one of these steps is completed, such as downloading a 3D file from Thingiverse or slicing the 3D model into printing layers in UltiMaker Cura, the participant experienced a lack of prompting and feedback on how to move on to the next step in a different interface.

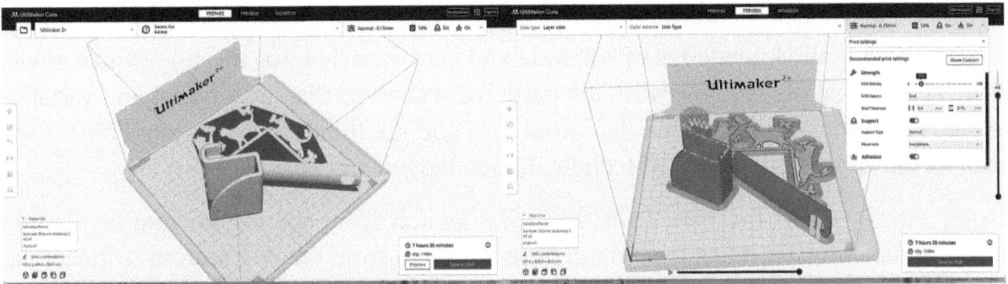

Fig. 6. 3D printing preparation with UltiMaker Cura software in between the sessions

This effect is more noticeable between the steps where the medium is changing back-and-forth from digital to analog; more explicitly, when exporting a gcode into an SD card and transferring it to the 3D printer and importing it through the digital interface of the 3D printer. This barrier hints at a design opportunity of an intermediary guiding, prompting and feedback interface between the steps, which is investigated further in the discussions section.

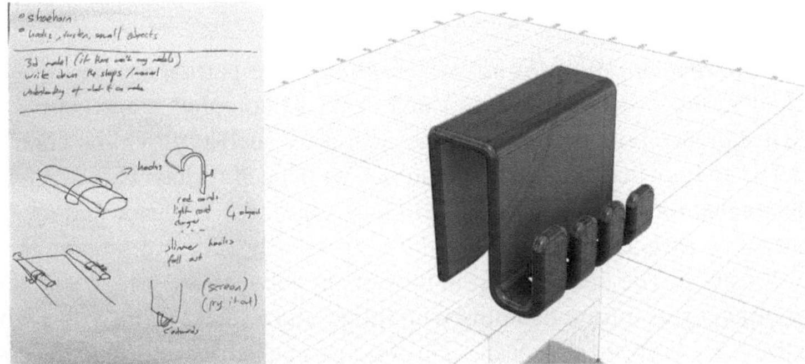

Fig. 7 Co-making sketches together with participant (left), 3D modelling (right)

Exploration of User Needs and Idea Generation. The co-making sessions involved discussions with the participant aided with sketching to generate ideas for 3D printable hacks that would alleviate their accessibility needs (see Fig. 7). The participant communicated with simple sketches and gestures to explain their need for a holder accessory to keep regularly used tools and products in accessible locations for their wheelchair and hospital bed. After further discussion to refine details, the hack idea is 3D modelled by the researcher to be 3D printed.

3.2 Making the Prototypes

Interacting with the 3D Printer. The process of 3D printing is much safer and approachable for the participant with reduced functioning relative to other production methods such as woodworking or power tools. However, it also required a level of technology literacy and knowledge of software and hardware that was missing from a novice user. The co-making sessions with the participant showed that the amount and variation of steps and interfaces between the initial idea and the finalized, 3D printed object was seen as intimidating in terms of technical knowledge and skill.

Using the SD Card for File Transfer. The switch from the digital interface to the physical data transfer interface did not have a prompt from the preparation software and participant required external instructions from the researcher. The physical interface of the SD card and related slots were tactilely discernible (8.4.3 Keys, tickets and fare cards). The preparation software had provided the option to connect to the 3D printer in the hospital makerspace wirelessly (11.2.4.5 Void - Multiple Ways), which would bypass the accessibility problem of having to change from digital to analog and back to digital interfaces while transferring files. However, the choice of using SD cards instead of the more seamless choice of wireless connection to transfer files was also observed in the university makerspace. When asked during the group session, the makers stated that this was the practice to ensure better control over a maker starting a 3D print remotely, resulting in unsupervised prints failing and damaging the 3D printers or wasting materials. By using the SD card method, they can better track when a user is starting a print and make sure the printing is supervised correctly.

Moving Around and Approaching the 3D Printer. The participant was a wheelchair user and had to move between stations and desks to complete steps. The 3D printer and where it stationed provided some of the clearances such as providing enough empty space underneath for wheelchair users to interact with the 3D printer (EN 301 549 criteria 8.3.2.3 Obstructed forward reach, 8.3.2.3.1 Clear space, 8.3.2.4 Knee and toe clearance width), but some aspects were limiting the user to fully access the features from the wheelchair position. The back-and-forth movement between the printer and the station with the computer was time consuming with little room to make turns with a wheelchair (criterion 8.3.4.3.2 Forward approach). This finding of a barrier informed the co-making of the second version of the holder hack for improving the wheelchair experience in the makerspace room (see Fig. 8).

Fig. 8 Second version of the holder hack for attaching maker tools on different wheelchairs

Powering-on and Shutting Down the Printer. The initial step of turning on the power for the printer was inaccessible for the participant because of the power-on button's location at the back of the printer. As a result of limited space and layout of the hospital makerspace, the participant could not approach the backside of the printer, limiting access to both power and filament control from the front (criteria 4.2.8 Usage with limited reach, and 8.3.2.3 Obstructed forward reach). This necessitated assistance by the researcher in the session.

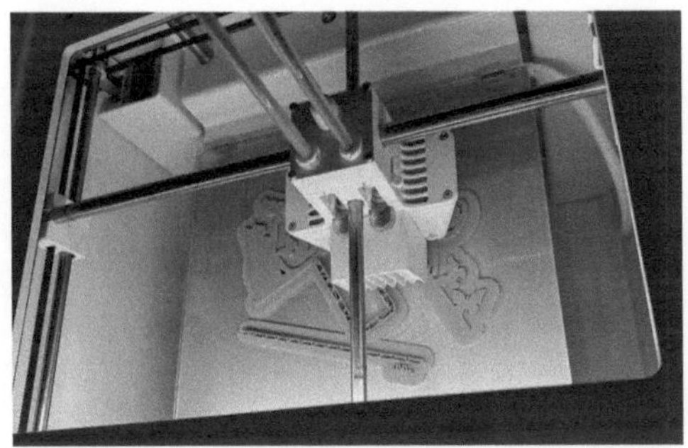

Fig. 9 The 3D print of the holder hack and models acquired from Thingiverse, top view

Reading the Digital Screen of the 3D Printer. The participant had difficulties reading the digital screen located at the bottom of the 3D printer which was in a vertical position. The participant was a wheelchair user with difficulties in moving their upper body leaning back and forth, which made interacting with and reading the small screen at the bottom side of the 3D printer less than ideal as the printer was in a fixed height (criterion 4.2.8 Usage with limited reach). The height was low enough to allow them to observe the beginning of the printing process, an important step of checking if it's a stable print (see Fig. 9), but it wasn't high enough to comfortably read and interact with the screen for the participant (criterion 8.3.5 Visibility).

One-Button Knob Interaction with the 3D Printer. The 3D printer interface was controlled solely by the knob-type button next to its digital screen, and no alternative method to control the screen was present (4.2.7 Usage with limited manipulation or strength, 5.5.1 Means of operation, 8.4.2.1 Means of operation of mechanical parts). It required turning for menu navigation and pressing for selection. The repetitive pressing of the button in consequent screens required the participant some getting used. The position of the button was reachable from a wheelchair (4.2.8 Usage with limited reach, 8.3.2 Forward reach). The selection of the interface elements was done by pressing in the knob with enough delay between repeating actions (5.7 Key repeat).

Glass Panel Install and Removal. The digital interfaces and the 3D printer interface provided the novice participant with warnings regarding the high temperature during the bedplate heating process. The physical hazard of hot bedplate was also shielded by a glass pane from the participant during the printing. The attachable glass panel, although not critical to the functioning of the 3D printer, is a safety feature to prevent injuries. The attachment details for the panel were in reach from a wheelchair position (4.2.8 Usage with limited reach, 8.3.2 Forward reach). However, the participant occasionally needed to hold onto a surface/desk to stabilize themselves with the wheelchair. This sometimes required them to do one hand interactions, requiring assistance from the researcher for install and removal of the glass pane (5.9 Simultaneous user actions).

3.3   Second Co-making Session

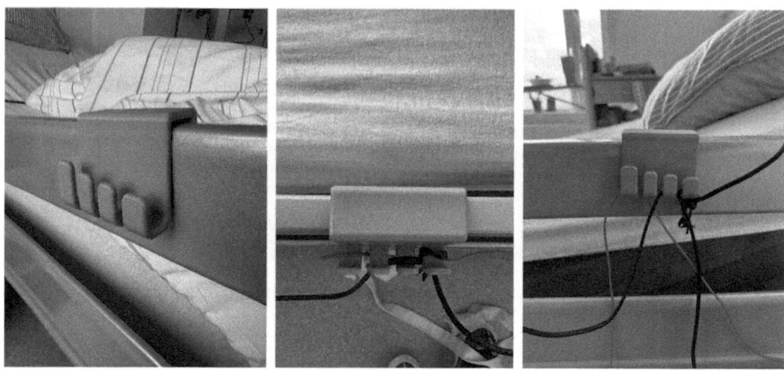

Fig. 10. 3D printed holder hack usage test and successful fit and use on the hospital bed

Testing the Accessibility Hack.   The suitability of the 3D printed object to the hospital bed environment was made sure by taking reference photographs of the bed frame. This is found to be an effective and easy-to-do method for measuring dimensions of the to-be-modified products and environment; can even be requested from the participants remotely. The holder hack printed after the first co-making session is tested on the participant's hospital bed and worked successfully with various room control interfaces and cords attached to it (see Fig. 10). The second, smaller version of the holder was printed and tested on the wheelchair.

Experiencing 3D Printing with the Hack.   *Removing the print and excess support filament materials.* Even though the build plate was reachable from a wheelchair position (4.2.8 Usage with limited reach), removing the second printed objects of the first session (the holder hack, the shoehorn and a picture frame) from the build plate required assistance from the researcher, as the surface area was bigger than the first introductory prints and required more force. (holding the print and scraping the bottom surface requiring two hands, 5.9 Simultaneous user actions). The participant used the first holder hack on their wheelchair while they prepared and printed the second version of the hack (see Fig. 11). The second print proved no difficulty in removing excess filaments.

In-Between Different Interfaces and Mediums.   There was a lack of information and guidance for the novice participant to follow while moving from one interface and medium to another. This resulted in them having to get assistance from the researcher

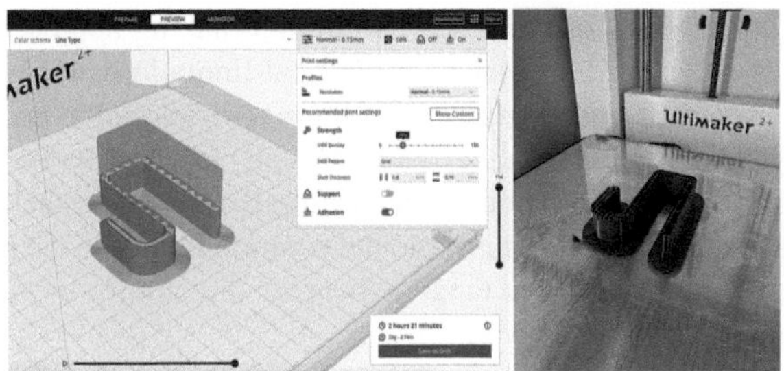

Fig. 11 The participant prepared, transferred the file and put the second version of the holder hack to print

and stated by the participant to potentially limit their agency in future trials of 3D prinitng for them. The university makerspace had produced hacks to tackle this guidance problem by providing a summary of the necessary steps the novice maker should take next to the rapid prototyping tools (see Fig. 12).

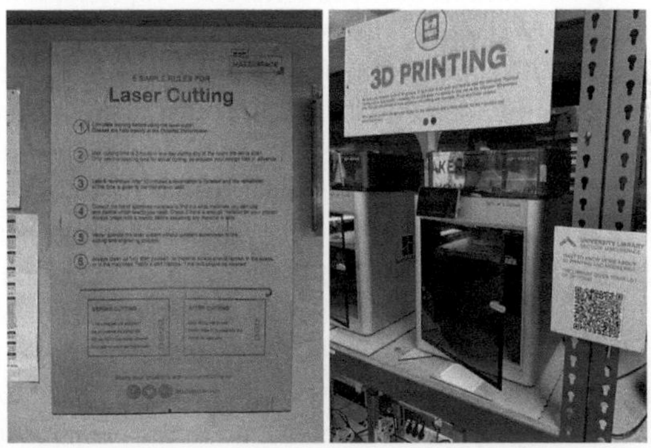

Fig. 12 The information on making steps provided by makerspace-made boards

4   Discussion

The research-through-making approach involving co-making with the participants showed great promise for the maker approach, mindset, and tools allowing makerspaces to make themselves more accessible and inclusive. The study focused on hacks to alleviate the existing barriers to accessibility in makerspaces. This focus needs to be emphasized because the barriers which the hacks intend to alleviate can be dealt with more effectively if makerspaces were designed to be accessible from the beginning or more accessible versions of 3D printers were used. However, the ability to produce its own hacks and modify itself to be more accessible incrementally is unique to makerspaces and their tools. Thus, the study endeavored to investigate that local production opportunity as it also allows the makerspace to respond to more personalized accessibility needs of its users.

The co-making sessions of our research-through-making approach also helped us ensure that the assistive product user with physical limitations was also motivated to participate in the research. First, acquisition of a functional prototype at the end of the transdisciplinary collaboration in makerspaces was an incentive, and second, by participating this research they increase their agency while also increasing their social inclusion in their immediate community (in this case, the community inside the hospital). Consequently, the research aimed to have tangible benefits directly for the users themselves, and to their local communities as well.

5 The Hacks for Accessibility

There seems to be three possible 'levels' for hacking the 3D printing process to improve accessibility. First is hacking on the 'maker' level, exemplified by the holder hack produced by the participant for their wheelchair. This level of hacks would focus on aiding the maker personally while they navigate and interact with the makerspace and tools. The second level is on the interface level, shown by the need of providing the user a connecting and guiding interface in-between different webpages, software and hardware interfaces. The third level of possible hacks are on the spatial, makerspace level. They would provide the accessibility improvements related to clearances, reach and approach distances when the makers interact with 3D printers inside the makerspace.

The holder hack, co-made with the participant had two versions for two different use contexts. In the first context it hacks the makerspace experience for the participant when the holder hack is attached to the wheelchair to provide easy access to tools and personal items without moving back-and-forth between stations. In the second context, the hack is modifying the hospital bed to allow for less physical effort in reaching and accessing tools and items around the bed while laying down. This is a result of both the location of the makerspace being inside the hospital, and the hack focusing on makers, so it is not bound to the makerspace and can extend to the hospital context.

Moreover, the accessible makerspace can help transform the hospital's in-house making competencies of assistive products or aids. Before the makerspace initiative, the hospital produced custom-made aids for their patients with a low-tech workshop operated by an experienced carpenter. Because of the level of skill and knowledge required to do carpentry, the built-up competency and knowledge of making patient-specific aids accumulated on this one employee and the knowledge and skills are hard-to-transfer. The accessibility of the recent makerspace with a lower skill threshold than carpentry will be an important enabler of making competency for more staff and patients.

The findings suggest there is a potential for user interface hacks. This addition can help narrow the current gap in continuity between the interfaces and mediums. Such interface hacks could act as guides in-between the separate software, webpages and analog interfaces. The interface could act as an overlay to guide the novice user throughout the experience, starting with finding the 3D models from webpages, exporting and preparing them on 3D printing preparation software, transferring the file to the 3D printer through the SD card, and controlling the 3D printer interface. Providing this holistic experience to connect separate interfaces and mediums would improve the accessibility of the 3D printing as a new experience for many users.

The study showed that there is, in fact, a more streamlined and accessible option provided by the interfaces and 3D printers, but this accessible option was competing with other motivations of the makerspace and was avoided by the makers. If the 3D printers in the hospital and the university makerspace were connected to the preparation software wirelessly, the SD card and one-button knob interfaces could be bypassed. This would solve the fragmented experience of 3D printing with multiple interfaces to some extent, but that would result in people maintaining the makerspace losing control over the printing process and safety (see Sect. 3.2). This suggests that even when the interfaces provide the necessary accessibility solutions, the less accessible options might be adopted by groups and organizations. Thus, making accessibility hacks for the less streamlined method (using SD cards) can be one of the ways to compromise between makerspace control and accessibility of the process.

Lastly, the 3D printed hacks produced by the makers in the university makerspace are examples of the third zone of accessibility hacks focusing on spatial level. 3D printed structures and modular holders and pockets allowed them to provide necessary tools and equipment in an accessible position close to the 3D printers (see Fig. 13). This incremental, modular approach to hacking the making environment gives flexibility to the makerspace, adapting to the makers' changing needs for various tools.

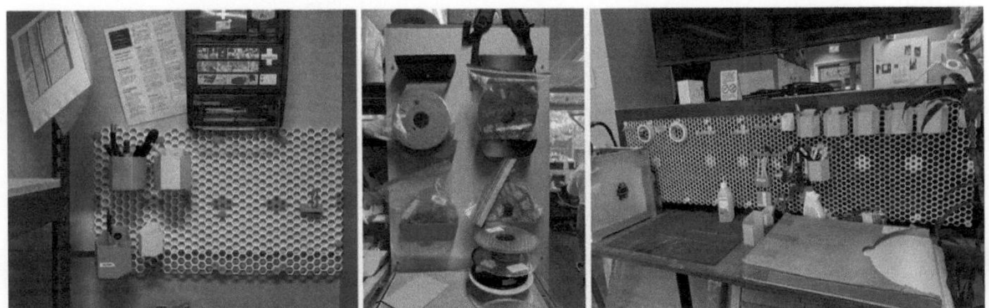

Fig. 13 The spatial accessibility hacks providing accessible and organized making tools

6 Agency and Independence

We argue that the goal of improving the accessibility of makerspaces is for these spaces to include more makers with varying abilities, which would mean more people with disabilities and limitations gaining access to means of making objects and tools for themselves. The more accessible makerspaces and tools become, the more independence people with physical limitations gain in making hacks, tools and objects that allow them to improve their agency in daily life. Our study showed that, agency of the participant as a rehabilitation patient acts both as a motivation and a result of participating in co-making activities in the makerspace. Their reduced agency stemming from physical limitations, long hospital stays, and busy rehabilitation programs motivates them to participate as a recreational activity. Then, the produced hacks improve their agency and independence from the hospital staff by making both the makerspace and the hospital experience more accessible.

7 Limitations and Future Research

The recruitment from the hospital's patients was done according to their availability to participate in the study. The initial sessions with the first participant showed the need for the study to diversify the types of physical disabilities or limitations, such as upper body and lower body limitations in participants, to reach its goal of alleviating wider accessibility problems in maker tools. As a result of busy rehabilitation programs of the patients, there weren't multiple patients available and willing to participate in the co-making sessions. To address the problem, the authors aimed to achieve variety of perspectives in co-making sessions by conducting a second workshop with a group of makers with varying experience levels. Although this improved the study to have a diversity of perspectives, more participation from the patients' perspective is needed to have a more robust understanding of accessibility barriers in makerspace contexts. We acknowledge that the hospital makerspace context of the first participant might positively influenced the accessibility motivations from the makerspace's side. Since the makerspace was a recent initiative by the hospital to involve their patients, they were arguably more inclined to put effort on improving accessibility than other makerspaces in public contexts. The possible directions for future research include diversifying the participants' disability and physical limitation types, and exploring and testing interface possibilities for providing a holistic and more accessible 3D printing experience.

Acknowledgements. This study was funded as part of a PhD research project by Technology, Art and Design Faculty, Innovation for Sustainability Program of OsloMet. The authors would like to thank Sunnaas Rehabilitation Hospital and OsloMet Makerspace for their collaboration.

References

Allen, K.H., Balaska, A.K., Aronson, R.M., Rogers, C., Short, E.S.: Barriers and benefits: the path to accessible makerspaces. In: Proceedings of the 25th International ACM SIGACCESS Conference on Computers and Accessibility, (pp. 1–14). **2**(5), 99–110 (2016)

Bosse, I.K., Linke, H., Pelka, B.: SELFMADE–self-determination and communication through inclusive makerspaces. In: International Conference on Universal Access in Human-Computer Interaction (pp. 409–420). Springer, Cham (2018)

Candy, L.: The Creative Reflective Practitioner: Research Through Making and Practice. Routledge. (2019)

Correa, I., Holbert, N.: Material-led research: a posthumanist methodology for maker education practitioners. Digital Cult. Educ. **14**(5). (2023)

da Silva, L.A., Medola, F.O., Rodrigues, O.V., Rodrigues, A.C.T., Sandnes, F.E.: Interdisciplinary-based development of user-friendly customized 3D printed upper limb prosthesis. In: Ahram, T.Z., Falcão, C. (eds.) AHFE 2018. AISC, vol. 794, pp. 899–908. Springer, Cham (2019). https://doi.org/10.1007/978-3-319-94947-5_88

ETSI: EN 301 549 v.3.2.1 "Accessibility requirements for ICT products and services" (2021). Retrieved from: https://www.etsi.org/human-factors-accessibility/en-301-549-v3-the-harmonized-european-standard-for-ict-accessibility

Gaver, W.: What should we expect from research through design? In: Proceedings Of The Sigchi Conference on Human Factors in Computing Systems, (pp. 937–946). (2012)

Gershenfeld, N., Gershenfeld, A., Cutcher-Gershenfeld, J.: Designing reality: How to survive and thrive in the third digital revolution. Hachette UK. (2012)

Kawano, M., Takamura, Y., Tachihara, M., Yokota, K., Yozu, A.: The relationship between motivation for rehabilitation and sense of agency in patients with cerebrovascular disease, and nurse support for patient agency. Int. J. Affect. Eng. **20**(3), 143–151 (2021)

Keitsch, M.M., Vermeulen, W.J. (Eds.).: Transdisciplinarity for sustainability: Aligning diverse practices. Routledge. (2020)

Kohtala, C.: Making "making" critical: how sustainability is constituted in fab lab ideology. Des. J. **20**(3), 375–394 (2017)

Lipschultz, A.: Modification and customization of medical equipment. Biomed. Instrum. Technol. **46**(5), 370–373 (2012)

Pohl, C., Hirsch Hadorn, G.: Principles for Designing Transdisciplinary Research. (2007)

Sarwar, S., Wilson, D.: Systematic literature review on making and accessibility. In: Proceedings of the 24th International ACM SIGACCESS Conference on Computers and Accessibility, (pp. 1–5). (2022)

Sivtseva, M.: Learning-by-making as a tool for provoking placemaking initiatives in Yakutsk, North-Eastern Siberia. Tradition Innov. Art Design Educ. **94**. (2020)

Stappers, P.J., Giaccardi, E.: Research through design. In: The encyclopedia of human-computer interaction, (pp. 1–94). The Interaction Design Foundation (2017)

Terzioğlu, N.: Do-Fix workshops: understanding users' product repair experience. In: PLATE: Product Lifetimes and the Environment, pp. 408–412. IOS Press. (2017)

Usó, V.G., Sandnes, F.E., Medola, F.O.: Using virtual reality and rapid prototyping to co-create together with hospitalized children. In: Di Nicolantonio, M., Rossi, E., Alexander, T. (eds.) AHFE 2019. AISC, vol. 975, pp. 279–288. Springer, Cham (2020). https://doi.org/10.1007/978-3-030-20216-3_26

Wherry, L.: Knowing Through Making. MInt (Prof) dissertation, University of Pretoria, Pretoria. LNCS Homepage, http://www.springer.com/lncs. Accessed 25 Oct 2023 (2015)

Gamifying Financial Literacy: A Digital Design Mobile Project to Promote Financial Literacy in Young Adults

Marisa Capa[1] and Jorge Brandão Pereira[2]([envelope]) [ORCID]

[1] Polytechnic Institute of Cávado and Ave, Design School, Barcelos, Portugal
a18775@alunos.ipca.pt

[2] Lnstitute for Research in Design, Media and Culture ID +, Barcelos, Portugal
jmpereira@ipca.pt

Abstract. The Financial literacy remains a significant challenge in Portugal, particularly among young adults who lack essential skills in saving, investing, and credit management. This study explores how gamification can enhance financial literacy through a digital design approach. A mobile app project was developed to make financial education engaging and interactive. Using the Design Thinking methodology – empathize, define, ideate, prototype, and test – the project focused on user-centered development. Gamification elements such as points, rewards, and interactive challenges were integrated to sustain motivation and daily engagement. Targeting users aged 18–30, the design process began with user research to define personas and usage scenarios, guiding the app's structure from onboarding to simulations. A site map ensured a logical information architecture, followed by low- and medium-fidelity wireframes to test navigation and layout. A vibrant visual identity was created to enhance usability and appeal. The high-fidelity prototype emphasized modularity and scalability, allowing future expansion and easy updates. Usability testing validated interface clarity and the effectiveness of gamified learning. Participants completed tasks like expense tracking, goal setting, and investment simulation, showing strong engagement and reduced friction. Findings suggest that a well-designed, gamified app can effectively boost financial literacy while promoting positive behavioral change. Key features – goal setting, simulations, and learning modules – make the experience both educational and enjoyable. This project highlights how digital design, grounded in user experience and gamification, offers an effective solution for addressing financial knowledge gaps among Portuguese youth.

Keywords: Financial Literacy · Gamification · Digital Design · User-Centered Design

1 Financial Literacy

The concept of financial literacy has undergone significant evolution over time. Noctor et al. [1] defined financial literacy as the set of knowledge necessary for individuals to make informed financial decisions, encompassing both the content acquired through

© The Author(s), under exclusive license to Springer Nature Switzerland AG 2026
M. Antona and C. Stephanidis (Eds.): HCII 2025, LNCS 16335, pp. 50–64, 2026.
https://doi.org/10.1007/978-3-032-12781-5_4

educational programs and the practical ability to apply that knowledge. Subsequently, Lusardi & Mitchell [2] define financial literacy as the combination of knowledge, skills, attitudes, and behaviors needed to make sound financial decisions and achieve financial well-being.

In general terms, financial literacy refers to the understanding of core financial concepts and the ability to confidently manage one's personal finances. This includes essential skills such as cash flow management, saving, credit usage, loans, and investments, as well as the knowledge required to evaluate options and make sound financial decisions [3]. Financial literacy can be described as a combination of awareness, knowledge, skills, and behaviors necessary to make appropriate financial choices with the aim of achieving personal financial well-being. Competencies such as money management, understanding credit and debt, risk assessment, and making decisions about saving and investing are central aspects of financial literacy [4].

Financial literacy plays a crucial role in financial stability, directly influencing consumer decision-making. Rutledge [5] and Kozup and Hogarth [6] highlight its importance in protecting consumers from fraud and excessive debt. Furthermore, Bačová et al. [7] emphasize the need for financial literacy interventions to empower individuals in making everyday decisions that impact their financial situations.

The importance of financial literacy is closely tied to financial well-being, which includes the ability to manage daily finances, cope with financial shocks, achieve goals, and maintain the freedom to make decisions that enhance quality of life. Moreover, financial literacy is vital for protecting individuals from risks in the digital world, such as financial fraud, while also equipping them to make more informed decisions about investments, savings, and debt management. It also plays a key role in mitigating impulsive behaviors facilitated by digital technologies and fintech solutions [3].

Financial literacy is essential for both personal and societal stability, assisting individuals in making informed decisions regarding financial products and services. This not only prevents over-indebtedness but also improves resource management. Individuals with a higher understanding of financial concepts tend to make more appropriate decisions regarding saving, investing, and consumption, thereby increasing their confidence in using financial products. Consequently, this contributes to a more dynamic and innovative economy. Financial education is, therefore, an essential tool for preventing financial exclusion, enabling individuals to plan and save more effectively. This capability is necessary for the proper functioning of competitive financial markets [8].

2 Gamification as a Strategy for Financial Education

Gamification, a concept that emerged in the early 2000s, refers to the application of game design elements in non-game contexts. The first definition was introduced in 2002, when Nick Pelling described it as "the application of a game-like interface to make electronic transactions more playful and efficient" [9]. However, a widely accepted definition is provided by Deterding et al. [10], who characterize gamification as the use of typical game elements – such as rewards, challenges, and interactivity – in everyday situations to engage and motivate individuals.

Gamification has emerged as a promising strategy to enhance financial literacy and promote education across various domains by incorporating game-like features into non-gaming contexts. According to Huber et al. [11] this approach goes beyond merely making activities more enjoyable; it involves creating experiences that actively encourage user participation. For instance, financial education platforms can implement interactive quizzes, where users earn points for correct answers, thereby fostering an engaging and playful learning environment. Gamification mechanisms act as motivational drivers, contributing to user engagement across a wide range of contexts and environments [12]. The individual's level of commitment to assigned tasks is reflected in the achievement of goals, influencing their immersion in a playful environment [13]. The degree of user engagement is a critical factor for the success of gamification [14] and is largely determined by the time spent in active interaction with other users or with the system itself.

Moreover, gamification aims to elicit positive emotions and leverage skills associated with reward-based behavior. It can be applied to activities that require behavioral stimulation and necessitate the adaptation of the user experience to products, services, or processes. Gamification has proven effective in retaining user attention by creating a unique and enjoyable environment [15]. During the learning process, gamification contributes not only to motivation but also to the cognitive development of learners [16].

With the advancement of technology, gamification has expanded into various fields such as healthcare, education, retail, and financial services. Hamari et al. [17] emphasize that gamification represents a form of value co-creation between the user and the service provider, enhancing intrinsic motivational values through game-like features. Huotari and Hamari [18] define gamification as a playful experience capable of improving the user experience and creating value in non-game contexts.

3   Gamification in Financial Education

Gamification has proven to be an increasingly effective tool in promoting financial education by incorporating typical game elements such as rewards, leaderboards, challenges, and continuous feedback. These playful components stimulate user interest and engagement in learning financial concepts, which are often perceived as difficult or unappealing. Through the use of digital rewards and ranking systems, users are encouraged to improve their financial literacy while interacting in an engaging and enjoyable manner with financial applications [19].

Moreover, mobile banking (m-banking) applications have increasingly integrated gamification to foster responsible financial behaviors. The introduction of immediate rewards, such as points or badges, has proven particularly effective in motivating users, encouraging them to perform secure financial transactions and adopt more efficient saving practices.

Gamification also plays a critical role in overcoming the lack of motivation that often hinders the success of traditional financial education programs. Studies show that incorporating immediate rewards into digital financial platforms can significantly increase user engagement, making the learning process more appealing and accessible [20].

These playful incentives reinforce positive financial behaviors, such as efficient savings management and prudent credit usage, thereby facilitating the adoption of sound financial practices [21].

Another important aspect of gamification in financial education is its ability to promote financial inclusion, particularly in emerging economies. Through gamified mobile applications, individuals with limited access to formal education can still learn fundamental financial literacy concepts – such as account management and the use of payment methods – while participating safely in digital transactions [19]. These platforms offer an interactive and accessible learning experience, contributing to the development of essential financial skills and encouraging more responsible financial behavior.

The growing adoption of digital financial services and the demand for more enjoyable and interactive experiences – especially in the post-pandemic context – highlight the relevance of gamification in financial education [22]. With the pandemic years accelerating the shift toward a "new normal," banking services have begun to offer more convenient and user-friendly solutions, making gamification even more pertinent [23]. According to [18], gamification not only increases user engagement but also contributes to customer experience value creation by shaping behavior and fostering a more dynamic learning environment.

4 Gamification, Human-Computer Interaction (HCI), and User Experience (UX)

In recent years, the rapid proliferation of software for computers and mobile devices has elevated these technologies to mass-market status. This significant increase in software presence in daily life has driven designers to seek innovative ways to motivate users to adopt and maintain engagement with their applications. Within this context, gamification plays a crucial role, influencing both Human-Computer Interaction (HCI) and User Experience (UX). According to the Interaction Design Foundation [24], HCI is a multidisciplinary field focused on designing computing technology and the interaction between humans and computers, encompassing all forms of information technology design.

With the popularization of personal computers, a growing need arose to simplify digital interfaces to reach a broader audience. This transition – from bulky systems to consumer-accessible devices – demanded more efficient and intuitive interactions [25, 26].

Although HCI is a relatively recent field, its applications have expanded beyond video games into numerous domains. The convergence of gamification, HCI, and UX not only reflects the evolution of these areas but also emphasizes the increasing demand for strategies that enhance effectiveness, motivation, and engagement [27] [28]. Gamification emerges as a valuable tool in this context, filling gaps identified in human-computer interaction.

User Experience (UX) is essential for software acceptance and adoption. While UX design aims to create useful, intuitive, and minimally restrictive systems [29, 30], gamification adds an additional layer of game-like elements to motivate users who may find interfaces otherwise unappealing.

There is a growing need not only for functional systems but also for motivational strategies that actively engage users. Gamification, with its characteristic game elements, provides this extra layer of motivation. Enjoyable game-like experiences encourage voluntary participation and significantly increase engagement. In contrast to traditional UX design – which prioritizes intuitive and easy-to-use systems – gamification introduces game design elements that foster a more immersive experience, encouraging users to explore and interact more deeply with digital systems [27, 31].

5   The Applied Project

This chapter details the project development process following the Design Thinking methodology [32, 33], which comprises five stages: empathize; define; ideate; prototype; and test [34].

The approach begins with identifying potential users through the creation of personas, followed by the presentation of the application's mechanics and dynamics. Based on these representations, the fundamental structures were developed using visual schemas such as sitemaps and user flows. Finally, various conceptual solutions were created through wireframes, which were subsequently transformed into final layouts and a functional prototype of the application.

5.1   Stage 1 – Understand

Although a prototype is essentially a mock-up of the intended product, before beginning the sketching of the mobile application concept, it was necessary to conduct a data gathering phase based on the existing state of the art and case studies. Subsequently, a questionnaire was implemented to obtain a comprehensive understanding of the target audience.

The goal was to understand the preferences of this target group regarding applications that incorporate gamification elements, thereby enabling the identification of the most appealing and motivating features and functionalities for young adults/participants. The selected method, based on closed-ended questions, allowed for the collection of valuable quantitative insights, minimizing the risk of bias during the project's development [35]. This information played a fundamental role in guiding the design and development of the application, ensuring it could fully meet the needs and expectations of the target audience [36].

5.2   Stage 2 – Define

In this stage, personas were defined based on the information collected through the questionnaire. Following this, the mechanics and dynamics of the application were presented. Simultaneously, specific scenarios for each persona and user flows were developed, alongside other information architectures, including the visual sitemap (Fig. 1).

The use of the Persona technique helps foster empathy with users and understand their behaviors, goals, and needs. Keeping potential users in mind guides decision-making aligned with their requirements, which in turn contributes to the creation of meaningful

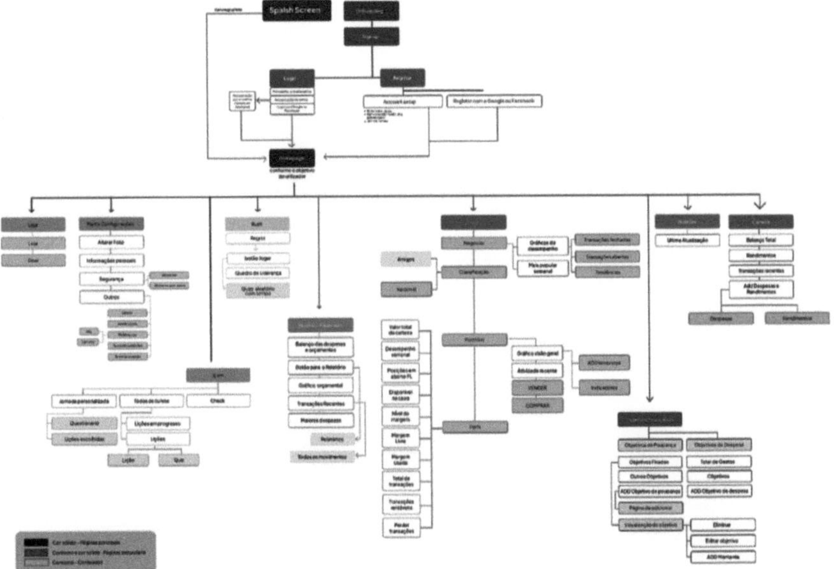

Fig. 1. Sitemap of the Finansify application. Source: Own formulation.

user experiences [37]. Thus, a persona is essentially a way to reduce a broad target audience into two or three fictional individuals who serve as profiles of that audience. To be accurate and representative, the personas must be based on research involving real users, such as interviews, field studies, or questionnaires. With this data, it is possible to create a set of typical users that summarizes all collected information, focusing only on the most significant details and characteristics of the group. Although imaginary, their attributes should be grounded in real user data.

Unger and Chandler [29] suggest that the minimum number of personas to create is three, while the maximum is seven; exceeding this number is uncommon. Furthermore, the number of personas should consider the target segments the product aims to address and the key differences between them. Consequently, the personas created for this project were based on the compiled data from the questionnaire. This led to the development of three personas and their respective user scenarios: a part-time working university student, a young professional, and an employed worker with potential investment interests.

It is also the stage to develop the dynamics and aesthetics of the app. The name 'Finansify' is a fusion of the words "Finance" and "Gamify." "Finance" reflects the core purpose of the application, which is to help users improve their financial literacy and efficiently manage their money. The suffix "-ify" alludes to gamification, indicating that the app incorporates game elements to make financial learning more engaging and enjoyable. Thus, the name Finansify embodies the application's goal to make personal finance more accessible, educational, and even fun for users (Fig. 2).

Information architecture refers to the process of structuring and organizing content within a digital platform, following a detailed analysis of user needs and preferences.

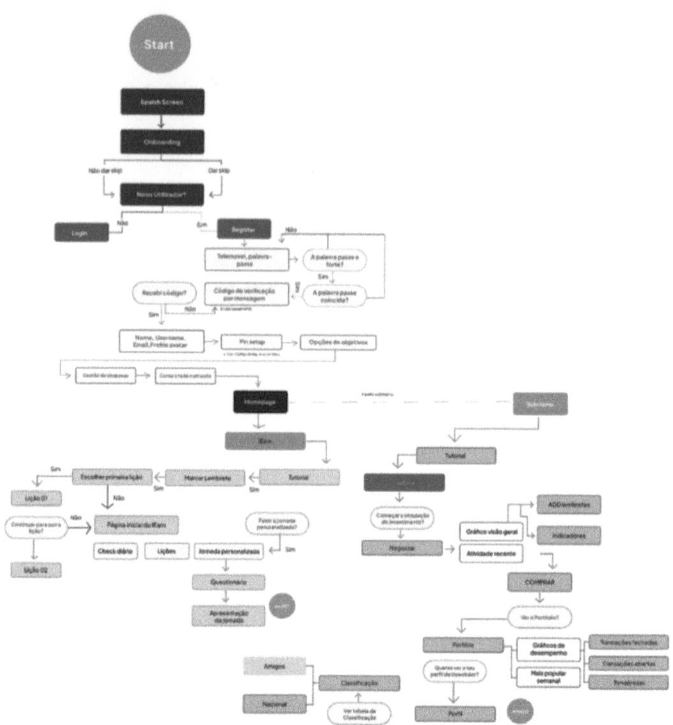

Fig. 2. Userflow of a specific persona. Source: own formulation.

Its primary objective is to facilitate navigation and interaction through a clear and intuitive arrangement of information. In the context of user experience (UX), information architecture is essential to ensure that content is logically organized with well-defined categories, easy-to-understand navigation systems, and informative labels that guide users. Effective information architecture not only improves usability but also enables users to quickly find what they are looking for, resulting in a more efficient and satisfying digital experience. By aligning the information structure with the target audience's behavioral patterns and expectations, information architecture guarantees a seamless and intuitive interaction with the platform.

In this phase, information architecture within UX was critical for organizing and categorizing the application's content to create a clear and intuitive structure. Visual navigation systems were designed with descriptive labels to help users locate and comprehend information rapidly. The main visual schemes employed were the Sitemap and User Flow diagrams.

Following the development of user flows, a sitemap was defined. Visual sitemaps are graphical representations of a website or application's structure, illustrating how pages and sections are organized and interconnected. Based on the personas' scenarios, it was observed that, despite some similarities, each persona had significantly different needs and goals when using the application. Consequently, distinct user flows were developed for each persona. A user flow is a diagram that represents the path a user follows while interacting with a product or site. It maps out the steps and decisions a user makes to achieve a specific goal.

5.3 Stage 3 – Ideation

In this stage, the visual identity of the application was developed along with the selection of a design system, including typography, color palette, and visual elements. Additionally, based on the visual navigation structure outlined in the user flows and sitemap, wireframes were created, providing a preliminary low-fidelity representation of the solution.

To attract new users, it is essential to create a visual identity that feels familiar and consistent. The product name and all brand elements should clearly convey the same message. The first step, already presented, was choosing the brand name: Finansify. Following this, the logo was created. The logo is an imagotype, where the symbol and text form the visual identity but function independently. The symbol features a stylized "F" formed by two overlapping lines and a small circle. The "F" prominently represents finance and suggests financial stability, growth, and trust (Fig. 3).

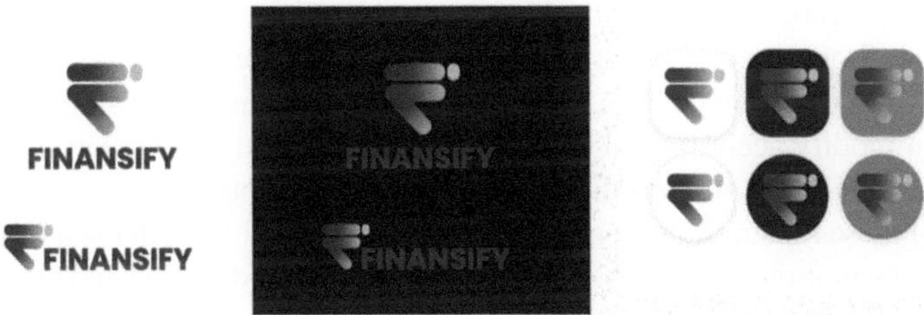

Fig. 3. Finansify logo proposal. Source: own formulation.

The choice of pink and blue colors in the financial gamification brand is strategic. Blue conveys trust, stability, and professionalism – key attributes in the financial sector – while pink adds warmth, friendliness, and accessibility, making finance appear more approachable. This combination balances seriousness with a touch of playfulness, making the application engaging and less intimidating. Moreover, it suggests modernity and innovation, encouraging user interaction and transforming financial management into a more pleasant and dynamic experience.

In interface design, visual consistency with the previously created identity and graphic elements was maintained, following the main style guidelines such as color usage. The application's primary colors are blue, lilac, and pink; however, other colors like orange and yellow were added to identify different functionalities. Text is displayed mainly in dark blue or white, depending on context. Red and green are occasionally used to indicate errors or differentiate expenses.

The use of grids in layout design is a key technique for creating organized and visually balanced compositions. It helps structure and align graphic elements efficiently, ensuring the design is both functional and aesthetically pleasing. For this application, a 4-column grid was used.

Typography. Text plays a crucial role in most interfaces, being fundamental to information transmission. According to Cooper [38], for optimal readability, it is preferable to use a clear sans-serif font with sizes above 10 pixels. Bearing this in mind, the font "Ubuntu Sans," designed by Dalton Maag and part of the OpenType family, was selected. This modern humanist-style font was created to reflect the Ubuntu personality across menus, buttons, and dialog boxes.

Icons. Icons were chosen for their easy recognizability and clear communication of functionalities, avoiding ambiguity. They play a fundamental role in guiding users and facilitating navigation within the application.

Illustrations. Illustrations were carefully selected and integrated to make the app more friendly and less intimidating, especially given the complexity of financial management topics. They help humanize the experience, providing a visually pleasant and welcoming environment. The illustrations follow the application's visual identity by using the predefined color palette. This alignment contributes to a consistent experience and reinforces the brand, clearly conveying the app's message in a harmonious way.

Illustrations were also used to explain financial concepts and application functionalities in a simplified and visually appealing manner, facilitating user comprehension and making navigation more intuitive and accessible. These illustrations were originally sourced from Storyset.com, a platform offering open-source visual resources. Storyset provides a vast collection of free, customizable illustrations that designers and content creators can modify according to their needs. The flexibility and creativity enabled by the open-source license support diverse project requirements.

Some of these illustrations were animated to significantly enrich the user experience. By introducing motion, animations make interactions more dynamic and engaging. They were used to draw attention to important features such as lesson completions and the user journey questionnaire, among others.

Components. The creation of components and variables followed the Atomic Design methodology, known for enabling modular and scalable design systems. Components are considered fundamental building blocks, constructed from atoms – simple elements like buttons, icons, or text fields. When combined, these atoms form molecules, such as reusable form groups, and then organisms, representing more complex interface sections. This modular structure allows for efficient and coherent development, where each component can be easily updated or reused across different parts of the application.

Variables play a key role as dynamic elements influencing component properties like colors, spacing, or sizes. Within Atomic Design, variables are applied consistently across the system to ensure a uniform visual experience. Defining a color palette or text sizes as variables allows their use across multiple atoms, molecules, and organisms, maintaining design coherence and facilitating global adjustments (Fig. 4).

Wireframes. They establish the organization of elements within the interface, serving as the starting point for the final visual design. They are considered the skeletons of the application, allowing for the analysis of structure, content, hierarchy, functionality, and user interaction [40]. They function as an essential design tool, offering a quick

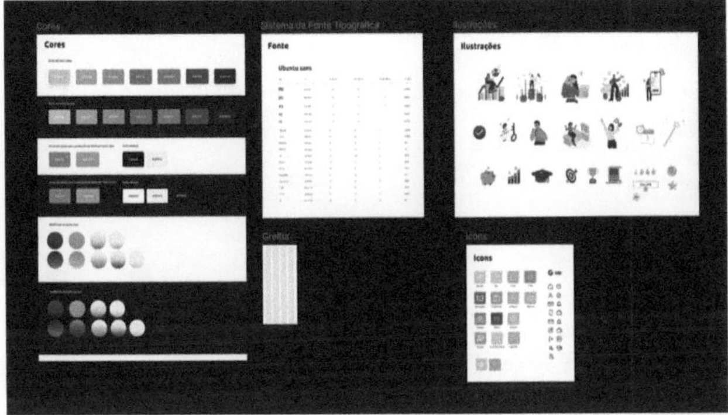

Fig. 4. Finansify design system and style guide. Source: own formulation.

overview of the layout and operation of elements on each screen. Wireframes define the hierarchical organization of content and how it will function and interact.

Wireframes are used by user experience (UX) designers to test the product's functionality and usability, and they represent an intermediate phase connecting information architecture to the final interface and should be simple, with few colors and graphic elements, to avoid distractions during layout analysis. This approach is the most effective way to test application functionality and identify problems early, saving time by making corrections on wireframes rather than on final interfaces. Additionally, it is the most suitable method for gathering user feedback.

The wireframe phase was divided into three stages, all optimized to obtain user feedback. The process began with some paper sketches to understand how many screens needed to be developed and how to organize the information. After this initial phase, the work progressed to Figma, where a more detailed definition of the content was carried out. Finally, layouts closer to the final product design were created, defining interactions between screens for an initial evaluation. A total of 134 screens were created to analyze interaction and information distribution across the interfaces. Being a low-fidelity prototype, this phase facilitated the possibility of making changes to improve the application as needed (Fig. 5).

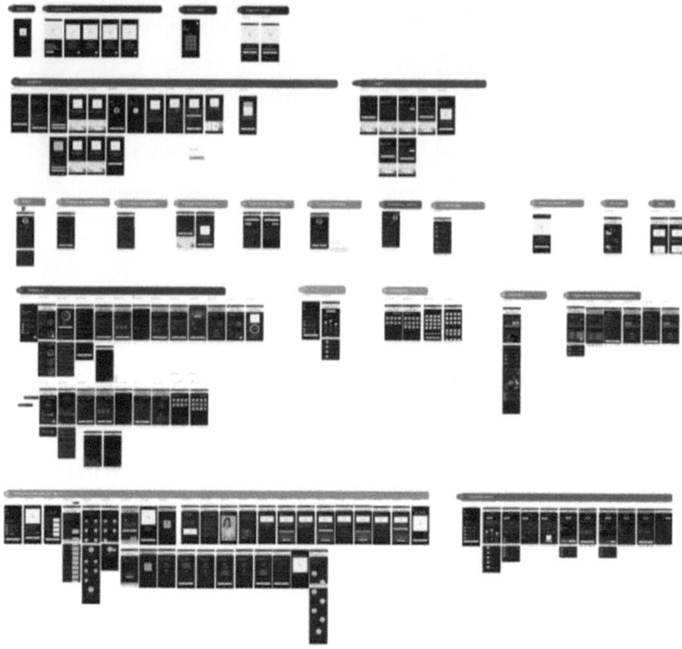

Fig. 5. All 134 wireframe screens of the Finansify application. Source: own formulation.

5.4   Stage 4 – Prototype

In this stage, with the wireframes and design system finalized, the first versions of the prototypes were developed. These allowed for testing and validating ideas to detect usability issues and confirm task flows, intended to be used in usability testing in the next phase. This prototype is an interactive version of the interface, which not only serves for testing but is also used throughout the design process to communicate ideas and gather feedback on the interface development.

The final prototype of this project[1] begins with an onboarding process, starting with a splash screen displaying only the application's logo. It then proceeds to a brief walkthrough that explains the application's functionalities. At this point, the user is given the option to skip the walkthrough, as this stage is purely informative about the application [39] (Fig. 6).

---

[1] The prototype was developed with FIGMA and is available to test and interact in the following link: https://www.figma.com/proto/Bucaf50n3NB9poXb7VcVhe/Finansify_app?page-id=1%3A11&node-id=1-29315&node-type=frame&viewport=-6147%2C-1088%2C0.76&t=IqY FIZr0Iti0sKuE-1&scaling=scale-down&content-scaling=fixed&starting-point-node-id=1%3A29307&show-proto-sidebar=1.

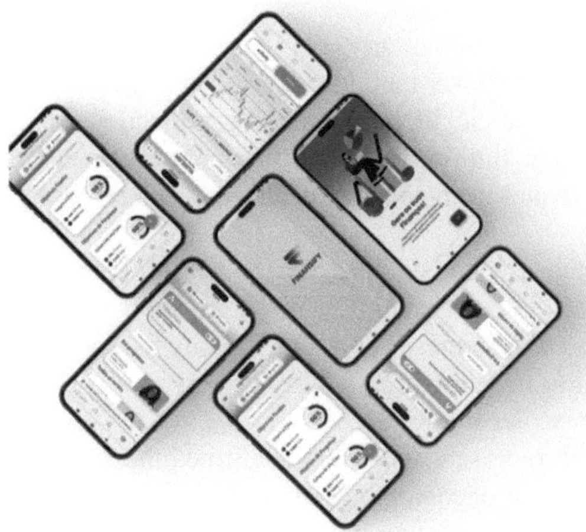

Fig. 6. Finansify prototype – sample screens. Source: own formulation.

5.5 Stage 5 – Test

Usability testing is an essential methodology for evaluating a product's effectiveness, allowing the identification of design flaws and opportunities for improvement. This process involves observing a representative sample of users as they perform specific tasks to detect navigation or interaction issues. Nielsen [40] highlights that testing with only six users can uncover up to 85% of usability problems.

For the usability testing of the application, a sample of five users was selected, with profiles representative of the developed personas. Each participant completed eight tasks in person, using a mobile phone and a high-fidelity prototype of the application, with an average session duration of 15 min. During the tests, the researcher acted solely as an observer, and a questionnaire was administered to participants afterward. To obtain concise responses and apply the System Usability Scale (SUS), adapted for this evaluation, a Likert scale response format from 1 to 5 was used.

The individual SUS scores from the five participants were as follows: User 1 scored 85, User 2 scored 77.5, User 3 scored 90, User 4 scored 95, and User 5 scored 85. These scores demonstrate that all users rated the application's usability positively, as all scores are above 68. The overall average score was 86.5, reflecting a generally satisfactory usability experience.

Based on these results, it can be concluded that the application has strong usability, though there remain opportunities for improvement in specific areas, particularly addressing difficulties reported by some participants. A more detailed analysis of the responses to individual questions could provide valuable insights into which features require refinement. Thus, despite the positive outcomes from the usability tests, minor adjustments could further enhance the user experience before the final product version is implemented.

6 Conclusion

This project aimed to develop a mobile financial management app for young adults in Portugal, promoting financial literacy through gamification. Many young people lack basic financial knowledge, limiting their ability to make informed decisions. The app not only educates but motivates users to adopt healthier financial habits by making learning engaging and fun.

The target audience is young adults aged 18–30 with limited knowledge in saving, credit, and investments. Personas and user flows guided the app's structure, supported by a clear sitemap and wireframes. The visual identity uses vibrant colors and modern typography to appeal to users. A high-fidelity prototype was developed using Atomic Design for a modular, scalable interface.

Usability tests with representative users confirmed the app's ease of use and effectiveness of gamification in encouraging regular engagement. Tasks included expense tracking, goal setting, and interacting with educational content. Feedback showed low frustration and positive motivation from reward systems. The project successfully created an innovative tool to improve financial literacy among young adults in Portugal, combining education with engaging gamified experiences. Usability results confirm the app's potential as a modern, effective solution to low financial literacy.

Acknowledgments. This work was supported by FCT – Fundação para a Ciência e Tecnologia, I.P. by project reference UID/04057: Research Institute for Design, Media and Culture.

Conflict of Interests. The authors have no competing interests to declare that are relevant to the content of this article.

References

1. Noctor, M., Stoney, S., Stradling, R.: Financial Literacy: A Discussion. OECD (1992)
2. Lusardi, A., Mitchell, O.S.: The importance of financial literacy: opening a new field. J. Econ. Perspect. **37**(4), 137–154 (2023)
3. Koskelainen, T., Kalmi, P., Scornavacca, E., Vartiainen, T.: Financial literacy in the digital age – a research agenda. J. Consum. Aff. **57**(1), 507–528 (2023)
4. Garg, N., Singh, S.: Financial literacy among youth. Int. J. Soc. Econ. **45**(1), 173–186 (2018)
5. Routledge, S.: Consumer Protection and Financial Literacy. The World Bank (2010)
6. Kozup, J., Hogarth, J.: Financial literacy, public policy, and consumers' self-protection – more questions, fewer answers. J. Consum. Aff. **42**(Summer), 127–136 (2008)
7. Bačová, M., Čonková, M., Bričová, Z.: Financial literacy of students in the Slovak Republic. In: The 7th International Days of Statistics and Economics, Prague (2013)
8. Khan, S., et al.: Financial literacy: key concepts and practical implications. J. Econ. Behav. Organ. **206**, 154–167 (2023)
9. Pelling, N.: The (Short) Prehistory of 'Gamification'... Funding Startups (& Other Impossibilities) (2012)
10. Deterding, S., Dixon, D., Khaled, R., Nacke, L.: From game design elements to gamefulness: defining "gamification". In: Proceedings of the 15th International Academic MindTrek Conference: Envisioning Future Media Environments, pp. 9–15. ACM (2011)

11. Huber, J., Hilty, L.M.: Gamification in the workplace: a scoping review. In: The 28th Bled eConference: Wellbeing (2015)
12. Zichermann, G., Cunningham, C.: Gamification by Design: Implementing Game Mechanics in Web and Mobile Apps. O'Reilly Media, Sebastopol, CA (2011)
13. Vianna, Y.: Gamification, Inc: como reinventar empresas a partir de jogos, 1ª MJV Press, Rio de Janeiro (2013)
14. Muntean, C.I.: Raising engagement in e-learning through gamification. In: The 6th International Conference on Virtual Learning (ICVL) (2011)
15. Campigoto, G., et al.: The use of gamification in education: a systematic review. Comput. Hum. Behav. **29**(3), 1–12 (2013)
16. Schmitz, B., Klemke, R., Specht, M.: Effects of mobile gaming patterns of learning outcomes: a literature review. Int. J. Technol. Enhance Learn. **4**(5–6), 345–358 (2012)
17. Hamari, J., Koivisto, J., Sarsa, H.: Does gamification work?—A literature review of empirical studies on gamification. In: 2014 47th Hawaii International Conference on System Sciences, Waikoloa, HI, pp. 3025–3034 (2014)
18. Huotari, K., Hamari, J.: Defining gamification: a service marketing perspective. In: 16th International Academic MindTrek Conference, pp. 17–22 (2012)
19. Ciunova-Shuleska, A., et al.: The impact of gamification on financial literacy and inclusion: evidence from emerging economies. J. Financ. Educ. **48**(2), 123–142 (2022)
20. Lau, P.Y., Ki, E.J.: The role of gamification in financial education: an analysis of its effectiveness. J. Financ. Literacy Educ. **18**(1), 45–63 (2021)
21. Garaialde, E., et al.: Gamification in financial literacy programs: a systematic review. Int. J. Educ. Manag. **35**(3), 511–528 (2021)
22. Lashitew, A., et al.: The role of gamification in improving financial literacy. J. Financ. Educ. **45**(1), 45–67 (2019)
23. Shahid, S., Islam, J., Malik, S., Hasan, U.: Examining consumer experience in using m-banking apps: a study of its antecedents and outcomes. J. Retail. Consum. Serv. **65** (2022)
24. Interaction Design Foundation. Human-Computer Interaction (HCI) (2024)
25. Preece, J., et al.: Interaction Design. Beyond Human-Computer Interaction. 2nd ed. Wiley (2007)
26. Vinney, C.: How to design intuitive user interfaces. UX Design Institute (2025). Accessed 15 June 2025
27. Tondello, G., Wehbe1, R., Diamond, L., Busch, M., Marczewski, A., Nacke, L.: The gamification user types hexad scale. In: CHI PLAY 2016: Proceedings of the 2016 Annual Symposium on Computer-Human Interaction in Play, pp. 229–243 (2016)
28. Suh, A., Wagner, C., Liu, L.: Enhancing user engagement through gamification. J. Comput. Inf. Syst. **58**(3), 204–213 (2016)
29. Chandler, D., Unger, R.: Smartphone applications: a new approach to encouraging sustainable transportation. J. Urban Technol. (2012)
30. Colin, C., Martin, A.: The user experience of low-techs: from user problems to design principles. J. User Experience **18**(2), 68–85 (2023)
31. Oprean, D., Balakrishnan, B.: From engagement to user experience: a theoretical perspective towards immersive learning. In: Schmidt, M., Tawfik, A.A., Jahnke, I., Earnshaw, Y. (eds.) Learner and User Experience Research – An Introduction for the Field of Learning Design & Technology (2020). https://edtechbooks.org/ux/10_from_engagement_t. Accessed 15 June 2025
32. Brown, T.: Design thinking. Harv. Bus. Rev. **86**(6), 84–89 (2008)
33. Tschimmel, K.: Design thinking as an effective toolkit for innovation. In: Proceedings of the XXIII ISPIM Conference: Action for Innovation: Innovating from Experience, Barcelona (2012). ISBN: 978-952-265-243-0

34. Dam, R.F., Siang, T.Y.: What Kind of Prototype Should You Create? Interaction Design Foundation (2019). https://www.interaction-design.org/literature/article/what-kind-of-protot ype-should-you-create?srsltid=AfmBOoqllAx_c3YQ_zsbjblkUYpZRtEJKwTtvqC-7fTJ2U zQ7SNCCx8t. Accessed 15 June 2025
35. Maxwell, J.: Designing a qualitative study. In: Bickman, L. (ed.) The SAGE Handbook of Applied Social Research Methods, pp. 214–253 (2009)
36. Lopes, A., Valentim, N., Moraes, B., Zilse, R., Conte, T.: Applying user-centered techniques to analyze and design a mobile application. J. Softw. Eng. Res. Dev. **6**, article number 5 (2018)
37. Jansen, J., Salminen, O., Jung, S., Data-driven personas for enhanced user understanding: combining empathy with rationality for better insights to analytics. Data Inf. Manage. **4**(1), 1–17 (2020)
38. Cooper, A.: About Face: The Essentials of Interaction Design, 4th ed. Wiley (2014)
39. Garrett, J.J.: The Elements of User Experience: User-Centered Design for the Web and Beyond, 2nd ed. New Riders (2010)
40. Nielsen, J.: Designing Web Usability: The Practice of Simplicity. New Riders (2000)

Educational Accessibility in STEM for Visually Impaired and Blind Students: A Literature Review on Challenges and Support

Rana Ghoneim[1]([⊠]) [iD], Wajdi Aljedaani[1] [iD], Asmaa Mansour Alghamdi[2] [iD], and Stephanie Ludi[1] [iD]

[1] University of North Texas, Denton, TX 76205, USA
{rana.ghoneim,wajdi.aljedaani,stephanie.ludi}@unt.edu
[2] Jazan University, Jazan, Saudi Arabia
amalghamdi@Jazan.edu.sa

Abstract. The incorporation of students with blindness and visual impairments into STEM (Science, Technology, Engineering, and Mathematics) has always posed challenges, and considerable attention has been directed toward closing the accessibility gap. This article constitutes a systematic literature review (SLR) of 44 articles from 2008 to 2024 that focused on identifying the fundamental issues surrounding these students and the aids provided to support their studies. It examines the barriers that hinder total participation in STEM subjects, including access, technological, and pedagogical barriers, among others. It also explores tools and resources, such as tactile aids, screen readers, web applications, and specialized software, designed to enhance the learning experience. In particular, web applications have emerged as a promising solution for delivering interactive and accessible STEM content, offering features such as real-time feedback, audio descriptions, and compatibility with assistive technologies. This paper, by integrating the results of previously conducted research, establishes an understanding of current developments in STEM education for blind and visually impaired learners, highlighting areas that still require active work to remove barriers to learning for all.

Keywords: STEM Education · Visually Impaired Students · Accessibility · Assistive Technologies · Tactile aids

1 Introduction

STEM education is often regarded as crucial to the advancement of technology and economic growth. Nevertheless, blind and visually impaired (BVI) students are significantly overlooked in these disciplines, primarily due to their limited access to visually oriented materials [17,54]. The curriculum in STEM subjects, for instance, cultivates a significant demand for charts, models, graphs, and other

© The Author(s), under exclusive license to Springer Nature Switzerland AG 2026
M. Antona and C. Stephanidis (Eds.): HCII 2025, LNCS 16335, pp. 65–86, 2026.
https://doi.org/10.1007/978-3-032-12781-5_5

techniques that are often considered unattainable for individuals with visual impairments [30,57]. Such tendencies create an explanation for why BVI students are in a disadvantageous position compared to their sighted peers in regard to participation in STEM disciplines [23].

Research has established that children with BVI can be as competent in STEM subjects as their sighted peers, provided necessary modifications are made, such as incorporating tactile models, explanatory audio, and kinetic elements [5–7,25,36]. Some initiatives, such as Independent Laboratory Access for the Blind (ILAB), have facilitated the use of multisensory approaches such as talking Lab Quest and other audio devices enabling blind chemistry students to perform experiments [21,48]. Such tools have been proven to enhance students' comprehension of scientific principles by enabling the delivery of auditory feedback to the students as the experiments are done [28].

In addition to these assistive technologies, web applications have emerged as a crucial tool in making STEM education more accessible for BVI students [54]. Online platforms now offer features such as screen reader compatibility, interactive simulations with audio descriptions, and real-time collaboration tools that allow students with visual impairments to engage in complex problem-solving alongside their peers [23,36]. Web-based learning environments, including coding platforms and virtual labs, provide alternative ways to access and interact with STEM content, reducing reliance on traditional visual materials and increasing opportunities for independent exploration [28,48].

Despite the presence of such assistive technologies, systemic issues persist. Many educators lack the requisite training to modify STEM content for students with BVI, resulting in passive learning when sighted counterparts perform the experiments for them [8,10,11,52,55]. This technique limits the chances of self-driven search for solutions, which is vital for developing an advanced understanding of concepts in science and mathematics [18]. Furthermore, the shift to remote and online education during the COVID-19 outbreak highlighted the unpreparedness of the digital transition for students with BVI [12,42].

Mentorship and community support are also vital in encouraging students with BVI to engage in STEM education. Studies are showing that mentorship programs such as the ones provided by the National Federation of the Blind's (NFB) National Center for Blind Youth in Science (NCBYS) develop and implement strategies to promote opportunities for blind youth in science and assist in improving self-efficacy and academic confidence for students with VI [2,40]. The ability to recall favorable images of more competent individuals is vital for these students, as it enables them to comprehend how to succeed in STEM careers despite the odds [43].

Nonetheless, the limited resources and competently qualified educators, as well as limited access to appropriate learning materials, remain substantial obstacles for BVI students pursuing STEM education [1,35]. As a result of these factors, there has been low participation of visually impaired students in higher levels of STEM education, which in turn has resulted in their underrepresentation in STEM professions [14,32].

The objective of this systematic literature review (SLR) is to evaluate the available literature on the inclusion of BVI students in STEM education. It deals with the integration of ATs, inclusive teaching methodology, and mentorship as factors that enhance equity in educational outcomes [38, 41]. In doing so, the review aims to inform the direction of future studies and subsequent policy formulation efforts that will contribute to increasing the diversity of STEM education in the United States [39].

2 Related Work

In this section, we examine the challenges faced by BVI students enrolled in STEM education and the different methodologies adopted in previous studies to illustrate how researchers have described these challenges.

2.1 Visual Impaired Community

BVI individuals face considerable challenges in education, particularly in STEM fields. These are social biases, low expectations from teachers, and a dearth of visually impaired role models in STEM careers [23, 57]. Further research shows that BVI students often have poor access to tactile and auditory resources needed to learn abstract concepts [13, 36]. In addition to this exclusion from STEM education, there are no adapted teaching materials. Examples include diagrams and visual aids that are critical for complex topics but often not accessible to BVI learners [21, 30].

With the rise of digital education, web applications have started to bridge some of these gaps by providing accessible learning platforms with built-in screen reader compatibility, audio descriptions, and interactive STEM simulations [18]. However, many web-based STEM resources still lack proper accessibility features, limiting their usability for BVI students [36].

2.2 STEM Education

Research shows that visually impaired students can succeed in STEM with accommodations such as tactile models and auditory support. For example, tactile graphics and interactive braille devices have enhanced understanding in STEM [17, 48]. Programs such as NASA's National Center for Blind Youth in Science have provided inclusive STEM education and mentorship [28, 37].

Despite this, mainstream STEM curricula often do not provide for BVI learners. Some educators are poorly trained to modify their teaching methods, often excluding students from classroom activities [30, 54]. Early interventions, including inclusive STEM camps, have been shown to address misconceptions and build confidence in BVI students [46].

Web applications also play a role in promoting accessibility in STEM education [42]. Platforms like accessible coding environments and virtual science labs allow BVI students to engage with STEM concepts interactively [52]. For example, coding platforms such as Code Jumper and Quorum provide non-visual programming interfaces, enabling students to develop coding skills independently [2]. Additionally, web-based collaborative tools facilitate teamwork by integrating real-time voice guidance and structured, accessible interfaces [12].

2.3 STEM Assistive Technologies

Technologies are an essential support in STEM for BVI students. For instance, 3D printing is employed to develop tangible models of molecular structures, as well as mathematical graphs, to make abstract concepts more understandable [18]. Automated transcription in Braille of STEM textbooks and voice-assisted education are other accessibility tools [14,40].

Additionally, interactive tools such as touch-based learning devices or accessible robotics kits have been developed for individuals with visual impairments. However, such tools often require significant customization to meet the needs of BVI students [19,35]. They need further innovation and refinement to ensure their efficacy and inclusion [2,57].

In addition to physical assistive technologies, web applications provide digital solutions that enhance STEM learning for BVI students [42]. Online platforms with haptic feedback simulations, audio-based equation solvers, and AI-driven accessibility features have the potential to revolutionize how BVI students interact with STEM content [28]. For example, EquatIO is a web tool that allows students to hear and interact with complex mathematical equations using speech-to-text and audio-based feedback, making mathematics more accessible [30].

Based on the studies referenced in this section, significant efforts have been made to improve STEM accessibility for BVI students, including the development of assistive technologies, tactile learning tools, and inclusive instructional strategies. Despite these contributions, no systematic literature review (SLR) has yet synthesized the specific challenges and solutions that BVI students face across the STEM disciplines. This paper fills that gap by being the first SLR to comprehensively analyze these issues, providing a structured understanding and a framework for future research and practice.

3   Research Questions

This study examines the barriers that BVI students face in STEM, along with potential solutions and supportive technologies. It offers insights for educators and policymakers on improving accessibility and inclusion. We also examine how web applications enhance STEM accessibility in the context of digital learning. The following research questions (RQs) are addressed:

RQ$_1$: What are the major barriers for BVI students to enroll in STEM education and succeed? This research question aims to identify the barriers and systemic challenges faced by BVI students in STEM learning environments. Additionally, it examines the role of web-based STEM resources and their accessibility shortcomings.

RQ$_2$: How have solutions and strategies been proposed and implemented to overcome the difficulties that BVI students are facing in STEM education? This research question explores interventions, accommodations, and practices designed to support BVI students in STEM education. It also evaluates the impact of web applications that provide interactive and accessible learning environments, such as online coding platforms, virtual science labs, and AI-driven tutoring systems.

RQ$_3$: How are tools and technologies implemented and developed for STEM education of BVI students? This research question explores assistive technologies, adaptive tools, and innovative methodologies that will enable BVI students to participate meaningfully in STEM subjects. It further explores how web applications, including screen-reader-friendly interfaces, audio-based simulations, and cloud-based collaborative platforms, are being integrated into STEM education to improve accessibility and engagement.

4   Study Methodology

This study reviews academic literature from 2008 to 2024 to synthesize current research and highlight key challenges facing BVI students in STEM education. It also explores emerging solutions, particularly the role of web applications in improving accessibility. The section is organized into three phases–planning, execution, and synthesis–detailing the process of identifying and selecting relevant studies.

4.1   Planning

In this approach, we improved literature search methodologies. Once the literature review was complete, we made a list of relevant terms for our inquiry, including keywords related to assistive technologies, web applications, and accessibility tools in STEM education for BVI students. Then, these terms were searched across various web databases.

Search Terms: A pilot study [9] was conducted to identify effective search phrases in two major databases, ACM and IEEE. It investigated the verbal equivalents and the terms commonly used to describe difficulties faced by visually impaired students in STEM education. The research, therefore, focused on abstracts and titles while also considering the role of web-based learning platforms and digital accessibility tools in modern education. The search query was formulated as follows:

```
Title:(''STEM*'' AND ''visual*impair*'' OR ''blind*'' OR ''loss of
vision'' OR ''low vision'') AND Abstract:(''education*'' OR
''teach*'' OR ''tactile aids'' OR ''screen reader'' OR ''special
software'' OR ''access barriers'' OR ''technological barriers'' OR
''pedagogical barriers'')
```

Online Databases: Literature research was conducted in several of the most esteemed online databases, including ACM Digital Library, IEEE Xplore, PubMed, ScienceDirect, SpringerLink, ERIC, Scopus, and Web of Science. These platforms provided academic resources relevant to our study, ensuring coverage of advancements in web applications and their integration into STEM education for BVI students. The list of queried databases is compiled in Table 1.

Table 1. Summary of online databases used for sourcing published studies

Digital Database	URL
ACM Digital Library	https://dl.acm.org/
IEEE Xplore	https://ieeexplore.ieee.org/
Web of Science	https://www.webofknowledge.com/
Scopus	https://www.scopus.com/
ScienceDirect	https://www.sciencedirect.com/
Springer Link	https://link.springer.com/
PubMed	https://pubmed.ncbi.nlm.nih.gov/
ERIC	https://eric.ed.gov/

Inclusion/Exclusion Framework: Applying strict inclusion and exclusion criteria allowed us to refine and organize search results while ensuring relevance to our research objectives. In addition to studies focusing on accessibility challenges and assistive technologies, we specifically included papers discussing web-based learning tools, online simulations, and digital accessibility features designed for BVI students in STEM education. This framework is summarized in Table 2, in which we ensured that the selected studies provided insights into both traditional accessibility solutions and emerging digital tools, including web applications, for improving STEM education among BVI students.

Backward/Forward Snowballing: We used snowballing as an additional method to enrich the collection of articles obtained through our automated search. This approach, as described [20], involves two steps: firstly, reviewing papers cited within a given study (backward snowballing) and secondly, identifying studies that have cited that paper (forward snowballing). To ensure thoroughness, we performed this process in a closed, iterative manner. Through snowballing, we identified 15 additional articles, out of which 9 met our inclusion criteria. These selected articles were then added to our final pool, bringing the total to 44 articles.

Table 2. Inclusion and Exclusion Framework

Inclusion Factors	Exclusion Factors
Studies focused on STEM education	Studies unrelated to STEM disciplines
Papers discussing visually impaired/blind students	Papers focusing solely on other disabilities
Research published in English	Non-English publications
Articles available in digital format	Papers not accessible online
Peer-reviewed journal articles	Papers Non-peer-reviewed sources (e.g., blogs, reports)
Studies published between 2008 and 2024	Studies published before 2008

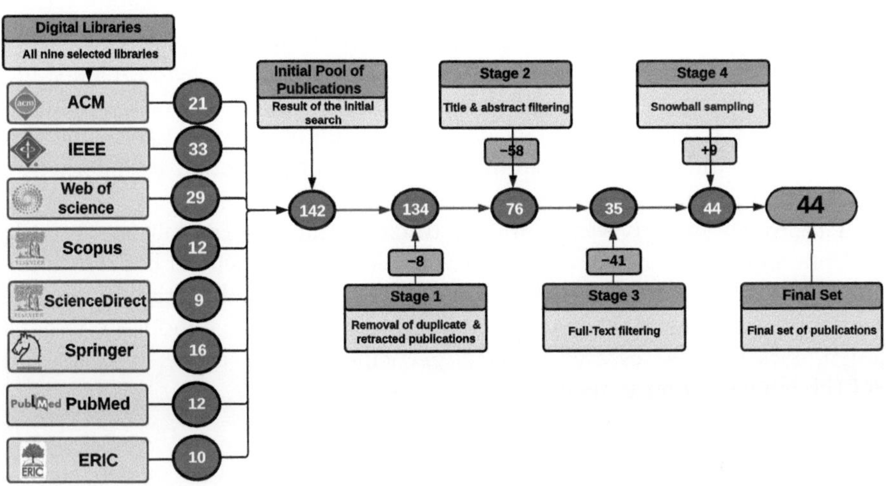

Fig. 1. Summary of the filtering process of the studies

Data Extraction Exclusion: During data extraction, we continued filtering articles based on relevance. Papers that only broadly discussed accessibility without focusing on BVI students in STEM or that focused on psychological theories rather than practical educational approaches [44] were excluded.

4.2   Execution

The initial search across all nine repositories yielded 142 articles. We employed a four-stage process to enhance the results and concentrate on the most relevant studies. In the first stage, we eliminated duplicate and retracted publications, resulting in a reduction of 8 articles, thereby yielding a total of 134. Subsequently, we assessed the titles and abstracts according to our inclusion and exclusion criteria. This step resulted in the elimination of 58 articles, including grey literature, non-peer-reviewed papers, and publications prior to the year 2008. At the conclusion of this stage, 76 articles were retained. Following that, we proceeded to full-text filtering, during which we precisely reviewed the remaining studies. This phase resulted in the elimination of 41 articles that did not meet our criteria, including those focused on non-STEM subjects or alternative disabilities. This resulted in a total of 35 articles. We employed forward and backward snowballing to identify further relevant studies. As a result of this process, we incorporated an additional 9 articles into our list. A total of 44 studies were selected for further analysis. This process, visualized in Fig. 1, ensured that the reviewed literature comprehensively covered both traditional accessibility approaches and modern web-based learning solutions for BVI students.

4.3   Synthesis

During the synthesis stage, we carefully analyzed the data we collected to ensure it could help us achieve our research objectives. To provide a clearer understanding of the challenges faced by BVI students in STEM education, we organized the studies by their year of publication and geographic focus. Each paper was examined in detail to extract relevant evidence, ensuring that all key information was captured accurately.

A thorough analysis was conducted to collect data on the barriers faced by students and the tools and strategies used to support their STEM education. For each study, we documented the study title, year of publication, purpose of the study, impairment category (e.g., visual impairment or blindness), research design, data sources, research location, participants (e.g., teachers or students), and the number of participants.

5   Study Results

This section presents the findings we derived from synthesizing the 44 selected studies in relation to the three research questions stated in this study. The key details of these studies are summarized in Table 3. The articles reviewed were published between 2008 and 2024, providing valuable insights that align with the objectives of this SLR.

In Fig. 2, we present the geographical distribution of the 44 studies analyzed. The data reveals that the majority of the studies were conducted in the USA, reflecting a significant focus on STEM education for BVI students in this region. Other countries with notable contributions include India, Austria, Mexico, and Nigeria, while all the other countries, such as Brazil and Canada, contributed one study each. These findings underscore the importance of encouraging further research in underrepresented regions to address the distinct challenges faced by BVI students in diverse educational and cultural contexts.

Table 3. Comprehensive data of the 44 studies: These papers reflect challenges and solutions for visually impaired or blind students in STEM education. The research papers are classified based on the year, impairment category, methodology, data collection method, data source, participants, sample size, and location

Studies	Year	Impairment Category	Methodology	Data Collection Method	Data Source	Participant	Sample Size	Location
[17]	2019	Visual Impairment	Ethnographic	Interviews	Indian Schools, Karnataka	Students, Teachers, Tech Designers	97 (75 VI, 22 Sighted)	India
[54]	2021	Visual Impairment	Qualitative	Photos, Notes, Memos	Arizona, USA	Students, Scientists, Interns	21 (9 Students, 8 Scientists, 4 Interns)	USA
[57]	2023	Visual Impairment	Mixed Methods	Surveys, Interviews	USA	Students, Teachers	10 Students	USA
[30]	2024	Visual Impairment	Qualitative	Case Studies, Literature Review	USA	K-12 Students	Not specified	USA
[23]	2019	Visual Impairment	Quantitative	Pre/Post-Tests, Surveys	Summer Camps	Students	22 Students	USA
[25]	2015	Visual Impairment	Experimental	Feedback, Lab Results	Arizona State University	Students	Not specified	USA
[36]	2015	Visual Impairment	Prototype Study	Device Evaluations	Massachusetts, USA	Blind Participants	2 Participants	USA
[48]	2014	Blindness, Low Vision	Qualitative	Event Participation	Towson University	BLV Students, Mentors	150 Students	USA
[21]	2015	Blindness, Visual Impairment	Experimental	Classroom Tests	Arizona State University	BVI Students, Adults	Not specified	USA
[28]	2023	Visual Impairment	Qualitative	Program Outcomes	Various USA Locations	VI Students	Not specified	USA
[55]	2024	Visual Impairment	Mixed Methods	Interviews, Questionnaires	Austria Schools	Pre-Service Teachers, VI Students	30 Participants	Austria
[52]	2023	Visual Impairment	Qualitative	Literature Reviews	Urban/Rural India	VI Students, Professionals	Not specified	India
[18]	2014	Visual Impairment	Mixed Methods	Interviews, Surveys	USA	Educators, Students	Not specified	USA
[12]	2008	Blindness	Mixed Methods	NASA and NFB Reports	USA	Blind Students	Not specified	USA
[42]	2023	Visual Impairment	Experimental	System Testing	Indian Locations	Students, Teachers	Not specified	India
[40]	2020	Visual Impairment	Literature Review	Literature Sources	Mexico Schools	Blind Students	Not specified	Mexico
[2]	2022	Visual Impairment	Survey	Questionnaires	Nigeria Schools	Teachers, Students	Not specified	Nigeria
[43]	2016	Visual Impairment, Blindness	Evaluation	Survey, Feedback Assessments	North Carolina	Students, Educators	9 Students	USA
[1]	2020	Blindness	Experimental	Classroom Observations	Nigeria Schools	Blind Students, Teachers	Not specified	Nigeria
[35]	2020	Blindness, VI	Autoethnography	Video Recordings	Canadian Locations	VI Children	25 Children	Canada
[32]	2019	Visual Impairment, Cognitive Disabilities	Review of Accessibility	Literature Reviews, Case Studies	Pisa, Italy	Students with Disabilities	Not specified	Italy
[14]	2019	Visual Impairment	Quantitative	Survey	USA Schools	Youth (Ages 10 18)	82 Youth	USA
[41]	2011	Visual Impairment	Mixed Methods	Teacher/Student Responses	Midwestern USA	Secondary Students, Teachers	13 Students, 15 Teachers	USA
[38]	2021	Blindness	Qualitative	Semi-Structured Interviews	USA	Post-Graduate STEM Students	2 Participants	USA
[39]	2019	Blindness/Visual Impairment	Challenge-Based Learning	Interviews, Field Notes	Mexico Schools	University Students	23 Students	Mexico
[13]	2018	Blindness	Survey	Survey Results	USA	Blind Teens, Adults	Not specified	USA
[37]	2015	Blindness	Qualitative	Literature Review	Austria Schools	Blind Students	Not specified	Austria
[46]	2014	Blindness/Low Vision	Case Study	Program Data, Feedback	USA	BLV Students	Not specified	USA
[19]	2018	Visual Impairment	Quantitative	Self-Efficacy Survey	USA Schools	VI Students	10 Students	USA
[47]	2016	Blindness/Low Vision	Mixed Methods	Interviews, Recordings	USA Schools	Secondary Students	6 Students	USA
[22]	2009	Visual Impairment, Spinal Injuries	Mixed Methods	Historical Research, Surveys, Interviews	USA	Impaired Individuals	Not specified	USA
[16]	2023	Blindness/Low Vision	Experimental	User Study	USA	BLV Students	19 Participants	USA
[24]	2021	Visual Impairment	Experimental	Observation, Feedback	Jordan Schools	VI Students	9 Participants	Jordan
[27]	2024	Visual Impairment	Qualitative	Focus Groups	USA Schools	Middle/High School Braille Users	11 Students	USA
[15]	2021	Visual Impairment	Qualitative	Semi-Structured Interviews	Brazil	VI Individuals	8 Participants	Brazil
[45]	2012	Blindness/Low Vision	Descriptive Research	Field Tests	USA Schools	Middle to Post-Secondary VI Students	Not specified	USA
[49]	2009	Blindness/Low Vision	Case Study	Adaptive Tools Testing	USA	BLV High School Students, Mentors	200 Participants	USA
[50]	2011	Blindness/Low Vision	Descriptive	Field Tests, Summer Camps	Caribbean (Tobago)	BLV Students	14 16 Students	Caribbean
[56]	2014	Blindness/Visual Impairment	Multi-Session Camps	Feedback Surveys	California, Maryland	BLV Students, Mentors, Instructors	10 Participants	USA
[31]	2020	Blindness/Low Vision	Descriptive Analysis	Tactile, Auditory Methods	USA Schools	Blind/Low Vision Students	Not specified	USA
[26]	2024	Visual Impairment	Qualitative	Interviews with Teachers	United Kingdom	Qualified Teachers of VI Students	2 Participants	UK
[34]	2022	Blindness/Visual Impairments	Descriptive, Exploratory	Observations, Interviews	North Carolina	Grades 2 9 VI Students	4 Students	USA
[51]	2010	Blindness/Low Vision	Mixed Methods	Field Tests in Science Classrooms	USA Schools	High School BLV Students	4 Participants	USA
[33]	2012	Blindness	Pre/Post-Test Design	Learning Activity Responses	University of Haifa, Israel	Late Blind Adults	4 Participants	Israel

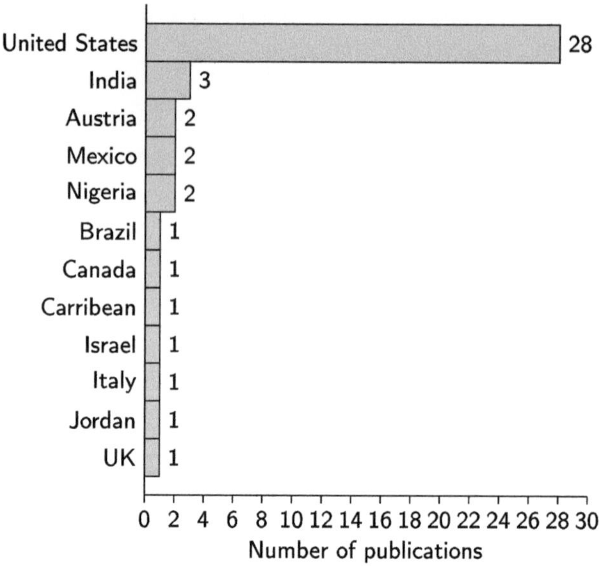

Fig. 2. Distribution of reviewed studies among different countries

The studies analyzed in this review were classified according to their methodologies and focus areas, as summarized in Fig. 3. Surveys, observations, interviews, and feedback were the most common methods, often conducted using tools such as online questionnaires, social media, video conferencing platforms, and accessible STEM resources. Additionally, the increasing role of web applications in STEM education was evident across multiple studies, emphasizing their ability to offer interactive and real-time learning experiences for BVI students. Platforms incorporating screen-reader-friendly interfaces, AI-driven tutoring systems, and collaborative cloud-based environments were found to enhance engagement and accessibility.

It is crucial to evaluate our findings in relation to the three research questions that this study addressed.

RQ$_1$: What are the major barriers for BVI students to enroll in STEM education and succeed? This research question explores the obstacles and systemic challenges BVI students face in STEM education, as identified across 44 studies. These challenges fall into four categories: technological barriers, educational challenges, accessibility issues, and social inclusion barriers.

(1) Technological Barriers: Several studies reported the lack of accessible technologies. Hasper et al. [25] noted that tactile graphics and 3D models were often unavailable or lacked sufficient detail. Murgaski [35] cited limited access to ICT tools in underfunded schools. Supalo et al. [49] found that existing tools often fail to meet the needs of BVI students. Singh et al. [42] highlighted the

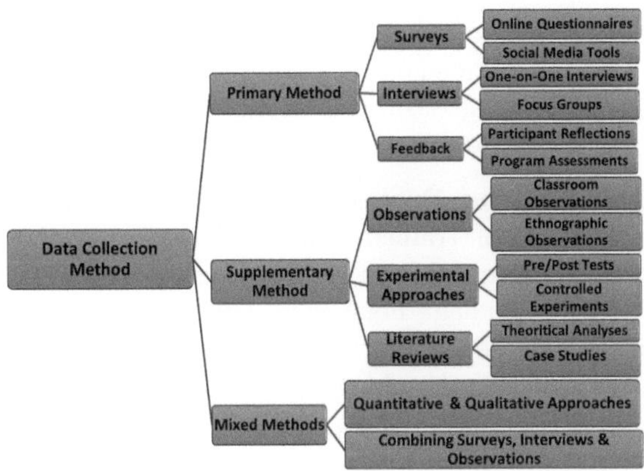

Fig. 3. An overview of the dataset types used in 44 studies

inaccessibility of web-based STEM platforms, which lacked screen reader compatibility.

(2) Educational Challenges: Teacher training and adapted materials were consistently lacking. Starling et al. [43] observed that many educators were unfamiliar with accessible STEM resources. Beck-Winchatz et al. [12] reported limited awareness of tactile or auditory aids. Koehler et al. [30] and Edwards et al. [18] highlighted a shortage of accessible materials in advanced subjects, such as calculus and physics.

(3) Accessibility Issues: STEM content often lacks non-visual alternatives. Supalo et al. [46] stressed the absence of tactile or auditory versions of diagrams and equations. Bell et al. [14] found that many e-learning platforms are incompatible with assistive technology. Wedler et al. [56] emphasized that STEM's visual nature creates barriers without proper adaptations.

(4) Social and Inclusion Barriers: Social exclusion and stereotypes were prevalent. Hong et al. [28] described the limited collaboration opportunities available to BVI students. Hamash et al. [24] discussed persistent low expectations from peers and educators. Hayes et al. [26] noted a lack of accommodations, which can lead to exclusion from STEM activities in mainstream classrooms.

RQ$_2$: How have solutions and strategies been proposed and implemented to overcome the difficulties that BVI students are facing in STEM education? This research question examines strategies from 44 studies designed to address the challenges faced by BVI students in STEM. These strategies fall into four main areas: technological innovations, teacher training, curriculum adaptation, and the creation of inclusive learning environments.

(1) Technological Innovations: Assistive technologies played a central role in many solutions. Namdev et al. [36] and Murgaski [35] highlighted the use of tactile graphics, 3D printing, and haptic feedback to support spatial understanding.

Wedler et al. [56] emphasized the importance of accessible digital platforms that are compatible with screen readers and braille displays. Surve [52] highlighted AI-driven tools, including voice-controlled coding platforms and real-time math transcription, which enhance digital accessibility in STEM.

(2) Teacher Training and Professional Development: Effective support for BVI students depends on trained educators. Starling et al. [43] and Koehler et al. [30] discussed programs that introduce teachers to accessible STEM tools and inclusive practices. Reynaga-Peña et al. [39] emphasized the importance of continuous professional development to keep educators informed about assistive technologies and accessibility standards.

(3) Curriculum Adaptation and Resource Development: Adapting STEM content was a common solution. Supalo et al. [46] redesigned labs using tactile and auditory tools. Beck-Winchatz [12] developed braille and audio materials, while Hasper et al. [25] described collaborative efforts to produce sonified datasets and 3D models tailored for BVI learners.

(4) Inclusive and Collaborative Learning Environments: Fostering peer collaboration was another key approach. Hong et al. [28] promoted group-based learning with sighted peers. Hamash [24] encouraged BVI student participation in STEM competitions. Miles et al. [34] highlighted community programs connecting BVI students with STEM mentors and professionals.

Together, these strategies provide a multi-faceted path toward inclusive and accessible STEM education through innovation, training, adaptation, and collaboration.

RQ$_3$: How are tools and technologies implemented and developed for STEM education of BVI students? This research question (RQ3) examines the role of innovative tools and technologies in addressing accessibility concerns for BVI students in STEM education. The analysis of 44 studies highlights the emergence of assistive technologies, tactile tools, and inclusive techniques that enhance their participation in STEM subjects. These solutions foster independence, hands-on learning, and equal involvement in STEM fields. Below is a detailed discussion of these advancements and their impact.

AI and Web-Based Assistive Technologies: AI-powered assistive tools have started to play a larger role in making STEM education more inclusive. Studies, for example, Singh et al. [42] highlighted AI-driven web applications that offer voice-assisted navigation, interactive equation solvers, and intelligent feedback systems to help BVI students engage with complex mathematical and scientific concepts independently.

Inclusive Design and Assistive Technologies: Inclusive design and assistive technologies play a critical role in enabling BVI students to engage with STEM education [3,4]. Wegwerth et al. [57] highlighted the Kasi Learning System, which combines tactile manipulatives and computer vision to create interactive and multi-sensory digital experiences, making complex STEM diagrams accessible. Similarly, Namdev et al. [36] described the development of a hyper-braille device enhanced with a mechanical XY gantry, which increases tactile resolution and allows users to explore STEM content using gestures such as zooming and panning. These devices provide intuitive access to abstract concepts. Additionally, Gonzales [21] introduced high-detail 3D tactile images crafted from HDPE materials using CNC milling. These tactile resources significantly improved BVI students' lab performance, with results showing a 60% increase in task success, showcasing the impact of tangible learning aids in STEM contexts.

Project-Based Learning and Collaboration: Project-based learning initiatives are instrumental in promoting collaboration and independence among BVI students. Tsinajinie et al. [54] discussed the Readiness Academy, an outdoor, inquiry-based STEM program that utilized assistive technologies and multisensory approaches to engage middle and high school students. The program emphasized collaboration, as students worked in teams to solve real-world problems. In informal STEM settings, tools like Bee-Bots, Lego Mindstorms, and Cubelets were adapted for BVI students, as documented by Hahn et al. [23], which showcased their success in teaching programming and robotics. Similarly, Hasper et al. [25] underscored the importance of resource adaptation in creating inclusive environments, highlighting tactile STEM kits as an effective means of engaging visually impaired students in collaborative learning.

Gamification and Hands-On Activities: Gamification and hands-on activities are increasingly used to make STEM subjects engaging and accessible for BVI students. Koehler et al. [30] explored the potential of gamified platforms, demonstrating how accessible games could enhance engagement and develop collaborative skills. Robotic tools such as Bee-Bots and Cubetto were adapted with tactile modifications to teach programming concepts effectively, as highlighted in Hahn et al. [23]. These activities not only facilitated hands-on learning but also provided an inclusive environment where BVI students could participate equitably, reinforcing the role of gamified and tactile-based strategies in STEM education.

Accessibility Challenges and Innovations: Accessibility remains a significant challenge in STEM education for BVI students, particularly in disciplines that rely heavily on visual materials. Supalo et al. [48] examined multi-sensory tablets that presented STEM graphics through vibrations and sound, finding them comparable in effectiveness to embossed tactile graphics. This study highlighted the potential for real-time digital solutions to complement traditional tactile methods. Meanwhile, Gonzales [21] focused on custom STEM kits and 3D tactile maps, which enabled students to explore abstract concepts, such as molecular structures. These tools, as supported by Hasper et al. [25], addressed the gap in accessible resources, ensuring that BVI students are not left behind in STEM education.

Educator and Institutional Support: The collaboration between educators and institutions is essential for implementing inclusive STEM education. Dey et al. [17] revealed the significance of collaborative initiatives, including NASA's tactile curriculum resources and the National Federation of the Blind's science academies, which offer organized pathways for students with BVI. Tsinajinie et al. [54] showed the urgent necessity for professional development to enable teachers to adapt instructional resources and methodologies for visually impaired students. This is particularly crucial in resource-limited areas such as India, where access to innovative technologies is restricted.

Emerging Technologies and Their Implications: Emerging technologies provide effective solutions for improving STEM accessibility for students with visual impairments. Reynaga-Peña [40] highlighted the use of 3D printing to create tactile models of complex molecular structures, enabling physical interaction and supporting the teaching of abstract chemistry concepts. Similarly, Laconsay et al. [31] developed smartphone apps, such as "Titration ColorCam," which utilize audio and vibrational feedback to support BVI students in titration experiments, providing real-time multisensory feedback in laboratory settings.

Laconsay et al. also introduced the sonification of infrared spectra, allowing BVI students to interpret chemical data through sound. Despite such innovations, Reynaga-Peña et al. [39] stressed the importance of balancing technological sophistication with affordability, particularly in low-resource settings, to ensure broad and sustainable adoption. Supalo et al. [47] reported that talking devices and audio feedback enhanced the independence of BVI students in labs, enabling data collection and analysis. Brown et al. [16] found that vibro-audio feedback and auditory overviews were as effective as verbal descriptions for interpreting graphical data. Supalo et al. [46] also showed that the Sci-Voice Talking LabQuest increased engagement and confidence through auditory feedback during summer programs.

In virtual learning, Ramdoss et al. [38] showed that platforms with multisensory tools and digital accessibility features helped students overcome learning barriers. Gould et al. [22] proposed standards for describing STEM images in digital talking books (DTBs), ensuring accessibility of non-textual content such as equations and charts. Meanwhile, Levy et al. [33] explored the Learning-to-Complexity (L2C) environment, which translates visual data into auditory cues to help students grasp complex systems, such as gas particle dynamics. Table 4 summarizes the characteristics and applications of these tools in supporting BVI students in STEM.

6   Study Discussion

Our literature review addresses the issues that BVI students experience in STEM education. We also evaluated innovative tools and technologies to overcome these challenges, as well as inclusive and equitable strategies. In this section, we present the key findings of our study and discuss their implications for future research.

Key Insight (1): Addressing Accessibility Barriers in STEM Education: The literature emphasizes that material inaccessibility remains a significant barrier for BVI students in STEM education. Hayes et al. [26] highlighted how tactile and 3D models, such as molecular geometries and planetary structures, provide an effective means of making abstract STEM concepts tangible

Table 4. Characteristics and usage of tools used in STEM education to support BVI students

Tool	Characteristics	Usage
Talking Balance	Provides verbal output for weight measurements.	Enables BVI students to independently measure mass in laboratory experiments.
Logger Pro Interface	Converts data from laboratory probes into audible output.	Supports independent collection and analysis of experimental data.
Sci-Voice Talking LabQuest	Gives real-time auditory feedback on data.	Assists in hands-on lab data collection and analysis.
3D Tactile Images	Created using CNC milling to depict images in tactile form.	Aids in understanding diagrams and visual STEM content.
Sound-Based Mediation	Transforms visual data into auditory cues.	Helps comprehend dynamic scientific phenomena.
Tactile and 3D Models	Physical models for abstract structures.	Enables tactile exploration of STEM concepts.
Braille-Labeled Equipment	Includes braille-labeled lab tools.	Enhances independent access in geoscience and other labs.
Audio-Tactile Graphs	Combines raised-line graphs with audio.	Allows exploration of data trends and equations.
Integrated STEM Kits	Inclusive manipulatives and diagrams.	Fosters accessible, collaborative STEM learning.
Accessible Periodic Tables	QR-enhanced periodic tables with audio info.	Provides accessible chemical reference for BVI students.
Tactile Talking Tablet (TTT)	Device giving tactile and auditory feedback.	Enables multisensory concept learning.
PIAF Tactile Graphic Maker	Produces raised-line tactile images.	Supports visual teaching material conversion.
Braille Rulers and Protractors	Measurement tools with braille/large print.	Supports geometry and measurement tasks.
Talking Calculators	Speaks operations and results aloud.	Enables independent math operations.
Liquid Level Indicator	Gives auditory alert when container is near full.	Helps safely measure liquids in science labs.
Talking Thermometers	Speaks temperature readings.	Facilitates temperature monitoring during experiments.
AI-Powered Equation Solvers	Converts equations to interactive voice format.	Promotes independent problem-solving in mathematics.
Virtual STEM Laboratories	Screen reader-friendly simulation platforms.	Allows full participation in accessible digital labs.
Web-Based Collaborative Learning	Cloud-based teamwork platforms with AI feedback.	Encourages inclusive real-time peer collaboration.

and accessible. Similarly, Supalo et al. [51] demonstrated the use of assistive tools, such as talking balances and Logger Pro interfaces, enabling BVI students to actively participate in laboratory experiments without assistance from sighted peers. These solutions highlight the crucial need to develop accessible learning resources specifically designed for the unique needs of BVI students.

In addition to physical tools, web applications have been identified as a key solution for addressing accessibility barriers [42]. AI-powered learning platforms with voice-guided navigation, digital braille support, and audio-enhanced mathematical notations are emerging as scalable alternatives to traditional teaching methods. These platforms enable BVI students to access real-time feedback and interactive simulations, improving engagement and comprehension in STEM subjects [42,52].

Key Insight (2): Enhancing Engagement with Technological Tools: Technological tools significantly enhance the learning experiences of BVI students by fostering engagement and independence. Levy et al. [33] explored sound-based mediation, a technique that translates visual data into auditory cues, helping students understand complex systems such as gas particle behaviors. Additionally, Adelakun [1] discussed the integration of tactile STEM kits in classrooms, screen-reader-friendly content, AI-assisted tutoring, and adaptive STEM assessments, which combine diagrams with multi-sensory feedback, promoting both collaboration and individual exploration among students. These advancements illustrate the potential of leveraging innovative tools to bridge accessibility gaps in STEM education.

Key Insight (3): The Role of Educators and Institutional Support: Effective STEM education for BVI students is heavily reliant on institutional support and educator preparedness. Miles et al. [34] highlighted the importance of braille-labeled equipment and voice-output devices in enabling BVI students to conduct independent experiments in geoscience. Furthermore, Reynaga-Peña et al. [39] emphasized the role of professional development in enabling teachers to adapt instructional materials more effectively and integrate assistive technologies into their classrooms. This finding underscores the importance of ongoing training and collaboration among educators, developers, and institutions.

Key Insight (4): Collaboration and Partnerships for Scalability: Collaboration between stakeholders is essential to scale up accessible STEM tools. Supalo [45] described the potential of partnerships among developers, educators, and policymakers in creating cost-effective and scalable solutions for under-resourced regions. For instance, initiatives to distribute affordable tactile materials and audio-enhanced STEM resources were found to significantly improve access for BVI students. Ramdoss [38] also stressed the importance of industry involvement, advocating for corporate social responsibility programs to supply assistive devices and technologies to schools.

Key Insight (5): Psychological and Social Inclusion: Addressing the psychological and social dimensions of STEM education is crucial for fostering an inclusive environment for BVI students. Beck-Winchatz et al. [12] identified emotional obstacles such as frustration and isolation experienced by students when learning STEM subjects. Providing access to supportive technologies and peer mentoring programs helped alleviate these challenges, thereby boosting the confidence and motivation of students. This highlights the need for holistic approaches that consider both the academic and emotional needs of BVI learners.

Key Insight (6): Emerging Technologies Transforming Accessibility: Emerging technologies are revolutionizing accessibility in STEM education. Starling et al. [43] highlighted the role of 3D-printed tactile models in teaching molecular structures, while Singh et al. [42] described the use of audio-tactile graphs to help BVI students interpret data trends. These innovations demonstrate the potential of multi-sensory tools in delivering immersive and effective STEM learning experiences. He also emphasized that AI-powered web applications, such as voice-interactive math solvers and haptic simulations, enhance STEM accessibility by enabling real-time, multi-modal learning. Their integration into mainstream curricula is key to fostering inclusive education [42]. However, Murgaski [35] emphasized the importance of balancing technological sophistication with affordability to ensure equitable access.

6.1   Recommendations for Future Research

✏ Future research can explore ways to refine and optimize assistive technologies, such as tactile models, sound-based systems, and multi-sensory tools. While these technologies have shown promise, studies like Levy et al. [33] and Starling et al. [43] suggest the need for enhancements in usability, portability, and customization to address diverse learning styles and requirements.
Scholars could examine the integration of artificial intelligence or adaptive interfaces to make these tools more responsive and effective. Additionally, researchers could investigate how AI-powered web applications can enhance these tools by providing adaptive interfaces, real-time feedback, and personalized learning experiences for students with BVI.

✏ Emotional and psychological barriers remain significant obstacles for BVI students in STEM fields, as highlighted in Beck-Winchatz [12]. Future research could explore strategies to reduce stress, build confidence, and enhance resilience in BVI STEM students through mentorship, peer support, and AI-driven interventions, offering new insights into these challenges.

✏ Stakeholder collaboration plays a crucial role in the success of accessible STEM education, as emphasized in Ramdoss et al. [38] and Supalo [45]. Future researchers can explore the potential for strengthening partnerships among educators, policymakers, and technology developers to create scalable and cost-effective solutions. Investigating cloud-based platforms as centralized hubs for resource sharing and accessibility innovation could be a valuable approach.

✏ The adequacy of funding and resource distribution is a recurring concern, as indicated in Miles et al. [34]. Future studies could analyze the extent to which institutions receive government or private funding to procure and maintain assistive devices for students with BVI. Additionally, investigating the feasibility of low-cost, web-based accessibility solutions could help bridge the resource gap and expand STEM opportunities for BVI students, especially in underserved regions.

7   Threats to Validity

This study is subject to specific threats to validity that must be considered, as with other SLR [29,53]. Our research examines tools, technologies, and methodologies designed for STEM education in the BVI, based on insights from 44 studies. While comprehensive, the following threats to validity are acknowledged:

Scope of Focus: The study focuses specifically on STEM education for BVI students. While the findings provide valuable insights, they may not fully address the needs of students with other disabilities or interdisciplinary areas where STEM merges with other domains. Expanding future research to broader aspects of accessibility and inclusion in education could address this limitation.

Data Completeness: The completeness of the dataset used in this SLR represents a potential threat. Despite employing a rigorous search strategy across multiple digital libraries and databases, some relevant studies might not have been included due to variances in terminology, indexing practices, or limited access to specific publications. To mitigate this, we employed an iterative search strategy and applied snowballing techniques to identify additional studies cited in the literature, thereby reducing data gaps.

Selection and Interpretation Bias: Another threat to validity lies in the potential for biases during the study selection and data synthesis phases. To counteract this, each paper underwent independent evaluation by multiple reviewers, with discrepancies resolved through discussion and consensus. Additionally, findings were synthesized based on themes identified across multiple studies rather than the perspective of a single reviewer, ensuring a balanced and objective representation of the evidence.

8   Conclusion

This study presents a systematic literature review (SLR) of the tools, technologies, and strategies that facilitate STEM education for BVI students. The findings indicate the progress in assistive technologies, including multisensory tools and tactile models, while underscoring the need for scalable and cost-effective solutions to ensure accessibility across various contexts. Also, Web applications, including AI-driven platforms and virtual labs, offer real-time feedback and adaptive learning to bridge these gaps. Future efforts should focus on refining these digital tools for seamless integration into education, thereby ensuring greater inclusivity in STEM fields. This study advances the existing literature by identifying deficiencies and offering practical recommendations for enhancing inclusion in STEM education. Building on these findings, collaboration among educators, policymakers, technologists, and researchers is key to creating a more inclusive STEM education system. Leveraging web-based platforms as collaborative hubs will expand access to STEM resources, break down barriers, and empower BVI students to fully participate and reach their potential.

References

1. Adelakun, S.A.: Exploring stem kit diagrams for braille readers in inclusive classrooms. J. Sci. Educ. Students Disabil. **23**(1), 45–60 (2020)
2. Adelakun, S.A., Abdulsalaam, A.O., Chukuka, U.E., Kehinde, M.A., Shittu, M.A.: How can the blind and visually impaired be involved in stem disciplines in Nigeria. Res. Square (2022). https://doi.org/10.21203/rs.3.rs-1787639/v1

3. Alghamdi, A.M., Aljedaani, W., Eler, M.M., Ludi, S.: Accessibility guidelines and standards: analyzing stack overflow posts. In: Proceedings of the 21st International Web for All Conference, pp. 118–122 (2024)
4. Alghamdi, A.M., Aljedaani, W., Jalali, H., Ludi, S., Eler, M.M.: Understanding developer challenges and trends in web accessibility: a stack overflow analysis. Univers. Access Inf. Soc. 1–17 (2024)
5. Aljedaani, W., Aljedaani, M., AlOmar, E.A., Mkaouer, M.W., Ludi, S., Khalaf, Y.B.: I cannot see you-the perspectives of deaf students to online learning during COVID-19 pandemic: Saudi Arabia case study. Educ. Sci. **11**(11), 712 (2021)
6. Aljedaani, W., Aljedaani, M., Mkaouer, M.W., Ludi, S.: Teachers perspectives on transition to online teaching deaf and hard-of-hearing students during the COVID-19 pandemic: a case study. In: Proceedings of the 16th Innovations in Software Engineering Conference, pp. 1–10 (2023)
7. Aljedaani, W., et al.: The state of accessibility in blackboard: survey and user reviews case study. In: Proceedings of the 20th International Web for All Conference, pp. 84–95 (2023)
8. Aljedaani, W., Eler, M.M., Parthasarathy, P.: Enhancing accessibility in software engineering projects with large language models (LLMs). In: Proceedings of the 56th ACM Technical Symposium on Computer Science Education V. 1, pp. 25–31 (2025)
9. Aljedaani, W., Krasniqi, R., Aljedaani, S., Mkaouer, M.W., Ludi, S., Al-Raddah, K.: If online learning works for you, what about deaf students? Emerging challenges of online learning for deaf and hearing-impaired students during COVID-19: a literature review. Univ. Access Inf. Soc. **22**(3), 1027–1046 (2023)
10. Aljedaani, W., Parthasarathy, P., Eler, M.M., Joshi, S.: Sprint to inclusion: embedding accessibility sprint in a software engineering course. In: Proceedings of the 56th ACM Technical Symposium on Computer Science Education V. 1, pp. 32–38 (2025)
11. Aljedaani, W., Parthasarathy, P., Joshi, S., Eler, M.M.: Accessibility insights from student's software engineering projects. In: Proceedings of the 56th ACM Technical Symposium on Computer Science Education V. 1, pp. 39–45 (2025)
12. Beck-Winchatz, B., Riccobono, M.A.: Advancing participation of blind students in science, technology, engineering, and math. Adv. Space Res. **42**(12), 1855–1858 (2008). https://doi.org/10.1016/j.asr.2007.05.080
13. Bell, E.C., Silverman, A.M.: The impact of attitudes and access to mentors on the interest in stem for teens and adults who are blind. J. Blind. Innov. Res. **8**(2) (2018)
14. Bell, E.C., Silverman, A.M.: Access to math and science content for youth who are blind or visually impaired. J. Blind. Innov. Res. **9**(1) (2019)
15. Bonfim, C.S., de Souza Mól, G., Pinheiro, B.C.S.: (in)visibility of visually impaired people in science, technology, engineering, and mathematics: perceptions and perspectives. Revista Brasileira de Educação Especial **27**, 605–620 (2021). https://doi.org/10.1590/1980-54702021v27e0220
16. Brown, J.R., Doore, S.A., Dimmel, J.K., Giudice, N., Giudice, N.A.: Comparing natural language and vibro-audio modalities for inclusive stem learning with blind and low vision users. In: The 25th International ACM SIGACCESS Conference on Computers and Accessibility (ASSETS '23), p. 17 (2023). https://doi.org/10.1145/3597638.3608429
17. Dey, S., Vidhya, Y., Bhushan, S., Neerukonda, M., Prakash, A.: Creating an accessible technology ecosystem for learning science and math: a case of visually impaired children in Indian schools. In: Workshop on Being (More) Human in

a Digitised World, Association of Information Systems–India Chapter Workshop, Kolkata (2019)

18. Edwards, K.M., Green, S.L.: Working with Learners with Visual Impairments in STEM, chap. 10, pp. 144–160. Nova Science Publishers (2014)

19. Farrand, K.M., Shaheen, N., Wild, T., Averil, J., Fast, D.: Improving student self-efficacy: the role of inclusive and innovative out of school programming for students with blindness and visual impairments. J. Blind. Innov. Res. **8**(2) (2018)

20. Ghoneim, R., Aljedaani, W., Bryce, R., Javed, Y., Khan, Z.I.: Why are other teachers more inclusive in online learning than us? Exploring challenges faced by teachers of blind and visually impaired students: a literature review. Computers (2073-431X) **13**(10) (2024)

21. Gonzales, A.: Development and analysis of new 3D tactile materials for the enhancement of STEM education for the blind and visually impaired. Master's thesis, Arizona State University (2015). https://www.proquest.com/docview/1587678

22. Gould, B., Ferrell, K.A., O'Connell, T.: Accessible science: how to describe stem images. AER J. Res. Pract. Vis. Impair. Blind. **2**(1), 52–54 (2009)

23. Hahn, M.E., Mueller, C.M., Gorlewicz, J.L.: The comprehension of stem graphics via a multisensory tablet electronic device by students with visual impairments. J. Vis. Impair. Blind. **113**(5), 404–418 (2019)

24. Hamash, M., Mohamed, H.: Basaer team: the first Arabic robot team for building the capacities of visually impaired students to build and program robots. Int. J. Emerg. Technol. Learn. (iJET) **16**(24), 91–103 (2021). https://doi.org/10.3991/ijet.v16i24.27465

25. Hasper, E., et al.: Methods for creating and evaluating 3D tactile images to teach stem courses to the visually impaired. J. Coll. Sci. Teach. **44**(6), 92–99 (2015). https://www.jstor.org/stable/43632001

26. Hayes, C., Proulx, M.J.: Turning a blind eye? Removing barriers to science and mathematics education for students with visual impairments. Br. J. Vis. Impair. **42**(2), 544–556 (2024). https://doi.org/10.1177/02646196221149561

27. Herzberg, T.S., McBride, C.R.: Middle and high school students with visual impairments describe their experiences in learning a new braille code for mathematics and science. J. Vis. Impair. Blind. 0145482X241257526 (2024)

28. Hong, S., Topor, I., Park, J., Alshuli, T.A., Topor, I.L.: Out-of-school stem program for students with visual impairments: adaptations and outcomes during the COVID-19 pandemic. J. Sci. Educ. Students Disabil. **26**(1), 1–10 (2023)

29. Kitchenham, B., Brereton, O.P., Budgen, D., Turner, M., Bailey, J., Linkman, S.: Systematic literature reviews in software engineering - a systematic literature review. Inf. Softw. Technol. **51**(1), 7–15 (2009)

30. Koehler, K.E., Picard, K.M.: Making stem accessible for students with visual impairments: implications for practice. Teach. Except. Children **XX**(X) (2024). https://doi.org/10.1177/00400599241231211

31. Laconsay, C.J., Wedler, H.B., Tantillo, D.J.: Visualization without vision-how blind and visually impaired students and researchers engage with molecular structures. J. Sci. Educ. Students Disabil. **23**(1), 1–21 (2020)

32. Leporini, B., Buzzi, M.: Education and STEM on the web. In: Yesilada, Y., Harper, S. (eds.) Web Accessibility. Human–Computer Interaction Series, pp. 651–678. Springer, London (2019). https://doi.org/10.1007/978-1-4471-7440-0_33

33. Levy, S.T., Lahav, O.: Enabling people who are blind to experience science inquiry learning through sound-based mediation. J. Comput. Assist. Learn. **28**, 499–513 (2012). https://doi.org/10.1111/j.1365-2729.2011.00457.x

34. Miles, R.G., Zambone, A., Manda, A.: Perceptions of earth science using assistive and supportive technologies by students who are blind or visually impaired. J. Sci. Educ. Students Disabil. **14**(1), 45–60 (2022). https://doi.org/10.14448/jsesd.14.0004

35. Murgaski, S.: Using inclusive design to improve the accessibility of informal STEM education for children with visual impairment. Master's thesis, OCAD University, Toronto, Ontario, Canada (2020)

36. Namdev, R.K., Maes, P.: An interactive and intuitive stem accessibility system for the blind and visually impaired. In: Proceedings of the 8th ACM International Conference on Pervasive Technologies Related to Assistive Environments, pp. 1–7 (2015)

37. Petz, A., Miesenberger, K.: Supporting blind students in stem education in Austria. Stud. Health Technol. Inform. **217**, 417–423 (2015). https://doi.org/10.3233/978-1-61499-566-1-417

38. Ramdoss, S., Liu, D., Kumar, S., Lee, K.: A qualitative study: perceptions of students with blindness in post-graduate distance learning in stemfields. J. Blind. Innov. Res. **11**(2) (2021)

39. Reynaga-Peña, C.G., Fernández-Cárdenas, J.M., Morales, L.D.G., de León Lastras, A.D., Capetillo, A.J.C.: Engineering for inclusive stem education: an interdisciplinary collaboration project for the design and creation of accessible and inclusive learning materials. In: Latin American Conference on Learning Technologies (LACLO) (2019). https://doi.org/10.1109/LACLO49268.2019.00057

40. Reynaga-Peña, C.G., Suero, C.L.: Strategies and Technology Aids for Teaching Science to Blind and Visually Impaired Students, chap. 2, pp. 35–56. IGI Global (2020). https://doi.org/10.4018/978-1-5225-8539-8.ch002

41. Rule, A.C., Stefanich, G.P., Boody, R.M., Peiffer, B.: Impact of adaptive materials on teachers and their students with visual impairments in secondary science and mathematics classes. Int. J. Sci. Educ. **33**(6), 865–887 (2011). https://doi.org/10.1080/09500693.2010.506619

42. Singh, P., Kapoor, I., Goyal, A.: Educational software system for teaching stem to visually impaired people. J. Phys. Conf. Ser. **2570**, 012030 (2023). https://doi.org/10.1088/1742-6596/2570/1/012030

43. Starling, L.P., Brauner, D.: Engaging students with visual impairments or blindness through comprehensive and accessible engineering experiences. In: American Society for Engineering Education Conference (2016)

44. Sternberg, R.: Applying psychological theories to educational practice. Am. Educ. Res. J. (2008)

45. Supalo, C.A.: The next generation laboratory interface for students with blindness or low vision in the science laboratory. RIT Scholar Works, pp. 34–42 (2012)

46. Supalo, C.A., Hill, A.A., Larrick, C.G.: Summer enrichment programs to foster interest in stem education for students with blindness or low vision. J. Chem. Educ. **91**(8), 1257–1260 (2014). https://doi.org/10.1021/ed400585v

47. Supalo, C.A., Humphrey, J.R., Mallouk, T.E., Wohlers, H.D., Carlsen, W.S.: Examining the use of adaptive technologies to increase the hands-on participation of students with blindness or low vision in secondary-school chemistry and physics. Chem. Educ. Res. Pract. **17**, 1174–1189 (2016). https://doi.org/10.1039/c6rp00141f

48. Supalo, C.A., Isaacson, M.D., Lombardi, M.V.: Making hands-on science learning accessible for students who are blind or have low vision. J. Chem. Educ. **91**, 195–199 (2014). https://doi.org/10.1021/ed3000765

49. Supalo, C.A., Mallouk, T.E., Amorosi, C., Lanouette, J., Wohlers, H.D., McEnnis, K.: Using adaptive tools and techniques to teach a class of students who are blind or low-vision. J. Chem. Educ. **86**(5), 587 (2009)
50. Supalo, C.A., Wohlers, H.D., Humphrey, J.R.: Students with blindness explore chemistry at "camp can do". J. Sci. Educ. Students Disabil. **15**(1), 1–9 (2011)
51. Supalo, C.A.: Teaching chemistry and other sciences to blind and low-vision students through hands-on learning experiences in high school science laboratories. Ph.D. dissertation, The Pennsylvania State University (2010)
52. Surve, I.: Exploring stem education for the visually impaired in India: leveraging technology for improvement. Int. Educ. Res. J. **9**, 68–72 (2023)
53. Torres-Carrión, P.V., González-González, C.S., Aciar, S., Rodríguez-Morales, G.: Methodology for systematic literature review applied to engineering and education. In: 2018 IEEE Global Engineering Education Conference (EDUCON), pp. 1364–1373. IEEE (2018)
54. Tsinajinie, G., Kirboyun, S., Hong, S.: An outdoor project-based learning program: strategic support and the roles of students with visual impairments interested in STEM. J. Sci. Educ. Technol. **30**(1), 74–86 (2020). https://doi.org/10.1007/s10956-020-09874-0
55. Ulbrich, E., Andic, B., Lichtenegger, B., Ulbrich, M., Lavicza, Z.: Visualizations and pictures for the visually impaired and its connection to stem education. J. Math. Arts (2024). https://doi.org/10.1080/17513472.2024.2365086
56. Wedler, H.B., et al.: Nobody can see atoms: science camps highlighting approaches for making chemistry accessible to blind and visually impaired students. J. Chem. Educ. **91**(2), 188–194 (2014)
57. Wegwerth, S.E., Manchester, G.J., Winter, J.E.: A feasibility study of the Kasi learning system to support independent use of stem diagrams by students with visual impairments. J. Vis. Impair. Blind. **117**(2), 162–174 (2023). https://doi.org/10.1177/0145482X231169713

Inclusive and Assistive IT Design: Pedagogical and Practical Insights from Two Iterations of a Service-Learning Computer Science Course

Julia Hermann[(✉)] and Aysegül Dogangün

Institute of Positive Computing, Ruhr West University of Applied Sciences,
Lützowstraße 5, 46236 Bottrop, Germany
`{julia.hermann,ayseguel.doganguen}@hs-ruhrwest.de`

Abstract. This article presents the design, implementation, and evaluation of *Inclusive IT Design*, a service-learning course in which computer science and HCI students from two German universities collaborated with people with diverse disabilities and support needs to develop inclusive or assistive digital technologies. Conducted across two consecutive semesters, the module tasked student teams with co-designing software prototypes that address the real-life needs of people with cognitive, physical, or emotional disabilities. The research draws on end-of-semester surveys and in-depth, semi-structured interviews with both cohorts to analyze course structure, student learning outcomes, and the evolution of the pedagogical approach. Our findings indicate that the combination of iterative, interactive fieldwork, theoretical frameworks, and sustained user participation is associated with increased student empathy, heightened awareness of inclusive design challenges, and the development of practical skills. While many students self-reported significant gains in understanding assistive and inclusive design, genuine co-creation with people with disabilities was often experienced as a challenge rather than a consistently realized outcome. Our results highlight persistent challenges: preparing students for complex real-world user engagement, balancing documentation with practical design, and sustaining project outcomes beyond a single semester. The experience also revealed institutional and organizational barriers that must be addressed for long-term curricular integration. We conclude our article with practical recommendations for educators seeking to embed inclusive, socially grounded design experiences into computing and HCI curricula.

Keywords: Inclusive IT Design · Service Learning · Accessibility · Assistive Technology · Participatory Design · Co-Creation · User-Centered Design · Computer Science Education · Disability

1 Introduction

Information and communication technology permeates nearly all aspects of modern life, yet people with disabilities, particularly those with higher support needs,

© The Author(s), under exclusive license to Springer Nature Switzerland AG 2026
M. Antona and C. Stephanidis (Eds.): HCII 2025, LNCS 16335, pp. 87–108, 2026.
https://doi.org/10.1007/978-3-032-12781-5_6

still face barriers in accessing digital tools [13, 18]. Although efforts toward universal and inclusive design have grown in recent years, many software systems remain insufficiently adaptable or accessible, and participation often relies on the availability of effective assistive technologies [28]. Based on personal teaching experience, human-centered approaches, especially those involving direct interaction with marginalized user groups, still play a subordinate role in computer science curricula. Students and lecturers alike tend to rely on their own abilities and ideas when envisioning potential users, a phenomenon referred to as "I-methodology" [22]. Some academic programs predominantly focus on theoretical concepts or educators' assumptions about user needs, which can lead to the specific perspectives and requirements of people with disabilities being overlooked.

To address this shortcoming, we developed a semester-based, service-learning course titled *Inclusive IT Design*, which actively engages computer science (CS) and human-computer interaction (HCI) students from two German universities in participatory projects with people with diverse disabilities and support needs. While the course is named to emphasize a broad commitment to *inclusion*, its design explicitly addresses the challenge of bridging inclusive and assistive IT design in practice. In line with current research, we define *inclusive design* as an approach aimed at removing barriers for as many users as possible and fostering equal participation. In contrast, *accessible* design focuses on removing barriers for people with disabilities in general, while *assistive* approaches address the specific needs of individuals who rely on tailored support or dedicated assistive technologies [8, 25]. Because many of our course participants had substantial support and assistance needs, the teaching format necessarily combines both principles: aiming for broad inclusion where feasible, but also developing highly specific solutions to enable participation for people with complex or individualized requirements [11, 21]. The goal is to promote participation and self-determination by creating digital solutions that enable meaningful inclusion, even where highly specific or assistive adaptations are required. In cooperation with organizations providing day-structuring measures and vocational workshops for people with disabilities, student teams collaborated closely with people with disabilities to design software prototypes tailored to the specific needs arising from daily and work-related routines. Participants varied considerably in their support needs, prompting students to adapt both their communication approaches and design strategies accordingly.

Given that people with disabilities who require more extensive support remain largely invisible in everyday contexts, computer science students typically have limited exposure to their experiences and requirements. Courses addressing inclusive or accessible IT Design [5, 17] highlight that unfamiliarity with disability contexts necessitates careful preparation to ensure meaningful interactions and a practical understanding of supportive technologies. Our service-learning model emphasizes social responsibility and ethical reflection, integrating academic objectives with community engagement [2, 4], guided by Design Science Research [14], Participatory Design [30], and Positive Computing [7].

By fostering direct interaction with user groups exhibiting a wide spectrum of cognitive, physical, and emotional disabilities, we examine how educational settings can promote both broader participation (inclusion) and address specific support needs (assistive technologies). This dual approach reflects the realities of our course context and underpins the user-centered strategies described in the following sections. We report on two iterations of our course, describing the structure, methodological approaches, and iterative refinements of assistive software prototypes developed in collaboration with end-users and their support staff. Our central research question is:

How do students perceive and evaluate the structure, methods, and practical experiences provided by a participatory, service-learning course on inclusive and assistive IT design across two consecutive iterations?

The contribution of this paper is a transferable model for a semester-based, participatory educational format that fosters direct collaboration between students and people with diverse, often complex support needs. In our context, this included not only general principles of inclusion, but also the practical development of accessible and, where necessary, assistive digital solutions to enable meaningful participation for people with disabilities.

2   Related Work

Research on inclusive, assistive, and participatory approaches in computer science education has grown in recent years. The implementation in our course extends beyond generic inclusivity. *Inclusive design* strives to ensure that digital tools and environments are usable by as many people as possible, regardless of ability, by considering diversity from the outset [8,11]. In contrast, *accessible and assistive design* specifically addresses the removal of barriers through targeted adaptations and the development of assistive technologies, responding to the needs of users who would otherwise be excluded [25,32]. However, in practice, and especially with user groups who have higher or more complex support needs, the boundaries between these concepts become fluid. Our course thus positions itself at the intersection of these paradigms: students are challenged to pursue the broad goals of inclusion, while learning to recognize when and why highly specific support is essential to enabling participation and agency for a specific user. This pragmatic, context-sensitive approach reflects the current consensus in design research, which increasingly advocates for a "both–and" strategy: combining the ethos of universal and inclusive design with the targeted problem-solving of assistive technology development [11,25]. By making these distinctions explicit, the course equips students not only to reflect on the ethical and conceptual foundations of inclusion and assistants, but also to make informed, empathetic design decisions in real-world, heterogeneous contexts.

These practical complexities are mirrored not only in approaches to inclusion and accessibility, but also in the ways users are involved throughout the design process. In the following, we adopt established definitions of key participatory design paradigms—while acknowledging that, in our own course, boundaries between them were often blurred by the realities of user needs, communication styles, and project constraints. *Participatory Design* (PD) describes design processes where end-users are intentionally involved as co-creators and share substantial decision-making power, with the aim of achieving empowerment and agency [30]. *Co-Design* is often used as a broader term for collaborative activities in which users and stakeholders contribute ideas or feedback, yet the final design authority may still predominantly reside with the professional design or development team [27]. In our course context, these boundaries were frequently blurred: While the ambition was participatory design in the sense of shared agency, the reality often reflected co-design or HCD patterns, especially where users faced communicative or cognitive barriers, or where practical constraints limited ongoing direct participation. We address these methodological tensions and their implications for student learning in the analysis and discussion sections.

To provide a foundation for this analysis, we first situate our course in the context of existing research. The following section reviews prior studies on service learning, participatory and inclusive design, and established educational strategies for teaching accessibility and fostering collaboration with people with disabilities.

2.1   Service Learning in Computer Science Education

Research on service learning demonstrates its potential to enhance students' academic achievement and reinforce their sense of social responsibility [1,33]. Bringle and Hatcher [4] illustrate how service learning effectively connects theoretical concepts with practical applications, particularly in technology-oriented programs, by immersing students in authentic projects. Service learning specifically aimed at accessibility and inclusion is gaining traction. Iniesto and Rodrigo [15], for example, describe a service-learning model in which computer science students evaluate the accessibility of city council websites, thereby promoting a deeper understanding of inclusive design through hands-on assessment activities. Unlike participatory formats, their model centers on practical exposure to accessibility standards and challenges from the evaluator perspective. These studies highlight that service learning can enhance students' technical skills and social awareness by situating learning in real-world contexts and encouraging active engagement. However, most existing models, particularly in the context of accessibility and inclusion, tend to emphasize relatively well-defined evaluation tasks or practical exposure to standards, rather than sustained, direct collaboration with people with disabilities. As a result, questions remain about the effectiveness of service learning in preparing students for more complex, participatory, or co-creative design settings, especially when working with users with diverse or high support needs.

2.2 Accessibility and Inclusive Design in Computer Science Education

Numerous barriers remain to fully accommodating the diversity of user needs in computer science education, particularly for students with disabilities and for those engaged in the design of inclusive technologies. A recurring theme in the literature is that, despite growing awareness, accessibility and inclusive design remain insufficiently embedded in computer science curricula. Weisberg et al. [31] argue that while inclusive design is increasingly recognized as essential, its practical integration into coursework and institutional structures is still lacking.

The studies examined methodological approaches for better consideration of accessibility and participation in computer science education contexts. Ferreira and Castro [10] discuss the adaptation of participatory and inclusive design methodologies for different teaching scenarios, emphasizing the importance of student engagement with real user needs. Ding et al. [9] provide evidence that direct student interaction with user communities, rather than abstract case studies, can significantly enhance learning outcomes and empathy for diverse perspectives. There is also empirical support for explicit accessibility training: Martin-Escalona et al. [19] demonstrate that targeted accessibility education improves students' technical performance and comprehension of disability-related challenges, especially when delivered within authentic project settings. Ludi [17] highlights the benefits of requirements-engineering exercises that focus on accessibility, showing that such tasks broaden students' appreciation for the spectrum of disability and user needs. Curricular strategies for integrating accessibility are varied. Ko and Ladner [16] review multiple models, from standalone modules to cross-curricular infusion, and underscore the value of flexible, context-sensitive integration approaches. Rosmaita [26] advocates for early and sustained attention to accessibility across courses, suggesting that repeated exposure is key to fostering genuine engagement and deeper understanding. Taken together, these works demonstrate the value of explicit, diverse, and participatory accessibility training in computer science education. However, as observed in both research and practice, ongoing and sustained collaboration with user groups who have complex or high support needs remains relatively rare in educational settings.

2.3 Participation and Co-creation: Benefits and Challenges

Direct interaction with people with disabilities has repeatedly proven valuable in shifting student perceptions and assumptions [5,29]. Shinohara et al. [29] found that interaction with users with disabilities helped student designers challenge and move beyond preconceived notions. Brinkley et al. [5] noted substantial logistical, ethical, and pedagogical challenges associated with participatory design and co-creation, highlighting the need for ongoing reflection and iterative adjustment. Much of the existing literature focuses on users with specific types of disabilities, such as sensory, physical, or certain neurodivergent conditions. However, disability and support needs exist along a broad and intersecting spectrum, shaped by context, individual experience, and diverse requirements for participation. Research involving participatory or co-design with people who have complex, multiple, or higher support needs, such as limited verbal communication, combinations of physical, cognitive, and psychosocial disabilities, or greater reliance on daily assistance, remains scarce. There is a particular lack of studies that reflect this diversity and complexity in authentic, real-world settings, rather than isolating disability categories or focusing only on "easy to involve" user groups. Our approach therefore intentionally avoids rigid classification and instead foregrounds the interrelatedness and diversity of access needs and lived experience in inclusive design processes.

2.4   Research Gap and Contribution

Despite significant progress in accessibility- and inclusion-focused education and participatory design approaches, existing research seldom combines comprehensive service-learning formats with sustained, direct collaboration involving users with complex support needs. In many service-learning models, students may work on projects for or about the target group, but do not always engage in repeated, hands-on interaction with the people who will ultimately use the solutions [15,29]. Many studies limit themselves to relatively straightforward cases, indirect involvement, or controlled environments. Thus, a gap remains regarding how service-learning models can effectively engage students with more challenging and realistic scenarios of disability and inclusion, addressing both technical and ethical complexities inherent in real-world settings.

3   Module Structure and Implementation

Jointly organized by two German universities (Ruhr University Bochum (RUB) and the University of Applied Sciences Ruhr West (HRW)), the module was offered as an elective at both institutions. Structurally, it was a semester-long module (6 ECTS), open to bachelor's and master's students from various computer science and HCI programs from the fifth semester onwards. The course was delivered across two semesters, in 2023 and 2024. Across both iterations, students engaged consistently with real user groups at partner facilities, developing prototypes through iterative cycles of observation, co-creation, and feedback. Student teams typically consisted of 4–5 members. These teams collaborated throughout the semester with existing groups of approximately 5–15 people with disabilities, who were themselves diverse in their support needs, abilities, and interests. The user groups were not composed according to type or degree of disability, but were formed in the practice settings (e.g., vocational workshops) based on shared interests and workplace skills. This ensured a heterogeneous, inclusive group dynamic reflecting real-world workplace diversity. The number of participating students varied substantially between the two cohorts (30 in 2023, 16 in 2024), primarily because the module was offered as an elective and was subject to competition with other elective courses each semester. As a result, the size and number of student teams, as well as the specific work areas chosen (e.g., office services, horticulture, assembly work), differed between cohorts. Students selected their preferred work area without prior knowledge of the exact composition of the user group they would engage with.

Despite these organizational differences, the core objectives remained: grounding technical skills in participatory, user-centered design practices, and promoting iterative refinement based on authentic, diverse user needs and ongoing feedback from all stakeholders. Three key components defined the module in both cohorts:

1. **Extended Block Sessions** (approximately five hours each, in weeks 2, 6, 10, and 14), held on campus, served multiple purposes. Alongside introducing theoretical frameworks, such as Design Science Research (DSR), participatory methods, Positive Computing, and accessibility standards, these sessions emphasized interactive learning and collaboration. Students worked together in their teams and across groups, regularly engaging with instructors, peers, and external partners as well as members of the target user group. The format prioritized joint problem-solving, method application, and peer feedback, with student demonstrations and discussion rounds fostering ongoing exchange between all stakeholders. This integrative and interactive approach helped bridge the gap between theory and practice and encouraged reflection on group dynamics and participatory processes.

2. **Fieldwork in Partner Institutions with the Target Group** constituted the core of the co-creation and participatory approach. Rather than merely observing routines, students actively engaged in ongoing collaboration with people with disabilities, staff, and caregivers at the partner sites. This included joint workshops, iterative feedback sessions, and hands-on prototyping, where students and users developed, tested, and refined ideas and solutions together. In the 2023 iteration, fieldwork consisted of one primary visit early in the semester and a final evaluation session. However, students, lecturers and partners reported that this format limited authentic participation and opportunities for meaningful iteration. In response, the 2024 module mandated at least two additional structured visits per team: one focused on collaborative idea generation (immersion in the solution space), and another dedicated to co-creation and prototyping workshops with the user group. These extended interactions fostered trust, allowed for reciprocal learning, and supported continuous integration of user perspectives throughout the design process, significantly enhancing both the quality of the prototypes and the students' understanding of participatory methods.

3. **Digital Impulses** (online sessions, 45–90 min), conducted approx. every two weeks, facilitated immediate peer-to-peer feedback, discussed emerging technical and ethical issues, and provided targeted theoretical and methodological guidance. The 2024 iteration placed increased emphasis on helping students effectively bridge feedback from multiple field visits.

Table 1 summarizes the methodological flow of both course iterations, marking changes introduced in 2024.

Table 1. Course Phases and Methodological Focus

Phase	Content and Activities	Methodological Emphasis
Kick-Off & Early Sessions	Basic orientation on DSR, Positive Computing, inclusive and assistive design, introduction to practice partners, team formation	Aligning theoretical frameworks with real-world contexts
Fieldwork & User Contact	Observations and contextual interviews at partner sites, co-creation workshops, initial user feedback (one main site visit in 2023; four in 2024)	Gathering authentic requirements, uncovering constraints, enabling user-driven design decisions
Prototyping Cycles	Development of prototypes, digital impulses for interim discussions, refinement guided by any new user insights (limited iteration in 2023; multiple cycles in 2024)	Implementing accessibility, integrating staff feedback, testing partial solutions in design loops
Final Demonstration	Presentation of prototypes to peers, partners, target group and instructors, reflection on both technical and ethical lessons	Summative evaluation, highlighting the extent of user involvement and social responsibility

4 Methodological Aspects of the Course Module

The course aimed to prepare students specifically for challenges in developing inclusive and assistive technologies through collaboration with people with diverse and often complex support needs. The module combined blended learning, project-based teamwork, and multiple field visits to community partners (workshops and day-structuring programs for people with disabilities). By situating collaborative projects within the context of daily routines and vocational activities, the course explicitly aimed to support real-world inclusion and participation, addressing not only technical accessibility but also the broader goal of social inclusion in everyday (work) life.

Two primary learning objectives guided our course: firstly, to heighten students' awareness of the lived experiences, constraints, and everyday participation challenges faced by people with disabilities, motivating them to incorporate genuine user perspectives at each stage of design; secondly, to foster social responsibility by enabling authentic interaction between students and people with disabilities, moving beyond designing "for" users to designing "with" them.

To fulfill these objectives, the course initially employed a Design Science Research (DSR) framework [14,24], guiding students systematically through identifying real-world barriers (Problem Space) and developing practical solutions (Solution Space). In 2023, we explicitly introduced Contextual Design [3] as a participatory framework, aiming to immerse students in the everyday contexts of the target groups. However, in 2024, we moved away from the formal Contextual Design framework toward a more flexible combination of participatory methods, responding to feedback that the strict structure of Contextual Design was less suitable given the diverse needs of our target groups. Instead, students were provided with a curated set of inclusive and participatory design methods, ranging from structured observation protocols and user interviews to adapted workshop formats, that were specifically chosen to accommodate the needs of people with diverse and sometimes complex support needs. They were encouraged to select from these methods, adapt them as needed, and document any further modifications for their target group. This approach ensured methodological rigor while allowing for individualization, enabling student teams to implement and reflect on communication and design strategies also tailored to settings with non-verbal or limited-verbal participants.

Throughout both iterations, Positive Computing principles [7,23] were consistently emphasized, encouraging students to move beyond a deficit-oriented approach to disability. Students were instructed to actively consider user autonomy, competence, relatedness, and emotional well-being, thus expanding traditional "assistance and accessibility" perspectives to include psychosocial dimensions. Ethical considerations, such as informed consent, respect for autonomy, and safeguarding vulnerable participants, were addressed explicitly through preparatory workshops, ongoing reflective discussions, and close supervision by instructors and support staff.

4.1 The Role of Community Partners in the Service-Learning Approach

The effectiveness of the course depended significantly on sustained partnerships with community-based organizations, ensuring that students' projects remained grounded in authentic, context-specific needs. Service-learning inherently integrates academic learning with active community involvement [2,4]. Our partner organizations, offering day-structuring and vocational activities for people with disabilities, provided critical insights into real-world constraints and user needs. According to Giles and Eyler [12], maintaining continuous and effective partnerships is crucial for successful service-learning experiences, a point we reinforced through structured dialogues and iterative feedback loops. Feedback sessions occurred during and after each course iteration, involving partner representatives, people with disabilities, course instructors, and students. This feedback was collected and analyzed to identify critical areas for improvement. Adjustments based on input included, e.g., increasing the number of mandatory field visits in 2024. We observed that transparent communication and clearly managing expectations helped mitigate challenges arising from partner organizations' desires for concrete outcomes versus the educational priorities of the course [6].

5   Evaluation

Our evaluation follows a mixed-methods design to systematically examine how the *Inclusive IT-Design* module's service-learning approach affects students' attitudes, competencies, and design practices in the development of assistive and inclusive technologies. The study integrated quantitative survey data and semi-structured interviews data collected at the end of each semester. While extensive data were collected at four points in time during each semester, this article focuses on the summative end-of-semester survey and the corresponding final-round interviews for each cohort. This deliberate narrowing of scope allows for a targeted, retrospective analysis of pedagogical and methodological outcomes, emphasizing how students experienced and reflected on the course structure, design process, and their own development after completing the module.

5.1 Quantitative Surveys with Open-Ended Questions

At the end of the semester, students at both universities completed an online evaluation. This survey formed the primary quantitative data source for the summative assessment of each cohort. In 2023, 19 students participated; in 2024, 12 students took part. The closed-ended items were rated on a 5-point Likert scale from 1 ("very good"/"strong agreement") to 5 ("poor"/"strong disagreement") and addressed dimensions such as instructor fairness, course structure and time management, and the relevance of user collaboration. Open-ended prompts solicited students' reflections on the most and least helpful aspects of the course as well as suggestions for improvement. Descriptive statistics were calculated for each item. Open-ended responses were systematically categorized into key thematic areas (e.g., scheduling, documentation-practice balance, value of user engagement). All responses were submitted anonymously and could not be attributed to individual participants (Table 2).

Table 2. Core Focus Areas in the End-of-Semester Evaluation

Focus Area	Example Items or Prompts
Instructor Fairness and Clarity	"Is the instructor fair in dealing with students?" "The instructor responds to questions clearly."
Course Structure & Time Management	"The course sessions are well structured and the scheduling is appropriate." "I felt we had enough time to implement prototypes effectively."
Practical Engagement and Prototyping	"How relevant was the collaboration with practice partners for your learning?" Open-ended: "What aspects of real-world involvement helped you the most?"
Overall Quality and Recommendation	"Rate the course overall from 1 ('very good') to 5 ('poor')." "Would you recommend this module to others?"
Suggestions and Feedback	Open-ended: "What did you like best about this course?" and "What should be improved?"

5.2 Qualitative Interviews

A subset of students participated in semi-structured interviews. Participation was voluntary and not tied to course credit; however, students who participated in all four interview time points were compensated with a € 50 honorarium. In 2023, 9 interviews were conducted; in 2024, 7 students participated for the last interview in the series. Interviews were conducted within one week following survey completion, lasted approximately 30–60 min, and took place in a private setting. All sessions were audio-recorded with informed consent and transcribed verbatim. Translations from German into English were performed after the qualitative analysis had been completed to ensure coding fidelity based on the original language. Participants were selected based on availability and willingness, with an emphasis on capturing a diversity of project experiences and backgrounds. While the full interview schedule covered a broad range of topics, for the purposes of this article, we analyzed only those sections from the fourth-round interviews that directly aligned with the standardized survey constructs (e.g., time management, instructor support, practical relevance) and established challenges in service-learning contexts (e.g., documentation load, iterative design). Interviews encouraged participants to reflect on both individual and team-level experiences.

5.3   Data Analysis and Quality Assurance

Quantitative data were compared across cohorts. Open-ended survey responses and interview transcripts were analyzed using qualitative content analysis according to Mayring [20]. An initial deductive coding frame was developed based on survey constructs and expanded inductively during analysis. Survey themes and interview findings were compared and integrated, with particular attention to topics recurring across both methods.

No formal university ethics committee existed at the time of data collection. To ensure responsible research practice, all participants were informed about the voluntary and confidential nature of participation, the right to withdraw at any time, and the intended use of data for research purposes. All participants gave written informed consent. Pseudonymization was applied in all records, and particularly sensitive information was omitted from analysis and reporting.

6   Evaluation of "Inclusive IT Design": Results from 2023 and 2024

6.1   Participants and Demographics (Quantitative Survey)

Among the respondents of the survey in 2023, nearly 40% were in their sixth semester or higher, and approximately 58% were employed alongside their studies (either part-time or full-time). Only 12.5% received study support from their employer. These figures reflect the characteristics of those who actually filled out the evaluation, not of the entire course cohort.

In semester 2024, 7 respondents were students from RUB and 5 from University of Applied Science Ruhr West (HRW). Within this sample, 57% were enrolled in a Master's program and 43% in a Bachelor's program; semester levels ranged from 2nd to "more than 10th" semester. All students participated voluntarily, motivated primarily by personal interest in the topic (71%) and the course's practical orientation (57%). Attendance was very high within this group: 86% reported attending "practically always." The reported weekly time investment was substantial.

6.2   Quantitative Evaluation Results

Overall course ratings were positive in both years. In 2023, the average overall grade was 2.2 (median 2.0); 63% rated the course "good" (2), and 16% "very good" (1). 89.5% said they would recommend the course to others, indicating strong overall satisfaction. In 2024, the average was 2.1, again corresponding to "good" to "very good."

Students consistently gave high marks to the instructors' engagement, teaching quality, and support. In 2023, agreement that "the instructor takes students seriously and shows interest in their learning" was high (mean = 1.3), as were clarity of explanation and audibility (mean $\approx$ 1.1). At 2024, the converted mean for "instructor well-prepared" was 1.3, and "conveyed enthusiasm" 1.6. These strong scores demonstrate consistent appreciation for instructional quality.

However, several aspects were evaluated more moderately. The structure and scheduling of sessions, and especially the workload, received mixed or only moderately positive marks. In 2023, the structure was rated at 2.7, and the appropriateness of workload and balance between theory and practice at 2.3. In 2024, students also indicated that the workload was demanding (difficulty mean $\approx$ 3.3; pace mean $\approx$ 2.3), and some felt that organizational clarity could be improved (converted mean $\approx$ 2.3).

6.3   Open Answers and Thematic Analysis

Participation and Target-Group Engagement: Working with real user groups was repeatedly described as a unique and valuable aspect. In 2023, students highlighted the importance of "working on real problems and making a contribution," and valued being "on site and in contact with the people for whom one is developing the prototype." In 2024, students described as strengths "the actual work with people with disabilities during the field visits" and "valuable practical experience" gained through community partnerships and the instructors' "great support." However, both cohorts also noted room for improvement in organizing the fieldwork and wished for more preparatory input on disability awareness: e.g., "It would help to address more the different types of disabilities, e.g. which ones exist and how to deal with them."

Documentation Effort and Time Management: Both cohorts saw the documentation workload and tight schedule as major challenges. In 2023, "it was far too little time for development" and "the preparation phase must be significantly shortened and the development phase correspondingly lengthened" were frequent suggestions. One student wrote: "Focus more on practice if the prototype is the focus, too much effort and time to find an idea, but too little for implementation and evaluation." In 2024, students echoed: "by far too many working hours in relation to the given credits" and "permanent stress due to time pressure, causing neglect of other important life areas... to get everything done." The recommendation was often to extend the module to two semesters or reduce the documentation and research scope.

Handling of Open Task Structure: The open, student-driven structure was both a strength and a challenge. In 2023, students requested "a clear task description with clearly formulated expectations" and noted that "tasks were sometimes not clearly formulated." The iterative, evolving requirements led to some uncertainty. In 2024, students similarly asked for "a more precise explanation of the tasks" and more structured opportunities for peer feedback and interim checkpoints. Both years saw suggestions to improve guidance and feedback throughout the open project process.

Didactic Design and Support: Instructor commitment and the overall learning atmosphere were praised in both cohorts. Comments highlighted "very pleasant" class environments, supportive and motivating instructors, and project-based assessment. One 2024 student described "subject-matter expertise," "interactive teaching methods," and a "clearly structured course plan." Block sessions and blended learning formats were appreciated for providing structure, though some students desired even more flexibility (e.g., digitizing block sessions).

Perceived Learning Gains and Career Relevance: A major outcome was the recognition of practical, transferable skills. In 2023, students noted: "You had the feeling of learning something you can really use later in your job," and listed "new competencies" and "Positive Computing concepts" as key gains. In 2024, students confirmed the course "promotes practical knowledge and experience that would not be possible in a purely on-campus course," and described meaningful shifts in attitudes toward disability and inclusion. Despite workload complaints, many viewed the experience as rewarding and impactful for their professional growth.

6.4   Interview Findings and Integration

The participants were students aged 20 to 34 from various degree programs, particularly applied computer science, IT security, and human-technology interaction, some of whom were pursuing bachelor's degrees and others master's degrees. The group included both full-time students and students who were working alongside their studies. The main reasons given for choosing the *Inclusive IT Design* module were interest in inclusion, practical relevance, user centricity, and interdisciplinary work.

Time pressure, documentation load, and the challenge of iterative, open-ended projects emerged as central themes. Participants described learning to let go of deficit-oriented perspectives, developing empathy and respect for users' competencies, and grappling with nonverbal communication and diverse support needs.

A recurring point was the value of direct user engagement. Students recounted moments when "observing a user interact with the app with visible joy" made the project meaningful (C1-d), or when the collaboration helped them "attribute more competence to users and evaluate more individually" (C1-c). At the same time, many interviewees struggled with team coordination and balancing project demands: "We spent too much time on design methods and had only a week or two to develop and evaluate" (C1-g), and "repeated or overlapping writing tasks reduced the time and energy available for creative and technical work" (C1-j).

In 2024, the added structure and extra field visits were seen as improvements, but concerns about time and task clarity persisted: "I think it would have helped if we had sent the test plan two or three days earlier. . . it was definitely too late" (C2-e). Some students struggled with abstract frameworks like Design Science Research: "DSR stands or falls with the pressure to deliver" (C2-e), though others found the service-learning model ultimately motivating once its purpose became clear (C2-g). Teamwork, as in 2023, was often positive but sometimes hampered by uneven skill distribution and communication lapses.

6.5   Comparative Synthesis and Lessons Learned

Both years of "Inclusive IT Design" yielded strong engagement and substantial learning gains, but also highlighted structural challenges. Students valued authentic, participatory engagement with users and recognized the course's relevance for real-world design. However, documentation and time management issues were persistent, and the open structure, while rewarding, required more scaffolding and feedback. The iterative improvements from 2023 to 2024, especially the addition of more user visits and earlier prototyping, were appreciated, but did not fully resolve all tensions.

Overall, the evaluation demonstrates that immersive, participatory teaching formats can be highly impactful, but require careful balancing of open-endedness, documentation, and practical development time. Continuous adaptation and close instructor engagement are crucial for supporting students' learning and well-being in such intensive, real-world project courses.

7   Discussion

Across two consecutive iterations, the **Inclusive IT-Design** module has demonstrated that inclusive or assistive, user-centered, and participatory design in computer science education is not only feasible but can be profoundly impactful for both student learning and social participation. The positive effects of the module are not only reflected in student interviews, but are also corroborated by high overall satisfaction ratings and strong recommendations to peers, as evidenced by end-of-semester survey data from both years. Students in both cohorts valued the opportunity to engage directly with people with disabilities, rating this aspect among the most important for their learning outcomes, both in closed survey items and in numerous open-ended responses.

By requiring students to work not only *for*, but *with* people with disabilities in genuine co-creation processes, the module moved beyond traditional classroom projects. The participatory structure, where requirements emerged directly from ongoing interaction with user groups, rather than being predetermined by instructors, posed unfamiliar challenges for many students, sometimes leading to initial confusion or frustration, as reflected in both qualitative interviews and open survey comments. Nonetheless, the integration of field-based learning with theoretical grounding confirms prior findings on the efficacy of experiential, service-learning formats [1,4]. Both the 2023 and 2024 cohorts engaged in projects requiring iterative design, direct collaboration, and ongoing critical reflection on their own development as technologists and team members.

A central development between the cohorts was the increased frequency and structure of user engagement in 2024. Survey data and open responses from 2024 underscore that repeated and structured field visits fostered trust and enabled more effective iteration of design solutions. This improvement is reflected not only in the interviews, where students described second or third contact moments as crucial for recognizing and correcting misconceptions, but also in open survey answers highlighting "valuable practical experience" and "the actual work with people with disabilities during field visits" as particular strengths of the revised module. Quantitative ratings for perceived practical relevance and learning gains in 2024 confirm these qualitative impressions, with students indicating even greater confidence in their ability to integrate user feedback into their design process compared to the first cohort.

In terms of personal development, students across both years reported that direct, sustained engagement with people with disabilities challenged their preconceptions, fostered empathy, and deepened their understanding of accessibility and inclusion. These outcomes are reflected consistently across all data types: interviews, survey ratings of learning gains, and open comments in which students described the fieldwork as "transformative" and "something I can really use later in my job." Notably, the shift to more frequent user contact in 2024 correlated with an increase in students reporting greater confidence and enjoyment in their interactions, as well as a more nuanced appreciation of user diversity.

Despite these strengths, both cohorts faced persistent structural challenges, particularly regarding time pressure, documentation workload, and uneven skill distribution within teams. These issues were highlighted in survey ratings (e.g., lower scores for workload appropriateness and organizational clarity), and further elaborated in open responses and interviews. In both cohorts, students recommended reducing documentation requirements or extending the module duration, citing the difficulty of balancing technical, practical, and reflective tasks within a single semester: "by far too many working hours in relation to the given credits" (2024) and "too much effort and time to find an idea, but too little for implementation and evaluation" (2023). While the iterative improvements from 2023 to 2024, especially increased field visits and earlier prototyping, were widely appreciated, time management and workload remained prominent concerns.

Team composition and skill distribution also emerged as ongoing challenges, noted in both interview data and open survey responses. Students described difficulties arising from unequal prior experience with tools and methods, suggesting that more explicit skill mapping and peer support at the outset could further improve collaborative outcomes in future iterations.

The question of sustainability and continuity after the course concluded was raised by both students and community partners, in interviews and in open-ended survey responses. While some student groups successfully created prototypes with lasting impact, others struggled to ensure ongoing use or handover after the semester. This underscores the need for curricular strategies, such as project archives or mentorship between cohorts—to support longer-term impact, a challenge also highlighted in the accessibility literature [16].

Taken together, the findings from both quantitative and qualitative data sources demonstrate that immersive, participatory teaching formats can deliver substantial educational benefits and foster more inclusive design mindsets among future technologists. The observed differences between cohorts highlight the value of iterative curricular refinement, particularly regarding the structure and frequency of user engagement. However, they also point to enduring challenges that require ongoing attention, including balancing depth of engagement with feasibility, supporting team development, and ensuring long-term continuity for participatory projects.

7.1   Lessons Learned: Implications for Teaching Inclusive IT Design

Based on our evaluation, several concrete recommendations can be derived for instructors seeking to embed participatory, accessible or inclusion-oriented methods into computing curricula.

Prioritize Relationship-Building and User Understanding over Deliverables
A central tenet of the Inclusive IT-Design module is that genuine understanding of the needs, abilities, and perspectives of people with disabilities must precede technical solution-building. Students are expected not only to develop functional prototypes, but to invest significant time and effort in building trust, engaging in dialog, and critically reflecting on their own assumptions. This process of relationship-building and empathetic engagement is deliberately weighted in the course assessment and is considered equally, if not more, important than the technical sophistication of final products. By shifting the emphasis away from rapid prototyping toward authentic, iterative engagement with the user group, instructors can foster a more ethical, user-centered, and sustainable design mindset among students. Clarifying this expectation at the outset is crucial for aligning student motivation with the broader learning goals of inclusion, participation, and social responsibility.

Balance Depth with Feasibility: Respect the Limits of a Single Semester
Students repeatedly emphasized that meaningful co-design or empowered participation with people with disabilities requires time, particularly when communication interaction is complex. While the second iteration improved, many students still described their prototypes as incomplete due to time pressure. Particularly for teams lacking prior experience with inclusive, assistive technology or

visual prototyping, additional time buffers are essential. Rather than adding content, instructors should consider reducing the number of deliverables or offering optional documentation formats to leave more space for iterative design.

Document Less, Reflect More

While written documentation is an essential part of responsible design, students in both cohorts questioned the balance between required paperwork and opportunities for genuine engagement with users. The aim of documentation in this context should not be bureaucratic fulfillment, but rather structured reflection and deepening of user understanding. Our experience suggests that rigid or repetitive reporting can obscure this purpose and even create resistance. Instead, course design should emphasize **meaningful, flexible reflection formats**, such as guided debriefs, design walkthroughs with user input, or concise process portfolios, that support critical analysis without overwhelming students. By clarifying the rationale behind documentation and explicitly linking it to user-centered design goals, instructors can foster a reflective mindset that prioritizes learning and adaptive problem-solving over mere compliance.

Provide Scaffolded Tools for Navigating Ambiguity

Many students expressed uncertainty in interpreting user needs, especially in interactions with people with complex support needs or those who primarily communicate non-verbally. Simple methods, such as observation protocols, icon libraries (e.g., Metacom), or structured debriefs with support staff (including group leaders, educators, or other professionals involved in daily activities), proved essential for bridging communication gaps and building mutual understanding. These approaches should not be optional, but systematically embedded into the course structure. One team, for instance, fundamentally revised their interaction design after realizing that their users struggled with touch-based input.

Foster Ethical Confidence, Not Just Technical Skills

Students reported moments of hesitation or insecurity when interacting with vulnerable users for the first time. However, they also described these moments as transformative. *"I was afraid of doing something wrong at first, or of saying something inappropriate. But actually, they were all really open and happy that we were there."* (C1-b). Offering early, low-threshold exposure (e.g. Q&A with disability advocates, caregivers) can lower initial barriers. More importantly, embedding ethical reflection throughout the course, not just at the end, can help students develop confidence in their own judgment when navigating ambiguity and responsibility.

Clarify the Role and Limitations of Design Frameworks

Some students struggled to apply abstract methodological models, such as Design Science Research, to real-world co-design situations. Rather than presenting such frameworks as universal solutions, instructors should explicitly discuss their strengths and limitations, modeling how to adapt and critically evaluate methods based on the unique demands of participatory settings. This reflective teaching approach can empower students to make informed methodological choices and foster the flexibility needed for authentic collaboration with diverse user groups.

Make Team Composition and Skill Distribution Explicit
Several students mentioned imbalances within teams, not necessarily due to engagement levels, but because key technical or design skills were lacking. For instance, a team without Figma experience spent "hours learning basics" instead of refining their prototype (C2-h). Making explicit skill-mapping part of the onboarding phase, and enabling low-threshold peer teaching, can mitigate these gaps early on.

Sustain Real-World Impact Beyond the Semester
Students and practice partners alike expressed a desire to maintain collaborations or extend the usefulness of prototypes. However, limited time and unclear pathways after the course end inhibited continuity. Providing handover templates or offering small grants for continuation (e.g., via volunteer follow-up or bachelor theses) can enhance long-term value without overburdening instructors.

7.2   Future Directions and Outlook

While our results demonstrate the potential of participatory, inclusive and accessible design formats in higher education, several open challenges and development opportunities remain. Future iterations of the **Inclusive IT Design** course will deepen the focus on early-stage empathy-building and methodological clarity, including more explicit expectation management for students regarding the centrality of relationship-building and user engagement. Strengthening partnerships with community organizations will remain essential for ensuring both contextual relevance and long-term continuity for all stakeholders.

A central challenge for future work concerns the sustainability and transferability of the course model. Not all institutions have access to local partner organizations or the resources required for intensive fieldwork. Research should investigate which boundary conditions (e.g., team size, group composition, digital vs. face-to-face collaboration) enable or constrain meaningful inclusion and co-design, and how digital or hybrid approaches might be leveraged when in-person contact is limited.

Open questions also remain regarding the depth and authenticity of user participation. While we aimed for co-creative, empowering engagement, many student teams still struggled to move beyond traditional "design for" paradigms, and only a subset realized genuinely participatory workshops. Continued didactic and institutional innovation is needed to enable more equal participation and shared decision-making, both in project work and in assessment.

From a research perspective, longitudinal studies are required to explore whether such experiential formats lead to lasting changes in students' attitudes, competencies, and professional choices, and how such courses impact the lives and opportunities of people with disabilities involved as co-designers. Further, future work should address how the outcomes of student projects, including prototypes and partnerships, can be sustained and meaningfully transferred beyond the classroom, for example, through open-source dissemination, project archives, or alumni mentoring schemes.

Finally, we see substantial potential in interdisciplinary and international collaboration. Pairing computer science students with those from occupational therapy, education, or social work, as piloted elsewhere [9,10], may further enhance both the breadth and depth of inclusive technology design. Ultimately, realizing true participation and sustainable impact in inclusive IT education will require ongoing reflection, stakeholder involvement, and institutional commitment far beyond individual courses.

Overall, our course **Inclusive IT Design** offers a framework for embedding social responsibility, participatory principles, and ethical awareness into technical education.

8   Conclusion

This paper has presented the design, implementation, and iterative refinement of the *Inclusive IT Design* module, an educational initiative that integrates inclusive and accessible IT design, service learning, and real-world collaboration with people with cognitive, emotional, physical, and multiple or severe support needs. Drawing on data from two consecutive cohorts, our study demonstrates how the combination of theoretical frameworks, such as Design Science Research, Positive Computing, and Participatory Design, with repeated, authentic user interaction can foster both technical and social competencies in computer science students. Notably, student feedback across both years emphasized that the greatest perceived value of the course lay in its participatory approach, namely, the opportunity for sustained, direct engagement with people with disabilities in real-world contexts. This hands-on collaboration was consistently described as transformative, promoting not only deeper understanding of accessibility and inclusion, but also self-reflection, empathy, and a heightened sense of social responsibility.

Students reported that the module deepened their understanding of accessibility, enhanced their teamwork and communication skills, and challenged preconceived notions about disability. These findings were substantiated by quantitative survey data and enriched by in-depth qualitative interviews, which revealed that exposure to authentic user contexts enabled students to move from abstract understanding to situated empathy and actionable design decisions. Iterative engagement with users, especially the shift to more frequent, structured contact in the second cohort, emerged as a key driver for learning outcomes and the overall quality of student solutions.

At the same time, the results highlight persistent tensions between practical and structural demands. Students consistently mentioned the documentation burden, the challenge of uneven team skill sets, and the pressure of addressing complex user needs within a single semester. While the participatory approach was widely valued, interview data also revealed that genuine, deep participation was not achieved by all groups; in many cases, more extensive training or ongoing guidance in co-creation methods would have been necessary to fully empower users and balance decision-making power. Practice partners expressed the wish for sustained collaboration, raising the issue of prototype continuity beyond the course. These challenges mirror broader issues in inclusive and accessible computing education and underscore the need for robust curricular scaffolding and long-term stakeholder engagement, including clearer pathways for project handover and continuation.

Overall, the *Inclusive IT Design* module illustrates the potential of immersive, socially engaged learning formats in computer science. By situating students in ethically grounded, community-linked design processes, the module not only supports professional growth but also delivers tangible benefits for underserved user communities. As a replicable model, it offers practical insights for educators aiming to place accessibility, empathy, and real-world impact at the heart of computing curricula.

Acknowledgments. This work was conducted as part of the project "DescPos", a joint initiative between Ruhr University Bochum and Ruhr West University of Applied Sciences. The project was funded by the Stiftung Innovation in der Hochschullehre (Foundation for Innovation in Higher Education). The responsibility for the content of this publication lies solely with the authors.

The authors would like to thank Christian Maske, Florian Brachten, and Markus Jelonek from Ruhr University Bochum for their valuable support in the organization and implementation of the course, as well as their contributions to the course structure and the qualitative data collection.

Parts of the language editing, restructuring, and improvement of the manuscript were supported by generative AI tools (OpenAI ChatGPT). All conceptualization, data analysis, interpretation, and scientific conclusions were exclusively performed by the author(s). The use of AI tools was limited to phrasing, clarification of wording, and editorial support, in accordance with current scientific publishing guidelines.

References

1. Astin, A.W., Vogelgesang, L.J., Ikeda, E.K., Yee, J.A.: How service learning affects students. Technical report, Higher Education Research Institute, University of California, Los Angeles, Los Angeles, CA (2000). https://heri.ucla.edu/PDFs/HSLAS/HSLAS.PDF. Accessed 16 June 2025
2. Backhaus-Maul, H., Roth, C.: Service learning an Hochschulen in Deutschland: Ein erster empirischer Beitrag zur Vermessung eines jungen Phänomens, 1 edn. Springer VS Wiesbaden (2013). https://doi.org/10.1007/978-3-658-00124-7
3. Beyer, H., Holtzblatt, K.: Contextual design: defining customer-centered systems (1997)
4. Bringle, R.G., Hatcher, J.A.: Implementing service learning in higher education. J. High. Educ. **67**(2), 221–239 (1996). https://doi.org/10.1080/00221546.1996.11780257
5. Brinkley, J.: Participation at what cost? Teaching accessibility using participatory design: an experience report. In: Proceedings of the 51st ACM Technical Symposium on Computer Science Education, SIGCSE 2020, pp. 114–120. Association for Computing Machinery, New York, NY, USA (2020). https://doi.org/10.1145/3328778.3366931

6. Butin, D.W.: Service-Learning in Theory and Practice. Palgrave Macmillan US, New York (2010). https://doi.org/10.1057/9780230106154
7. Calvo, R.A., Peters, D.: Positive Computing: Technology for Wellbeing and Human Potential. MIT Press (2014)
8. Clarkson, J., Coleman, R.: Inclusive design. J. Eng. Des. **21**(2-3), 127–129 (2010). https://doi.org/10.1080/09544821003693689
9. Ding, S., Smith, J.B., Garrett, S., Magerko, B.: Redesigning EarSketch for inclusive CS education: a participatory design approach. ACM. https://par.nsf.gov/biblio/10508200
10. Ferreira, R.D.S., de Castro, T.H.C.: Participatory and inclusive design models from the perspective of universal design for children with autism: a systematic review. Educ. Sci. **14**(6) (2024). https://doi.org/10.3390/educsci14060613. https://www.mdpi.com/2227-7102/14/6/613
11. Gilbert, R.M.: Inclusive Design for a Digital World. Apress, Berkeley, CA (2019). https://doi.org/10.1007/978-1-4842-5016-7
12. Giles, D.E.J., Eyler, J.: Theoretical roots of service-learning in John Dewey: toward a theory of service-learning. Mich. J. Commun. Serv. Learn. **1**, 77–85 (1994)
13. Hackett, S., Parmanto, B., Zeng, X.: Accessibility of internet websites through time. In: Proceedings of the 6th International ACM SIGACCESS Conference on Computers and Accessibility, Assets 2004, pp. 32–39. Association for Computing Machinery, New York, NY, USA (2003). https://doi.org/10.1145/1028630.1028638
14. Hevner, A.R., March, S.T., Park, J., Ram, S.: Design science in information systems research. MIS Q. Manag. Inf. Syst. **28**(1), 75–105 (2004)
15. Iniesto, F., Rodrigo, C.: Exploring the accessibility evaluation of city council websites by computer science students using a service-learning approach (2024). https://doi.org/10.1145/3657242.3658591
16. Ko, A.J., Ladner, R.E.: AccessComputing promotes teaching accessibility. ACM Inroads **7**(4), 65–68 (2016). https://doi.org/10.1145/2968453
17. Ludi, S.: Introducing accessibility requirements through external stakeholder utilization in an undergraduate requirements engineering course. In: 29th International Conference on Software Engineering (ICSE 2007), pp. 736–743 (2007). https://doi.org/10.1109/ICSE.2007.46
18. Lussier-Desrochers, D., et al.: Bridging the digital divide for people with intellectual disability. Cyberpsychol. J. Psychosoc. Res. Cyberspace **11**(1), Article 1 (2017). https://doi.org/10.5817/CP2017-1-1. https://cyberpsychology.eu/article/view/6738
19. Martin-Escalona, I., Barcelo-Arroyo, F., Zola, E.: The introduction of a topic on accessibility in several engineering degrees. In: 2013 IEEE Global Engineering Education Conference (EDUCON), pp. 656–663 (2013). https://doi.org/10.1109/EduCon.2013.6530177
20. Mayring, P.: Qualitative Content Analysis: Theoretical Foundation. Basic Procedures and Software Solution. Beltz, Weinheim (2014)
21. Newell, A.F., Gregor, P.: "user sensitive inclusive design" – in search of a new paradigm. In: Proceedings on the 2000 Conference on Universal Usability, CUU 2000, pp. 39–44. Association for Computing Machinery, New York, NY, USA (2000). https://doi.org/10.1145/355460.355470
22. Oudshoorn, N., Rommes, E., Stienstra, M.: Configuring the user as everybody: gender and design cultures in information and communication technologies. Sci. Technol. Hum. Values **29**(1), 30–63 (2004). https://doi.org/10.1177/0162243903259190
23. Pawlowski, J.M., et al.: Positive Computing. Bus. Inf. Syst. Eng. **57**(6), 405–408 (2015). https://doi.org/10.1007/s12599-015-0406-0

24. Peffers, K., Tuunanen, T., Rothenberger, M., Chatterjee, S.: A design science research methodology for information systems research. J. Manage. Inf. Syst. **24**(3), 45–77 (2007). https://doi.org/10.2753/MIS0742-1222240302
25. Petyaeva, A., Hosking, I.M., Goodman-Deane, J., Clarkson, P.J.: What is the difference between accessibility, usability, and inclusion? Understanding and addressing the confusion in the design of digital products and services. In: Goodman-Deane, J., et al. (eds.) New Frontiers for Inclusion, pp. 25–35. Springer Nature Switzerland, Cham (2025)
26. Rosmaita, B.J.: Accessibility now! Teaching accessible computing at the introductory level. In: Proceedings of the 8th International ACM SIGACCESS Conference on Computers and Accessibility, Assets 2006, pp. 277–278. Association for Computing Machinery, New York, NY, USA (2006). https://doi.org/10.1145/1168987.1169053
27. Sanders, E.B.N., Stappers, P.J.: Co-creation and the new landscapes of design. CoDesign **4**(1), 5–18 (2008). https://doi.org/10.1080/15710880701875068
28. Shinohara, K., Bennett, C.L., Pratt, W., Wobbrock, J.O.: Tenets for social accessibility: towards humanizing disabled people in design. ACM Trans. Access. Comput. **11**(1) (2018). https://doi.org/10.1145/3178855
29. Shinohara, K., Bennett, C.L., Wobbrock, J.O.: How designing for people with and without disabilities shapes student design thinking. In: Proceedings of the 18th International ACM SIGACCESS Conference on Computers and Accessibility, ASSETS 2016, pp. 229–237. Association for Computing Machinery, New York, NY, USA (2016). https://doi.org/10.1145/2982142.2982158
30. Simonsen, J., Robertson, T.: Routledge international handbook of participatory design. In: Routledge International Handbook of Participatory Design, pp. 1–300 (2012). https://doi.org/10.4324/9780203108543
31. Weisberg, L., Barrett, J., Israel, M., Miller, D.: A review of arts integration in K-12 CS education: gathering STEAM for inclusive learning. Comput. Sci. Educ. **35**(1), 123–152 (2025). https://doi.org/10.1080/08993408.2024.2359854
32. Wobbrock, J.O., Kane, S.K., Gajos, K.Z., Harada, S., Froehlich, J.: Ability-based design: concept, principles and examples. ACM Trans. Access. Comput. **3**(3) (2011). https://doi.org/10.1145/1952383.1952384
33. Yorio, P.L., Ye, F.: A meta-analysis on the effects of service-learning on the social, personal, and cognitive outcomes of learning. Acad. Manag. Learn. Educ. **11**(1), 9–27 (2012). https://doi.org/10.5465/amle.2010.0072

Visible Sound: The Impact of Sign Language Interpreter Picture Size and Speed on Viewer Comprehension and Satisfaction in News Broadcasts

Jingyan Li, Yankuan Liu, and Pei-Luen Patrick Rau

Department of Industrial Engineering, Tsinghua University, Beijing 100000, China
rpl@tsinghua.edu.cn

Abstract. This study aims to optimize the picture size and interpreting speed of sign language in news broadcasts to enhance comprehension and satisfaction among deaf viewers, while considering the impact on hearing audiences. We conducted an experiment with equal numbers of deaf and hearing participants who watched news clips featuring varying sign language overlay sizes and interpreting speeds. The results indicate that larger sign language windows and moderately slowed interpreting speeds significantly improve both comprehension and satisfaction for deaf viewers. In contrast, hearing viewers' comprehension remained unaffected, but their satisfaction decreased with larger sign language overlays. This research provides empirical evidence and practical guidelines for broadcasters to adjust sign language presentations, enhancing accessibility for the deaf community without compromising the viewing experience for hearing audiences.

Keywords: Deaf people · Sign language interpreting · Usability · Comprehensibility · News broadcasts

1 Introduction

Deafness, characterized by partial or complete hearing loss, leads many individuals to use sign language—a visual-manual system of hand shapes and movements (Soleman & Bousquat, 2021; Amangeldy et al., 2022). In China, where the hearing-disabled population exceeds 6.7 million (China Disabled Persons' Federation, 2023), television remains widely used by the deaf community, with subtitles and sign language serving as standard accessibility tools (Hu, 2008; Li, 2013). By the end of 2023, there are 37 provincial-level television sign language programs and 272 prefecture-level television sign language programs nationwide (China Disabled Persons' Federation, 2023). Deaf people's media consumption habits are similar to those of hearing individuals, with television being the most commonly owned and frequently used medium, often for extended periods of time. Both adult and young deaf individuals prefer to obtain information from television news, which is also one of the favorite television programs among deaf youth (Hu, 2008). In 2006, China signed the Convention on the Rights of Persons with Disabilities, which

© The Author(s), under exclusive license to Springer Nature Switzerland AG 2026
M. Antona and C. Stephanidis (Eds.): HCII 2025, LNCS 16335, pp. 109–120, 2026.
https://doi.org/10.1007/978-3-032-12781-5_7

emphasized the importance of providing adequate support to ensure that individuals with disabilities can access information, encouraging the use of sign language, and enhancing the accessibility of television programs for the deaf. These measures have significantly contributed to the progress of sign language interpretation in television news, framing it as a crucial element in upholding human rights and fostering an inclusive social environment (Gao & Liu, 2015).

Deaf viewers primarily focus on interpreters, while hearing viewers prioritize pictorial content (Wehrmeyer, 2014). However, studies on the comprehensibility of sign language interpretation in news broadcasts highlight several challenges faced by Deaf viewers, including small interpreter picture size, interpreter performance, viewers' proficiency, and background (Wehrmeyer, 2015). Another study showed that understanding interpreters can be difficult due to cohesion issues, errors, language influence, high speed, and lack of preparation (Napier & Barker, 2004).

For example, in China, significant comprehension disparities exist due to inadequate interpreting quality. Xiao et al. (2015) found deaf viewers comprehended only 24% of news content compared to 96% by hearing viewers. Many deaf viewers did not like sign language news, with only about 34% understanding more than half of the sign language used (Ran, 1998; Jiang, 2004). Common issues cited include inability to understand sign language, small and unclear images, and fast interpretation (Xiao & Li, 2011; Shen & Zhao, 2021). Moreover, Gao and Liu (2015) highlighted the need for standardized training for interpreters, improvements in the quality of sign language interpretation, and the development of more inclusive practices to meet the needs of deaf audiences effectively. Therefore, this project aims to enhance both the comprehension and satisfaction of the deaf audience by improving sign language interpretations in live news broadcasts, thereby advancing accessibility in television media. The key research questions are:

- How do picture size and interpreting speed affect viewer comprehension and satisfaction?
- Is there an optimal combination that meets the needs of both deaf and hearing audiences?

"Picture size" refers to the interpreter's area, while "interpreting speed" pertains to the rate of translation into sign language. Using a mixed experimental design, the study explores various combinations to identify a configuration that maximizes comprehension and satisfaction for deaf viewers while considering hearing audiences.

2   Literature Review

Initially, sign language interpretation in media involved pre-recorded segments with interpreters placed in a corner of the screen, using minimalistic graphics a method limited by early technological constraints including black-and-white broadcasting and limited screen space for multiple visual elements (Horton, 2004). The incorporation of sign language interpretation was minimal and seen as an afterthought, with the real breakthrough coming in the 1990s with more sophisticated closed-captioning systems (Horton, 2004). In the 2000s, digital TV and streaming platforms allowed for better integration, while legislation such as the Americans with Disabilities Act (ADA) in the

US pushed for more accessibility, encouraging the inclusion of sign language interpreters in more mainstream media (Clarke, 2012). Recently, there are some real-time interpreting technologies, such as virtual avatars and AI-driven systems emerging as alternatives to human interpreters, offering more seamless and adaptive sign language interpretation (Thomas & Brown, 2017). The introduction of customizable accessibility features on platforms like Netflix, allowing viewers to select sign language interpretation, marks a shift towards more inclusive, user-centered media (Smith & Robinson, 2021).

Research highlights the crucial role of sign language interpreters in bridging communication gaps and supporting the linguistic and cultural identity of the Deaf community (Schmitt, 2017; Moores, 2001). Integrating sign language into television programming enhances accessibility and comprehension, promoting inclusivity and equitable information dissemination (Moores, 2001). During emergencies like the COVID-19 pandemic, the need for accessible content becomes even more critical (Adigun et al., 2022). Studies have underscored challenges faced by sign language interpreters during such times, emphasizing the need for specialized training and clear communication strategies (McKee, 2014; Stankevič & Mankauskienė, 2021).

Understanding the cognitive mechanisms involved in sign language comprehension reveals the complexities that differentiate it from spoken language. Sign language comprehension in news broadcasts involves complex visual-spatial processing, unlike spoken language, which is primarily auditory. Cognitive load theory suggests that excessive visual stimuli or rapid movements in sign language interpretation can impede comprehension (Sweller et al., 2011). As cognitive load increases, visual working memory is affected, decreasing the ability to retain and manipulate information (Baddeley, 2003), which is particularly relevant in fast-paced news broadcasts. Additionally, dual coding theory (Paivio, 2006) posits that information is processed through separate verbal and visual systems. Since sign language is visual-gestural, it relies on the visual processing system. The size of the interpreter's image influences comprehension—too small an image may obscure critical details, while an overly large image can disrupt visual flow and increase cognitive load.

Studies show a preference for larger interpreter windows and customizable interfaces, including adjusting avatar size, subtitles, and animation speed (Nolte et al., 2023). A study in South Korea by Ji Hyun Yi et al. (2021) found that 13 out of 30 participants preferred a news broadcast layout with a large sign language interpreter occupying one-third of the screen and no background, as this configuration was considered the most efficient and clear for information delivery. This preference for larger sign language windows is echoed in Ugulino de Araújo et al.'s (2013) research on Brazilian digital TV systems, which highlighted the importance of allowing users to resize the sign language interpreter's window on digital TV systems, concluding that larger windows significantly improve visibility and comprehension for deaf users by enhancing the clarity of the signs.

Alexander and Rijckaert (2021) found that Deaf viewers often struggled with the high speed of live sign language interpretation during news broadcasts, affecting their comprehension. Additionally, Lan Ni (2015) reported 120–130 words per minute, compared to normal signing speeds of 70–90 words per minute. Yuan Wei (2016) analyzed the sign language presentation rate on Chinese TV, finding it ranged from 75 to 114 gestures per minute. The survey from the study also showed that Deaf viewers preferred slower-paced programs, which received higher satisfaction ratings.

Most international studies have relied solely on questionnaires, focus group discussions, or interviews, without incorporating user research. Chinese research has primarily focused on examining the existing situation of Chinese television sign language news programs, emphasizing descriptive analysis rather than experimental manipulation and empirical research on variables such as sign language speed. In addition, as in the case of the study conducted in Korea, the research conducted on the aspect of screen size included only two size settings and did not discuss the different levels of screen size. Furthermore, the audience of most news programs includes hearing people and hearing-impaired people, and most previous studies have not analyzed hearing people's preference and satisfaction with television programs with sign language interpreters.

To address these identified gaps in accessibility and comprehension, the current study seeks to investigate the effects of varying screen sizes and interpreting speeds on the comprehension and satisfaction of both Deaf and hearing viewers with news broadcasts. Specifically, this study tests the following hypotheses:

H1: Comprehension and satisfaction levels for Deaf audiences are lower than those for hearing viewers.
H2: The larger the picture size, the more comprehensible and satisfying the news program will be for Deaf audiences.
H3: Larger picture sizes may lead to decreased satisfaction among hearing viewers but do not affect their comprehension.
H4: A slower sign language interpreting speed will enhance comprehension and satisfaction for Deaf audiences.
H5: Slower sign language interpreting speed may lower satisfaction for hearing viewers but does not affect their comprehension.

In this context, "picture size" refers to the interpreter's area, while "interpreting speed" pertains to the rate of translation into sign language. Using a mixed experimental design, the study explores various combinations to identify a configuration that maximizes comprehension and satisfaction for deaf viewers while considering hearing audiences.

3 Methodology

3.1 Participants

We recruited 24 participants (14 females) aged 21–29 years (M = 24, SD = 2.13), including 12 hearing participants from Tsinghua University and 12 deaf participants from the Special Education College of Beijing Union University or Tianjin University of Technology. All participants had normal or corrected vision with no color blindness. Deaf participants were native sign language users with first-degree hearing impairment. This study has received ethics approval from Tsinghua University Science and Technology Ethics Committee (Humanities, Social Sciences and Engineering).

3.2 Variables

In assessing viewers' comprehension and satisfaction with the translated news in sign language, we focused on three independent variables: group (hearing and deaf), picture size and interpreting speed. Picture size was categorized into three classes: small (original size, $0.15\times$ the length and $0.20\times$ the width of the broadcast), medium (1.33 times the original size, $0.20\times$ the length and $0.27\times$ the width of the broadcast) and large (1.67 times the original size, $0.25\times$ the length and $0.33\times$ the width of the broadcast). In this setting, "small" represents the original screen ratio of the program, whereas in the "large" setting, the height of the sign language presenter was made close to that of the hearing presenter, based on the eye-tracking study by Ji Hyun Yi et al. (2021), which suggested setting the maximum image size to one-third of the screen for sign language news broadcasts.

Drawing on the findings of Ni (2015) and Yuan (2016), this study argues that aligning the speed of sign language news with the tempo of everyday sign language communication is equivalent to approximately 0.70 times the regular speed. Therefore, we defined three interpreting speeds: fast (1.00 times the regular speed), medium (0.85 times the regular speed), and slow (0.70 times the regular speed).

The experimental material consisted of three news clips from CCTV's "Focus Interview" program, each with small, medium and large, labeled a1, a2, and a3 respectively (Fig. 1). Each video clip also had the playback speed adjusted to three different settings, b1 (fast), b2 (medium), and b3 (slow), resulting in nine unique video combinations (a1b1, a1b2, a1b3, a2b1, etc.). All video clips were in 720p resolution, and the original video duration was 5 min.

Fig. 1. Levels of Picture Sizes in Clips.

We randomly assigned 12 deaf and 12 hearing participants into three groups (b1, b2, b3) with four individuals per group. Each participant watched three videos with the same interpreting speed but different picture sizes. Therefore, picture size was a within-group variable, while speed was a between-group variable. To control for fatigue and practice effects, the video sequence was randomized for each participant.

3.3 Measures

Comprehension was measured through both objective questions (15 multiple choice items related to video content) and a subjective questionnaire. The questionnaire was based on Jim Lewis's (1991) After-Scenario Questionnaire and consisted of three subjective items. Participants were asked to rate their level of Comprehension on a 1–7 scale. Satisfaction was measured only through a questionnaire, which was based on Arnie Lund's (2001) USE (Usefulness, Satisfaction, and Ease of use) questionnaire and consisted of nine items rated on a 1–7 scale.

Reliability tests revealed excellent internal consistency for the satisfaction scale (Cronbach's $\alpha = 0.970$) and good reliability for the comprehension scale (Cronbach's $\alpha = 0.868$). Factorability was confirmed with Kaiser-Meyer-Olkin (KMO) values of 0.929 for satisfaction and 0.820 for comprehension, exceeding the recommended threshold of 0.5.

3.4 Procedure

At the beginning of the test, all participants had read and signed an informed consent form. The experiment began with the playback of the first video. Following each video, participants were presented with objective questions related to the video content. Upon completion or after 5 min, the experimenter collected the responses and distributed the questionnaires for comprehension and satisfaction rates. This process was repeated for the remaining two videos. At the end of the three videos, participants were given the opportunity to provide feedback on the experiment.

A 75-inch MAXHUB SM75CA screen was used to display the videos, with a fixed 4.5 m distance between the participant and the screen, which was in accordance to recommendations from the Society of Motion Picture and Television Engineers.

Participant responses and questionnaire data were analyzed using Python (version 3.10) and R (version 4.2.2) to generate descriptive and inferential statistics on the effects of picture size and interpreting speed on viewer comprehension and satisfaction. Mixed-ANOVA and non-parametric tests were used when appropriate, with a significance level of 0.05.

4 Results

4.1 Descriptive Analysis

Tables 1 and 2 show that for deaf individuals, both comprehension and satisfaction increase steadily with larger Picture Sizes and slower Interpretation Speeds. For hearing individuals, Satisfaction decreases significantly with larger Picture Sizes.

Table 1. Descriptive statistics of Picture Size.

Group	Variable	Small Mean $\pm$ SD	Medium Mean $\pm$ SD	Large Mean $\pm$ SD
Deaf	Objective Comprehension	7.35 ± 3.76	9.29 ± 3.71	10.25 ± 2.23
	Subjective Comprehension	11.83 ± 4.75	12.58 ± 5.28	15.83 ± 5.47
	Satisfaction	29.75 ± 14.35	35.67 ± 15.57	38.17 ± 15.43

(*continued*)

Table 1. (*continued*)

Group	Variable	Small Mean ± SD	Medium Mean ± SD	Large Mean ± SD
Hearing	Objective Comprehension	15.48 ± 2.99	16.00 ± 4.16	16.08 ± 3.18
	Subjective Comprehension	19.83 ± 2.17	19.50 ± 3.75	18.50 ± 3.09
	Satisfaction	50.75 ± 12.87	48.67 ± 14.11	36.08 ± 8.23

Table 2. Descriptive statistics of Interpreting Speed.

Group	Variable	Fast Mean ± SD	Medium Mean ± SD	Slow Mean ± SD
Deaf	Objective Comprehension	6.98 ± 4.13	9.06 ± 2.23	10.85 ± 2.72
	Subjective Comprehension	11.33 ± 6.29	13.00 ± 4.75	15.92 ± 4.06
	Satisfaction	22.25 ± 9.01	38.25 ± 14.08	43.08 ± 13.72
Hearing	Objective Comprehension	14.58 ± 3.60	16.77 ± 2.67	16.21 ± 3.70
	Subjective Comprehension	18.08 ± 4.06	20.17 ± 1.19	19.58 ± 3.00
	Satisfaction	46.50 ± 14.93	39.00 ± 6.73	50.00 ± 15.26

4.2 Statistical Analysis

In the statistical analysis, Satisfaction and Objective Comprehension for the Hearing group, as well as Satisfaction for the Deaf group, met normality and homogeneity of variances criteria, permitting the use of Mixed-ANOVA.

For non-normal distributions identified in Objective and Subjective Comprehension within the Deaf group, and Subjective Comprehension in the Hearing group, we used Aligned Rank Transform (ART) ANOVA to examine the effects of the three independent variables, including group.

The results of the Mixed-ANOVA and Aligned Rank Transform ANOVA revealed that the main effect of Group was significant for all three variables: Satisfaction ($F = 6.75$, $p = 0.018$), Objective Comprehension ($F = 37.20$, $p < 0.001$), and Subjective Comprehension ($F = 14.47$, $p = 0.001$), indicating that the Hearing group consistently scored higher than the Deaf group (see Fig. 2).

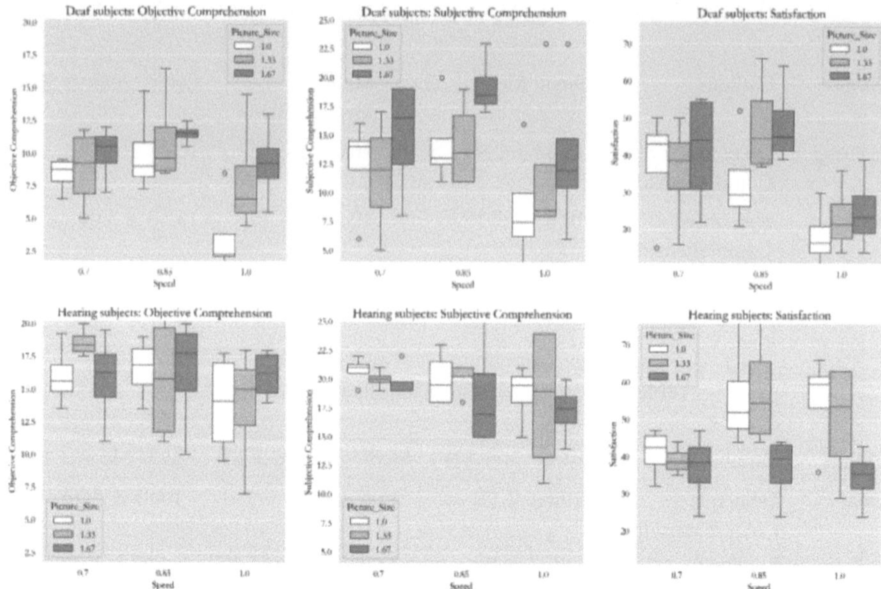

Fig. 2. Distributions of Outcomes.

Furthermore, a significant interaction between Group and Picture Size was found for both Satisfaction (p < 0.001) and Subjective Comprehension (p < 0.001), suggesting that Picture Size influences Satisfaction and Subjective Comprehension differently for Deaf and Hearing groups. Therefore, it was worth conducting further analysis for each group. Additionally, the main effect of Picture Size was significant for Objective Comprehension (p = 0.009).

Subjective Comprehension. The Friedman test revealed a significant effect of Picture Size on Subjective Comprehension for the Deaf group (Q = 7.256, p = 0.027), highlighting that variations in Picture Size materially affect their comprehension. The Wilcoxon signed-rank tests showed that significant differences emerged when comparing the largest Picture Size 1.67–1.00 (p = 0.439) and 1.33 (p = 0.020), indicating that increasing to the largest Picture Size significantly promotes Subjective Comprehension. For the Hearing group, non-parametric tests revealed that neither Interpretation Speed nor Picture Size significantly influenced Subjective Comprehension.

Objective Comprehension. The Friedman test for the variable Picture Size in the Deaf group yielded significant results (Q = 7.167, p = 0.028). Subsequent post-hoc Wilcoxon signed-rank tests revealed specific contrasts between Picture Sizes: significant differences were observed when comparing Picture Sizes 1.00–1.33 (p = 0.016) and 1.00–1.67 (p = 0.005), suggesting that increasing to these larger sizes notably affects Objective Comprehension. The Kruskal-Wallis H test indicated a significant effect of Interpreting Speed on Objective Comprehension (H = 6.656, p = 0.036) in the Deaf group. Additional post-hoc Mann-Whitney U tests showed a significant difference between speeds

1.00× and 0.85× (p = 0.019). For the Hearing group, Mixed-ANOVA findings indicated that neither Interpretation Speed, Picture Size, nor interaction terms significantly influenced Objective Comprehension.

Satisfaction. For the variable of Satisfaction within the Deaf group, Mixed-ANOVA indicated a significant effect of Picture Size (p = 0.024). The effect size for the Satisfaction variable was moderate (Cohen's d = 0.565), suggesting a discernible impact of Picture Size on viewer Satisfaction. For the Hearing group, a significant effect of Picture Size on Satisfaction was observed (p = 0.002, p-GG-corr = 0.009), accompanied by a substantial negative effect size (Cohen's d = -1.358), indicating that larger Picture Sizes substantially decreased Satisfaction. Post-hoc analyses showed that satisfaction significantly decreased with the largest picture size, comparing 1.00–1.67 (p = 0.036) and 1.33–1.67 (p = 0.043). Additionally, for the Hearing group, analyses indicated that Interpretation Speed and interaction terms had no significant impact on Satisfaction.

5 Discussion

In this study, we examined comprehension and satisfaction levels among deaf and hearing participants regarding different picture sizes and interpreting speeds. Our results show that increasing the picture size and slowing the interpreting speed to 0.85× improved comprehension and satisfaction for deaf viewers, while the largest picture size reduced satisfaction for hearing participants. Therefore, we recommend broadcasters increase the interpreter's picture size to 1.33 times the original and reduce the interpreting speed to 0.85×.

Our analysis of three dependent variables—objective comprehension, subjective comprehension, and satisfaction—revealed that hearing participants consistently scored higher than deaf participants, confirming our first hypothesis. This highlights the greater challenges faced by deaf individuals in understanding news content and achieving satisfaction, consistent with Xiao et al. (2015). However, our findings suggest that adjusting picture size and interpreting speed can alleviate these challenges for deaf viewers.

For deaf participants, increasing picture size to the largest option resulted in the highest scores across all variables, confirming Hypothesis 2 and supporting Xiao & Li (2011), who found that small, unclear sign language pictures hinder comprehension. These results also align with Ji Hyun Yi et al. (2021), but our study offers a more detailed examination with three size ratios. For hearing participants, larger picture sizes did not affect comprehension but reduced satisfaction, supporting Hypothesis 3. Since a medium-sized picture enhances comprehension for deaf viewers without negatively affecting hearing participants, a moderate increase to 1.33 times the original size is recommended.

From the perspective of cognitive load theory (Sweller, 1988), the increase in picture size reduces extraneous cognitive load by improving visual clarity. This allows deaf viewers to more easily allocate cognitive resources to processing the linguistic content of sign language, rather than spending excessive cognitive effort on interpreting unclear or small images. Conversely, when the image is too large, the cognitive load for hearing viewers increases due to the intrusion of the interpreter's picture into their primary focus, which aligns with the principles of Gestalt visual perception (Wertheimer, 1923). Excessively large pictures can disrupt visual coherence and increase cognitive load, reducing overall satisfaction.

For deaf participants, slower interpreting speeds improved objective comprehension, supporting Hypothesis 4 and aligning with Wei Yuan (2016), who found the highest comprehension at interpreting speeds of 98–106 words per minute. This suggests that current interpreting speeds may be too fast for deaf individuals. Our results differ from Lan Ni (2015), who suggested a normal signing speed of 70–90 words per minute (0.70× speed); however, our deaf participants found 0.70× too slow. A speed of 0.85× thus seems optimal for deaf viewers, as Cognitive processing theory (Anderson, 2005) suggests that for efficient learning and understanding, processing time must be matched with the complexity of the material being presented. A slower speed gives viewers more time to parse visual information without overwhelming their working memory. Faster speeds may reduce comprehension, while slower speeds may disrupt engagement.

For hearing participants, changes in interpreting speed had no impact on comprehension or satisfaction. Based on these findings, slowing the interpreting speed to 0.85× improves deaf participants' comprehension without affecting hearing viewers. The results have significant implications for news broadcasts, particularly in enhancing accessibility for deaf audiences. Increasing the interpreter's picture size improves both subjective and objective comprehension for deaf viewers, while slower interpreting speeds boost comprehension, suggesting current speeds may be too fast. However, larger picture sizes decrease satisfaction for hearing viewers, highlighting the need for balance.

To enhance inclusivity in news broadcasting, broadcasters should integrate adjustable interpreter picture sizes and speeds within the production workflow, ensuring that both deaf and hearing viewers can customize their viewing experience. Increasing the interpreter's picture size by 1.33 times the original and reducing the interpreting speed to 0.85× can be achieved through digital layout modifications and post-production video editing. During live broadcasts, dynamic overlay systems could facilitate real-time adjustments to both picture size and speed based on ongoing viewer feedback, which could be collected through interactive platforms or app-based surveys. Additionally, implementing dual-stream technology would enable broadcasters to offer separate video feeds for the main program and the sign language interpretation, allowing deaf viewers to select a larger, slower feed while hearing viewers can opt for a smaller window or even disable the interpreter feed altogether. This customization would be further supported by integrating these features into smart TVs and streaming platforms, where users could seamlessly adjust settings according to their preferences. Post-broadcast, feedback mechanisms would allow viewers to fine-tune their choices and inform future production decisions. Collaborating with deaf community experts and sign language interpreters throughout this process is essential to ensuring that these changes align with the cognitive needs of deaf viewers and contribute to improved comprehension without compromising the integrity of the interpretation. Ultimately, incorporating these technologies and practices would foster an inclusive viewing experience that accommodates the diverse needs of all audiences.

6 Conclusion

This study examines how picture size and interpreting speed affect comprehension and satisfaction for both hearing and deaf audiences, identifying optimal settings as 1.33 times the interpreter's picture size and 0.85× speed. It highlights the importance of optimizing these factors in sign language interpretation for news broadcasts. Current broadcasts fail to meet most deaf viewers' needs. By providing empirical evidence, this study fills a gap left by prior research relying on surveys and interviews. Our findings offer practical guidelines for broadcasters to optimize news programs, ensuring accessibility and satisfaction for both audiences. By emphasizing deaf viewers' preferences, we support more inclusive broadcasting standards and underscore the potential of technological solutions like adjustable sign language frames and customizable interpreting speeds, suggesting broader applications across different contexts.

Disclosure of Interests. The authors have no competing interests to declare that are relevant to the content of this article.

References

Soleman, C., Bousquat, A.: Health policies and definitions of deafness and hearing impairment in the SUS: a monologue? Cadernos de Saúde Pública **37**(8) (2021). https://doi.org/10.1590/0102-311X00206620

Amangeldy, N., Kudubayeva, S., Kassymova, A., Karipzhanova, A., Razakhova, B., Kuralov, S.: Sign language recognition method based on palm definition model and multiple classification. Sensors **22**(17), 6621 (2022). https://doi.org/10.3390/s22176621

Hu, L.: An empirical study on media use among hearing-impaired adolescents in Shanghai. Master's Thesis, Tongji University (2008)

Li, D.X.: The current situation, problems, and suggestions of accessibility development of TV media in China. Mod. Commun. J. Commun. Univ. China **5**, 7–13 (2013)

Bowe, F.: Television Accessibility: Closed Captioning, Subtitling, and Sign Language Interpretation. Gallaudet University Press, Washington, DC (2002)

Gao, Y., Liu, Y.: TV news sign language interpreting in China: status and prospects. Mod. Spec. Educ. **4**, 57–61 (2015)

Wehrmeyer, J.: Eye-tracking Deaf and hearing viewing of sign language-interpreted news broadcasts. J. Eye Mov. Res. **7**(1), 1–16 (2014). https://doi.org/10.16910/jemr.7.1.3

Wehrmeyer, E.: Comprehension of television news signed language interpreters. Interpreting **17**(2), 195–225 (2015). https://doi.org/10.1075/intp.17.2.03weh

Napier, J., Barker, R.: Accessing university education: perceptions, preferences, and expectations for interpreting by Deaf students. J. Deaf Stud. Deaf Educ. **9**(2), 228–238 (2004). https://doi.org/10.1093/deafed/enh024

Xiao, X., Chen, C., Palmer, J.: Chinese Deaf viewers' comprehension of sign language interpreting on television. Interpreting **17**, 91–117 (2015)

Ran, M.H.: Investigation and reflection on sign language news viewing. Disabil. in China **9**, 11–13 (1998)

Jiang, X.: A survey report on the opinions of some Deaf individuals and teachers of schools for the Deaf in Beijing regarding the promotion of Chinese Sign Language. Chin. Spec. Educ. **7**, 33–37 (2004)

Xiao, X.Y., Li, F.Y.: Quality evaluation of media interpretation. Chin. Transl. J. **32**(2), 68–72 (2011)

Shen, Y., Zhao, Q.: Survey of sign language comprehension in the CCTV programme. In: Lü, Y., Li, W. (eds.) Focus On, vol. 6 2015, pp. 175–182. De Gruyter Mouton, Berlin, Boston (2021). https://doi.org/10.1515/9783110711790-016

Horton, J.: Television and disability: early adaptations for accessibility. Media Stud. Rev. **18**(1), 45–63 (2004)

Clarke, M.: The impact of legislation on media accessibility for the Deaf community. J. Media Accessibil. **15**(2), 123–140 (2012)

Thomas, G., Brown, T.: Advancements in media accessibility: virtual avatars in live broadcasting. Digit. Media J. **11**(3), 56–72 (2017)

Smith, L., Robinson, P.: AI avatars and their role in real-time sign language interpretation in broadcasting. J. Commun. Technol. **28**(4), 234–248 (2021)

Schmitt, P.: Representations of sign language, Deaf people, and interpreters in the arts and the media. J. Media Cult. Stud. **26**(4), 541–558 (2017). https://doi.org/10.1080/02701367.2017.1325784

Moores, D.F.: Measuring usability with the USE questionnaire. STC Usabil. SIG Newsl. **8**(2), 3–6 (2001)

Adigun, O.T., Mosia, P.A., Olujie, C.T.: Television as a source of COVID-19 information: a qualitative inquiry into the experiences of the Deaf during the pandemic. EUREKA: Soc. Human. **4**, 67–81 (2022). https://doi.org/10.21303/2504-5571.2022.002316

McKee, R.: Breaking news: sign language interpreters on television during natural disasters. Interpreting **16**(1), 107–130 (2014). https://doi.org/10.1075/intp.16.1.06kee

Sweller, J., Ayres, P., Kalyuga, S.: Cognitive Load Theory. Springer, New York (2011)

Baddeley, A.: Working memory: looking back and looking forward. Nat. Rev. Neurosci. **4**, 829–839 (2003). https://doi.org/10.1038/nrn1201

Paivio, A.: Mind and Its Evolution: A Dual Coding Theoretical Approach, 1st ed. Psychology Press, New York (2007). https://doi.org/10.4324/9781315785233

Stankevič, N., Mankauskienė, D.: Interpreting of live press conferences into Lithuanian Sign Language under extreme conditions of the COVID-19 pandemic. Vertimo studijos (2021)

Nolte, A., Gleißl, B., Heckmann, J., Wallach, D., Jochems, N.: "I want to be able to change the speed and size of the avatar": assessing user requirements for animated sign language translation interfaces. In: Extended Abstracts of the 2023 CHI Conference on Human Factors in Computing Systems (CHI EA 2023), Article 167, pp. 1–7. ACM, New York (2023). https://doi.org/10.1145/3544549.3585675

Yi, J.H., Kim, S., Noh, Y.-G., Ok, S., Hong, J.-H.: Design proposal for sign language services in TV broadcasting from the perspective of people who are Deaf or hard of hearing. Appl. Sci. **11**(23), 11211 (2021). https://doi.org/10.3390/app112311211

de Araújo, T.M.U., et al.: Automatic generation of Brazilian sign language windows for digital TV systems. J. Braz. Comput. Soc. **19**(2), 107–125 (2012). https://doi.org/10.1007/s13173-012-0086-2

Alexander, D., Rijckaert, J.: News with or in sign language? Case study on the comprehensibility of sign language in news broadcasts. Perspect. Stud. Transl. Theory Pract. **30**(4), 627–642 (2022). https://doi.org/10.1080/0907676X.2021.1936088

Yuan, W.: An investigation into the speed of sign language anchoring on TV in China and reflections on the cultivation of sign language anchor persons. Chin. J. Spec. Educ. **10**, 14–18 (2016)

Ni, L.: News interpretation speed. Mod. Commun.: J. Commun. Univ. China **5**, 7–13 (2015)

Xiao, X., Li, F.: Sign language interpreting on Chinese TV: a survey on user perspectives. Perspectives **21**(1), 100–116 (2012). https://doi.org/10.1080/0907676X.2011.632690

Wertheimer, M.: Laws of organization in perceptual forms. In: Ellis, W.D. (ed.) A Source Book of Gestalt Psychology, pp. 71–88. Kegan Paul, Trench, Trubner & Company, London (1938)

What is the Key Difference Between Legal Accessibility Guidelines and Real Users' Experience?

Jungmuk Oh[1], Yuahn Shin[1], Hyunjin Jang[1], Hyun K. Kim[1(✉)], Seyeon Lee[2],
Youngkyung Jung[2], Miyoung Lee[2], and Jiyu Lee[2]

[1] Kwangwoon University, Seoul, Republic of Korea
`hyunkkim@kw.ac.kr`
[2] Corporate Design Center, Samsung Electronics, Seoul, Republic of Korea

Abstract. Legal accessibility standards often fail to reflect the real experiences of users with disabilities. Focusing on visually impaired users, we conducted a comparative analysis of international accessibility guidelines and performed empirical testing with 10 participants using smartphone-based scenarios. The study identified 51 key pain points not captured by existing standards, including issues related to feedback clarity, interface responsiveness, and customization. These findings were synthesized into actionable design guidelines to bridge the gap between compliance and actual usability. While the study is limited to visual impairments and smartphone usage, it lays the groundwork for broader application across diverse disability types and ICT devices. This research highlights the importance of aligning accessibility standards with the actual usability needs of visually impaired users.

Keywords: Accessibility · User Experience · Visually Impaired · Disability · Design Solution · Design Guidelines

1 Introduction

Ensuring accessibility of information and communication technology (ICT) devices for individuals with disabilities has become a key issue worldwide. Access to information is regarded as a fundamental right in the digital age and various legal and technical efforts are being made globally to guarantee this right. The Americans with Disabilities Act (ADA) in the U.S., the European Accessibility Act (EAA), and the web content accessibility guidelines (WCAG) established by the World Wide Web Consortium (W3C) are important legal frameworks aimed at securing the rights of individuals with disabilities [1, 2, 5]. These legal frameworks establish standards for digital accessibility to ensure that disabled individuals can use digital devices and services.

However, often, these legal frameworks fail to ensure the actual user experience (UX) of individuals, particularly in relation to people with visual impairments [11]. ICT devices that comply with legal standards often do not sufficiently resolve the discomfort

© The Author(s), under exclusive license to Springer Nature Switzerland AG 2026
M. Antona and C. Stephanidis (Eds.): HCII 2025, LNCS 16335, pp. 121–131, 2026.
https://doi.org/10.1007/978-3-032-12781-5_8

or limitations faced by disabled users during use, as highlighted in multiple studies [4, 14, 16]. The challenges faced by visually impaired users in using ICT devices highlight the limitations of current legal frameworks [40]. Accessibility not only encompasses the ability to use a device but also the overall experience of the user while interacting with the device [8]. However, current research on accessibility and legal guidelines has mainly focused on functional requirements, with significant gaps remaining in terms of UX [14]. From the perspective of visually impaired users, merely satisfying these requirements does not necessarily guarantee a satisfactory UX [14].

This study aims to revisit the concepts of accessibility and user experience (UX) for individuals with disabilities, and to systematically identify the challenges they face by analyzing existing accessibility-related laws and guidelines. Through this process, the study seeks to identify key pain points and ultimately provide solutions for inclusive design within the scope of accessibility standards.

2   Law and Guideline Analysis

2.1   Method

In this study, various international and national accessibility laws and guidelines were analyzed to derive common structures applicable for providing ICT device accessibility for visually impaired users. The relevant laws and guidelines are presented in Table 1.

Table 1. Accessibility laws and guidelines used in the study (revised from [20]).

Title of Law & Guideline	Contents
EN 301 549 v3.2.1	Guidelines for regulating the accessibility of public ICT products and services in the European Union (EU) state that they should be designed for all users with disabilities to use ICT devices and services. EN 301 549 contains regulations related to the WCAG, specifically addressing accessibility requirements for the visually impaired
WCAG 2.2	Guidelines developed by the World Wide Web Consortium (W3C) to define that web content should be designed to be accessible to people with disabilities around four principles: perceivable, operable, understandable, and robust
Section 508	It defines access to ICT products used by public institutions in the United States and specifies ICT accessibility standards for various disabled people, including the visually impaired
CVAA	U.S. legislation to ensure communication and video accessibility in the 21st century, regulating access to communication and media platforms, such as telephone, broadcast, and video content

These legal frameworks and guidelines provide critical standards for ensuring the accessibility of ICT devices. In this study, we compared and analyzed these laws and guidelines, focusing on their evaluation based on the experiences of visually impaired users.

2.2 Result

By analyzing 603 clauses from various laws and guidelines, 106 clauses directly related to smartphone accessibility for the visually impaired were identified. These clauses were clustered based on their main themes, leading to the identification of common structures within the legal frameworks and guidelines. Table 2 provides examples of the criteria derived by clustering visual accessibility elements from the legal frameworks analyzed.

Legal guidelines focus primarily on technical requirements but do not fully address the real-world discomfort experienced by users. This underscores the necessity of developing user-centered accessibility UX criteria. Based on this analysis, in this study, we aim to provide specific indicators that can improve the overall UX.

3 User Testing with Visually Impaired Participants

In this study, user testing was conducted using a high-fidelity prototype based on the empirical testing method proposed by Kim et al. [2016] [3]. The visually impaired users were instructed to use their smartphones in a set of predefined scenarios. After completing each scenario, the users were asked to explain why they performed certain actions. The experiment aimed to identify the problems faced when using smartphones and establish an accessibility UX model.

3.1 Method

Participants. The experiment involved 10 visually impaired participants divided into three groups: totally blind (TB) (three participants), profoundly visually impaired (PV) (five participants), and color vision deficient (CVD) (two participants) [40].

TB participants were unable to detect light, while PV participants had visual impairments from optic nerve atrophy or narrowed fields of vision, making it impossible to use mobile phones without accessibility features. CVD participants had difficulty distinguishing colors, particularly green and red combinations. The participants were selected based on their frequent use of accessibility features on Samsung smartphones, and 90% of them used their smartphones over three hours daily. The accessibility features varied, but all participants except those with CVD used TalkBack, a screen reader function.

Device Used in the Experiment. A single android-based device was used in the experiment. The device was equipped with the latest operating system (OS) as of 2024 and included key accessibility features for individuals with visual disabilities, such as screen magnification, voice guidance, and color inversion (Fig. 1).

Procedure. The experiment replicated daily smartphone usage scenarios. Participants started by configuring accessibility settings on the device and then performed tasks, such as sending messages, taking pictures using the camera, browsing the gallery, and

Table 2. Example of criteria for clustering visual accessibility elements.

Main Category	Sub-Category	Description	Relevant Law & Guideline
Screen	Content-background separation	Each content must be distinguishable by color, shape, etc. from other content and backgrounds	WCAG 2.2
	Screen magnification	Screen and content must be zoomed in	EN 301 549 v3.2.1
Text	Text resizing	Text size must be above the appropriate level and adjustable	WCAG 2.2, EN 301 549 v3.2.1
	Text brightness contrast	Text should have a background and more than appropriate contrast ratio	WCAG 2.2, EN 301 549 v3.2.1
	Line-to-line/align	When representing text, user must have an appropriate level of line-to-line and alignment	WCAG 2.2, EN 301 549 v3.2.1
	Line/letter/word spacing	When representing text, user must have an appropriate level of spacing between each text	WCAG 2.2, EN 301 549 v3.2.1
Color	Identify color-independent content	The information displayed on the screen must be identifiable without relying on color recognition	WCAG 2.2, EN 301 549 v3.2.1, Section 508
	Adjust color	Must be able to adjust the color contrast of the screen	Section 508
	Adjust brightness	Must be able to adjust the brightness contrast of the screen	WCAG 2.2, EN 301 549 v3.2.1, Section 508

conducting Internet searches. Each task was based on realistic scenarios for visually impaired users, such as sending a message by entering a designated number and typing "Hello." After completing each scenario, feedback was collected in real time. At the end of the experiment, an in-depth interview was conducted to gather further insights into the UX (Figure 2).

Fig. 1. Experimental environment.

Data Analysis. The collected data were analyzed using the Affinity Diagram method [36]. This technique helped clustering the common problems and inconveniences experienced by participants, leading to the identification of key pain points. A qualitative analysis of the feedback provided further insights into how to improve the quality of the UX. Subsequently, each pain point was classified based on the common structure derived in Sect. 2.

3.2 Result

The experiment produced 192 user feedback items, divided into 69 from the TB group, 110 from the PV group, and 13 from the CVD group. Through this feedback, we identified pain points, revealing persistent usability barriers: unclear voice guidance, limited customization, inconsistent focus control, slow responsiveness, and inadequate color adjustment options. Several issues encountered by the TB and PV groups overlapped. Based on this analysis, 51 main pain points were developed to assess the accessibility UX for visually impaired users. These pain points are essential for categorizing user discomfort and providing specific improvement measures for accessibility features. Table 3 presents examples of the pain points and requirements derived from the user tests. The classification in Table 3 was organized based on the sub-categories in Table 2.

Certain pain points, such as cognitive load, were identified through user testing but were not addressed in existing legal accessibility standards.

Table 3. Example of pain point derived from user test and its classification.

Type of Disability	Pain Point	Requirement	Classification
TB	Voice guidance does not give user much feedback on user's progress	Need more specific and frequent feedback	Voice guidance
	Low accuracy of speech recognition	Need the device to be well aware of user input	Voice input
	Focus changed to unwanted place while using TalkBack	Need the ability to maintain consistent focus	Navigation guarantee
PV	Screen enlargement region control icon overlaps other UI	Need a way to adjust the magnification area without colliding with UI elements	Screen magnification
	Keyboard's font size is small	Need to be able to increase the size of the keyboard as well	Screen component
	Risk of security leakage when using passwords while using voice guidance	Need the voice guidance should not read personal information	Personal information protection
CVD	Narrow spectrum for adjusting color calibration values	Need the wide color-adjustment spectrum	Adjust color
	Color calibration does not calibrate only the desired color	Need an option to change only the color user want so it doesn't affect other content.	Adjust color

4   Discussion

4.1   Comparison of Legal Guidelines and Usability Testing Results

Park et al. (2023) mentioned that in the case of kiosks, basic accessibility guidelines, such as voice support and high-contrast functions were not followed [40]. However, smartphones fulfill legal standards better than other ICT devices. Despite this, among the contents derived from user opinions, there were also pain points that accessibility laws and guidelines could not address.

Table 4 provides examples of pain point derived from user testing that cover aspects not addressed by legal frameworks, and summarizes the requirements of each pain point. This highlights the gap between legal guidelines and users' real-world experiences.

Table 4. Examples of pain point from user test excluded in Law.

Pain Point	Requirement
Too many features to understand	Need a simplified interface or guided mode that reduces initial cognitive load
Slow response time of voice guidance and operation often not be recognized due to slow response speed when using the function	Need faster system responsiveness and more immediate feedback to user inputs
When setting the accessibility function, not only the color of the desired area changes, but the entire color changes, making it uncomfortable	Need to separate functional color settings from overall system appearance to avoid unintended visual changes
Inconvenient because there are apps that do not have accessibility features	Need system-level support or warnings to notify users when an app lacks accessibility features

Based on user testing, this study identifies key pain points experienced by visually impaired users and proposes specific design directions for each. These insights emphasize how accessibility features should be adapted to align with real usage contexts. Table 5 is an example of design guidelines according to each pain point.

Table 5. Examples of pain point from user test excluded in Law.

Pain point	Design Guideline
Voice guidance does not give user much feedback on user's progress	Accessibility features should provide periodic and contextual feedback through voice prompts. For instance, when a screen reader guides a user through a form, it should verbally confirm each completed step and notify the current position.
Screen enlargement region control icon overlaps other UI	When implementing screen magnification, designers must ensure that control icons do not obstruct interactive elements. Dynamic icon positioning or collapsible control panels can minimize interference with the primary interface.
Narrow spectrum for adjusting color calibration values	Color and contrast settings should offer more granular control, including expanded ranges and presets for various types of color vision deficiency. Real-time preview and customization should also be integrated.
Too many features to understand	Accessibility menus should be structured hierarchically and provide onboarding or simplified modes for novice users. Progressive disclosure and contextual help messages can reduce the initial learning burden.

These findings call for a shift from static feature provisioning to adaptive accessibility, where functions respond intelligently to user contexts. Through precise calibration of each design element: feedback, layout, control, and responsiveness; accessibility tools can provide not only compliance but also confidence and clarity for visually impaired users.

The key difference between legal accessibility guidelines and user testing is that legal guidelines focus primarily on technical requirements. While these guidelines are designed to enable individuals with disabilities to perform basic tasks on ICT devices, they differ significantly from the qualitative aspects of the real UX. Legal guidelines often consider accessibility to be fulfilled as long as the feature is provided such as assuming that offering a screen magnification function is enough. Through practical user testing, this study confirmed that aspects such as intuition, responsiveness, and ease of manipulation of detailed functions are critical to UX of disabled users. Therefore, it is necessary to emphasize the need for intuitive design guidelines that integrate accessibility and UX criteria, and provide support.

4.2   Limitations and Future Research Directions

This study acknowledges several limitations. Firstly, due to practical constraints such as the number of accessibility functions to be tested, challenges in participant recruitment, and budgetary limitations, the research was confined to visually impaired users. As a result, the findings presented herein do not fully address the needs of users with other types of disabilities, such as auditory, motor, or cognitive impairments. Future research should aim to expand the demographic scope to encompass a more diverse range of disability types, with the objective of developing more inclusive and universally applicable design guidelines. Secondly, this study specifically examined the accessibility features of smartphones. Although smartphones are among the most commonly used ICT devices, the accessibility challenges encountered by users can vary significantly depending on the device type and usage context. Devices such as smart TVs, desktop computers, and public kiosks present distinct interaction paradigms and accessibility requirements. Future research should consider these various device categories and usage scenarios to derive context-specific accessibility UX guidelines and ensure that inclusive design practices are comprehensively applied across digital ecosystems. Lastly, the user test in this study was conducted based on a limited set of predefined smartphone usage scenarios. While these scenarios were designed to reflect common daily tasks, there is a possibility that some usability issues remain unaddressed due to the constraints of scenario selection. Expanding the range of usage contexts in future studies will be crucial to uncover a broader spectrum of accessibility challenges and refine the accessibility UX model accordingly.

5   Conclusion

This study examines the disparity between legal accessibility standards and the actual user experience (UX) of visually impaired individuals utilizing smartphones. Through a comprehensive analysis of international accessibility laws and guidelines, coupled with a user study involving visually impaired participants, seeking bridge the gap between technical compliance and user-centered design. The findings underscore that, while existing legal standards provide a foundational basis for accessibility, they inadequately address the nuanced challenges users encounter during real-world interactions. By identifying 51 pain points and translating them into actionable design guidelines, this research underscores the significance of a UX-integrated approach to accessibility. Future accessibility guidelines should go beyond merely meeting legal requirements and evolve in a more inclusive direction by incorporating actual user pain points.

Acknowledgments. This research was supported by Samsung Electronics. Additionally, it was supported by the Ministry of Science and ICT (MSIT) Korea under the ICAN (ICT Challenge and Advanced Network of HRD) program (IITP-2024-RS-2022–00156215), supervised by the Institute of Information & Communications Technology Planning & Evaluation (IITP).

Disclosure of Interests. The authors have no competing interests to declare that are relevant to the content of this article.

References

1. Americans with Disabilities Act of 1990, Pub. L. No. 101–336, 104 Stat. 327 (1990)
2. European Union. European Accessibility Act. Directive (EU) 2019/882 (2019)
3. Kim, H.K., Han, S.H., Park, J., Park, J.: The interaction experiences of visually impaired people with assistive technology: a case study of smartphones. Int. J. Ind. Ergon. **55**, 22–33 (2016)
4. Power, C., Freire, A., Petrie, H., Swallow, D.: Guidelines are only half of the story: accessibility problems encountered by blind users on the web. In: Proceedings of the SIGCHI Conference on Human Factors in Computing Systems (CHI 2012), pp. 433–442. Association for Computing Machinery, New York, NY, USA (2012)
5. Caldwell, B., et al.: Web content accessibility guidelines (WCAG) 2.0. WWW Consortium (W3C) (2008). https://www.w3.org/TR/WCAG20/
6. Hassenzahl, M., Tractinsky, N.: User experience – a research agenda. Behav. Inf. Technol. **25**(2), 91–97 (2006)
7. Vigo, M., Arrue, M., Brajnik, G., Lomuscio, R., Abascal, J.: Quantitative metrics for measuring web accessibility. In: Proceedings of the 2007 international cross-disciplinary conference on Web accessibility (W4A) (W4A 2007), pp. 99–107. Association for Computing Machinery, New York, NY, USA (2007)
8. Lee, Y., Park, S., Park, J., Kim, H.K.: Comparative analysis of usability and accessibility of kiosks for people with disabilities. Appl. Sci. **13**(5), 3058 (2023)
9. Sauer, J., Sonderegger, A., Schmutz, S.: Usability, user experience and accessibility: towards an integrative model. Ergonomics **63**(10), 1207–1220 (2020)
10. Vigo, M., Brajnik, G.: Automatic web accessibility metrics: where we are and where we can go. Interact. Comput. **23**(2), 137–155 (2011)
11. Sullivan, T., Matson, R.: Barriers to use: usability and content accessibility on the Web's most popular sites. In: Proceedings on the 2000 conference on Universal Usability (CUU 2000), pp. 139–144. Association for Computing Machinery, New York, NY, USA (2000)
12. Brajnik, G.: Beyond conformance: the role of accessibility evaluation methods. In: Web Information Systems Engineering – WISE 2008 Workshops. WISE 2008. Lecture Notes in Computer Science, vol. 5176. Springer, Berlin, Heidelberg (2008)

13. Iwarsson, S., Ståhl, A.: Accessibility, usability and universal design – positioning and definition of concepts describing person-environment relationships. Disabil. Rehabil. **25**(2), 57–66 (2003)
14. Petrie, H., Kheir, O.: The relationship between accessibility and usability of websites. In: Proceedings of the SIGCHI Conference on Human Factors in Computing Systems (CHI 2007), pp. 397–406. Association for Computing Machinery, New York, NY, USA (2007)
15. Aizpurua, A., Harper, S., Vigo, M.: Exploring the relationship between web accessibility and user experience. Int. J. Hum. Comput. Stud. **91**, 13–23 (2016)
16. Petrie, H., Bevan, N.: The evaluation of accessibility, usability, and UX. Univ. Access Handb. **1**, 1–16 (2009)
17. Rusu, C., Rusu, V., Roncagliolo, S., González, C.: Usability and user experience: what should we care about? Int. J. Inf. Technol. Syst. Approach **8**(2), 1–12 (2015)
18. Gonçalves, R., Rocha, T., Martins, J., Branco, F., Au-Yong-Oliveira, M.: Evaluation of e-commerce websites accessibility and usability: an e-commerce platform analysis with the inclusion of blind users. Univ. Access Inf. Soc. **17**, 567–583 (2018)
19. Oswal, S.K.: Breaking the exclusionary boundary between UX and access: steps toward making UX inclusive of users with disabilities. In: Proceedings of the 37th ACM International Conference on the Design of Communication (SIGDOC 2019), pp. 1–8. Association for Computing Machinery, New York, NY, USA, Article 12 (2019)
20. Park, J., Han, S.H., Kim, H.K., Cho, Y., Park, W.: Developing elements of user experience for mobile phones and services: survey, interview, and observation approaches. Hum. Fact. Ergonom. Manuf. Serv. Ind. **23**, 279–293 (2013)
21. Yesilada, Y., Brajnik, G., Vigo, M., Harper, S.: Exploring perceptions of web accessibility: a survey approach. Behav. Inf. Technol. **34**(2), 119–134 (2013)
22. Harper, S., Chen, A.Q.: Web accessibility guidelines. World Wide Web **15**, 61–88 (2012)
23. International Organization for Standardization, 2008. ISO 9241-171:2008: Ergonomics of Human-System Interaction – Part 171: Guidance on Software Accessibility. Technical Specification International Organization for Standardization. ISO – International Organization for Standardization, Switzerland
24. International Organization for Standardization, 2019. ISO 9241-210:2019: Ergonomics of Human-System Interaction – Part 210: Human-Centred Design for Interactive Systems
25. Cooper, M., Kirkpatrick, A., Campbell, A., Bradley Montgomery, R., Adams, C.: Web Content Accessibility Guidelines (WCAG) 2.2. W3C Recommendation (2023)
26. Velleman, E., Strobbe, C., Koch, J., Velasco, C.A., Snaprud, M.: A unified web evaluation methodology using WCAG. In: Universal Access in Human-Computer Interaction. Applications and Services. UAHCI 2007. Lecture Notes in Computer Science, vol. 4556. Springer, Berlin, Heidelberg (2007)
27. Hackett, S., Parmanto, B., Zeng, X.: Accessibility of Internet websites through time. In: Proceedings of the 6th international ACM SIGACCESS conference on Computers and accessibility (Assets 2004), pp. 32–39. Association for Computing Machinery, New York, NY, USA (2003)
28. Carvalho, M.C.N., Dias, F.S., Reis, A.G.S., Freire, A.P.: Accessibility and usability problems encountered on websites and applications in mobile devices by blind and normal-vision users. In: Proceedings of the 33rd Annual ACM Symposium on Applied Computing (SAC 2018), pp. 2022–2029. Association for Computing Machinery, New York, NY, USA (2018)
29. Lopes, R., Carriço, L.: The impact of accessibility assessment in macro scale universal usability studies of the web. In: Proceedings of the 2008 International Cross-Disciplinary Conference on Web Accessibility (W4A) (W4A 2008), pp. 5–14. Association for Computing Machinery, New York, NY, USA (2008)
30. Bailey, J., Burd, E.: Towards more mature web maintenance practices for accessibility. In: 9th IEEE International Workshop on Web Site Evolution, Paris, France, pp. 81–88 (2007)

31. Calvo, R., Seyedarabi, F., Savva, A.: Beyond web content accessibility guidelines: expert accessibility reviews. In: Proceedings of the 7th International Conference on Software Development and Technologies for Enhancing Accessibility and Fighting Info-exclusion (DSAI 2016), pp. 77–84. Association for Computing Machinery, New York, NY, USA (2016)
32. Brooke, J.: SUS: a quick and dirty' usability scale. Usability Eval. Ind. **189**, 4–7 (1996)
33. Lewis, J.R.: The system usability scale: past, present, and future. Int. J. Hum. Comput. Interact. **34**(7), 577–590 (2018)
34. Laugwitz, B., Held, T., Schrepp, M.: Construction and evaluation of a UX questionnaire. In: HCI and Usability for Education and Work. USAB 2008. Lecture Notes in Computer Science, vol. 5298. Springer, Berlin, Heidelberg (2008)
35. Hassenzahl, M., Burmester, M., Koller, F.: AttrakDiff: Ein Fragebogen zur Messung wahrgenommener hedonischer und pragmatischer Qualität. In: Szwillus, G., Ziegler, J. (eds.) Mensch & Computer 2003. Berichte des German Chapter of the ACM, vol. 57 (2003)
36. Beyer, H., Holtzblatt, K.: Contextual Design: Defining Customer-Centered Systems. Elsevier (1997)
37. The Rehabilitation Act Amendments (Section 508). https://www.access-board.gov/ict/
38. U.S. Congress. Communications and Video Accessibility Act of 2010 (CVAA). Pub. L. No. 111–260, 124 Stat. 2751 (2010). https://www.fcc.gov/cvaa
39. Global Accessibility Reporting Initiative (GARI). Global Accessibility Reporting Initiative (2023). https://www.gari.info
40. Park, S., Kim, H.K., Lee, Y., Park, J.: Kiosk accessibility challenges faced by people with disabilities: an analysis of domestic and international accessibility laws/guidelines and user focus group interviews. Univ. Access Inf. Soc. 1–17 (2023)

Enhancing the Accessibility for Museum Exhibition: An Explorative Study on Digital Storytelling Design Strategies for Cognitively Impaired Audiences

Chen Peng[✉]

Universiti Sains Malaysia, 11800, Gelugor, Penang, Malaysia
1142370994@qq.com

Abstract. In recent years, user experience research has increasingly focused on inclusivity and social equity, especially strategies to enhance the experience of disadvantaged people through accessible design. As a place where different groups of people gather, museum visitors include healthy people and people with cognitive disabilities. Cognitively impaired people have different mental impairments in thinking, memory, attention, etc. Attention to their needs not only enhances the motivation of the public to visit but also improves the quality of social services. However, current museums mainly rely on the exhibition form of text and images, which has limited friendliness to people with cognitive disabilities. Digital storytelling, as an important means of enhancing interaction and sustaining interpersonal relationships, has demonstrated the potential to enhance audience content understanding in exhibition design. Although studies have shown the positive effects of digital narratives on enhancing content understanding in exhibitions, research on how to design storytelling formats for people with cognitive disabilities needs to be further explored to contribute to the goals of inclusiveness and social equity.

Keywords: Digital storytelling · accessibility · cognitively impaired people

1 Introduction

The fields of human-computer interaction, museum studies, and design research have devoted sustained attention to museum exhibitions [1]. With the emergence of new technologies and media, art, science and technology, and design are combined to offer creative exhibition content, enriching the exhibition form and improving the audience visiting experience [2].

The visitor population of the museum exhibition not only includes healthy people but also covers vulnerable groups. Notably, cognitively impaired people, people are those who have different degrees of impairment in thinking, memory, attention, language, problem-solving, and other cognitive functions. Such a consideration of cognitively impaired people in museum exhibitions provides important contributions to. An accessible world [3].

© The Author(s), under exclusive license to Springer Nature Switzerland AG 2026
M. Antona and C. Stephanidis (Eds.): HCII 2025, LNCS 16335, pp. 132–148, 2026.
https://doi.org/10.1007/978-3-032-12781-5_9

Digital storytelling [5, 6] is an important instrument for exhibitions. Storytelling is a means of social interaction that creates and sustains human connections and relationships [6]. While Research has shown that storytelling enhances visitors' understanding of exhibition content [4, 7], it is not clear how storytelling can be designed to enhance the understanding of exhibition content by people with cognitive disabilities.

To address this research gap, this study explores two research questions:

RQ1: What are the obstacles and opportunities for cognitively impaired people to experience exhibits in museums?
RQ2: What are the design strategies for storytelling that promote accessibility in museum exhibitions?

This study aims to contribute to two research fields. In the field of accessibility design, we propose design strategies that encourage diversity in cognitive populations. For the field of museum exhibition, this study deepens the exhibition mechanism and design strategy of storytelling, providing manners for borrowing multiple media to convey information and express the historical connotation of museum artifacts. Practically, we contribute to a better understanding of the needs of people with cognitive disabilities to improve design approaches and methods in museums.

2 Literature Review

2.1 Digital Storytelling and Museum Exhibition

Digital storytelling and museum exhibitions [8] are planning activities for the public to display their collections or short-term exhibition items and tell their stories through the use of digital technology, mainly by placing various types of objects such as cultural relics, artworks, natural specimens, and other items reasonably in a specific space, combining traditional narrative techniques and modern digital tools to convey knowledge to the audience, to inspire thinking, and to show the results of cultural relics, art or scientific development. Digital storytelling and museum exhibitions are understood as peer-to-peer activities such as cultural dissemination and popularization of science, which are often felt to have greater interactivity, visual impact, and information visualization. Corresponding research is frequent in the fields of museum studies, exhibition planning, education, and human-computer interaction [9].

Numerous studies have explored different display methods such as traditional display displays, interactive displays [10], multimedia displays, holographic projection displays, object and restoration displays, mobile exhibitions, thematic exhibitions, art installations and experiential displays, educational displays, and digitally-assisted displays, especially digitally-assisted [11] displays, for example, Amy hurst [12] from the perspective of accessibility design, using digitalization and multi-modal interaction to design interactive maps to help museum visitors understand the complex layout of the museum. Timo partial [13] uses human-computer interaction technology to design tablet-based animated AR to help visitors better navigate the museum from the perspective of user experience. Huang and coauthors [14] use human-computer interaction technology to observe and evaluate participant journey maps from the perspective of participatory design. To observe and evaluate participant journey maps to design a more humanized interactive and fun museum display model. Zhou [13] provided a novel idea for digital display and storytelling in museums by studying and understanding shared-control VR from the perspective of user experience, using human-computer interaction technology.

Storytelling is the art and skill of presenting a story through narration, expression, or presentation. It can be done verbally, in writing, in images, in music, etc., and its purpose is to convey emotions, ideas, or information and to create an emotional connection with the viewer or listener. At the same time, people also turn their attention to digital instrument [15], digital instruments refer to digital technology, electronic devices, or information processing related things, digital technology is widely used in all aspects of life, in the museum has been applied to explore the use of digital and storytelling to create and tell stories. For example, the Singapore Museum has made VR experience and interactive video theatre to achieve an immersive [16] learning experience, which shows that digital storytelling [17] can stimulate the audience's emotions, inspire thinking, and even influence behaviors, which has a positive effect on the exhibition.

2.2 Designing for Mild Cognitively Impaired People

Mild Cognitive Impairment (MCI) is essentially a state of mild cognitive decline that usually manifests itself as a decrease in memory, thinking, or judgment. Cognitive impairment [18], on the other hand, is defined as a significant decline in an individual's cognitive functioning, which subsequently affects daily living and independent living. This group of people generally presents with memory problems, decreased attention and concentration, language problems, decreased judgment and decision-making abilities, spatial orientation, and visual recognition [19] problems.

A large number of studies have explored how to enhance experience, learning, memory, and social equality in people with cognitive impairment from different perspectives. Niharika Mathur [20] introduced a set of conversational aids to assist MCI in improving ease of living. Huang [21] introduced a set of green natural learning methods to assist MCI learning outcomes.

Cognitively impaired people are also important visitors to exhibitions in museums, but most studies have focused on the normal population, and there are differences between the normal population and cognitively impaired people in terms of cognitive functioning, impact on daily life, emotional and behavioral performance, as well as memory and learning ability, such as cognitively disorganized memories of recent events, but good retention of familiar events or past experiences, and a preference for exhibitions with concise and clear information, interactive, recall and associative exhibition formats, etc. The user experience needs to pay more attention to their cognitive, and emotional needs [22] and social needs [23] to better help them make sense of the information, maintain their independence, and promote their active participation.

3 Research Methods

We conducted an interview study to develop an understanding of the barriers, as well as opportunities, that people with cognitive disabilities encounter during museum visits and browsing. Specifically, we focused on the role of storytelling strategies in enhancing the experience for people with cognitive disabilities. Our goal was to reveal the barriers and claims encountered, further elaborate on the design elements of storytelling, and then propose a series of design strategies and a guiding framework for accessible digital storytelling.

3.1 Respondents and Demographics

Participant recruitment consisted mainly of simple random sampling, searching for people in cognitively impaired rehabilitation facilities, canvassing the internet, and posting on social media platforms. A snowball sampling approach was also adopted, as some respondents recommended several other participants. We accordingly adhered to the principle of maximizing variation by looking for individuals from different work environments, different cultural backgrounds, and different regions of the country. To see if there were shared patterns in these cases. We actively contacted and carefully screened 12 candidate participants for the interview study. After an initial understanding and communication with the participants, we interviewed eight of them. All of these participants identified themselves as people with cognitive impairment or as family members or healthcare workers, and all eight had experience of museum browsing (e.g., regular semi-monthly visits). They were the audience who were considered to be vocal in this aspect of the browsing experience.

Our small sample size, while lacking in data scalability, allowed us to explore in-depth the experiences of our respondents. Therefore, we prioritized solid data and depth over breadth.

Our participants ranged in age from 20 to 48 years old. They were located in three different countries for work or study: China, Malaysia, and the United States. Thus, the different cultural backgrounds and geographical features in their browsing visit experiences made the range very large. Tables 1 and 2 then consolidate this information.

Table 1. Information about our participant

Participants	Nationality	Age	Gender	Occupation	Discipline
P1	China	28	Male	Woodworking	Self-employed
P2	China	30	Female	High School Teachers	Art & Design
P3	Malaysia	23	Male	Undergraduate students	Social Psychology
P4	Hong Kong, China	26	Female	High school research assistant	Computer
P5	China	48	Female	Secondary School Teacher	Education Sector
P6	China	21	Female	Model	Self-employed
P7	Malaysia	32	Female	Nurse practitioner	Rehabilitation Hospital

(continued)

Table 1. (*continued*)

Participants	Nationality	Age	Gender	Occupation	Discipline
P8	United States of America	21	Male	Undergraduate student	Energy Engineering

3.2 Data Collection

We used a semi-structured interview methodology. Most of the interviews were conducted in the fall of 2024, either through real-time online meetings or offline face-to-face via communication software. For example, P1, 2, 4, 5, 6, and 8 were online meetings, while P3 and 7 were conducted via offline face-to-face. Each interview lasted approximately forty minutes, and each participant signed an informed consent form. Through semi-structured interviews, we were able to go deeper to obtain the real feelings and concerns of people with cognitive disabilities during their travel experiences and adjusted the interview questions during the interview process to make our focus more focused.

We developed a series of tightly themed interview questions that encompassed understanding the demographics and details of the lives of people with cognitive disabilities, browsing experiences, specific cases, behaviors and reactions at the time, experiences and claims afterward, and potential opportunities. We also asked about the status, impediments, claims, and opportunities for people with cognitive disabilities to browse in museums, their projected design outputs, and design strategies to encourage interviewees to suggest improvements. Interview questions are summarized in Table 2. As the interviews proceeded, we also asked appropriate questions and appropriately adapted them based on the information articulated to us.

Table 2. Interview Questions

Demographics and experience

   Age, gender, work and life details

   Level of cognitive impairment (none/mild/moderate/severe)

   How often do you visit museums? (e.g. every half month, 1-2 times a month)

   How much do you participate in it?

Browsing experiences and specific cases

   What difficulties did you encounter during your visit?

   What would you like to see improved? (e.g., the way the exhibition is organized)

   Do you know how digital storytelling is used in museums? Can you tell us about a specific case?

   What is your acceptance of digital storytelling? (e.g., 20%/30%/50%/80% etc.) Are there any barriers to use? Do these technologies help to increase the independence of the visitor?

Self-appeal

   Using digital storytelling as an example, how do you think it should be designed to improve your engagement interactions? (e.g., interactive narrative/traditional narrative, immersive narrative approach, etc.)

   How was your acceptance after the modification? Are there still barriers?

   What would change in your attention span? (e.g., images, interactive devices, bright colors, adaptive fonts)

Experiences and specific behaviors at the time

   What was your experience in it? (e.g., percentage, mood, etc.)

   After the modification, did you have a deeper or a lighter impression of the content of the exhibit?

   What do you feel you gained from using storytelling? (e.g., better understanding of the exhibits, more willingness to go to the museum, self-satisfaction, etc.)

   Does the process of storytelling resonate with you emotionally? (e.g., no, a little, a lot)

Opportunities and Challenges

   Describe what digital storytelling has brought to you and your industry/museum.

   How has the introduction of digital storytelling in museums changed the industry?

   Regarding the use of digital storytelling in museums: what current challenges are being addressed?

   Regarding the use of digital storytelling in your industry: what opportunities are being worked on?

3.3 Data Analysis

This study uses thematic analysis to explore the obstacles and claims of people with cognitive disabilities experiencing exhibits in museums. Thematic analysis is a common qualitative research method used to identify and understand the main themes and patterns in the data [23, 24]. The researcher will repeatedly read and review the interview and observation data and carry out preliminary coding to mark key points related to the experience, such as "complexity of information", "the guiding tool is not friendly". By identifying and summarizing these codes, the researcher can extract the core themes that affect the museum experience for people with cognitive disabilities, revealing the main obstacles and potential demands they face.

We started with transcribing the data and becoming familiar with its content, open coding was performed by the researchers to generate an initial list of codes. Based on this, I summarized this information and completed the initial code in a discursive process. We repeatedly read relevant excerpts to review the code and went back to think about patterns, themes, and differences. Next, the codes were then organized into broader categories.

Through iterative review and refinement, these categories were summarized into different themes, each supported by relevant examples from the data. This process aids in a nuanced understanding of the phenomenon under study and provides valuable insights for further explanation and discussion. In summary, I organized the data from the bottom up, identifying patterns and forming a model.

4   Results

Our findings are organized into five sections. First (1) the purpose and potential value of an accessible digital storytelling design are articulated; (2) the process experiences and experiences of navigating the museum for people with cognitive disabilities are described; (3) the obstacles encountered by people with cognitive disabilities and their aspirations are illustrated; and (4) an outlook on the expected outputs and the potential opportunities for the future is given, as well as the impacts of the study.

4.1   The Purpose and Potential Value of Accessible Storytelling Design

This interview exposes the unique advantages that digital storytelling exhibits in museum browsing for people with cognitive disabilities, as well as design strategies.

In terms of display, the original means of museum display is mainly point-to-point, two-dimensional display, but with the advancement of technology, the means of the display have gradually become point-to-point, three-dimensional, or multi-dimensional display. Correspondingly, the value of storytelling has evolved with the development of other technological fields/means, such as augmented virtual reality and HCI.

Impact on museums: convenience, inclusivity, accessibility, effectiveness. One of the prominent ways in which digital Storytelling affects potential value is by impacting the accessibility and effectiveness of existing means of display extremely well. An example is the dramatic enhancement of the effectiveness of the museum's means of display, such as enhancing accessibility when navigating the museum for people with cognitive disabilities. While these improvements are based on improvements to existing problems, they still create significant value for museum displays.

Accessibility reflects an important value dimension of museums, and previously, people attended museums with more consideration for healthy people. However, it is difficult for people with cognitive disabilities to perform these behaviors. Like P1 in the browsing process, usually because of their cognitive disabilities, it is difficult to independently and autonomously browse through the museum or deeply understand the exhibits, and after using digital storytelling, P1 can independently and autonomously browse and visit the museum, understand the exhibits, and significantly improve the degree of participation with the museum. P5, a secondary school teacher, gave a similar example as she navigated through the museum, "I think we use digital storytelling to improve areas that we had neglected. Like, if people with cognitive disabilities can't engage with the museum, it goes against the public nature of the museum itself."

P2's real-life case also emphasized the necessity of digital storytelling as a means of display. While browsing a museum, she found that a certain area where digital storytelling was applied had significantly more foot traffic than the area where digital storytelling was not applied, and people were inside interacting with the exhibits and communicating what they saw.

Stylized propositions like time, necessity, and comprehension can be integrated in a single case to form a new process. For example, when browsing museums, many people do not always fully understand the content of the exhibits and the thoughts and feelings expressed after seeing them, P3 dispels this problem, "Digital storytelling can be used in museums, immersive contextualized spaces, to make silent proclamations about the exhibits." Reducing the "distance" between people and museums."

Digital storytelling can also increase the level of understanding or interest in exhibits, as P3 says, "Wandering through complex interior spaces, we need a means of bridging the gap between us and the exhibits and the museum," sometimes to increase the level of understanding of the exhibits, sometimes to increase the level of interest in the exhibits. The great value lies in the ability to use digital storytelling to achieve increased convenience, accessibility, inclusivity, effectiveness, etc. As P4 said, we have been looking forward to a "bridge" connecting people and museums, rather than visitors looking at exhibits in isolation and having difficulty understanding and thinking about their content.

Of course, this is not possible without external technological developments, such as augmented virtual reality and HCI. P7 works in a rehabilitation hospital and is responsible for the basic rehabilitation of people with cognitive disabilities, while P8 has participated in social volunteer work, volunteering in museums on several occasions. The combined views of the two interviewees give us another perspective, that is, "Cognitively impaired people visit museums independently with the help of digital storytelling technology so that the 'bridge' proposed by P4 can be built successfully."

Therefore, design recommendations regarding digital storytelling: refine the consideration of the existing value of technology, such as HCI, and VR, to enrich digital storytelling. We found that current digital storytelling research and applications are mainly focused on healthy populations, with a focus on transforming museum information into more intuitive visual symbols or sensory experiences. On the contrary, in cognitively impaired populations such as MCI, AD, and ADHD populations, digital storytelling creates significant value as an aid to museum browsing.

According to the value to the individual, the sense of experience is enhanced, and the sense of flux is transformed. It has often been mentioned that the knowledge an individual possesses comes from specific educational experiences or socio-cultural environments, not from him/herself. Digital storytelling, as an important means of bridging the gap between visitors and museums, encompasses a wide range of disciplines: computers, design, psychology, sociology, museology, ergonomics, etc. P2 believes that museums should adopt digital storytelling as soon as possible, and after experiencing it firsthand, she feels that its potential value has been underestimated for a long time. P1 and P5, on the other hand, shared this view.

P8 extends around this idea by presenting a more in-depth view that people encounter obstacles when visiting museums due to their knowledge base and the level of cognitive impairment, and that digital storytelling can better ameliorate people's distress with unfamiliar exhibits and boring historical backgrounds.

The design of digital storytelling suggests that the user's demands and the actual user experience should be the primary consideration, and that the user's behavior is valuable data and the basis for the next step of improvement. At the same time, research has shown that there is a significant need and opportunity for the application of digital storytelling, which opens the possibility of exploring the barriers and opportunities for people with cognitive disabilities in museum navigation.

4.2   Tour Flow and Experience

In one subsection, I described the visit process and experience of navigating a museum for people with cognitive disabilities. In this context, it is interesting to note that most of the strategies are centered on pre-research and preparation. I found that most of the museum design focuses on the experience of healthy people and very little on the experience of people with cognitive disabilities.

The authentic flow and experience of a museum visit for people with cognitive disabilities may vary depending on individual circumstances and the level of the museum's facilities and services, but it usually includes the following key aspects and feelings:

1. **Preparations and challenges before entering the coffin.** Family members or accompanying persons of people with cognitive disabilities usually make appointments in advance to ensure that the museum is aware of the special needs of the visitors, as P1 said, "Every time I go to the museum, I need to communicate in advance by phone for fear of not being able to receive them or worrying about the disturbances of the visit" In the preliminary stage, visitors have already felt the difference in the visit process and perceived differences. In this preliminary stage, visitors have already felt the difference in the flow of the visit and the difference in perception.

2. **Entry and acclimatization.** Upon entering the museum, visitors are usually assisted by a chaperone to obtain a guide map or relevant information. P7 said: "As you know, in this case, it is almost difficult to complete a complete tour of the museum on one's own. This is not possible without the help of a chaperone, but you have to realize that many people are not assisted by a chaperone, so what are they supposed to do?" In this regard, I perceived the importance of digital storytelling and the difficulty that people with cognitive disabilities have in accessing information.

3. **The process of visiting.** The cognitively impaired people visited the museum with the assistance of a chaperone. P6 made an interesting point that "museums, because of the different exhibits they have on display, can express different historical stories and cultures, and in a state that is difficult for the healthy population to fully comprehend, it is even more of a challenge in front of the eyes of the cognitively impaired people."

Our data analysis revealed several design recommendations for digital storytelling. These recommendations include supporting the improvement of the browsing process in museums, including convenient booking methods, good spatial layout, and welcoming services. The rationality, convenience, and accessibility of the browsing process are important areas to consider for people with cognitive disabilities, which is crucial for their visiting experience.

In reality, some families may encounter communication difficulties, especially when museums do not clearly label related services, which can add a lot of uncertainty, and people with cognitive disabilities may feel anxious or confused about sudden changes in the environment. On this point, P5 agrees, describing how "people with cognitive disabilities need a stable and harmonious environment, and sudden changes can make them feel uneasy and psychologically burdened, but unfortunately, many museums seldom take this into consideration and do not take the initiative to provide services."

The cognitively impaired people, because of their special characteristics, may lose patience or even experience mood swings in the face of more complex environments or large amounts of information intake or exhibitions that take a long time. Corresponding multi-sensory interactions can stimulate their interest. In this regard, P4 adds, "multi-sensory should be utilized reasonably, too much sensory stimulation is counterproductive."

On the other hand, if the environment is noisy or crowded, people with cognitive disabilities can feel uneasy. Individuals with a poor sense of direction, and complex layout of the premises may cause distress. P8 mentions this point, "Most museums do not realize this, and very often this difficulty needs to be solved by the cognitively impaired people themselves."

Our analysis also revealed several design recommendations for digital storytelling, which encompasses supporting the museum experience by signage, environmental layout, multisensory interactions, and color. Experience is a priority area for people with cognitive disabilities and should be an integral part of digital storytelling design.

4.3   Obstacles and Claims of People with Cognitive Disabilities

Cognitively impaired people may face various obstacles when visiting museums, and these obstacles come from the environment and services of the museums, as well as the characteristics of cognitively impaired people themselves. At the same time, they also have some specific demands in the process of visiting, hoping to get a better experience reasonably.

Our analysis revealed several obstacles. As an important place, the museum displays different exhibits every day, and the huge amount of information exacerbates the complexity of comprehension. P2 mentions that "the text of exhibition information is too long, and the complexity of specialized terms makes it difficult for people with cognitive disabilities to comprehend the content, and they tend to feel frustrated."

High footfall, harsh lighting, and loud noises can trigger anxiety, unease, and even mood swings, a point echoed by P3. In terms of understanding exhibits and effective dissemination of information, museums seldom consider the special characteristics of people with cognitive disabilities, and P6 mentions that "the lack of clear and concise introduction and the difficulty of museums to provide effective support during visits make it difficult to understand the exhibits and make a deep impression on them." Based on the characteristics of people with cognitive disabilities themselves, i.e., difficulty in remembering and understanding, easy to fluctuating emotionally, and difficulty in controlling behaviors, P8 puts forward the view that "in front of the huge amount of information in the museums, people with cognitive disabilities have difficulty in remembering complex information and have a weaker sense of experience."

Interviewees also provided several self-claims. People with cognitive disabilities may face unique challenges and claims when visiting museums. For example, "difficulties in guiding and understanding information", "environmental perception and adaptation", "control of time and pace", "social interaction and support", "memorization and retention of information".

"Difficulties in guided tours and information comprehension bear the brunt of the problem, trapping many cognitively impaired people, and challenging language comprehension, memory, and attention during the visit, as well as making it difficult to follow traditional guided tours. There is an urgent need to provide multi-sensory guided tours, such as VR and tactile maps," said P1.

P3 expressed his opinion on the point of "social interaction and support", "People with cognitive disabilities often have communication barriers with staff or other visitors when visiting museums, which stems from their lack of confidence and causes problems." It is hoped that conversational and interactive guided tours will be conducted to increase the sense of participation."

The museum is like a huge information distribution center, and it is difficult for people with cognitive disabilities to quickly understand the meaning of it, as stated in P7: "Many people with cognitive disabilities have difficulty in remembering what they have learned or in creating a lasting experience of the visit," as an example of "memory and retention of information". Therefore, it is hoped that the use of personalized animated ARs and push-button illustrated brochures will lead to better participation and retention.

P6 mentioned "environmental perception and adaptation" because people with cognitive disabilities face unfamiliar and huge spaces, they can't easily locate the specific exhibition area, they can't locate where they are by color or text cues, multi-language signs or abstract symbols may confuse them. People with cognitive disabilities who face unfamiliar and large spaces cannot easily locate specific areas of the exhibition by using color or text cues; multi-lingual signs or abstract symbols may cause confusion; too much light or too little light may interfere with visual perception; too many exhibits may lead to visual information overload, which may cause cognitive processing difficulties; language and symbols are not well understood, e.g., metaphors, academic language, or professional terminology in the exhibition cannot be easily understood; and the interactivity of the exhibits is too demanding, e.g., more complicated operation requirements or quick response interactive experiences may lead to frustration. "Control of time and pace", in which P8 puts forward its point of view: people with cognitive disabilities may have difficulty in perceiving the passage of time, which may lead them to stay too long in front of some exhibits or hastily skip others; on the other hand, if the information of the exhibition is delivered too fast (such as dynamic multimedia On the other hand, if the information in an exhibition is delivered too quickly (such as dynamic multimedia displays or rapid explanations), people with cognitive disabilities may have difficulty keeping up with the pace, leading to anxiety or abandonment of understanding; they may not be able to adhere to the traditional continuous visiting mode and need to take multiple breaks within a short period, and they need personalized pacing, which may require them to spend more time in front of some exhibits while skipping over exhibits they are not interested in instead of passively following the guided tour timeline.

Digital storytelling design suggestions: Effective improvement through digital storytelling design, reasonable solution to the complexity of information and understanding of the obstacles, to make up for the lack of emotional resonance, and to properly deal with environmental perception and adaptation, the obstacles encountered by cognitively impaired people and their aspirations are the new development point of digital storytelling design.

4.4 Expected Outputs and Potential Opportunities

Expected Outputs.

1. Enhancing the museum experience for people with cognitive disabilities

Through digital narrative design, the experience of people with cognitive disabilities during museum visits can be significantly improved, including increased ease of access to information, depth of understanding of exhibits, as well as increased sense of participation and self-confidence. In particular, the combination of multi-sensory interaction, virtual reality (VR), and augmented reality (AR) technologies can effectively reduce barriers to information comprehension and help people with cognitive disabilities participate more deeply in cultural and educational activities.

2. Exemplary cases of digital transformation in museums

This study provides a practical framework for integrating digital technologies into museum design, showing how to create more inclusive and pervasive cultural and educational spaces by combining innovations such as human-computer interaction (HCI), multi-sensory interaction, and virtual technologies. These experiences can be adopted by other cultural institutions to promote the overall digital upgrade of the industry.

3. Data-driven design improvement

By analyzing the behavioral data and demanding feedback from people with cognitive disabilities, the research results will provide an important basis for museums to formulate future digital narrative strategies and optimize user experience. At the same time, it also lays the foundation for museums to develop personalized services (such as exclusive guided tours or customized educational content).

Potential Future Opportunities.

1. Interdisciplinary collaboration and technological innovation

Research has shown that the needs of people with cognitive disabilities provide a special scenario for technological innovation. This field could further stimulate cross-border collaboration between disciplines such as computer science, design, psychology, sociology, and museology. For example, optimizing information push through artificial intelligence algorithms or enhancing the immersion of exhibitions through brain-computer interface technology.

2. Expansion of Services for Diverse Social Groups

The application of digital narratives is not only limited to people with cognitive disabilities but can also be extended to other special groups such as the elderly, children, and foreign language visitors. The research results can provide a more comprehensive service model for museums to meet the needs of diversified social groups and enhance the public and inclusive nature of cultural facilities.

3. Extension in Education and Rehabilitation

The findings and design ideas of this study can also be useful in the fields of education and rehabilitation. For example, applying digital narrative technology to the rehabilitation training of cognitively impaired patients or special education programs not only helps to enrich the learning style but also may improve the learning effect.

Implications for Research.

1. Practical implications of inclusive design

The study provides a real-world example of inclusive design, showing how technological and design innovations can be used to eliminate inequities faced by socially challenged groups and enhance the public value and social responsibility of cultural institutions.

2. Promoting the redefinition of the role of museums

While traditional museums are often seen as passive spaces for knowledge transfer, the introduction of digital narrative technologies has transformed museums into active places of cultural interaction. Through this transformation, museums can better fulfill their role as a platform for public education and cultural dissemination.

3. Stimulating society's attention to cognitively impaired groups

The wide dissemination of the study will help raise public awareness of the needs of people with cognitive disabilities, prompting society to provide supportive services for this group in more scenarios, and promoting fairness and inclusiveness in society as a whole.

In conclusion, this study not only has direct practical significance for the optimization of the museum experience for people with cognitive disabilities but also provides important inspiration for the digital transformation of cultural institutions and the design of social inclusiveness, as well as a direction for future interdisciplinary research and technological innovation.

5   Concluding Remarks

Digital storytelling design suggestions: Effective improvement through digital storytelling design, reasonable solution to the complexity of information and understanding of the obstacles, to make up for the lack of emotional resonance, and to properly deal with environmental perception and adaptation, the obstacles encountered by cognitively impaired people and their aspirations are the new development point of digital storytelling design.

This study aims to contribute to two research fields. Contribution to the field of accessible design: In the field of accessible design, design often lacks sufficient relevance and comprehensiveness for people with cognitive disabilities, a highly diverse group. This study will deeply analyze the unique needs of people with cognitive disabilities in terms of information perception, comprehension, and memory, and propose a series of innovative design strategies to better meet their experiential needs in the museum environment. For example, through careful study of different types of cognitive disabilities (e.g., memory loss, distraction, language comprehension difficulties, etc.), a guiding signage system that can adapt to a variety of cognitive conditions will be designed. These signs will not only be visually more eye-catching and concise, but will also combine graphics, symbols, and short, easy-to-understand text to convey information in a variety of ways, helping people with cognitive disabilities find their way around and understand and exhibit information more easily. This innovation in design strategy will break the monolithic pattern of traditional design, encourage full consideration of cognitive diversity in accessible design, and make the design more relevant to the actual needs of people with different cognitive abilities.

Deepening the exhibition mechanism and design strategy of storytelling: Storytelling has always been an important means of conveying information and cultural connotations in museum exhibitions, but when targeting people with cognitive disabilities, existing storytelling methods often need to be further optimized and expanded. This study will explore how to adjust and improve the exhibition mechanism of storytelling according to the cognitive characteristics of people with cognitive disabilities.

For example, in the selection of story content, more attention is paid to the simplicity, coherence, and emotional resonance of stories. Complex plots and excessive details are avoided, and themes that are relevant to the life experiences of people with cognitive disabilities and easy to understand are selected to enhance their sense of immersion and interest in the stories. In terms of storytelling, a multi-sensory approach is used, adding elements such as tactile displays and interactive experiences in addition to traditional textual explanations and audio guides. For example, for a historical artifact, a touch model related to it can be made so that people with cognitive disabilities can feel the shape and texture of the artifact through touch, while at the same time, together with a simple audio explanation, the story behind the artifact can be told, so that they can understand the historical value and cultural significance of the exhibits from multiple perspectives. Through these in-depth studies and practices, museums are provided with richer and more effective storytelling strategies in exhibition design for people with cognitive disabilities.

This study has some limitations in using storytelling strategies to enhance the museum tourism experience for people with cognitive disabilities, and it also clarifies the direction for subsequent research.

First, we describe sample and methodological limitations and improvements: The sample selection was limited and did not comprehensively cover people with cognitive disabilities with different demographic characteristics, and geographic and cultural backgrounds, thus affecting the generalizability of the study. Meanwhile, although the qualitative study of thematic analysis is applicable, the sample size is small and susceptible to subjective bias of the researchers. In the future, the diversity of the sample should be expanded to cover cognitively impaired people of all ages, geographical and cultural backgrounds, and different occupations. Comprehensive observation methods should be used to record their visiting behaviors; questionnaires should be used to collect extensive feedback; and experimental methods should be used to accurately analyze the effects of the strategy. Furthermore, focusing only on the current storytelling strategy, the interactive design strategy is not sufficiently explored. In the future, interactive prototypes can be developed and tested in different scenarios for various user groups to clarify the applicability and effectiveness of the strategy in reality and promote the development of human-computer interaction and design practice.

Acknowledgments. We are grateful to all the participants of this study.

Disclosure of Interests. None.

References

1. Salecha, R.G.: Server-Based Curator for Museums: Wireless Communication—A Boon to Mankind Design and Implementation of the Assistive Listening Devices. LAP Lambert Academic Publishing, Koln, Germany (2012)
2. Huang, H.-Y., Liem, C.C.S.: Social inclusion in curated contexts: insights from museum practices. In: Proceedings of the 2022 ACM Conference on Fairness, Accountability, and Transparency (FAccT'22), pp. 300–309. Association for Computing Machinery, New York, NY, USA (2022). https://doi.org/10.1145/3531146.3533095
3. Mueller, J.P.: Accessibility for Everybody: Understanding the Section 508 Accessibility Requirements. Apress, New York, USA (2003)
4. Chu, S., Garcia, B., Quance, T., Geraci, L., Woltering, S., Quek, F.: Understanding storytelling as a design framework for cognitive support technologies for older adults. In: Proceedings of the International Symposium on Interactive Technology and Ageing Populations (ITAP 2016),

pp. 24–33. Association for Computing Machinery, New York, NY, USA (2016). https://doi.org/10.1145/2996267.2996270

5. Chittaro, L., Zuliani, F.: Exploring audio storytelling in mobile exergames to affect the perception of physical exercise. In: Proceedings of the 7th International Conference on Pervasive Computing Technologies for Healthcare (Pervasive Health 2013), pp. 1–8. ICST, Brussels, Belgium (2013). https://doi.org/10.4108/icst.pervasivehealth.2013.252016

6. Burova, A., et al.: Promoting local culture and enriching airport experiences through interactive storytelling. In: Proceedings of the 18th International Conference on Mobile and Ubiquitous Multimedia (MUM 2019), pp. 1–7. Association for Computing Machinery, New York, NY, USA (2019). https://doi.org/10.1145/3365610.3365640

7. Chowdhury, S.: Pintail: a travel companion for guided storytelling. Master's thesis, Massachusetts Institute of Technology, Cambridge, MA (2018)

8. Smith, J.: Digital storytelling in the classroom: exploring the impact on student engagement. J. Educ. Technol. **35**(4), 45–60 (2022). https://doi.org/10.1016/j.jedtech.2022.01.004

9. Norman, D.A.: Affordance, conventions, and design. Interactions **6**(3), 38–43 (1999). https://doi.org/10.1145/301153.301168

10. Heath, C., Lehn, D.V., Osborne, J.: Interaction and interactives: collaboration and participation with computer-based exhibits. Public Underst. Sci. **14**(1), 91–101 (2005). https://doi.org/10.1177/0963662505047343

11. Li, X., Liao, Y., Liu, Q.: AI-assisted learning: exploring the impact of digital assistants on user performance. In: Proceedings of the 2020 ACM Conference on Human Factors in Computing Systems (CHI'20), pp. 1234–1243. ACM, New York, NY, USA (2020). https://doi.org/10.1145/3313831.3376841

12. Hurst, A.: An accessible solution to unlock museums. Commun. ACM **67**(11), 92 (2024). https://doi.org/10.1145/3656371

13. Mast, D., Broekens, J., de Vries, S.I., Verbeek, F.J.: Participation patterns of interactive playful museum exhibits: evaluating the participant journey map through situated observations. In: Proceedings of the 2023 ACM Designing Interactive Systems Conference (DIS' 23), pp. 1861–1885. Association for Computing Machinery, New York, NY, USA, July 2023. https://doi.org/10.1145/3563657.3595985

14. Huang, Y., Zhou, Y., Zhao, H., Fang, L., Riedel, T., Beigl, M.: ExTea: an evolutionary algorithm-based approach for enhancing explainability in time-series models. In: Machine Learning and Knowledge Discovery in Databases. Applied Data Science Track, pp. 429–446 (2023). https://doi.org/10.1007/978-3-031-70381-2_27

15. Wang, L., Zhang, X.: Machine learning algorithms for big data. J. Digit. Comput. **30**(2), 123–135 (2023). https://www.jdcjournal.com/learningalgorithms

16. Williams, K., Zhou, L.: Virtual Reality Exploration in Space. VR Studios (2022). https://www.vrspaceexploration.com

17. Jain, R.P., Satriadi, K.A., Drogemuller, A., Smith, R., Cunningham, A.: Once upon a data story: a preliminary design space for immersive data storytelling. In: Companion Proceedings of the 2024 Conference on Interactive Surfaces and Spaces (ISS Companion' 24), pp. 63–68. Association for Computing Machinery, New York, NY, USA (2024). https://doi.org/10.1145/3696762.3698054

18. Hocine, N., Sehaba, K.: A systematic review of online personalized systems for the autonomous learning of people with cognitive disabilities. Hum.-Comput. Interact. **39**(3–4), 174–205 (2023). https://doi.org/10.1080/07370024.2023.2242364

19. Chen, Y., Liu, Z.: Visual Recognition Systems for Interactive Museum Exhibits. Museum Technologies Research Group (2021). https://www.museumtechresearch.com/visualrecognition

20. Mathur, N., Dhodapkar, K., Zubatiy, T., Li, J., Jones, B., Mynatt, E.: A collaborative approach to support medication management in older adults with mild cognitive impairment using Conversational Assistants (CAs). In: Proceedings of the 24th International ACM SIGACCESS Conference on Computers and Accessibility (ASSETS' 22), Article 42, pp. 1–14. Association for Computing Machinery, New York, NY, USA (2022). https://doi.org/10.1145/3517428.3544830

21. Huang, Y.-C., Huang, T.-S.: A study of green natural learning method at the improvement of cognitive function: take the elderly with mild dementia as an example. In: Proceedings of the 2017 International Conference on Deep Learning Technologies (ICDLT' 17), pp. 28–35. Association for Computing Machinery, New York, NY, USA (2017). https://doi.org/10.1145/3094243.3094253

22. Johnson, M., Lee, R.: Understanding emotional needs in virtual assistants. In: Proceedings of the ACM Conference on Affective Computing, San Francisco, CA, USA, pp. 45–56. ACM (2018). https://www.acmaffective2018.com/emotional-needs

23. Davis, K., Nguyen, P.: Identifying Social Needs in Low-Income Communities. Social Policy Institute (2020). https://www.socialpolicyinstitute.com/social-needs-report

24. Terry, G., Hayfield, N., Clarke, V., Braun, V.: Thematic analysis. In: The SAGE Handbook of Qualitative Research in Psychology, 2nd edn. SAGE (2017)

25. Braun, V., Clarke, V.: Qualitative research in psychology using thematic analysis in psychology. Qual. Res. Psychol. **3**(2), 77–101 (2006)

Collaborative Marketing Platforms in Tourism: Acceptance Factors and Impact on Consumer Behaviour

Célia M. Q. Ramos[1]([✉]) [iD], Teresa Costa[2] [iD], Maria de Lurdes Calisto[3] [iD], and Ana Teresa Machado[4] [iD]

[1] CinTurs and ESGHT – Universidade do Algarve, Faro, Portugal
cmramos@ualg.pt
[2] Escola Superior de Ciências Empresariais, Instituto Politécnico de Setúbal, Setúbal, Portugal
teresa.costa@esce.ips.pt
[3] CiTUR and Escola Superior de Hotelaria e Turismo do Estoril, Estoril, Portugal
Lurdes.Calisto@eshte.pt
[4] Escola Superior de Comunicação Social, Instituto Politécnico de Lisboa, Lisboa, Portugal
amachado@escs.ipl.pt

Abstract. Collaborative marketing on digital platforms has revolutionised business-to-business (B2B), business-to-consumer (B2C), and consumer-to-consumer (C2C) interactions, creating new opportunities for value co-creation and strategic partnerships. This study explores the key factors influencing the adoption of collaborative marketing platforms in the tourism sector and their impact on consumer behaviour. Grounded in the Unified Theory of Acceptance and Use of Technology (UTAUT2) and the Technology Acceptance Model (TAM), the research assesses performance expectancy, effort expectancy, social influence, facilitating conditions, compatibility with needs, data privacy, trust and security, innovation and differentiation, and expected satisfaction as determinants of platform adoption. A partial least squares structural equation model (PLS-SEM) was applied to survey data. Findings reveal that compatibility with needs, effort expectancy, and expected satisfaction significantly influence behavioural intention to adopt these platforms. Interestingly, while data privacy and trust remain critical concerns, they did not exhibit statistically significant direct effects on adoption. The study underscores the importance of user-centric design, seamless workflow integration, and perceived value in driving platform adoption. These insights offer practical guidance for developers and marketers seeking to optimise collaborative marketing strategies in the digital tourism landscape.

Keywords: Collaborative Marketing · Digital Platforms · Tourism · Technology Adoption · UTAUT2 · PLS-SEM

© The Author(s), under exclusive license to Springer Nature Switzerland AG 2026
M. Antona and C. Stephanidis (Eds.): HCII 2025, LNCS 16335, pp. 149–168, 2026.
https://doi.org/10.1007/978-3-032-12781-5_10

1   Introduction

Collaborative marketing, in its B2B (business-to-business), B2C (business-to-consumer) and C2C (consumer-to-consumer) aspects, has grown significantly due to the advancement of digital platforms. These platforms facilitate direct interaction between companies and consumers, enabling value co-creation, strategic partnerships and peer-to-peer exchanges. In the B2B context, tools like LinkedIn and specialised marketplaces allow companies to share resources and knowledge, increasing operational efficiency [1]. In B2C, social media and evaluation applications encourage consumer participation in brand building, strengthening trust and engagement [2].

The C2C model, driven by platforms such as eBay and Facebook Marketplace, democratises commerce, allowing consumers to trade with each other autonomously. Studies highlight that trust and digital reputation are critical factors for the success of these transactions [3, 4]. Furthermore, recommendation algorithms and evaluation systems optimise the correspondence between supply and demand, reducing information asymmetries [5]. Thus, digital platforms expand the scope of collaborative marketing and redefine market dynamics.

In addition to collaborative marketplaces, social networks and co-creation tools have become essential elements for business success in the digital age. Platforms like Instagram, TikTok and LinkedIn allow brands to develop highly targeted marketing strategies, increasing consumer engagement and driving sales [1]. Collaborative marketplaces, such as Shopify and Mercado Livre, democratise access to e-commerce, enabling small entrepreneurs to compete on a global scale [6] and facilitating peer-to-peer transactions, expanding access to niche markets and reducing barriers to entry [7] Furthermore, co-creation tools, such as crowdsourcing platforms and digital design thinking, facilitate open innovation by allowing consumers to participate actively in developing products and services [8]. The synergy between these tools is redefining relationships between companies and consumers. Recent studies highlight that co-creation in digital environments generates greater perceived value and customer loyalty [9]. Collaborative marketplaces, in turn, depend on advanced reputation systems and artificial intelligence to ensure secure and personalised transactions [10]. In parallel, social networks function as dynamic feedback channels, allowing companies to quickly adapt their strategies based on real-time data [11]. This combination of technologies creates a more agile, user-centric business ecosystem geared toward continuous innovation.

Understanding the factors determining the acceptance and effectiveness of digital collaborative marketing platforms is crucial to maximising their strategic potential. Recent research highlights that adopting these technologies depends not only on perceived usefulness, but also on elements such as trust, ease of use and alignment with user needs [12]. Models based on the UTAUT2 reveal that user experience and social value generated are key predictors of engagement [1]. Furthermore, contextual factors, such as organisational culture in B2B or digital habits in B2C/C2C, significantly moderate the results [13]. The absence of this understanding can lead to misdirected investments and underutilisation of platforms.

The growing adoption of digital platforms for collaborative marketing (B2B, B2C and C2C) has redefined the interaction dynamics between companies and consumers, creating new opportunities and strategic challenges. This study's main objective is to examine the key factors that affect the adoption of these online platforms and evaluate how users behave in relation to their expectations for their level of satisfaction. As the digital environment evolves, it becomes essential to understand the factors that drive or inhibit the adoption of these tools, both by organisations and end users, filling gaps identified in the current literature [1].

To guide this investigation, two central research questions are proposed: (1) What factors influence the adoption of collaborative platforms by companies and consumers? and (2) How is this adoption reflected in measurable changes in consumer behaviour through assessment of expected satisfaction? By examining dimensions such as perceived usefulness, ease of use, trust, innovation and differentiation and social influence, there are still disagreements about how emerging factors, such as algorithmic trust and data privacy, affect this process [14]. This study seeks to provide valuable insights for platform managers and developers and contribute to the academic literature on technology and digital marketing. Understanding these elements is essential to optimising the effectiveness of collaborative marketing strategies in the digital age.

2 Collaborative Marketing and Acceptance Factors in Tourism

2.1 Collaborative Marketing

Collaborative marketing is a strategy in which two or more businesses, or even individuals, join forces to jointly promote a product, service, or cause, mutually benefiting from shared resources, audiences, and expertise. This approach is based on cooperation rather than competition, allowing participants to achieve common goals more efficiently. According to Hunt and Morgan [15], collaborative marketing is rooted in the theory of comparative advantage, where strategic partnerships create superior value for all parties involved.

Initially, collaborative marketing was predominantly offline, taking the form of co-branded events, shared sponsorships, or cross-promotions in retail spaces. With the advent of the internet and social media, this strategy migrated to the digital environment, gaining greater scale and precision. Platforms like Instagram, TikTok, and LinkedIn facilitate partnerships between brands and influencers, while data analytics tools enable real-time impact measurement. Kumar et al. [2] state that digitalisation has transformed collaborative marketing, making it more accessible, measurable, and global.

Collaborative marketing has emerged as a key strategy in today's business landscape, primarily due to its ability to expand reach, optimise resources, and strengthen audience engagement. In an increasingly competitive and digitised market, partnerships between brands, influencers, and even consumers enable the creation of more authentic and impactful campaigns. This approach reduces operational costs and enhances the credibility of the brands involved, as association with trusted partners reinforces consumers' perception of value [16]. Furthermore, collaborative marketing fosters continuous innovation, as exchanging knowledge and resources among participants leads to more creative and market-aligned solutions [17].

Another crucial aspect of collaborative marketing is its role in audience engagement and community-building around brands. By joining forces, businesses can access new consumer segments and foster more meaningful interactions, particularly on digital platforms. Studies show that collaborative campaigns generate stronger emotional engagement and higher conversion rates, as they combine the trust and affinity of different audiences [18]. This strategy also has proven effective in adapting to rapid market changes, since collaboration enables agile responses to trends and crises when brands partner to launch impactful social and commercial initiatives [19].

Beyond these advantages, collaborative marketing drives audience engagement, since joint campaigns generate greater interaction by combining distinct communities. Open innovation is another significant benefit, as collaboration between brands or between brands and consumers enables the co-creation of products and campaigns better aligned with market needs. Additionally, reduced operational and marketing costs are critical, especially for small and medium-sized enterprises (SMES), which can share production, distribution, and promotional expenses. According to Gummesson [20] in his study on relational marketing, strategic partnerships not only optimise resources but also accelerate market adaptation, making organisations more agile and competitive.

Collaborative marketing significantly boosts audience engagement, as partnership-driven campaigns merge different follower bases, amplifying reach and interaction. Research shows that collaborations between brands and digital influencers generate up to 50% higher engagement rates than standalone campaigns [21]. Furthermore, the authenticity of partnerships strengthens emotional connections with audiences, as demonstrated by Murtas et al. [18] in analyses of social media co-branding.

Developing a collaborative marketing platform with advanced features could revolutionise tourism management and promotion, fostering stakeholder synergies and enhancing visitor experiences. For example, a collaborative tourism offerings map enables hotels, guides, and restaurants to highlight their offerings and create integrated packages, boosting destination appeal [22]. An automated commission management system ensures transparent transactions between partners in joint sales, incentivising cooperation and reducing conflicts [23, 24]. A shared multimedia repository (photos, videos, text) accessible to accredited partners promotes consistent destination storytelling, enriching marketing campaigns [25]. A campaign co-creation tool allows DMOS, agencies, local suppliers, residents, and tourists to collaborate on authentic, engaging strategies [26]. A real-time tourism dashboard tracks visitor flows, preferences, and campaign performance, enabling rapid adjustments (e.g., redirecting promotions to underutilised attractions) [27]. Finally, a verified review system, where only tourists who used a service can leave feedback, enhances recommendation credibility [28]. These features could transform the platform into a digital tourism ecosystem, integrating technology, collaboration, and data intelligence to drive sustainable sector growth.

Investigating the factors influencing the acceptance and adoption of collaborative marketing platforms is critical. As highlighted by Ertz and Sarigöllü [29] and Fleury and Chaniaud [30], understanding these dynamics helps optimise engagement strategies, increase user uptake, and maximise the impact of such tools in the competitive digital landscape.

2.2 Acceptance of Collaborative Online Marketing Platforms

The acceptance of collaborative online marketing platforms has been extensively studied based on established technology adoption models such as TAM and UTAUT. Research highlights that perceived usefulness and ease of use [31, 32] are critical factors for adopting these platforms, particularly in collaborative business contexts [29]. Furthermore, studies applied to tourism and digital marketing demonstrate that integrating features such as automated partnership management and content co-creation tools significantly enhances users' perceived value [26].

Social influence and organisational support also emerge as key determinants, as evidenced by research adapting UTAUT2 for B2B environments [33]. These findings reinforce the need to go beyond traditional models by integrating specific dimensions of collaborative marketing, such as commission transparency and review validation [24].

Recent advances highlight the importance of real-time indicators and personalisation as facilitators of acceptance. Leal et al. [23] demonstrate that dynamic dashboards with performance metrics increase continued usage intention, while Amorim et al. [22] emphasise the role of system interoperability. However, gaps remain in understanding how cultural and sectoral factors moderate adoption, suggesting directions for future research. In summary, current literature converges on the idea that collaborative platforms require hybrid models, combining TAM/UTAUT with relational and ecosystem variables [30].

Performance Expectancy (PE). Performance expectancy constitutes a decisive factor in adopting collaborative marketing platforms, reflecting users' belief that these tools will significantly improve their marketing campaign results [22, 33]. Marketing professionals value these platforms' ability to optimise processes, increase return on investment, and provide clear performance metrics - factors that justify their use over traditional methods.

Furthermore, the expectation that these platforms will enhance collaborative efficiency between teams and commercial partners emerges as another critical adoption motivator [26, 34]. The potential to simplify complex workflows, share resources in real-time, and coordinate strategies in an integrated manner is perceived as a decisive competitive advantage in today's digital marketing landscape, where agility and stakeholder coordination are crucial for success. In this context, the following hypothesis was formulated:

H_1: Performance expectancy positively influences the intention to use collaborative marketing platforms.

Effort Expectancy (EE). Effort expectancy represents a crucial factor in the initial adoption of collaborative marketing platforms, reflecting users' perceptions of the system's ease of learning and use [31, 35]. When users believe the platform has an intuitive, user-friendly interface requiring minimal training for basic operations and low cognitive effort, initial adoption barriers are significantly reduced. This positive perception is directly linked to Davis's [31] original theory of perceived ease of use, adapted to the contemporary context of digital collaborative tools.

Recent studies show that platforms with low perceived effort requirements achieve up to 40% higher adoption rates than complex solutions [36]. Interface simplicity and shallow learning curves are fundamental in collaborative environments where multiple stakeholders with varying digital literacy levels must interact with the system. When users perceive they can quickly master basic functionalities without mental overload, their willingness to try and adopt the platform increases substantially. In this context, the following hypothesis was formulated:

H_2: Effort expectancy positively influences the intention to use collaborative marketing platforms.

Social Influence (SI). Social influence factors significantly impact the adoption of collaborative marketing platforms, particularly in sectors where technological trends and professional networks play crucial roles [9]. When respected field professionals recommend a platform [37] or when there is a clear perception that one's professional network values users of these tools [38], adoption rates tend to accelerate. This dynamic is especially relevant in digital marketing contexts, where reputation and peer recognition are often associated with technological innovation adoption.

Moreover, perceptions of sector-wide trends toward collaborative platforms and the reputation of the solution's development team also strongly influence adoption decisions [37]. In competitive environments, professionals and companies seek operational efficiency and alignment with field best practices. Combining these social factors creates network effects that can accelerate technology diffusion, establishing it as a sector standard. In this context, the following hypothesis was formulated:

H_3: Social influence positively influences the intention to use collaborative marketing platforms.

Facilitating Conditions (FC). Users' perceptions of available support resources are fundamental in reducing uncertainty during collaborative marketing platform adoption [39]. Expectations that the development team will provide adequate training and clear tutorials [40] increase user confidence in mastering the platform, especially in collaborative contexts requiring multi-stakeholder coordination. This anticipation of promised support and planned resources is particularly relevant for complex platforms where learning curves may present significant obstacles.

Recent studies highlight that technological compatibility and ongoing support are decisive for successful platform adoption [35]. When users perceive seamless integration with existing workflows and access to responsive technical support, their willingness to adopt the technology increases considerably [36]. These conditions are especially critical in digital marketing environments where cross-team coordination and system interoperability are essential for operational success. In this context, the following hypothesis was formulated:

H_4: Facilitating conditions positively influence the intention to use collaborative marketing platforms.

Compatibility with Needs (CN). The compatibility between collaborative marketing platforms and existing tools/processes is a determining factor for successful adoption.

When professionals perceive seamless integration with current systems (like Google Analytics and CRM) and adaptation to established workflows, resistance to change decreases significantly [24]. This alignment perception is crucial as it reduces extensive training needs and minimises daily operation disruptions. Moreover, when functionalities specifically address user needs, the platform is viewed not as another management burden but as a genuine value-adding solution [41].

The vision of how the platform can be implemented organisation-wide also strongly influences adoption decisions. Studies show professionals are more likely to embrace new technologies when they can visualise practical applications within their organisational context [42]. This perceived compatibility with collective needs and integration with established systems creates an adoption-friendly environment where platforms are seen as natural extensions rather than disruptive solutions requiring radical workflow changes. In this context, the following hypothesis was formulated:

H_5: Compatibility with needs positively influences the intention to use collaborative marketing platforms.

Data Privacy (DP). Personal and professional data protection concerns constitute a critical barrier to adopting collaborative marketing platforms [43]. When users lack confidence that a platform ensures adequate security for storing and sharing sensitive information [44], their willingness to adopt the technology decreases significantly. This apprehension is particularly relevant in collaborative contexts where multiple stakeholders access the same data, increasing potential vulnerabilities. Compliance with regulations like GDPR (General Data Protection Regulation) is not just a legal requirement but also a decisive factor in building user trust perception [38].

Studies show that perceived privacy risks can reduce digital platform usage intention by up to 35% [44]. Marketing professionals demand explicit guarantees about encryption policies, access controls, and audit procedures before sharing client data or business strategies. When platforms effectively communicate their security measures and regulatory compliance [38], they mitigate concerns and transform data privacy into a competitive advantage. In this context, the following hypotheses were formulated:

H_6: Data privacy positively influences the intention to use collaborative marketing platforms.
H_7: Data privacy positively influences the security perception and trust of collaborative marketing platforms.

Platform Trust and Security (TS). Trust and security are fundamental pillars for adopting collaborative marketing platforms, especially when they involve sharing sensitive campaign and client data. Recent studies emphasise that users require robust guarantees about a platform's ability to protect critical information from unauthorised access and system failures [45]. This trust is built through tangible mechanisms like end-to-end encryption, multi-factor authentication, and compliance with international security standards (e.g., ISO 27001), collectively reinforcing system reliability perceptions. Perceived security becomes crucial in collaborative ecosystems where multiple parties access and manipulate the same datasets, exponentially increasing vulnerability risks [46].

Beyond technical aspects, institutional trust in the organisation behind the platform plays an equally vital role in adoption decisions. Research demonstrates that transparent security policies, data protection track records, and independent certifications significantly increase users' willingness to share strategic information [45]. When marketing professionals recognise that a platform implements proactive security protocols and maintains a proven record of data protection, their trust in the solution becomes a decisive adoption factor [46]. This dimension grows even more critical in stringent regulatory contexts like GDPR, where compliance is not just a legal requirement but a central element in building user trust relationships. In this context, the following hypothesis was formulated:

H_8: Platform trust and security positively influence the intention to use collaborative marketing platforms.

Innovation and Differentiation (ID). The perception of innovation and differentiation is crucial for attracting early adopters to collaborative marketing platforms. When users recognise that a solution offers unique capabilities superior to existing market alternatives [47], their willingness to trial the technology increases significantly. This competitive advantage expectation is particularly relevant for marketing professionals seeking cutting-edge tools featuring predictive AI analytics, multi-channel campaign automation, or blockchain-secured transactions [48]. The mere promise of innovative capabilities can generate enthusiasm and motivate initial experimentation, especially among technological segments.

Some authors considered that perceived technological differentiation can accelerate early adopter adoption processes by up to 50% [49]. Innovative professionals value platforms that integrate emerging technologies and apply them meaningfully to solve specific collaborative marketing challenges. When users identify that proposed functionalities address unmet needs in their current workflows and represent tangible advances over conventional solutions [48], their willingness to overcome initial learning curves and advocate organisational adoption increases proportionally. In this context, the following hypotheses were formulated:

H_9: Innovation and differentiation positively influence trust and security in collaborative marketing platforms.
H_{10}: Innovation and differentiation positively influence the intention to use collaborative marketing platforms.

Expected Satisfaction (ES). Expected satisfaction determines user retention on collaborative marketing platforms, reflecting users' belief that the solution will deliver tangible work benefits. When professionals believe a platform will outperform existing alternatives and become a differentiator in their activities [44], the likelihood of adoption and continued use increases significantly. Positive anticipation proves particularly relevant when users envision how advertised functionalities will solve specific workflow problems, creating value expectations that motivate initial experimentation and long-term commitment [50].

Moreover, confidence in post-launch support and the platform's ability to deliver promised functionality reinforces expected satisfaction. Studies demonstrate that users are more willing to overcome initial adaptation challenges when they perceive clear alignment between platform capabilities and their professional needs [44]. Expected satisfaction thus functions as a psychological mechanism that facilitates initial adoption and establishes foundations for loyalty, especially when actual user experience confirms or exceeds these positive expectations [50]. In this context, the following hypothesis was formulated:

H_{11}: Expected satisfaction positively influences the intention to use collaborative marketing platforms.

Behaviour Intention (BI). Recent research highlights that future usage intention is strongly influenced by platform claim credibility and perceived compatibility with professional needs [13, 16]. When users foresee how solutions might optimise workflows and generate competitive advantages, their willingness to allocate resources (time, data, and eventually money) increases proportionally [51]. This positive intention predicts initial adoption and is an essential precursor for long-term retention, especially when experience confirms expectations created during pre-launch phases. Considering the above hypotheses, the research model examined in this study is presented in Fig. 1.

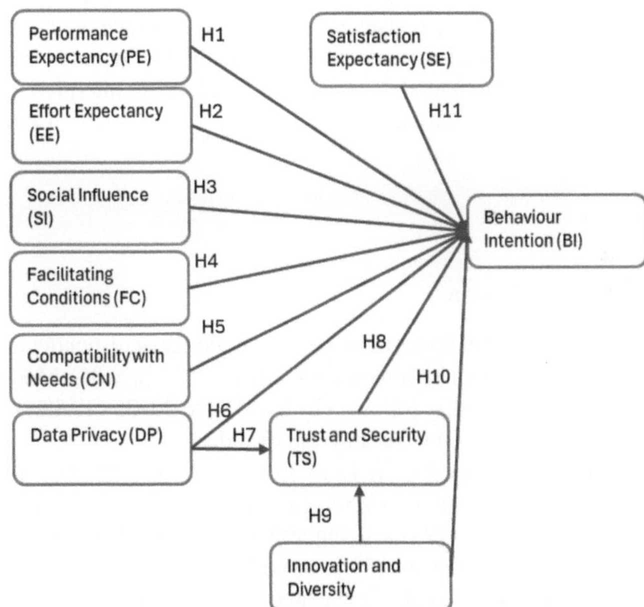

Fig. 1. Marketing Collaboration Acceptance Model (MCAM).

Future usage intention represents a critical indicator of collaborative marketing platforms' potential success, reflecting users' concrete predisposition to adopt the solution post-launch. When professionals demonstrate immediate willingness to trial the platform and migrate portions of their operations to the new system [13], this suggests a genuine perception of potential value. This behavioural intention proves particularly relevant in competitive contexts where willingness to recommend platforms to colleagues can significantly accelerate market diffusion [51]. Openness to considering paid subscriptions, contingent on functional promise fulfilment, further indicates advanced levels of potential solution commitment.

3 Methodology

Following the definition of the research hypotheses, the review of relevant literature, and the clarification of the research problem, the study's methodology was structured around these key stages: 1) designing the survey; 2) gathering data; 3) filtering and encoding the collected data; 4) choosing appropriate data analysis methods and techniques; and 5) interpreting the findings.

The survey was conducted in April 2025, yielding 93 valid responses. The target sample consisted of professionals and undergraduate and graduate students of Marketing or Tourism studying their perception of the effects that the acceptance and use of Collaborative Marketing platforms could have on the business and professionals in the area, selected through convenience sampling, a non-probabilistic sampling method approach where participants are chosen based on their willingness and ease of access. Once the data were collected, responses were coded to facilitate analysis. Descriptive statistics were used to profile the sample, while a structural equation model (SEM) was employed to assess the research model. Finally, the results were interpreted, conclusions were drawn, and the study's limitations and potential future research directions were discussed.

4 Results

4.1 Sample Characterisation

The survey sample consisted of 93 participants. The majority of respondents were female (64.4%, $n = 58$), while male participants accounted for 37.6% ($n = 35$). Most respondents were aged 18–25 (64.5%, $n = 60$), followed by those aged 26–35 (25.8%, $n = 24$). Only a small proportion (9.7%, $n = 9$) were 36 years or older.

The participants' ages ranged from 19 to 59 years, with an average (mean) age of 26.05 years and a standard deviation of 9.87 years, indicating moderate variability in age distribution. The minimum age (19 years) suggests that the sample primarily consisted of young adults, while the maximum age (59 years) reflects some representation from older age groups. However, the relatively low mean age (26.1) confirms that most respondents were in their early to mid-20s, aligning with the earlier finding that 63.8% of participants were aged 18–25. The standard deviation (9.9 years) indicates that while most responses clustered around the mean, there was a reasonable spread, with some respondents significantly younger or older than the average. This variation should be considered when interpreting results, as different age groups may have distinct perspectives or behaviours.

The highest level of education among participants was a bachelor's degree (64.5%, $n = 60$), while 16.1% ($n = 15$) had completed secondary education (high school). A smaller percentage held a master's degree (9.7%, $n = 9$), a PhD (6.5%, $n = 6$), or other qualifications (3.2%, $n = 3$).

Most respondents were students (64.5%, $n = 60$), while 35.5% ($n = 33$) were employed by someone else. The largest proportion of participants were from Algarve (41.9%, $n = 39$), followed by other locations (35.5%, $n = 33$), while Lisboa had 22.6% ($n = 21$).

The sample is predominantly female, young (18–25 years old), highly educated (bachelor's degree holders), and student-based, with a strong representation from Faro and other unspecified regions. This demographic profile suggests an academic and young-adult-oriented sample, which should be considered when analysing and generalising the findings.

4.2 Evaluation of the Research Measurement Model

Following the selection and coding of data, appropriate methods and techniques were identified for data analysis. The structural equation model (SEM) was selected to measure multidimensional and non-directly observable concepts, also known as constructs or latent variables [52]. As Gefen et al. [53] highlighted, SEM has become the standard approach for validating measurement instruments and testing relationships between theoretical constructs. The study specifically employed variance-based SEM, or partial least squares path modelling (PLS-SEM). This methodological choice is justified by its suitability for exploratory research phases, which do not require strict assumptions about data normality and demonstrate good performance even with smaller samples [54, 55].

Model validation followed a rigorous three-stage process. Initially, the measurement model was evaluated to ensure convergent validity using the average variance extracted (AVE) criterion. As Fornell and Larcker established [56], all AVE values must exceed 0.5 to confirm appropriate model convergence, as presented in Table 1.

Secondly, internal consistency was analysed through Cronbach's alpha (CA) and composite reliability (CR) values, the latter represented by Dillon-Goldstein's rho. The established parameters require CA values above 0.6 (with 0.7 being ideal), while CR values must surpass 0.7 (with 0.9 indicating excellent consistency), as referenced by Chin [54] and Ringle et al. [55].

Table 1 presents the research model results, showing that all AVE values meet the minimum 0.5 criterion as recommended by Henseler et al. [57]. Furthermore, the CA and CR values satisfactorily meet the established thresholds, confirming the model's statistical robustness. This rigorous methodological approach ensures the validity and reliability of the analysed constructs, providing a solid foundation for research inferences and conclusions.

In the third stage, the evaluation of discriminant validity allows for the examination of independence between latent and other variables. This analysis can be conducted in two ways: by observing cross-loadings, where indicators should have higher factor loadings on their respective latent variables compared to observed variables, or by applying the Fornell and Larcker criterion, which compares the square roots of the AVE (Average Variance Extracted) values of each latent variable with the Pearson correlations between

Table 1. Values of the Adjustment Quality of the Research Model.

	Cronbach's Alpha	Composite Reliability (rho_a)	Composite Reliability (rho_c)	Average Variance Extracted (AVE)
BI	0.906	0.909	0.941	0.841
CN	0.763	0.766	0.894	0.808
DP	0.948	0.957	0.975	0.951
EE	0.822	0.837	0.88	0.647
ES	0.887	0.891	0.922	0.747
FC	0.767	0.772	0.852	0.593
ID	0.841	0.857	0.895	0.682
SI	0.780	0.808	0.857	0.604
TS	0.871	0.875	0.921	0.795

them. According to this criterion, the square roots of the AVES must be greater than the correlations between the latent variables.

In the first method, the cross-loadings of observed variables on their latent variable are consistently higher than those on other latent variables. This indicates that the variables are more strongly associated with the construct they intend to measure, confirming the model's discriminant validity, as Chin [54] established.

In the second method, based on the data in Table 2, the variance captured by the AVE must exceed the variance shared between observed variables and other latent variables in the model. In practice, discriminant validity is confirmed when the square root of the AVE for each construct is greater than the correlation values between latent and observed variables [58]. As shown in Table 2, the research model demonstrates discriminant validity, as verified by the first method, since the square roots of the AVES (presented in the main diagonal) are higher than the correlations between latent variables, in line with the Fornell and Larcker criterion [59].

Once discriminant validity has been confirmed in the assessment of the measurement model (indicating that adjustments to the measurement model are complete), the next step is to evaluate the structural model.

4.3   Evaluation of the Structural Model

The assessment of the structural model begins by examining the Pearson's correlation coefficient (R2) for the endogenous latent variables. This study analysed two such variables: TS, with an R2 of 0.606, and BI, with an R2 of 0.752. These values indicate the proportion of variance in the endogenous variables that the structural model can explain [58].

A further consideration is the model's predictive capability, which is assessed using the Cohen indicator (f2), linked to effect size (Hair et al., 2014), presented in Table 3. The f2 evaluates the relative contribution of each construct to the model's explanatory power.

Table 2. Values of the Correlations Between the Latent Variables and the Square Roots of the AVE Values (On the Main Diagonal).

	BI	CN	DP	EE	ES	FC	ID	SI	TS
BI	**0.917**								
CN	0.741	**0.899**							
DP	0.168	0.071	**0.975**						
EE	0.610	0.533	0.395	**0.804**					
ES	0.700	0.479	0.318	0.466	**0.864**				
FC	0.618	0.527	0.392	0.726	0.540	**0.770**			
ID	0.594	0.367	0.519	0.415	0.713	0.597	**0.826**		
SI	0.556	0.403	0.323	0.419	0.723	0.598	0.606	**0.777**	
TS	0.288	0.129	0.693	0.345	0.440	0.432	0.663	0.337	**0.891**

Table 3. Indicators' Values of Effect Size.

	BI	TS
CN	0.383	
DP	0.041	0.423
EE	0.071	
ES	0.108	
FC	0.001	
ID	0.064	0.319
SI	0.000	
TS	0.001	

The evaluation of the structural model concludes with an examination of the individual path coefficients [58, 59]. This involves assessing each coefficient's sign, magnitude, and statistical significance, which should exceed 1.96 (for a two-tailed test at a 5% significance level) to be considered meaningful.

Further insight can be gained by analysing the model's direct effects. As presented in Table 4, the DP (Data Privacy), FC (Facilitating Conditions), ID (Innovation and Differentiation), SI (Social Influence) and TS (Platform Trust and Security) t-test value of 1.5125 suggests that the null hypothesis (H_0) should be accepted, indicating no significant direct effect on the Future Use Intention (BI). Similarly, the DP (Data Privacy), with t-test values below 1.96, also show no measurable impact on TS (Platform Trust and Security).

However, the CN (Compatibility with Needs), EE (Effort Expectancy), and ES (Expected Satisfaction) demonstrate a statistically significant effect on Future Use Intention (BI), ID (Innovation and Differentiation), and DP (Data Privacy) in TS (Platform Trust and Security).

This finding suggests that Marketing Collaborative platforms are more likely to be adopted, considering whether the compatibility characteristics meet marketers' needs and whether they perceive that professional satisfaction will increase using this type of platform.

Table 4. Direct Effects in the Structural Relationships Between the Latent Variables.

	Original sample (O)	Sample mean (M)	Standard deviation (STDEV)	T statistics (|O/STDEV|)	P values	Hypotheses
CN → BI	0.405	0.390	0.089	4.551	**0.000**	**Supported**
DP → BI	-0.148	-0.203	0.117	1.267	0.205	Not supported
DP → TS	0.477	0.574	0.167	2.865	**0.004**	**Supported**
EE → BI	0.211	0.203	0.098	2.157	**0.031**	**Supported**
ES → BI	0.290	0.295	0.099	2.918	**0.004**	**Supported**
FC → BI	0.031	0.054	0.098	0.313	0.754	Not supported
ID → BI	0.230	0.237	0.134	1.712	0.087	Not supported
ID → TS	0.415	0.347	0.158	2.623	**0.009**	**Supported**
SI → BI	-0.006	-0.005	0.097	0.059	0.953	Not supported
TS → BI	-0.026	0.017	0.152	0.169	0.866	Not supported

5 Discussion

The results confirmed that compatibility with user or organisational needs significantly influences adoption intentions. This aligns with the Diffusion of Innovations Theory [47], which emphasises that innovations are more readily adopted when they align with existing values, practices, and experiences. Recent empirical studies reinforce this premise: Abubakar and Al-Mamary [60] and Fan and Li [61] demonstrated that compatibility between platform features and users' functional or professional needs enhances behavioural intentions, particularly in educational and mobile learning contexts. In the marketing domain, such compatibility translates to alignment with branding, customer engagement, and workflow strategies, thus improving platform receptivity.

Effort expectancy—defined as the perceived ease of using a platform—was also shown to significantly influence adoption. As posited by UTAUT [32], lower effort expectations lead to higher acceptance likelihood. Empirical support was found in various sectors: Sengkalit and Khairal Abdullah [62] observed that user-friendly design strongly influenced technology adoption among Indonesian SMEs. Similarly, Fan and

Li [61] confirmed that ease of use directly enhances user attitudes and behavioural intentions in mobile learning environments. These findings underscore the importance of intuitive interface design and minimal cognitive load in driving collaborative marketing platform adoption.

Expected satisfaction emerged as a consistent predictor across B2B, B2C, and C2C contexts. In B2B, firms adopt platforms anticipating strategic gains such as customer insight and innovation [63, 64]. In B2C, satisfaction expectations are linked to customer loyalty and repurchase behaviour [65]. C2C platforms benefit from users' anticipated personal value and identity alignment [66]. This confirms that users and organizations adopt platforms not solely for functionality, but for the anticipated value experience.

Both innovation and differentiation (ID) and data privacy (DP) were validated as influential factors shaping perceptions of trust and security (TS)—critical precursors to platform engagement. Otieno [67] emphasized that privacy-by-design frameworks enhance user confidence in e-commerce systems, while Jones [68] argued that ethical AI innovation promotes transparency and mitigates consumer concerns. In technological ecosystems such as IoT finance, Wang [69] demonstrated how privacy-preserving analytics foster trust. These findings underscore that a dual focus on innovation and data protection is essential to cultivating user trust in collaborative marketing platforms.

Contrary to prior expectations, trust and security did not significantly affect the intention to adopt collaborative platforms. This deviates from the TAM [31] and UTAUT frameworks, which regard trust as foundational to technology acceptance. However, recent literature suggests a contextual shift: trust and privacy may now serve as baseline requirements rather than differentiating motivators, especially in settings where platforms are institutionally endorsed or digitally familiar [68]. The decline in sensitivity to trust concerns may also reflect "risk fatigue" in high-frequency tech users.

The hypothesis that social influence (SI) affects behavioural intention was also not supported, challenging its traditional role in the UTAUT model. Contemporary findings suggest SI's impact is highly contingent on user context. For example, Agrawal [70] found that while social influencers shape perceptions in social commerce, their impact varies by platform and audience. For more autonomous, experienced users, adoption tends to be driven by perceived utility and system fit rather than social approval.

Similarly, facilitating conditions (FC)—such as access to infrastructure and support—did not significantly impact adoption intentions. While UTAUT highlights FC as a usage enabler, their effect appears to wane in digitally mature environments where infrastructure is assumed. Wut et al. [71] found that while FCs were adequately present in online platforms, factors like content quality were more influential in shaping user behaviour. This indicates that FCs may be necessary for continued use, but not compelling enough to spark initial adoption.

In summary, the results reinforce that adoption in voluntary, user-driven environments is shaped primarily by internal drivers—compatibility, ease-of-use, and expected satisfaction—rather than external enablers like trust, support systems, or social pressure. These insights emphasise the need for user-centred platform design that prioritises functional alignment and experiential value.

6 Conclusions

This study examined the factors influencing the adoption of collaborative digital marketing platforms, focusing on behavioural intention (BI) through the lens of extended technology acceptance models. Using structural equation modelling (PLS-SEM) on data from 93 respondents, the findings revealed that compatibility with user needs (CN), effort expectancy (EE), and expected satisfaction (ES) are the most significant predictors of future use. These results suggest that users are more inclined to adopt platforms that align well with their current workflows, are easy to use, and promise a positive experience. In contrast, facilitating conditions (FC), social influence (SI), and platform trust and security (TS) did not significantly impact behavioral intention. Although data privacy (DP) and innovation and differentiation (ID) were found to significantly affect perceptions of platform trust and security, the latter did not directly influence users' intention to use the platform.

Theoretically, this study contributes to the existing literature by reinforcing the centrality of perceived compatibility and ease-of-use within voluntary adoption settings, while extending technology acceptance models through the inclusion of expected satisfaction as a forward-looking predictor. Furthermore, the findings challenge the assumed direct influence of social norms and institutional support in user-driven adoption scenarios, suggesting that in digitally mature environments, internal perceptions of value and fit take precedence over external influences.

Practically, the study offers actionable insights for platform designers and digital marketing strategists. Systems should be developed with strong alignment to user needs and existing practices, emphasizing intuitive interfaces and clearly communicated benefits to encourage adoption. Rather than focusing on social persuasion or support infrastructure during early rollout phases, stakeholders should prioritize delivering immediate, perceived value to users. While trust and data protection remain important, they may serve more as threshold factors than primary motivators in initial adoption decisions.

Several limitations should be acknowledged. The sample was largely composed of young (18–25 years old), predominantly female university students, which limits the generalizability of the results to more diverse or professional populations. The study was also geographically restricted, and data were collected cross-sectionally, precluding conclusions about temporal dynamics or causality. Additionally, constructs such as algorithmic transparency, ethical considerations, and sustainability, emerging as critical in platform use, were not included in the current model.

Future research should extend these findings by including more demographically and professionally diverse populations, adopting longitudinal designs to capture the evolution of user perceptions and behaviours over time, and integrating emerging concerns such as digital ethics and environmental impact. Moreover, mixed-methods approaches could deepen understanding of the subjective and contextual drivers behind platform adoption, moving beyond structural factors to explore the lived experiences and motivations of users.

In conclusion, this study highlights the primacy of practical alignment, ease-of-use, and outcome expectations in shaping the adoption of collaborative digital platforms. By focusing on these internal, user-centred drivers, platform developers and marketers can more effectively design, position, and scale tools that meet the real-world needs of modern digital collaborators.

Acknowledgments. This research was financed by national funds provided by the FCT—the Foundation for Science and Technology—through project number UIB/04020/2020 (CinTurs) and under the SHIFT project (Sustainability-oriented, Highly interactive, and Innovation-based Framework for Tourism marketing), with the reference PTDC/EDE-OGE/2146/2021.

References

1. Dwivedi, Y.K., et al.: Setting the future of digital and social media marketing research: perspectives and research propositions. Int. J. Inf. Manage. **59**, 102168 (2021)
2. Kumar, V., Ramachandran, D., Kumar, B.: Influence of new-age technologies on marketing: a research agenda. J. Bus. Res. **125**, 864–877 (2022)
3. Hong, Y., Sawang, S., Yang, H.P.: How is entrepreneurial marketing shaped by E-commerce technology: a case study of Chinese pure-play e-retailers. Int. J. Entrep. Behav. Res. **30**(2/3), 609–631 (2024)
4. Pavlou, P.A., Gefen, D.: Building effective online marketplaces with institution-based trust. Inf. Syst. Res. **15**(1), 37–59 (2004)
5. Tadelis, S.: Reputation and feedback systems in online platform markets. Ann. Rev. Econ. **8**(1), 321–340 (2016)
6. Dallocchio, M., Lambri, M., Sironi, E., Teti, E.: The role of digitalization in cross-border e-commerce performance of Italian SMEs. Sustainability **16**(2), 508 (2024)
7. Um, T., Lee, Y., Koo, J.: Economic impacts of digital home-sharing platform: creative destruction in the hospitality industry. Tour. Econ. **31**(2), 201–220 (2025)
8. Bogers, M., et al.: The open innovation research landscape: established perspectives and emerging themes across different levels of analysis. Ind. Innov. **24**(1), 8–40 (2017)
9. Kamboj, S., Sharma, M.: Social media adoption behaviour: consumer innovativeness and participation intention. Int. J. Consum. Stud. **47**(2), 523–544 (2023)
10. Benitez, J., Ruiz, L., Castillo, A., Llorens, J.: How corporate social responsibility activities influence employer reputation: the role of social media capability. Decis. Support. Syst. **129**, 113223 (2020)
11. Sheth, J.: New areas of research in marketing strategy, consumer behavior, and marketing analytics: the future is bright. J. Mark. Theory Pract. **29**(1), 3–12 (2021)
12. Alalwan, A.A., et al.: Fintech and contactless payment: help or hindrance? The role of invasion of privacy and information disclosure. Int. J. Bank Mark. **42**(1), 66–93 (2024)
13. Gligor, D.M., Pillai, K.G., Golgeci, I.: Theorizing the dark side of business-to-business relationships in the era of AI, big data, and blockchain. J. Bus. Res. **133**, 79–88 (2021)
14. Belanche, D., Casaló, L.V., Flavián, C.: Artificial Intelligence in FinTech: understanding robo-advisors adoption among customers. Ind. Manag. Data Syst. **119**(7), 1411–1430 (2019)
15. Hunt, S.D., Morgan, R.M.: The comparative advantage theory of competition. J. Mark. **59**(2), 1–15 (1995)
16. Kumar, A., Sikdar, P., Gupta, M., Singh, P., Sinha, N.: Drivers of satisfaction and usage continuance in e-grocery retailing: a collaborative design supported perspective. J. Res. Interact. Mark. **17**(2), 176–194 (2023)
17. Ojasalo, J., Kauppinen, H.: Collaborative innovation with external actors: an empirical study on open innovation platforms in smart cities. Technol. Innov. Manag. Rev. **6**(12), 49–60 (2016)

18. Murtas, G., Pedeliento, G., Mangiò, F., Andreini, D.: Co-branding strategies in luxury fashion: the Off-White case. J. Strateg. Mark. **33**(4), 484–503 (2025)
19. Nan, M., Huang, L.: Innovation ecosystems: a cross-industry examination of knowledge flows and collaboration dynamics. J. Knowl. Econ. **16**(1), 26–64 (2025)
20. Gummesson, E.: Total Relationship Marketing. Routledge, London (2011)
21. Palmatier, R., Steinhoff, L.: Relationship Marketing in the Digital Age. Routledge, London (2019)
22. Amorim, R.C., Castro, J.A., Rocha da Silva, J., Ribeiro, C.: A comparison of research data management platforms: architecture, flexible metadata and interoperability. Univers. Access Inf. Soc. **16**, 851–862 (2017)
23. Lee, J.M., Kim, H.J.: Determinants of adoption and continuance intentions toward Internet-only banks. Int. J. Bank Mark. **38**(4), 843–865 (2020)
24. Nam, K., Dutt, C.S., Chathoth, P., Khan, M.S.: Blockchain technology for smart city and smart tourism: latest trends and challenges. Asia Pac. J. Tour. Res. **26**(4), 454–468 (2021)
25. Leal, F., Malheiro, B., Veloso, B., Burguillo, J.C.: Responsible processing of crowdsourced tourism data. J. Sustain. Tour. **29**(5), 774–794 (2020)
26. Gretzel, U., Sigala, M., Xiang, Z., Koo, C.: Smart tourism: foundations and developments. Electron. Mark. **25**, 179–188 (2015)
27. Ivanov, S., Webster, C.: Automated decision-making: hoteliers' perceptions. Technol. Soc. **76**, 102430 (2024)
28. Filieri, R., Mariani, M.: The role of cultural values in consumers' evaluation of online review helpfulness: a big data approach. Int. Mark. Rev. **38**(6), 1267–1288 (2021)
29. Ertz, M., Sarigöllü, E.: Consumer intentions to use collaborative economy platforms: a meta-analysis. Int. J. Consum. Stud. **46**(5), 1859–1876 (2022)
30. Fleury, S., Chaniaud, N.: Multi-user centered design: acceptance, user experience, user research and user testing. Theor. Issues Ergon. Sci. **25**(2), 209–224 (2024)
31. Davis, F.D.: Perceived usefulness, perceived ease of use, and user acceptance of information technology. MIS Q. **13**(3), 319–340 (1989)
32. Venkatesh, V., Morris, M.G., Davis, G.B., Davis, F.D.: User acceptance of information technology: toward a unified view. MIS Q. **27**(3), 425–478 (2003)
33. Venkatesh, V., Thong, J.Y.L., Xu, X.: Unified theory of acceptance and use of technology: a synthesis and the road ahead. J. Assoc. Inf. Syst. **17**(5), 328–376 (2016)
34. Gretzel, U.: The Smart DMO: a new step in the digital transformation of destination management organizations. Eur. J. Tour. Res. **30**, 3002 (2022)
35. Alalwan, A.A., Baabdullah, A.M., Rana, N.P., Tamilmani, K., Dwivedi, Y.K.: Examining adoption of mobile internet in Saudi Arabia: extending TAM with perceived enjoyment, innovativeness and trust. Technol. Soc. **55**, 100–110 (2018)
36. Upadhyay, N., Upadhyay, S., Abed, S.S., Dwivedi, Y.K.: Consumer adoption of mobile payment services during COVID-19: extending meta-UTAUT with perceived severity and self-efficacy. Int. J. Bank Mark. **40**(5), 960–991 (2022)
37. Chen, C.H.: Extending the technology acceptance model: a new perspective on the adoption of blockchain technology. Hum. Behav. Emerg. Technol. **2023**(1), 4835896 (2023)
38. Zhang, J., Hassandoust, F., Williams, J.E.: Online customer trust in the context of the general data protection regulation (GDPR). Pac. Asia J. Assoc. Inf. Syst. **12**(1), 4 (2020)
39. Venkatesh, V., Thong, J.Y., Xu, X.: Consumer acceptance and use of information technology: extending the unified theory of acceptance and use of technology. MIS Q. **36**(1), 157–178 (2012)
40. Cheung, R., Vogel, D.: Predicting user acceptance of collaborative technologies: an extension of the technology acceptance model for e-learning. Comput. Educ. **63**, 160–175 (2013)
41. Li, H., Zhang, C., Kettinger, W.J.: Digital platform ecosystem dynamics: the roles of product scope, innovation, and collaborative network centrality. MIS Q. **46**(2), 739–770 (2022)

42. Rani, V.S., Sundaram, N.: Collaborative social media marketing in small scale business using artificial intelligence. ECS Trans. **107**(1), 5175 (2022)
43. Lu, B., Yi, X.: Institutional trust and repurchase intention in the sharing economy: the moderating roles of information privacy concerns and security concerns. J. Retail. Consum. Serv. **73**, 103327 (2023)
44. Ruiz-Alba, J.L., Abou-Foul, M., Nazarian, A., Foroudi, P.: Digital platforms: customer satisfaction, eWOM and the moderating role of perceived technological innovativeness. Inf. Technol. People **35**(7), 2470–2499 (2022)
45. Marth, S., Hartl, B., Penz, E.: Sharing on platforms: reducing perceived risk for peer-to-peer platform consumers through trust-building and regulation. J. Consum. Behav. **21**(6), 1255–1267 (2022)
46. Das, D.K.: Exploring the symbiotic relationship between digital transformation, infrastructure, service delivery, and governance for smart sustainable cities. Smart Cities **7**(2), 806–835 (2024)
47. Yu, P.: Diffusion of innovation theory. In: Rapport, F., Clay-Williams, R., Braithwaite, J. (eds.) Implementation Science, pp. 59–61. Routledge, London (2022)
48. Reinhardt, R., Gurtner, S.: Differences between early adopters of disruptive and sustaining innovations. J. Bus. Res. **68**(1), 137–145 (2015)
49. Schofield, P., Crowther, P., Jago, L., Heeley, J., Taylor, S.: Collaborative innovation: catalyst for a destination's event success. Int. J. Contemp. Hosp. Manag. **30**(6), 2499–2516 (2018)
50. Ofori, K.S., Anyigba, H., Adeola, O., Junwu, C., Osakwe, C.N., David-West, O.: Understanding post-adoption behaviour in the context of ride-hailing apps: the role of customer perceived value. Inf. Technol. People **35**(5), 1540–1562 (2022)
51. Sin Tan, K., Chong, S.C., Lin, B.: Intention to use internet marketing: a comparative study between Malaysians and South Koreans. Kybernetes **42**(6), 888–905 (2013)
52. Hoyle, R.H.: The structural equation modeling approach: basic concepts and fundamental issues. In: Hoyle, R.H. (ed.) Structural Equation Modeling: Concepts, Issues and Applications, pp. 1–15. Sage, Thousand Oaks (1995)
53. Gefen, D., Straub, D., Boudreau, M.C.: Structural equation modeling and regression: guidelines for research practice. Commun. Assoc. Inf. Syst. **4**(1), 7 (2000)
54. Chin, W.W.: How to write up and report PLS analyses. In: Esposito Vinzi, V., Chin, W., Henseler, J., Wang, H. (eds.) Handbook of Partial Least Squares. Springer Handbooks of Computational Statistics, pp. 655–690. Springer, Berlin, Heidelberg (2010). https://doi.org/10.1007/978-3-540-32827-8_29
55. Ringle, C.M., Silva, D., Bido, D.D.S.: Modelagem de equações estruturais com utilização do SmartPLS. REMark **13**(2), 54 (2014)
56. Hair, J.F., Hult, T.M., Ringle, C.M., Sarstedt, M.: A Primer on Partial Least Squares Structural Equation Modeling (PLS-SEM). SAGE, Los Angeles (2014)
57. Henseler, J., Sarstedt, M.: Goodness-of-fit indices for partial least squares path modeling. Comput. Statistics **28**, 565–580 (2012)
58. Pinto, P.: Modelos de equações estruturais com variáveis latentes, fundamentos da abordagem Partial Least Squares. Bnomics, Lisboa (2016)
59. Henseler, J., Ringle, C.M., Sinkovics, R.R.: The use of partial least squares path modeling in international marketing. Adv. Int. Mark. **20**, 277–319 (2009)
60. Abubakar, A., Al-Mamary, Y.: Exploring factors influencing the intention to use social media and its actual usage in higher education: a conceptual model of effectiveness, effort, communication, self-awareness, social influence, and facilitating conditions. Interact. Learn. Environ. **33**(6), 3833–3857 (2025)
61. Fan, J., Li, C.: Factors influencing the behavioral intention to use mobile learning platform in higher education of Changsha, China. Int. J. Soc. Anthrop. Sci. Rev. **5**(1), 821–836 (2025)

62. Sengkalit, D., Khairal Abdullah, T.M.: Factors influencing technology adoption among SMEs: a case study of Youtap and the role of performance expectancy and effort expectancy. J. Syntax Literate **10**(1), 322–333 (2025)
63. Haryanto, B., Alshoushan, A.J.: The influence of digital marketing on innovative performance with knowledge sharing as a mediation variable in five star hotels. J. Soc. Res. **4**(2), 93–106 (2025)
64. Baden-Fuller, C., Blair, J., Teece, D.: When should incumbent consumer goods producers ally with digital platforms? Calif. Manag. Rev. **67**(2), 141–163 (2025). 00081256241296915
65. Fitrianti, D., Halik, A., Budiarti, E.: The influence of brand image, product innovation, and social media marketing activity on repurchase decision through customer satisfaction as an intervening variable at Mixue in Bojonegoro. J. Soc. Res. **4**(2), 128–147 (2025)
66. Ana, A., Kustiawan, U.: Understanding the effects of social media marketing activities: mediation of social identification, perceived value and satisfaction. Jurnal Syntax Admiration **6**(1), 451–464 (2025)
67. Otieno, E.A.: Data protection and privacy in e-commerce environment: systematic review. GSC Adv. Res. Rev. **22**(1), 238–271 (2025)
68. Jones, M.: Navigating the privacy paradox in a digital age: balancing innovation, data collection and ethical responsibility. J. Ethics Entrep. Technol. **5**(1), 2–13 (2025)
69. Wang, W.: Privacy-preserving data analytics in 5G-enabled IoT for the financial industry (2025)
70. Agrawal, S.: The impact of social media influencers on consumer behaviour: trends, opportunities, and challenges. Int. Sci. J. Eng. Manag. (2025)
71. Wut, T.M., Lee, S.W., Xu, J.: How do facilitating conditions influence student-to-student interaction within an online learning platform? A new typology of the serial mediation model. Educ. Sci. **12**(5), 337 (2022)

Accessibility and Innovations in Intelligent Environments

Evaluating Brainwave Changes in Cognitive Function Tests for Early Dementia Detection

Kakeru Amano[1], Yasuyuki Matsuura[1,2], Kuwon Sumi[1], Akihiro Sugiura[3], Hirofumi Tahara[4], and Hiroki Takada[1(✉)]

[1] Department of Human and Artificial Intelligent Systems, Graduate School of Engineering, University of Fukui, Fukui 9108507, Japan
`takada@u-fukui.ac.jp`
[2] Education and Research Center for Data-Driven Science, Gifu City Women's College, Gifu 5010192, Japan
[3] Department of Healthcare Science, Gifu University of Medical Science, Gifu 5013892, Japan
[4] Bio Search Co., Ltd., Eiha Shinkawa 6F, 1-5-17 Shinkawa Chuoku, Tokyo, Japan

Abstract. In Japan, a rapidly aging society with a declining birthrate has led to an increased caregiving burden on younger generations. Dementia, often preceded by mild cognitive impairment (MCI), requires early intervention to prevent progression, which necessitates monitoring MCI and related brain changes. However, traditional methods, such as computed tomography (CT), magnetic resonance imaging (MRI), and medical electroencephalography (EEG), are costly and physically demanding for elderly individuals. This study examines the feasibility of using a simple headband-type EEG device during cognitive function tests to identify early dementia markers. This study investigates the effects of cognitive function testing on EEG activity by comparing EEG data obtained from two groups: younger healthy adults (19 subjects; mean age $\pm$ standard deviation (SD): 21.07 ± 1.38 years) and older healthy adults (15 subjects; mean age $\pm$ SD: 77.07 ± 5.37 years). The Mann-Whitney U test was used to analyze their EEG power spectral density (PSD). Significant differences were observed in the β and γ bands during the Clock Drawing Test (CDT) and in the δ band of the right hemisphere during the Spiral Drawing Test (SDT). However, no significant differences were observed on the Revised Hasegawa's Dementia Scale (HDS-R). These findings suggest that δ band abnormalities during the Spiral Drawing Test and β and γ band changes during CDT could serve as potential biomarkers for early MCI symptoms. Hence, this approach offers a less invasive and cost-effective alternative for early dementia detection, potentially easing the burden on healthcare systems while supporting timely interventions.

Keywords: Dementia · Rhythmic electroencephalogram · Cognitive function evaluation · Mild Cognitive Impairment (MCI) · Clock Drawing Test (CDT)

1 Introduction

Driven by the increase in average life expectancy globally, the proportion of individuals aged 65 years and older has been steadily increasing, thereby accelerating the progression of aging societies. Among these demographic trends, Japan exhibits one of the

© The Author(s), under exclusive license to Springer Nature Switzerland AG 2026
M. Antona and C. Stephanidis (Eds.): HCII 2025, LNCS 16335, pp. 171–182, 2026.
https://doi.org/10.1007/978-3-032-12781-5_11

highest aging rates worldwide, a level projected to persist in the coming decades [1, 2]. Consequently, Japan faces multifaceted challenges, particularly in healthcare, medical services, and social welfare. Among these, long-term care has emerged as one of the most critical challenges. The decline in physical and cognitive functions associated with aging frequently necessitates caregiving. Dementia represents the leading cause of long-term care needs (23.6%), followed by cerebrovascular diseases such as stroke (19.0%) and fractures or falls (13.0%) [3]. Furthermore, by 2025, one in five older adults in Japan will either have dementia or be in a pre-dementia stage [4], underscoring the urgency of dementia prevention and management.

Among the various diseases contributing to dementia, Alzheimer's disease (AD) is the most prevalent, accounting for 67.6% of cases [5]. The severity of dementia during definitive diagnosis significantly impacts subsequent health outcomes [6]. Dementia does not manifest abruptly but develops progressively as cognitive function deteriorates over time. In recent years, several pharmacological treatments for dementia have been approved, demonstrating efficacy in slowing the disease progression and others [7–9]. However, these treatments are often ineffective for advanced dementia, which emphasizes the importance of early detection. Additionally, among dementia-related disorders, some exhibit pronounced hemispheric asymmetry in cerebral dysfunction, while others present minimal asymmetry. Functional imaging studies have revealed that many dementia-related diseases display hemispheric differences in cerebral function decline [10–12].

Mild cognitive impairment (MCI) is regarded as an intermediate stage preceding dementia, characterized by cognitive and memory decline that does not significantly interfere with daily life. Therefore, MCI often goes unrecognized by affected individuals and their families, increasing the risk of progression to dementia. Numerous studies indicate that suitable interventions may prevent the transition from MCI to dementia or even improve cognitive function [13, 14].

Several non-invasive diagnostic tools are commonly employed to assess cognitive function in dementia. These include the Clock Drawing Test (CDT), which requires individuals to draw a clock face and set their hands to a specified time. Additionally, the mini-mental state examination (MMSE), is an 11-item questionnaire designed to evaluate cognitive function. However, these methods do not elucidate underlying pathology or disease progression. Previous studies have identified amyloid-β accumulation as a primary cause of neurodegeneration in dementia. Existing clinical applications for measuring biomarkers such as amyloid-β in cerebrospinal fluid or serum are highly invasive. Structural and functional brain imaging techniques such as computed tomography (CT), magnetic resonance imaging (MRI), and single-photon emission computed tomography (SPECT) are widely utilized in dementia diagnostics [15].

Electroencephalography (EEG) also serves as a valuable tool for assessing functional brain abnormalities non-invasively. When combined with other imaging modalities such as CT and MRI, EEG plays a pivotal role in diagnosing dementia. Aging leads to decreased normal EEG rhythm frequency [16–20]. Furthermore, EEG slowing has been observed in dementia cases [21, 22]. However, abnormalities often remain undetectable via EEG during the early stages of AD. Recent studies have demonstrated that portable EEG devices, such as headband-type systems, enable simple and quantitative assessments of cognitive function [23]. It has been suggested that early detection of MCI is possible using EEG.

This study investigates the effects of cognitive function testing on EEG activity by comparing EEG data obtained from two groups: younger healthy adults (young group) and older healthy adults (elderly group). EEG recordings were conducted during cognitive function tests and intergroup differences in brainwave activity were examined to determine how cognitive assessments impact neural responses.

2 Methods

In this study, 34 participants were enrolled, comprising 19 younger adults (4 males and 15 females; mean age $\pm$ standard deviation (SD): 21.07 ± 1.38 years) and 15 older adults (2 males and 13 females; mean age $\pm$ SD: 77.07 ± 5.37 years). Ethical approval was obtained from the Research Ethics Committee of the Graduate School of Engineering, University of Fukui (No. H2022001).

Figure 1 shows a band-type, telemetry-based, two-electrode portable EEG device (NeuroSky) employed to obtain EEG data. A band-pass filter with a frequency range of 1–49 Hz was applied. EEG signals were recorded from the left frontal region (Fp1) and the right frontal region (Fp2), with a reference electrode affixed to the right earlobe. Prior to participation, all individuals received a comprehensive explanation of the study protocol and provided written informed consent.

During the experimental session, participants performed the following tasks while EEG data were recorded:

1. Resting-state with eyes open for 3 min.
2. Resting-state with eyes closed for 3 min.
3. CDT, comprising three sequential subtasks: drawing only the clock face, drawing the entire clock, and setting the clock hands to indicate "10:10."
4. The Spiral Drawing Test, in which participants traced a pre-drawn spiral on paper.
5. The Revised Hasegawa's Dementia Scale (HDS-R), a cognitive screening test.

Figure 2 shows an experimental scene. For Task 3 (CDT), scoring was conducted based on the Kouno Method, with a maximum score of nine points[6]. Regarding Task 4 (Spiral Drawing Test), participants traced a pre-drawn spiral on paper; while various evaluation methods are available, this study employed visual inspection to count instances where the participant's traced line contacted the guideline, deducting points accordingly. A perfect score was defined as zero deductions. Task 5 (HDS-R) is a dementia screening tool developed by Dr. Kazuo Hasegawa, with a maximum score of 30 points; one point was deducted for each incorrect response [7]. The established cutoff score is 20 points, below which dementia is suspected.

Spectral analysis of EEG data was performed using statistical methods, with frequency bands defined as follows:

δ band: 1–4 Hz
θ band: 4–8 Hz
α band: 8–14 Hz
β band: 14–30 Hz

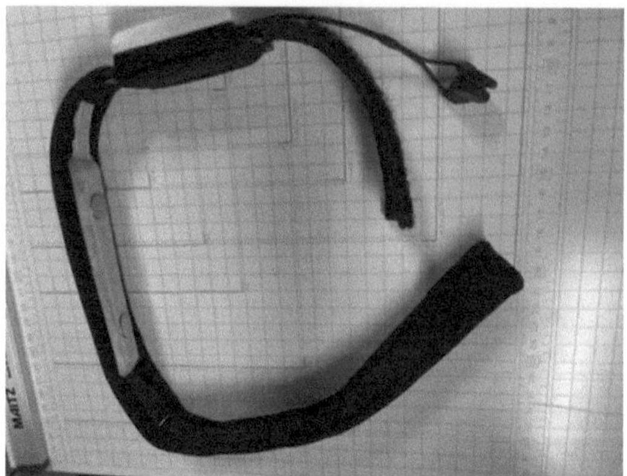

Fig. 1. Portable EEG device used in this study.

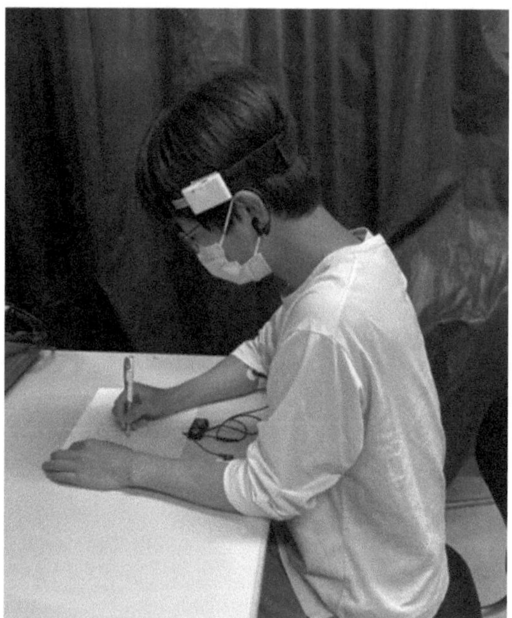

Fig. 2. Participant performing the CDT while EEG data are recorded.

γ band: 30–49 Hz

The Left-Right ratio (LR ratio) was calculated as the Fp1 value divided by the Fp2 value. EEG parameters (Fp1, Fp2, and LR ratio) between younger and older adult groups were compared using the Mann-Whitney U test, with statistical significance set at $p < 0.05$.

3   Results and Discussion

3.1   CDT

Figure 3 illustrates the results of the CDT and Fig. 4 depicts the distribution of scores. Comparative analyses were conducted between the older and younger groups. In the β band at Fp2, a trend toward significance was observed ($p < 0.1$). However, in the γ band, a significant difference was detected ($p < 0.05$) (Fig. 5). No significant differences were observable in the other bands.

The EEG comparison results between the two groups indicate that the β and γ bands exhibited increased activity during the CDT. The β band is generally associated with active cognitive processing and sustained attention, whereas the γ band is linked to consciousness and perceptual integration. The cognitive demands of recalling and drawing the clock likely account for the activation of these frequency bands. Based on the findings, we posit that these significant differences may serve as potential biomarkers for early symptoms of MCI. The significant differences observed in both left hemispheres suggest bilateral cerebral engagement during the CDT.

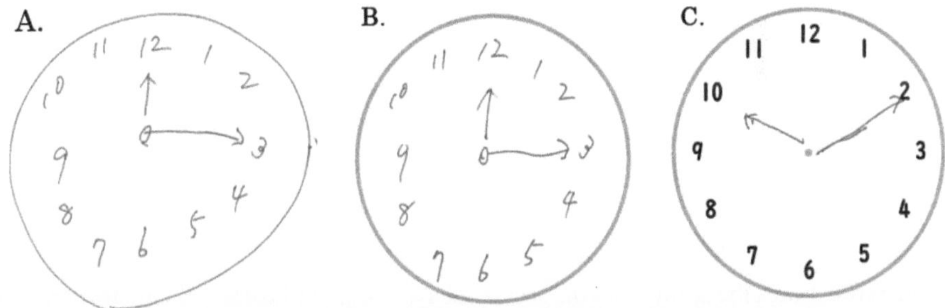

Fig. 3. Results of CDT (A: All, B: Dial, C: 10:10).

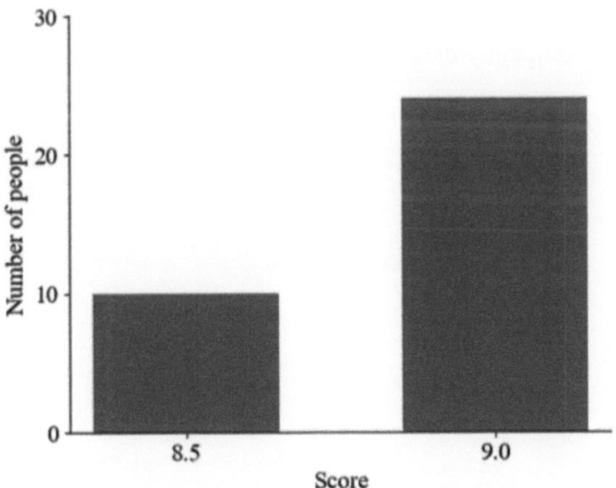

Fig. 4. Distribution of CDT scores.

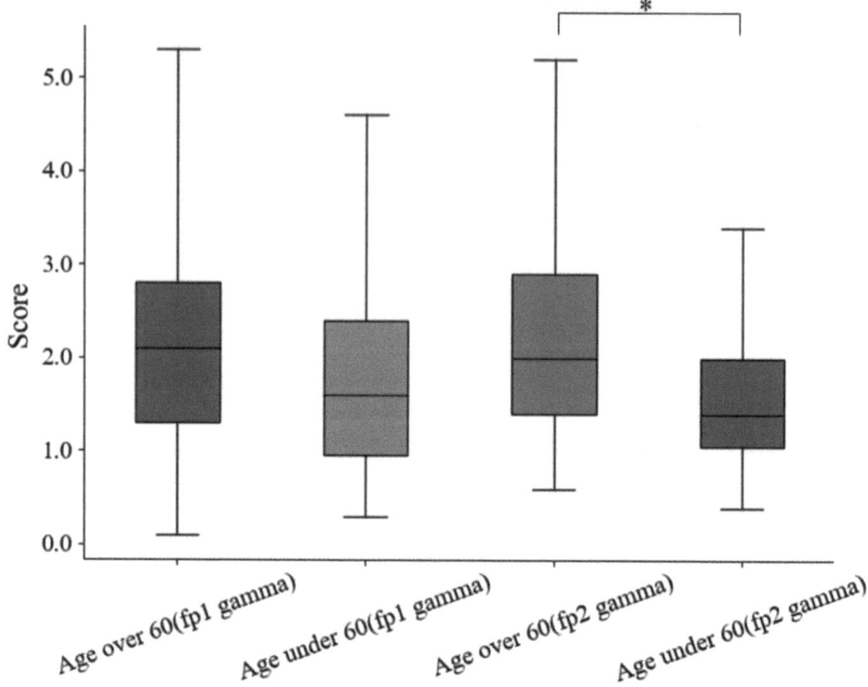

Fig. 5. Results of γ band and ratio in CDT (Mean $\pm$ SD).

3.2 Spiral Drawing Test

Figure 6 illustrates the spiral drawing test results and Fig. 7 illustrates the distribution of scores. The same comparative analyses as those conducted for the CDT were applied. The LR ratio yielded a trend toward significance in the θ band ($p < 0.1$). At Fp1, significant differences were observed in the δ and θ bands ($p < 0.05$). At Fp2 (Fig. 8), a significant difference was observed in the δ band ($p < 0.05$) (Fig. 9). No significant differences were noted in other frequency bands.

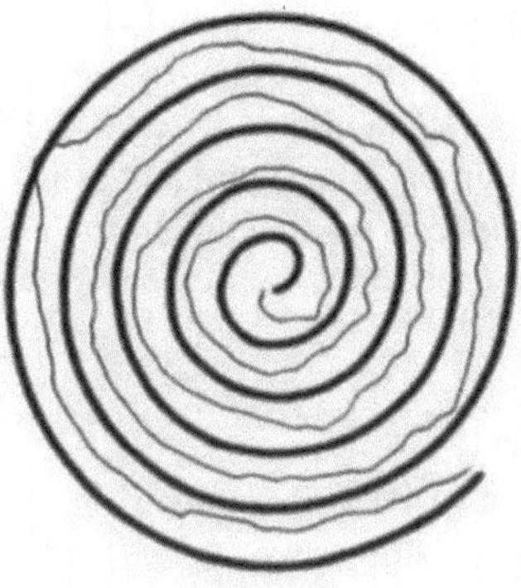

Fig. 6. Results of spiral drawing test.

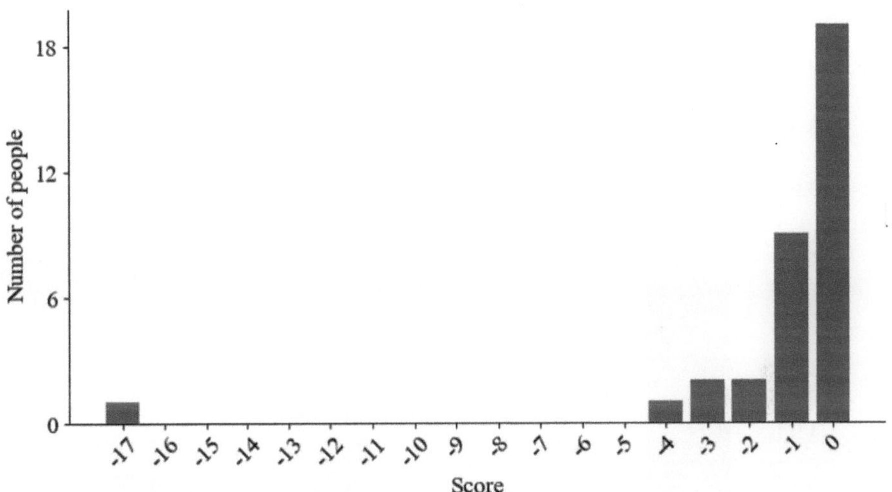

Fig. 7. Distribution of scores for spiral drawing test.

EEG comparisons between the two groups revealed that the δ band was activated during the spiral drawing test, with significant differences attributable to aging. The spiral drawing test was less complex than the CDT in terms of motor execution and cognitive demand. Thus, the significant differences were confined to the θ and δ bands—frequencies typically associated with attention and blinking. However, no significant differences were observed in the β and γ bands. The significant difference in the θ band for the LR ratio suggests greater involvement of the right hemisphere during the task. The left hemisphere is commonly implicated in linguistic and temporal processing. However, the right hemisphere is responsible for spatial recognition and processing. Because the spiral drawing task primarily engages spatial processing, the observed right hemisphere activation is consistent with these cognitive functions.

Previous studies have reported that abnormalities in the δ band may serve as early indicators of Alzheimer's disease. Rehabilitation programs for Alzheimer's disease often incorporate right hemisphere training. The significant difference observed in the δ band during the spiral drawing test suggests its potential utility as a biomarker for early-stage MCI.

3.3 HDS-R

Figure 10 shows the distribution of HDS-R scores. Comparative analyses between the two age groups revealed significant differences in the γ band at Fp1 and Fp2 ($p < 0.05$), as shown in Fig. 11. No significant differences were observed in the LR ratio.

The EEG findings suggest that, relative to the other tasks, the HDS-R entails many subtasks and requires more complex cognitive processing. Given that the γ band is activated during higher-order cognitive operations, the observed significant differences in this frequency band further corroborate this association.

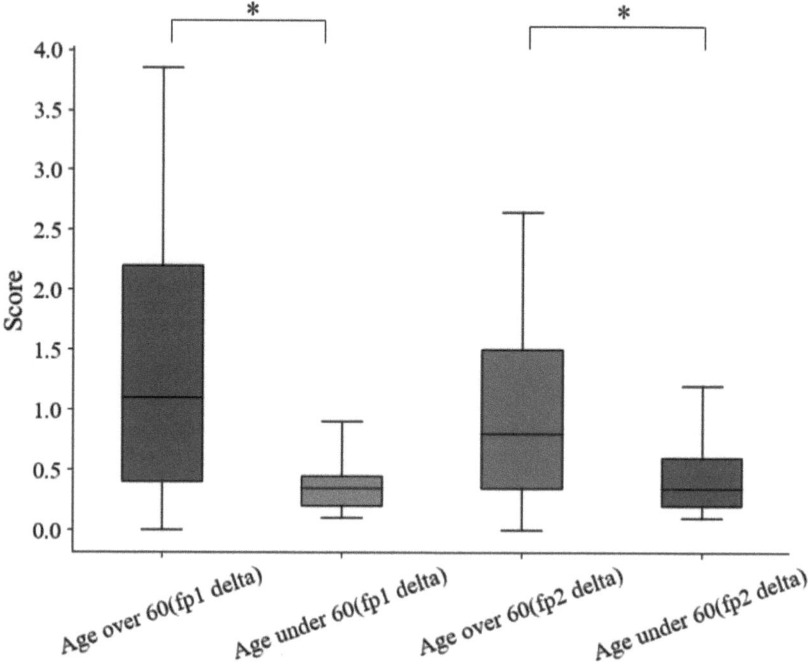

Fig. 8. Test results for δ band, Fp1 and Fp2 in the spiral drawing test (Mean ± SD).

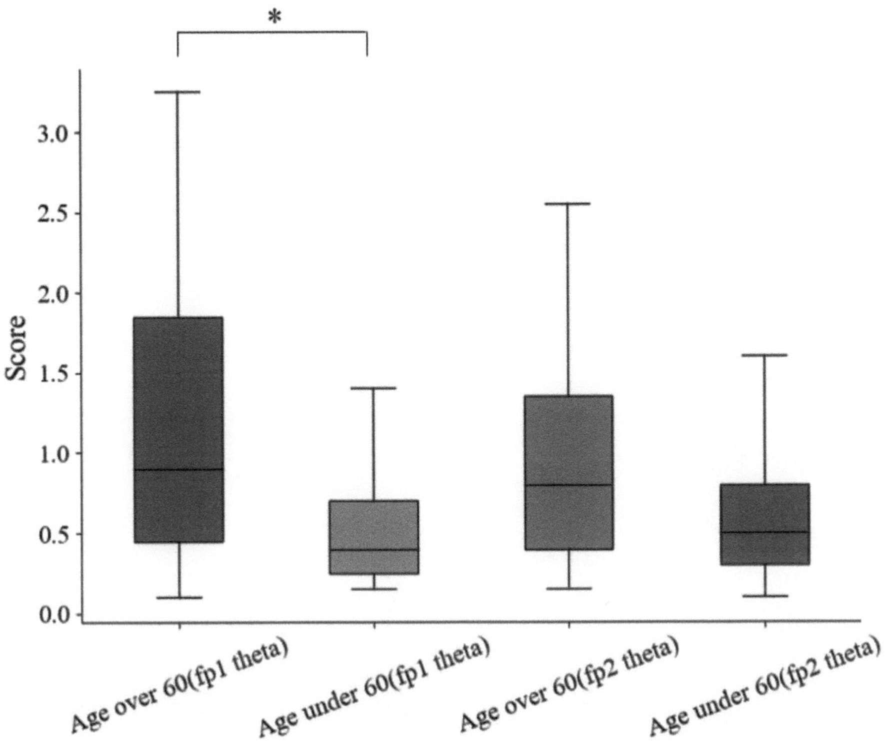

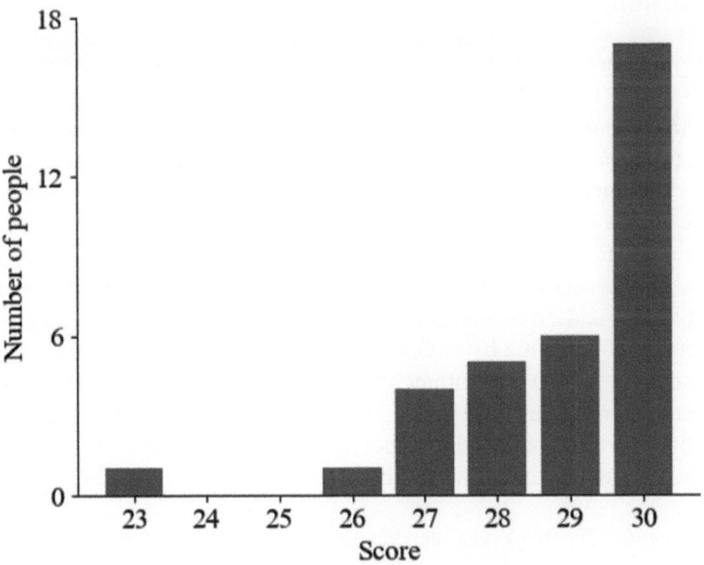

Fig. 9. Test results for θ band, Fp1 and Fp2 in the spiral drawing test (Mean ± SD).

Fig. 10. Distribution of HDS-R scores.

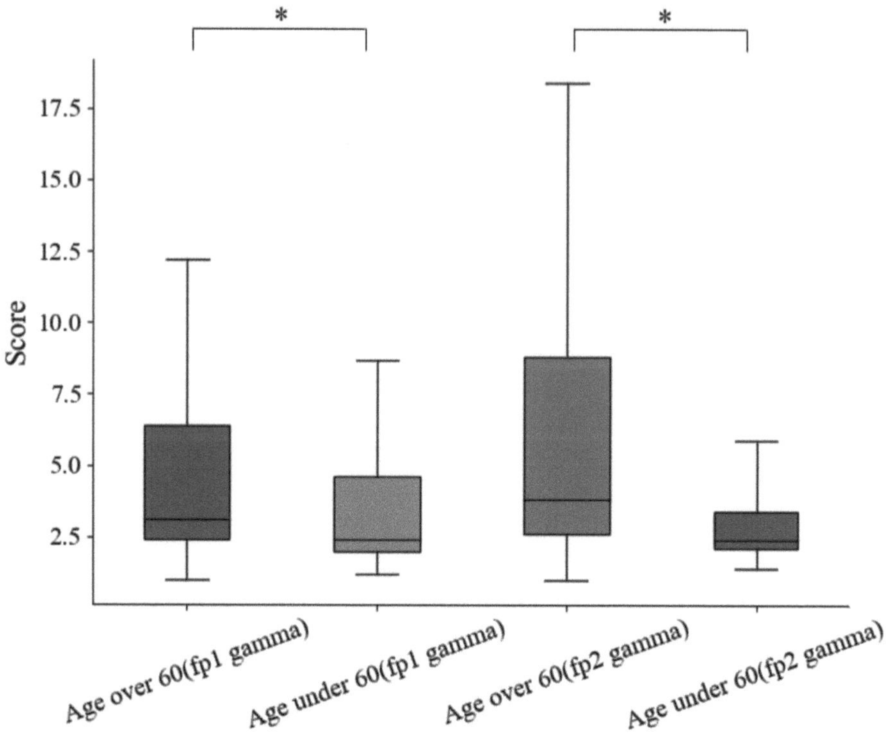

Fig. 11. Test results for γ band, Fp1 and Fp2 in HDS-R (Mean ± SD).

4 Conclusion

This study investigated the effects of cognitive decline on EEG activity by recording brainwaves during three cognitive assessments: CDT, HDS-R, and the Spiral Drawing Test. EEG data were analyzed and compared across different age groups. The findings revealed significant differences in the γ band during the CDT and HDS-R. However, significant differences were observed in the δ and θ bands during the Spiral Drawing Test. These results suggest that higher-frequency bands are preferentially activated in cognitively demanding tasks such as the CDT and HDS-R, whereas lower-frequency bands show significant differences in simpler tasks, such as the Spiral Drawing Test.

These findings underscore the potential of portable EEG devices for use in detecting early symptoms of dementia by evaluating brainwave activity during various cognitive tasks. Future work will involve further analyses of the collected data. This also includes the administration of these cognitive assessments within an fMRI environment and comparing results with those obtained from portable EEG, thereby providing deeper insights into brain activity during cognitive testing.

Acknowledgments. This work was supported in part by the Japan Society for the Promotion of Science, and Grant-in-Aid for Scientific Research (B) (Grant number 23K28367) and (C) (Grant numbers 20K12528 and 22K12141). Portions of this paper contain revised versions of the co-author's thesis [23, 24].

Disclosure of Interests.   The authors have no competing interests to declare that are relevant to the content of this article.

References

1. Cabinet Office of Japan: Annual Report on the Aging Society: 2024 (2024)
2. United Nations: 2024 Revision of World Population Prospects (2024)
3. Ministry of Health, Labour and Welfare of Japan: Comprehensive Survey of Living Conditions: 2022 (2022)
4. Ministry of Health, Labour and Welfare of Japan: Comprehensive Strategy to Accelerate Dementia Measures (New Orange Plan) (2015)
5. Yoshimura, T., Maeshima, S., Osawa, A., Sekiguchi, E.: Clinical examination of the usefulness of the Clock Drawing Test (CDT). High. Brain Funct. Res. **28**(4), 361–372 (2008)
6. Kouno, K.: MCI (Mild Cognitive Impairment) from the perspective of the Kouno Method, 180–187 (2019)
7. Kato, S., Shimogaki, H., Onodera, A.: Development of the revised Hasegawa's Dementia Scale (HDS-R). Jpn. J. Geriatr. Psychiatry **2**(11), 1339–1347 (1991)
8. Fujiwara, K., Kano, H., Mitobe, K.: Proposal for the dual-task assessment using drawing and counting test in elderly and young people. Paper Hum. Interface Soc. **19**(1), 25–28 (2017)
9. Takada, H., Miyao, M., Takada, M., Kinoshita, F., Tahara, H.: Development of sports vision training system using virtual reality for prevention of mild cognitive impairment. Descente Sports Sci. **40**, 97–107 (2019)
10. Arai, H., et al.: Asymmetry of cerebral blood flow in patients with senile dementia of Alzheimer type by SPECT using I-123 IMP. Jpn. J. Nucl. Med. **27**(12), 1401–1410 (1990)
11. Kazui, H., Nishio, Y.: Symptomatology of dementia from the viewpoint of left-right difference in cerebral function. High. Brain Funct. Res. **40**(2), 169–170 (2020)
12. Kashibayashi, T., Takahashi, R., Akagawa, M., Kamimura, N., Kazui, H.: Difference of symptoms between left-and right-sided in dementia with Lewy body disease. High. Brain Funct. Res. **40**(2), 187–193 (2020)
13. Takanashi, J.: Electroencephalography of dementia. Jpn. J. Med. Technol. **66**(2), 55–61 (2017)
14. Kaneko, M.: The majority of dementia cases are lifestyle-related. J. Jpn. Mibyou Syst. Assoc. **14**(1), 30–33 (2008)
15. Matsuura, M.: Age-related changes in Electroencephalographic (EEG) patterns. Jpn. J. Electroencephalogr. Electronmyogr. **22**(2), 106–107 (1994)
16. Matsuura, M.: Interpretation of EEG in the elderly (1) Background activity and changes with activation procedures. Clin. Electroencephalogr. **45**(8), 447–453 (2003)
17. Otomo, E.: Electroencephalography (EEG) in the elderly. Clin. Electroencephalogr. **63**(6), 214–220 (1964)
18. Dustman, R.E., Shearer, D.E., Emmerson, R.Y.: EEG and event-related potentials in normal aging. Prog. Neurobiol. **41**(3), 369–401 (1993)
19. Nakano, T., Miyasaka, M., Ohtaka, T., Ohmori, K.: Longitudinal changes in computerized EEG and mental function of aged: a nine-year follow up study. Int. Psychogeriatr. **4**(1), 9–23 (1992)
20. Coben, L.A., Danziger, W.L., Storandt, M.: A longitudinal EEG study of mild senile dementia of Alzheimer type: changes at 1 year and 2.5 years. Electroencephalogr. Clin. Neurophysiol. **61**(2), 101–112 (1985)
21. Ishii, R., et al.: Electroencephalographic and physiological findings in relation to cognitive decline. Jpn. J. Geriatr. Psychiatry **23**(4), 420–428 (2012)

22. Mitsukura, Y., Sumali, B., Watanabe, H., Ikega, T., Nishimura T.: Frontotemporal EEG as potential biomarker for early MCI: a case–control study. BMC Psychiatry **22** (2022). https://doi.org/10.1186/s12888-022-03932-0
23. Suni, K., Takada, H.: Industrial application of simple electroencephalogram technology. Jpn. J. Hyg. **79**(suppl), S181–S181 (2024)
24. Sumi, K.: Research on early detection of mild dementia using simple electroencephalography and fMRI. Master's thesis in Department of Mechanical and System Engineering, School of Engineering, University of Fukui (2025)

Development of a Hand Hygiene Assessment Method Using Pix2pix

Fumiya Kinoshita[1]([✉]), Gaochao Cui[2], Miho Yoshii[3], and Hideaki Touyama[2]

[1] Mie University, Tsu, Mie, Japan
kinoshita@eng.mie-u.ac.jp
[2] Toyama Prefectural University, Toyama, Japan
[3] University of Toyama, Toyama, Japan

Abstract. In this study, we developed a hand hygiene assessment system using pix2pix, a type of generative adversarial network, by imaging the palms of nursing students after handwashing. For this, a fluorescent lotion was used for hand-wash training, and a black light was used to visualize the remaining residues after washing. In pix2pix, the adopted input image was a black light image obtained after handwashing, while the ground truth image was a binarized image created by extracting the residues remaining in the input image, as determined by a trained staff member. We used 433 paired images after handwashing as training data and employed 30 images for verification. To evaluate the training model, we used the intersection over union (IoU) metric to assess the degree of overlap between the generated image and the ground truth image. The results indicated that the IoU value was highest when the training model with data expansion was used ($p < 0.05$). Subsequently, the effectiveness of this assessment method was verified using data from six handwashing measurements performed on the nursing students each week. The results showed that the percentage of unwashed hands decreased significantly after the fourth measurement ($p < 0.05$).

Keywords: Hand hygiene · Direct observation method · Generative adversarial network (GAN) · pix2pix · Intersection over Union (IoU)

1 Introduction

The novel coronavirus disease that emerged at the end of 2019 (COVID-19) developed into a global pandemic with many deaths and has attracted great social concern [1]. COVID-19 exhibits community-acquired spread. When infected individuals enter or are transported to hospitals, it can develop into a nosocomial infection. The damage caused by nosocomial infections is enormous, as many elderly and vulnerable patients are admitted to hospitals. In such situations, the most important and basic measure for preventing infectious diseases is hand hygiene. Hand hygiene is a general term that applies to handwashing, hand disinfection, and surgical hand disinfection, and it refers to the process of removing organic matter such as dirt and transient bacteria from the hands [2]. Handwashing has been a cultural and religious practice for centuries, but scientific

© The Author(s), under exclusive license to Springer Nature Switzerland AG 2026
M. Antona and C. Stephanidis (Eds.): HCII 2025, LNCS 16335, pp. 183–195, 2026.
https://doi.org/10.1007/978-3-032-12781-5_12

evidence of its role in preventing disease only emerged in the early 19th century [3, 4]. The principle of hand hygiene is to reduce dirt and bacteria on the hands of healthcare workers as much as possible and to keep them clean while caring for patients. Maintaining clean hands ensures safety in medical care and nursing, benefiting not only the patients but also the medical staff. For hand hygiene methods, it is common to refer to the guidelines issued by the Centers for Disease Control and Prevention (CDC) and the World Health Organization (WHO) [5, 6]. These guidelines provide explanations based on a substantial amount of literature and research data, and they include recommendations that are easy to follow according to the situation [7].

Common methods for evaluating hand hygiene include indirect observation, which assesses the amount of hand disinfectant used, and direct observation, which monitors the timing of handwashing and disinfection methods with the naked eye. However, the WHO guidelines recommend direct observation by trained staff [7]. On the other hand, direct observation faces challenges such as securing trained staff and the time required to monitor multiple situations. Additionally, since direct observation is a subjective evaluation, the results may vary depending on the staff's level of proficiency [8]. Methods for quantitatively evaluating hand hygiene include the palm stamp method, ATP wipe test, and glove juice method [9–12]. The palm stamp method utilizes a special culture medium, and the number of bacteria on the hands is visualized by pressing the palm against this medium before and after handwashing. However, this method requires culturing the bacteria from the hands, which can be costly and time-consuming. The ATP wipe test analyzes adenosine triphosphate (ATP) present in living cells such as those from animals, plants, and microorganisms. In this method, ATP wiped from the palm emits light through a chemical reaction with a special reagent. The amount of light emitted is then evaluated as an indicator of contamination. Since the ATP wipe test does not use a culture medium, it is less costly and time-consuming than the palm stamp method. However, the results can vary based on how the wipe is used and the pressure applied with the wipe stick [13]. The glove juice method is an evaluation technique for hand hygiene recommended by the U.S. Food and Drug Administration (FDA). In this method, subjects wear rubber gloves into which a sampling liquid and a neutralizing agent are poured. Afterward, the bacterial liquid from the gloves is cultured, and the number of bacteria on the hands is measured to assess hand hygiene. However, the glove juice method evaluates the total number of bacteria within the entire rubber glove, making it unsuitable for assessing specific areas of the palm.

As mentioned above, there are several methods to quantitatively evaluate hand hygiene, but existing methods have various issues, such as the need for specialized measuring equipment and the costs and time required for evaluation. Therefore, there is a need for a quantitative hand hygiene evaluation method that addresses these problems, is simple to use, and does not require extensive time for feedback of results.

The author's group has been developing a quantitative hand hygiene evaluation method mainly based on image processing [14–16]. In a previous study, we proposed a method using pix2pix, a type of generative adversarial network (GAN), to determine the binarization threshold, with the hope that information beyond brightness values would be reflected in the results [16]. Pix2pix is an image generation algorithm that learns the relationship between two paired images (input image and ground truth image) and generates an estimated image that takes this relationship into account when an input image is provided [17–19]. In previous research, the input image was a black light image taken after handwashing, while the ground truth image was a binarized image in which the unwashed area was extracted from the input image by a trained staff member. As a result, it was confirmed that the learning model using pix2pix produces an image similar to the perspective of the trained staff member. However, the pix2pix learning model in the previous research demonstrated insufficient agreement in the unwashed area between the estimated image and the ground truth image when compared with image processing methods that do not use neural networks. In the present paper, we developed a quantitative evaluation method for hand hygiene using image processing, extracting the unwashed area using Otsu's binarization method and our proposed method employing pix2pix, and evaluated the degree of overlap with the ground truth image using the intersection over union (IoU). Additionally, by applying this evaluation method to palm images taken during weekly hand-wash practice sessions, we also investigated students' handwashing skills in relation to the number of lectures.

2 Experimental

At the Department of Nursing, Toyama University School of Medicine, we use a hand-washing evaluation kit (Spectro Pro Plus Kit, Moraine Corporation) to provide hand hygiene education to nursing students. Students applied a special fluorescent lotion (Spectro Pro Plus special lotion, Moraine Corporation) to the entire palm of their hands and wash their hands hygienically according to the guidelines recommended by the WHO. Afterward, students evaluated their handwashing skills by examining areas that were not washed under a black light. The palm images used in this experiment were taken of nursing students' palms during this hand-wash practice session. This experiment was conducted after obtaining approval from the Toyama Prefectural University Ethics Committee (H31-10) and was carried out in accordance with the Declaration of Helsinki and with the subjects' informed consent.

In order to standardize the environment for taking palm images, we developed a special shooting box. The dimensions of the shooting box were 30 cm in height, 30 cm in width, and 45 cm in depth. Two LED fluorescent lamps (RE-BLIS04-60F, Ryudo Co., Ltd.) and two black lights (PL10BLB, Sankyo Denki) were installed inside the shooting box (Fig. 1). When taking palm images, the black lights were turned on, the opening was covered with a black curtain, and the image was captured with a digital camera (PowerShot G7 X Mark II, Canon). The resolution of the captured image was 5,472 × 3,072 px, with shooting parameters set to a resolution of 72 ppi, an F value of 2.8, a shutter speed of 1/60 s, ISO sensitivity of 125, and a focal length of 20 cm. These parameters were chosen to prevent image overexposure when shooting with the fluorescent lamp on, while ensuring that the palm remained in focus. The method for capturing palm images is outlined below.

1. The subject applies fluorescent lotion to the entire palm of the hand and checks under black light to confirm that the lotion has been applied correctly.

2. The subject washes their hands thoroughly using running water and soap according to WHO guidelines. After washing, they dry their hands with a paper towel.
3. The subject places their right hand, palm up, in the shooting box, and the photographer takes one photo under fluorescent light and another under black light (Fig. 2).

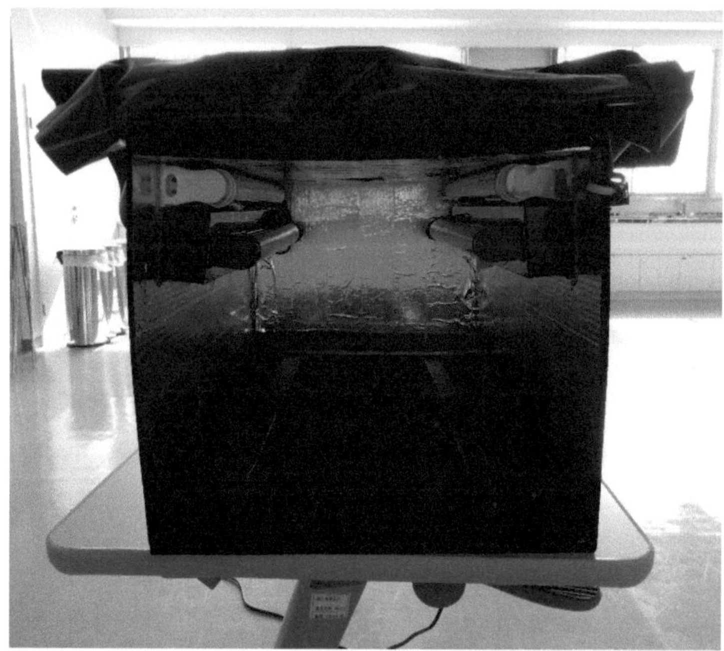

Fig. 1. Illustration of imaging box.

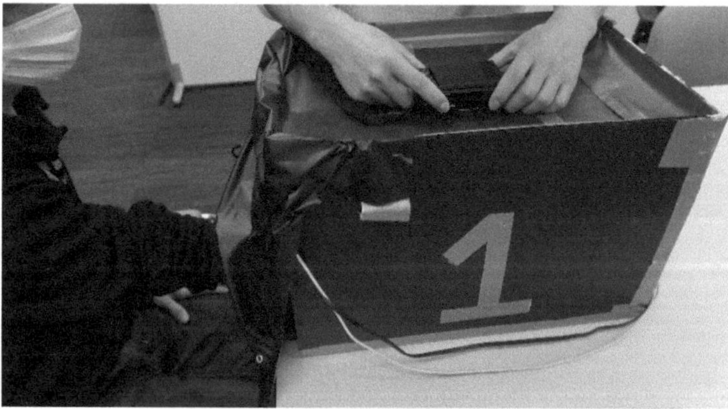

Fig. 2. Experimental scene.

3   Analysis Method

3.1   Preprocessing of Image Data

Through the hand-wash practice sessions, 463 palm images after handwashing were collected for this experiment. Contaminants on the floor of the shooting box, such as remnants of the fluorescent lotion, may affect image analysis. Therefore, the right arm was extracted from the image taken under black light using the image captured under fluorescent light. For contour extraction, edge detection using the Sobel method and basic morphological operations were performed using MATLAB's Image Processing Toolbox [20]. Figure 3a shows an image taken under fluorescent lighting, and Fig. 3b displays a binarized image in which the contours of the arm area were extracted from Fig. 3a, with the arm area painted white and the rest painted black. Figure 3c is an image taken under black lighting, overlaid with the results from Fig. 3b.

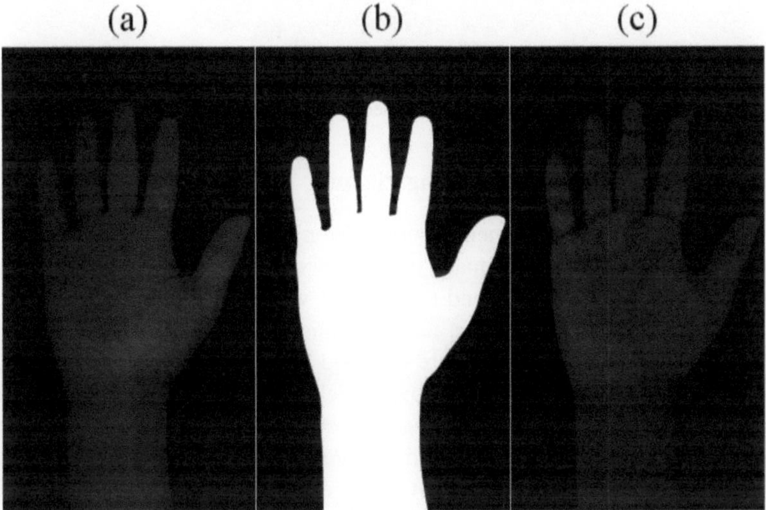

Fig. 3. Preprocessing method of captured image under (a) fluorescent light, (b) binarization, and (c) black light.

In this system, the arm-to-wrist area of the black light image, with the background painted black, was excluded from the analysis because the target was areas in the palm that had not been washed (Fig. 4a). Next, focusing on the luminance value of the black light image, binarization was performed so that areas visually identified by trained staff as unwashed were displayed in black (Fig. 4b). To adjust the pixel ratio of the vertical to horizontal directions to 1:1, black pixels were evenly distributed at the top and on the left and right sides of the image to ensure that the number of pixels in all black light images was 4,746 × 4,746 px. Additionally, because the purpose of this system is not to extract the outline of the palm, only the unwashed areas were displayed in black in the ground truth image.

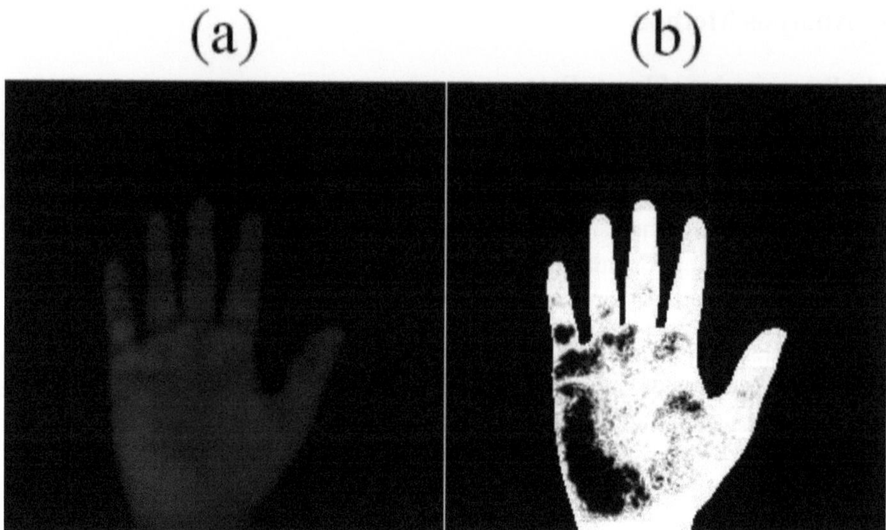

Fig. 4. Method for generating ground truth images: (a) Input image (brightness tripled for the paper), (b) binarized image showing the unwashed residues left.

3.2   Creating a Learning Model Using Pix2pix

In this paper, pix2pix was implemented with reference to the pix2pix-TensorFlow repository on GitHub [21]. The input image used for pix2pix was a black light image taken after handwashing, while the ground truth image was a binarized image in which the unwashed areas were extracted from the input image by one trained staff member. In this experiment, 463 palm images were obtained through the hand-wash practice sessions; however, when used for the learning model, there was a bias in the proportion of unwashed areas in the ground truth image. Therefore, we also investigated a learning model using a data augmentation method to equalize the proportion of unwashed areas in the ground truth image [22]. For data augmentation, we first created a histogram from the ground truth image, with the horizontal axis representing the proportion of unwashed areas (in 10% increments) and the vertical axis representing the number of images. Next, the bias in the proportion of unwashed areas was assessed from the created histogram, and for the group of images with a small number of samples, three processes—namely enlargement, reduction, and translation—were applied to augment the data. In the enlargement and reduction processes, the size of the palm was varied from 85% to 115% in 5% increments, and in the translation process, the position of the palm was shifted horizontally by ± 5 px and ± 10 px, respectively. Figure 5 shows histograms of the proportion of unwashed areas and the number of images before and after data augmentation. After data augmentation, the total number of paired images was 1,800.

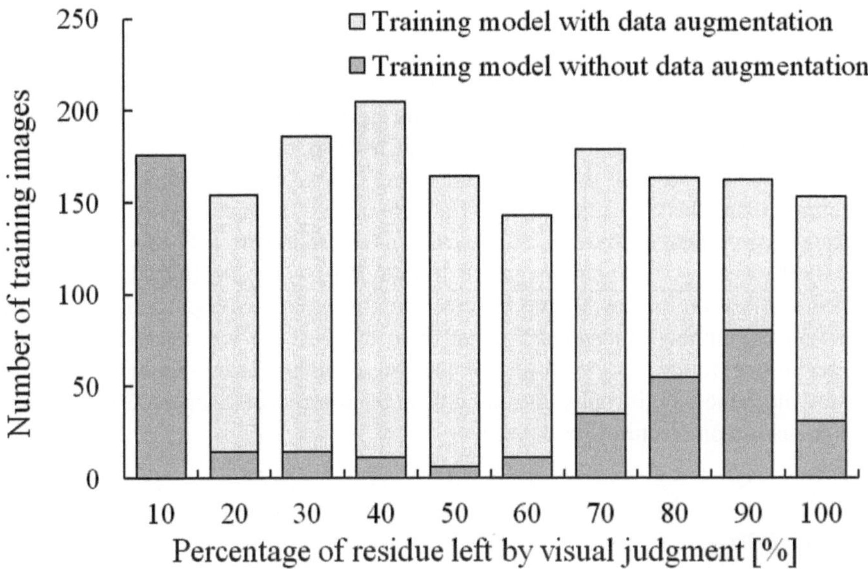

Fig. 5. Histogram of the number of training images and the percentage of residues left.

3.3 Validation Method of the Learning Model

To evaluate the learning model, leave-one-out cross-validation (LOOCV) was used, and validation images were randomly selected to include 10 black light images with a proportion of unwashed areas in the ground truth image of 30% or less, 30%–70%, and 70% or more. Additionally, Otsu's binarization was applied to the verification images to calculate the threshold at which the degree of separation was greatest, resulting in a binarized image that extracted the unwashed area from the verification image. The unwashed area was extracted using both the pix2pix method and Otsu's binarization, and the degree of overlap with the ground truth image was evaluated using IoU.

4 Results

For all verification images, the unwashed area was extracted using both the Otsu's binarization method and the pix2pix method. Examples of the input image, ground truth image, and estimated image generated from the verification image are shown in Fig. 6. Figure 6a is an example of a black light image with an unwashed area ratio of 30% or less, Fig. 6b is an example of a black light image with an unwashed area ratio of 30%–70%, and Fig. 6c is an example of a black light image with an unwashed area ratio of 70% or more. From the left, the order of images is: the input image, the ground truth image, the estimated image generated from Otsu's binarization, the estimated image generated from the learning model before data augmentation, and the estimated image generated from the learning model after data augmentation. The numbers in the bottom right corner of the binarized images indicate the percentage of black pixels in the palm. Next, the degree of overlap between the area of the estimated image and the ground truth image was evaluated using IoU (Fig. 7). For statistical analysis, one-way ANOVA was performed, followed by multiple comparisons using the Tukey-Kramer method. As a result, significant differences were observed in all comparisons of IoU, with the degree of overlap between the estimated image and the ground truth image being highest when the learning model after data augmentation was used ($p < 0.05$).

Next, the handwashing skills of students were investigated according to the number of lectures, using this evaluation method for palm images taken during all six hand-wash practice sessions held each week. The learning model following data augmentation was used for the analysis, and palm images of 15 individuals who attended all lectures were used as verification images. Figure 8 shows the change in the proportion of unwashed areas with the number of lectures. For statistical analysis, one-way analysis of variance was performed, followed by multiple comparisons using the Tukey-Kramer method. As a result, the values significantly decreased from the fourth lecture onwards compared to the first and second lectures ($p < 0.05$).

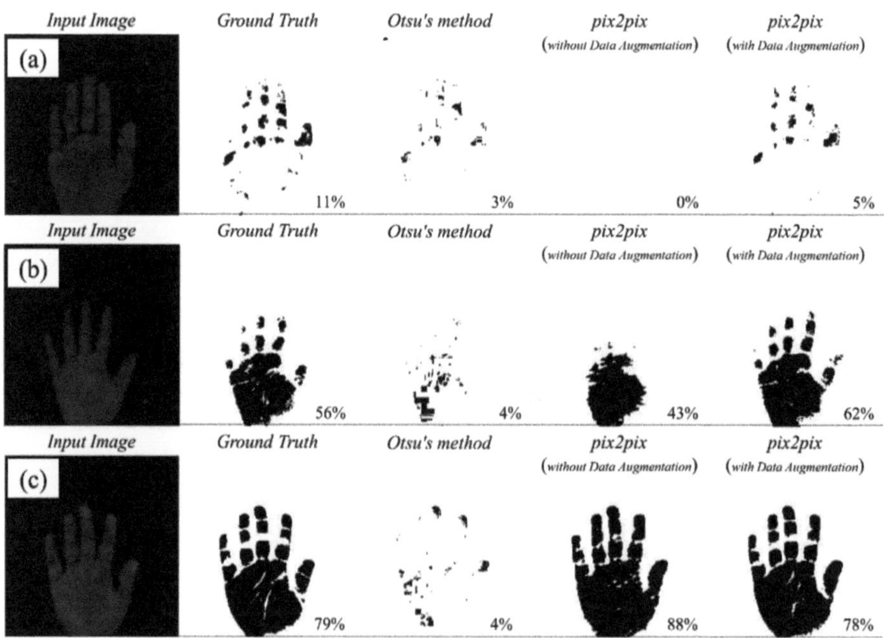

Fig. 6. Example of estimated images generated from verification images.

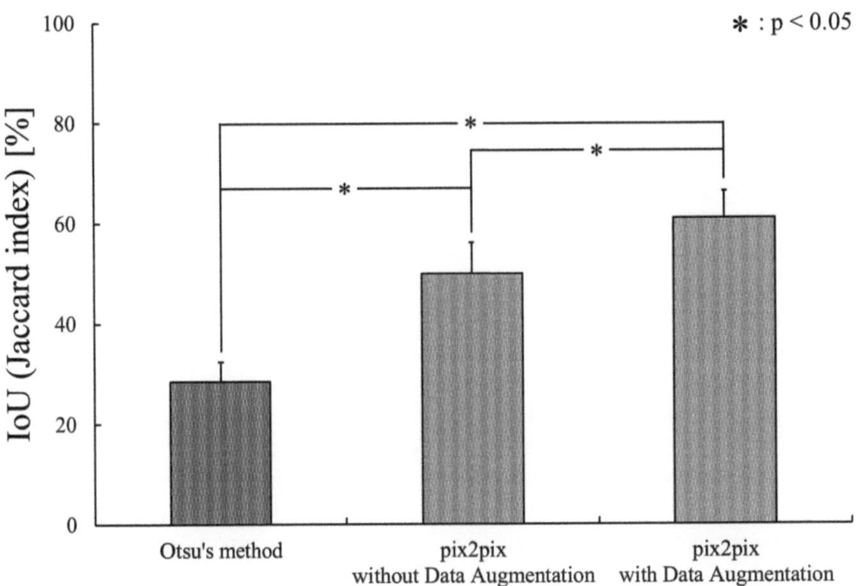

Fig. 7. Quantitative evaluation of each method using IoU (Mean ± SE).

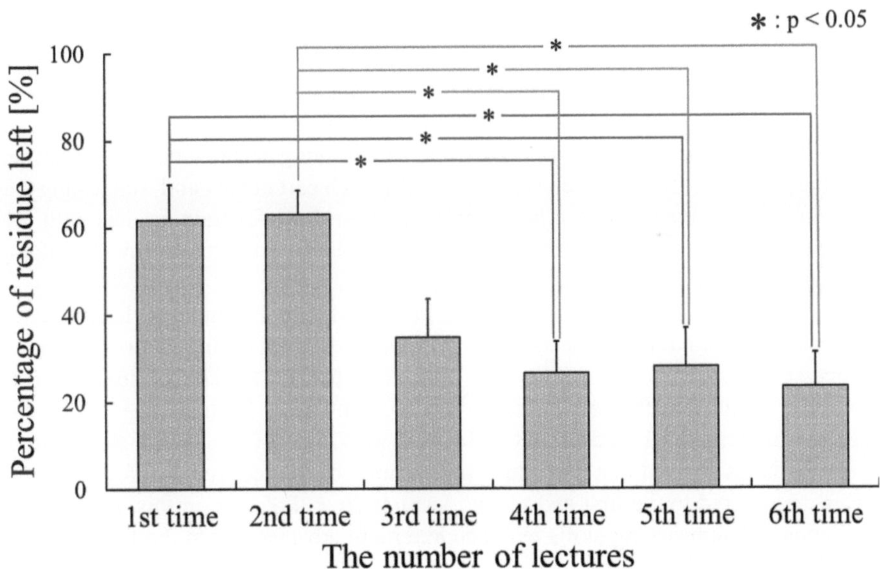

Fig. 8. Change in percentage of residues left with respect to number of lectures (Mean ± SE).

5 Discussion

The WHO guidelines recommend direct observation by trained staff as a method for evaluating hand hygiene. However, issues with direct observation have been identified, such as the need to secure trained staff and the time required to observe multiple scenarios.

Additionally, since direct observation is a subjective evaluation by staff, the results may vary depending on their skill level. In this paper, we focused on palm images after handwashing and developed a hand hygiene evaluation method that simulates the perspective of trained staff. For image processing methods, we concentrated on a method using Otsu's binarization and a method using pix2pix. The input image for pix2pix was a black light image taken after handwashing, while the ground truth image was a binarized image in which unwashed areas were extracted from the input image taken by a trained staff member. When the test image was input into the pix2pix learning model, the generated estimated image closely resembled the ground truth image. Next, unwashed areas were extracted from all the test images using both the Otsu's binarization method and the pix2pix method, and the degree of overlap with the ground truth image was evaluated using IoU. As a result, the IoU value was highest when the learning model after data augmentation was used. Here, Figs. 9 and 10 show examples where the accuracy of the estimated image improved and instances where it did not improve due to the data augmentation method. In Figs. 9a and 9b, the accuracy of the estimated image improved with data augmentation. On the other hand, in Fig. 10a, the accuracy of the estimated image improved with data augmentation, but the values were significantly different. Furthermore, in Fig. 10b, the accuracy decreased with data augmentation. There are two possible reasons for this. One reason may be that the light was not sufficiently blocked during the photographing process. Although the right arm was inserted and the opening was covered with a blackout curtain, insufficient light blocking emphasized parts of the hand other than the fluorescent lotion, which likely reduced accuracy. The other reason may be that the learning model was not effectively created with training data that contained few unwashed areas. With training data that has many unwashed areas, the entire palm is painted black, so the impact of unwashed areas is less significant depending on the part of the hand. Conversely, with training data that has few unwashed areas, the location of the unwashed areas varies for each part of the hand, suggesting that sufficient learning may not have been achieved. Therefore, for training data with few unwashed areas, the accuracy of the learning model is expected to improve by adding more data.

Finally, this evaluation method was used to investigate the students' handwashing skills based on the number of lectures for palm images taken during all six hand-wash practice sessions conducted each week. When we checked the change in the rate of incomplete washing with the number of lectures, the values fluctuated as the number of lectures increased: 61.73%, 62.98%, 34.76%, 26.47%, 28.07%, and 23.34%. Multiple comparisons showed that the values significantly decreased from the fourth lecture onwards compared to the first and second lectures ($p < 0.05$). From this, it is thought that students' handwashing skills may become more advanced from the fourth lecture onwards.

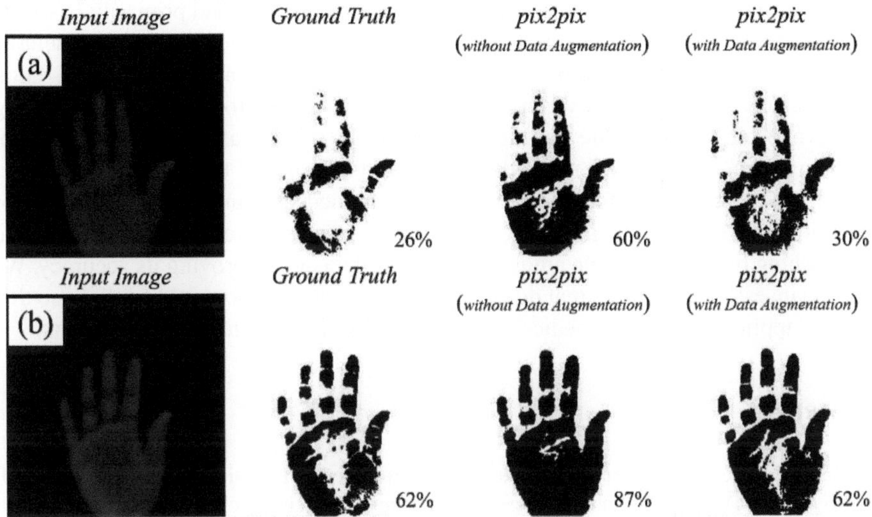

Fig. 9. Example of improved accuracy due to data augmentation.

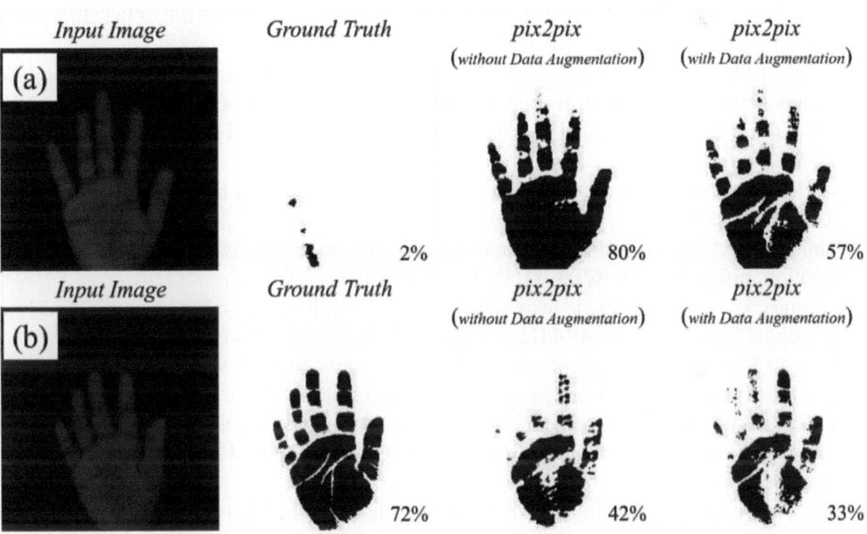

Fig. 10. Example of no improvement in accuracy due to data augmentation.

6   Conclusion

In response to the unprecedented infectious disease of COVID-19, various infection control measures have been implemented in the medical field according to the situation. The most important and basic measure for preventing infectious diseases is hand hygiene, for which it is common to refer to guidelines issued by the CDC and WHO. However, when it comes to evaluation methods, the subjective direct observation method is proposed as the gold standard. Therefore, in this paper, we focused on a method primarily based on image processing to develop a simple and quantitative hand hygiene evaluation method. We extracted unwashed areas using both the pix2pix method and Otsu's binarization and evaluated the degree of overlap of these areas with the ground truth image using IoU. As a result, the IoU value was highest when using pix2pix after data augmentation. This image processing-based method can address the issues of the conventional direct observation method, including the need to secure trained staff and the time required for evaluation. In the future, we aim to use this method as the first screening tool for hygienic handwashing by increasing the amount of training data and improving its accuracy. We will also investigate methods that do not require fluorescent lotion or black light so that it can be applied not only in medical settings but also in educational environments.

References

1. Kikuchi, T.: COVID-19 outbreak: an elusive enemy. Respir. Investig. **58**(4), 225–226 (2020)
2. Misao, H.: Thinking about hand hygiene: unchanging principles, changing evidence. Infect. Control ICT J. **11**(1), 7–12 (2016). (in Japanese)
3. Katz, J.D.: Hand washing and hand disinfection: more than your mother taught you. Anesthesiol. Clin. North Am. **22**(3), 457–471 (2004)
4. Labarraque, A.G.: XXI. Instructions and observations concerning the use of the chlorides of soda and lime. Am. J. Med. Sci. **1**(15), 207–210 (1831)
5. Boyce, J.M., Pittet, D.: Guideline for hand hygiene in health-care settings: recommendations of the Healthcare Infection Control Practices Advisory Committee and the HICPAC/SHEA/APIC/IDSA Hand Hygiene Task Force. Infect. Control Hosp. Epidemiol. **23**(12), S3–S41 (2002)
6. World Health Organization: WHO guidelines on hand hygiene in health care. World Health **30**(1), 270 (2009)
7. Ichinohe, M.: Basic hand hygiene techniques: How to choose the right method for your situation. Infect. Control ICT J. **11**(1), 19–25 (2016). (in Japanese)
8. Erasmus, V., et al.: Systematic review of studies on compliance with hand hygiene guidelines in hospital care. Infect. Control Hosp. Epidemiol. **31**(3), 283–294 (2010)
9. Kato, T.: Systematic assessment and evaluation for improvement of hand hygiene compliance. Jpn. J. Environ. Infect. **30**(4), 274–280 (2015). (in Japanese)
10. Sato, M., Saito, R.: Nursing students' knowledge of hand hygiene and hand hygiene compliance rate during on-site clinical training. Jpn. J. Environ. Infect. **34**(3), 182–189 (2019). (in Japanese)
11. U.S. Food and Drug Administration (FDA): Guidelines for effectiveness testing of surgical hand scrub (glove juice test). Fed. Regist. **43**, 1242–1243 (1978)
12. Hirose, Y., Yano, H., Baba, S., Kodama, K., Kimura, S.: Educational effect of practice in hygienic handwashing on nursing students. Jpn. J. Environ. Infect. **14**(2), 123–126 (1999). (in Japanese)
13. Murakami, K., Umesako, S.: Study of methods of examination by the full-hand touch plate method in food hygiene. Jpn. J. Environ. Infect. **28**(1), 29–32 (2013). (in Japanese)
14. Yamamoto, K., Yoshii, M., Kinoshita, F., Touyama, H.: Classification vs regression by CNN for handwashing skills evaluations in nursing education. In: Proceedings of the IEEE International Conference on Artificial Intelligence in Information and Communication (ICAIIC), Fukuoka, Japan, pp. 590–593 (2020)

15. Yamamoto, K., Yoshii, M., Kinoshita, F., Touyama, H.: Quantitative evaluation of hand washing skills based on convolutional neural network for nursing education. Forma **35**(1), 15–19 (2020)
16. Kinoshita, F., Nagano, K., Cui, G., Yoshii, M., Touyama, H.: A study on novel hand hygiene evaluation system using pix2pix. Adv. Sci. Technol. Eng. Syst. J. **7**(2), 112–118 (2022)
17. Shinozaki, T.: Recent progress of GAN–Generative Adversarial Network. Artif. Intell. **33**(2), 181–188 (2018). (in Japanese)
18. Goodfellow, I.J., et al.: Generative adversarial nets. In: Proceedings of the International Conference on Neural Information Processing Systems (NeurIPS), Quebec, Canada, pp. 2672–2680 (2014)
19. Isola, P., Zhu, J., Zhou, T., Efros, A.: Image-to-image translation with conditional adversarial networks. In: Proceedings of the IEEE Conference on Computer Vision and Pattern Recognition (CVPR), Hawaii, USA, pp. 5967–5976 (2017)
20. MathWorks: Detect cell using edge detection and morphology. Accessed 4 Apr 2022
21. TensorFlow: Pix2Pix tutorial. Accessed 4 Apr 2022
22. Shorten, C., Khoshgoftaar, T.M.: A survey on image data augmentation for deep learning. J. Big Data **6**(1), 1–48 (2019)

People's Interest in, and Experience of, Smart Home Technology – A Survey-Based Study

Martin Maguire[(✉)] and Hye Joo Cheong

School of Design and Creative Arts, Loughborough University, Leicestershire LE11 3TU, UK
m.c.maguire@lboro.ac.uk, jackie_0820@naver.com

Abstract. This paper reviews people's interest in and experience of smart home technology as well as barriers for its adoption. Two survey studies were carried out. The first, based in the UK, surveyed people's levels of interest in technology in the future smart kitchen. There was clear interest in innovations that increased safety and security, while designs that made life easier through better comfort and convenience were also appreciated. The second survey studied the impact of smart home technology on individuals in the UK and South Korea who were experiencing physical discomfort. It was found that while most participants were aware of smart home products, the take up of them was more limited. However, those that were currently using it were generally satisfied with it. Reasons for dissatisfaction and prioritised features for the smart home devices are also reported as well as recommendations for addressing smart home user issues.

Keywords: Smart home · Home automation · Intelligent home · Smart kitchen · Physical discomfort · People with disabilities

1 Introduction

A smart home is a residence designed or set up to provide people with enhanced security, comfort, convenience and energy efficiency, by use of devices or products connected to a central hub or network. The system is operated by the user either within the home or remotely. Many devices will be set up for automatic operation.

1.1 History of Home Automation

The idea of home automation has been around for a long time with devices like vacuum cleaners and refrigerators being invented in the early part of the twentieth century. Science fiction writers, such as Ray Bradbury, imagined a future where homes were connected and interactive, but could run themselves. In his short story, 'There Will Come Soft Rains', he describes an automated home that continues to function even after humans have died out (Bradbury 1950). The 1950s Jetson's cartoon also predicted futuristic home technology, some of which has come true such as video calling, hot food vending machines, and robot cleaners (Evans and Realtor 2024). In 1966 to 1967, James Sutherland designed and built the first integrated smart home system. His Echo

© The Author(s), under exclusive license to Springer Nature Switzerland AG 2026
M. Antona and C. Stephanidis (Eds.): HCII 2025, LNCS 16335, pp. 196–211, 2026.
https://doi.org/10.1007/978-3-032-12781-5_13

IV design was essentially a bespoke home computer which allowed consumers to create digital shopping lists, control the temperature of the home, turn appliances on and off, and to access weather forecasts, (Cortesi 2015).

The Millennium House was a British show-home opened in 1998 to demonstrate how running a home could be automated with computer-controlled heating, security, lights, doors and gardens. In 1999, Microsoft created their vision for a smart home located in Richmond, Washington. A video of its technological features, demonstrating its potential, was produced showing a family acting out a typical afternoon and evening in the home (Callaham 2023). While not all the ideas came true exactly as they were shown, many of them exist in some way today.

In the 21st century, smart home technologies became more affordable, modular and therefore viable for consumers. The Internet of Things (IoT) has bolstered this trend by integrating various home devices into a unified system that can be remotely controlled via a smartphone or digital assistant (Liu et al. 2023). The development of more accurate voice recognition technology via smart speakers has also provided convenient control of devices within the home. Assigning different smart speaker wake-up names for each person in the household can give each one independent control to a certain level.

Despite the development of many innovative features and gadgets, the growth of smart homes has been hampered by the lack of a common standard for communications between products and appliances. Different protocols have their advantages and disadvantages but, along with the proliferation of more stable routers, Wi-Fi has become the most common communications system for smart home networks. The ability to retrofit products using wireless or powerline connections has allowed householders to experiment with smart appliances and to build them up according to their needs.

Contemporary smart homes are particularly concerned with better security and greener living by helping ensure that homes are not expending unnecessary energy and by alerting the owner to intruders using remote video surveillance. Facilities such as automated lights, voice-controlled devices, and heating schedules learned from people's behavior patterns also offer greater convenience. Artificial Intelligence and IoT will continue to make home systems more intelligent, connected and capable. What is important though is how these developments impinge on the quality of life of the inhabitants.

1.2 Aim of the Paper

As the global population ages, the need for supportive home environments increases. Smart home technology adoption in the UK is growing quickly with 39% of households currently using devices such as smart speakers, thermostats and security systems. This percentage is predicted to increase to 50.2% by 2027, which may then be considered mainstream acceptance (Ukpanah 2024). The aim of this paper is to understand people's needs and their experiences of smart home technology (both positive and negative), so that improvements can be made and to encourage more sections of society, especially vulnerable groups, to benefit from it.

2 Literature Review

According to Marikyan et al. (2019), the aim of a smart home is to anticipate and respond to the needs of the occupants to enhance their quality of life and promote independent living. Functions that can assist with this are:

1. **Comfort and convenience**: Features that make activities and tasks in the home easier such as simple user interfaces and operating appliances with convenient modes of input within the home or remotely. These may include TVs, lighting, blinds, beds, cupboards or worktops.
2. **Automation**: Automated operation of functions such as movement sensing lights, robot vacuum cleaners, and smart thermostats that learn and operate on the patterns of movement within the home.
3. **Security**: Monitoring through smart cameras, sensors, and doorbell cameras; reporting (via smartphone) when suspicious activity or breaches occur, e.g. break-ins, water or gas leaks.
4. **Health and safety management**: Monitoring the health and well-being of an occupant and acting when their health status requires e.g. respiratory and sleeping disorder assessment, activity tracking, falls detection, telemedicine, or a hospital virtual ward.
5. **Environmental control**: Efficient use of energy in the home e.g. drawing from solar powered batteries during when energy costs are high, and the grid when rates are cheaper (smart grids).

2.1 Control Within a Smart Home

Control is a key issue with smart homes and how individuals share this, for example with parents and children having different levels of control or privileges (Greeng and Roesner 2019). Control is also concerned with automating various functions and services within the home and responding to information from outside the home, e.g. utility price signals. However, it is also said that the holy grail may be less about control over technology but matching it to the hectic chaotic and demands of people's lives which smart homes must accommodate. As Alam et al. (2012) state, smart homes require an understanding of human behavior and effective algorithms to solve the uncertainty problem within the home.

2.2 Barriers to Adoption

Nascimento (2023) analysed the focus of studies concerned with the benefits and barriers of smart home implementation. 84 studies addressed infringement and security as the main barrier to universalization, 24 documents cited technical complexity, and 22 dealt with doubts regarding the usefulness and reliability of the technology. Pricing was addressed in 16 documents, alongside other barriers faced by users such as a lack of prior knowledge, repair costs, maintenance, and reluctance to embrace new technologies.

Pal et al. (2018) conducted a survey to better understand the adoption of smart homes by elderly users. It was found that if potential users felt that smart technology was compatible with their home, if it provided improved convenience through automation and improved feelings of self-capability and satisfaction, then their likelihood of adopting smart home technology increased. However, if users perceive a potential loss of security, risk with their personal data, or that the perceived benefits did not justify the cost outlay, then it decreased. Lack of information is also a barrier. A survey of 200 elderly individuals revealed widespread anxiety about how they would use smart home technology (Zhou et al. 2024). Without directions for correct usage, they tended to distrust its apparent benefits.

Security is another barrier. Wilson et al. (2015) found that potential users were reluctant to introduce sensing technologies into their home as they could leave sensing trails that others could monitor and use as opportunities to break in when the house is empty. Primary concerns among consumers were found to be cybersecurity and potential attacks (Hammi et al. 2022). Technical problems can also occur with smart home technology that users may need to deal with and which may discourage take-up. They include compatibility challenges, internet connectivity problems, power source drain issues, and difficulties setting up the smart home equipment (Reolink 2024).

While there is support for more intelligent use of energy resources, there was also concern that monitoring use by energy companies may try to control demand. Paetz et al. (2012) argues that greater transparency and accountability on behalf of smart home developers, energy utilities and others is needed to make explicit how all stakeholders may benefit from smart home development.

2.3 Psychological Benefits and Satisfaction

According to an analysis of housing satisfaction conducted by the Korea Disabled People's Development Institute (KODDI), the daily life of individuals within their homes could be more independent and convenient if protective measures such as suitable systems or barrier-free environments were provided for those with disabilities (Kim et al. 2011).

For people with disabilities, smart home technology can therefore be crucial in enhancing their feelings of independence. In a study by Sohn et al. (2012) a smart home setup was constructed based on a preliminary survey reflecting disabled individuals' requirements. Three severely disabled individuals then resided there for 2 weeks. It was found that being in a smart home could be beneficial for them in performing their daily activities in contrast to relying on other people which, over time, can reduce their self-determination.

A study was conducted to find out what determines people's satisfaction with smart home technology and what influences rates of its adoption (Alexandr 2024). The research included 225 participants randomly selected from different age groups. They were asked to use three different smart home technologies and provide feedback. As a result, four main results were drawn. Firstly, satisfaction increased with longer and more frequent use. Secondly, combining various technologies boosted satisfaction and adoption rates. Thirdly, longer pre-training periods resulted in heightened satisfaction. Lastly, younger users showed greater positivity than older users who might therefore need more support for them to adopt smart home devices.

3   Survey of People's Interest in Smart Technology in the Kitchen

The kitchen is an important space in the home. To support easier use and independent living for older people, it is desirable to provide a kitchen environment so that tasks can be performed without unnecessary effort and strain. While good workspace design and physical ergonomics can help to achieve this, smart technology can potentially assist further.

3.1   Addressing Ergonomics Problems in the Kitchen

A UK Research Council funded Transitions in Kitchen Living or TiKL project studied older people's abilities, needs, likes and dislikes in relation to their current kitchen (Sims et al. 2011, Maguire et al. 2014). It was found that kitchen users with age-related disabilities can be affected in different ways:

Loss of Sight. Visual impairment can make it difficult to read instructions on packaging, see the labelling on appliance controls and displays on appliances, or judge the cleanliness of a kitchen floor.

Loss of Hearing. Hearing impairment will affect a person's ability to hear auditory signals such as a telephone or doorbell ringing, completion of a washing machine cycle, or a CO2 alarm. Simultaneous sounds from devices such as TVs and radios can increase this problem further.

Dexterity and Strength. Reduced strength due to health conditions such as arthritis can affect the user's ability to lift and carry pans, plates, kettles, and to open jars, bottles and cans. Standing for a period can also be difficult.

Movement and Balance. Chronic physical conditions can hamper a person when reaching up to cupboards or bending down to the floor e.g. to fill pet bowls. Balance can also be impaired preventing standing on a stool or steps to reach a high cupboard shelf.

3.2   Survey to Explore Requirements for Technological Support

Within the TiKL project a survey was carried out to determine people's interest in smart technology to manage potential problems in kitchen (Maguire et al. 2011). A list of potential innovations was created, such as a clothes iron that would turn itself off when the householder and other occupants left the home. A list of 15 smart kitchen innovations was created. Respondents were asked to indicate which ones they were interested in having. A comment could be added for each device as required. The sample consisted of 40 people (27 females, and 13 males, aged from 50 to 92 years) with an average age of 73. A summary of the survey results is shown in Table 1 in order of the number of participants interested in each innovation. The category of each innovation e.g., security, convenience, is also shown.

Participants were also asked to propose their own innovations. There was a requirement from two people for more help to be energy or water efficient in the kitchen. One suggested having a plug to cut down on energy use in the kitchen by avoiding standby

Table 1. User interest in and reactions to 'hi-tech' innovations in the kitchen (N = 40).

Innovation	% Would have	Comments
1. Shut off electrical equipment when you leave the house. **(Security)**	93%	It is easy to go out and forget that things are still on. It would be safer. It would save money on electricity not being used. Peace of mind.
2. Sensor alert if smoke, CO, fire or gas leak when you are out. **(Security)**	83%	It would help with safety. Good idea. Who would come to deal with it? If returned to the house and has been leak, putting on a light could cause fire.
3. Washing machine has only 6 buttons for easy use. **(Comfort/convenience)**	79%	Only use 2 or 3 programs most of the time. Less confusing. Too many programs are never used. I am happy with the simple dial of choices.
4. You or others alerted if water on the floor indicates possible flood. **(Security)**	79%	Useful – water can run a long time before noticed. It would be safer and avoid waste. Too many alarms may make you worry about too many minor things.
5. Quick cooling oven hob. **(Security)**	78%	It would be safer, especially for grandchildren. Good idea – have sometimes been caught out by residual heat on a ceramic hob.
6. Open/close windows and blinds with button press. **(Comfort/convenience)**	75%	It would be handy as my window is situated over the sink. It would make life easier as often I have to stretch to close them. It would be safer. Blind may hit items on windowsill. It would make us lazy.
7. Automatic task light when working in dark corner. **(Automation, Safety)**	73%	Very useful. I could see better and avoid eye strain. It could save energy. Safety and emergencies in the dark. Need good light all the time.
8. Lower worktop temporarily so can be used seated. **(Comfort/convenience)**	63%	Would enable people to keep their interest in cooking and their independence longer. Very practical for disabled or wheelchair users or someone who cannot stand for long. Loss of storage space below.

(continued)

while other suggested a better mixer tap so that hot water was delivered quickly rather than running it until it warmed up. Three people suggested a fridge facility to help assess

Table 1. (*continued*)

Innovation	% Would have	Comments
9. Cupboards adjustable in height (manually or remote controlled) (**Comfort/convenience**)	57%	Wonderful for older people. Safer than climbing steps. Would it be expensive? It would require work surface below to be kept clear.
10. Water sensor welfare alert if taps not run for some time. (**Security**)	55%	My daughter regularly checks I'm OK. Useful for emergencies e.g. if someone has fallen. You would have to be able to cancel the system if you went on holiday.
11. Food product placed on reader so cooking instructions are read out. (**Comfort/convenience**)	50%	Cooking temperature and time often in tiny writing. Great for those with limited sight. Another gadget to clutter up kitchen. Too technical. Just need bigger print.
12. Recipe display on wall so easier to follow when cooking. (**Convenience**)	48%	May make it more efficient and save writing recipe's down. Don't follow recipes. Prefer to print with large font. Interested to see prototype.
13. Press button on fridge to read out food items present or run out of. (**Convenience**)	38%	Would help with shopping. Good idea for freezer where more food is stored. Opening the door less saves energy. Unsure of the technology behind it. Would you trust it? I would also need to know if items are within date. I would need to log food items in and out.
14. Simple touch screen to order shopping and have delivered. (**Convenience**)	35%	Save carrying heavy shopping. Prefer the choice or to check quality in store. It feels too complicated for the people intended to help. If became disabled, friends would assist.
15. Instructions read out (vocalize) for food preparation and cooking actions. (**Convenience**)	28%	Cooking is an effort so it could help if tired. It would be useful if you couldn't read the cooking instructions label. I know how to cook things. I prefer to cook at my pace.

food quality e.g. *"Have the eggs or cheese gone off?"* Two people wanted to hand over complete tasks to technology: *"Something to do the ironing"* and *"A robot that could cook, clean, serve food, do the shopping and the washing and drying up"*.

One participant suggested extending welfare monitoring to include non-use of all water taps, toilet, bath etc. Another suggestion was a built-in ironing board that could be pulled out from a cupboard unit, be set at a reasonable working height with hanger storage above. Other ideas were a long arm grabber for lifting things off high shelves and a signal system to tell the householder when the inside of the oven needed cleaning.

3.3 Discussion

As the results show, there was strong interest in security/alarm-related innovations to make kitchens safer (e.g., sensor alerts and quick cooling hobs). There was also significant interest in innovations that provided more comfort or convenience through reduced mental or physical task load. These included simpler washing machine controls, remote control of blinds and windows, and the ability to lower and raise a worktop and cupboard with motors for more convenient use. However, there was concern that lowering a cupboard could collide with items on the worktop underneath. There was less support for features that seemed too technologically advanced, for example reading out the contents of a fridge or food packaging instructions. The idea of reading out cooking instructions lacked support as they seemed unnecessary for some respondents or could be out of step with the person performing the task.

As shown in Table 1, while technological innovations in the kitchen may seem useful, it is important that they are based on real user needs and tailored to the way users want to work. In accordance with Zhou et al.'s (2024) findings, potential customers may need more information and demonstrations of smart kitchen devices before they are willing to purchase them.

4 Survey on Smart Home Technology with People Suffering from Medical Conditions or Discomfort

One of the key groups that should be able to benefit from smart home technology is people who suffer from medical conditions or experience discomfort to enhance convenience in their lives. A questionnaire survey was carried out to consider the impact of smart home technology on this group of people in the UK and South Korea. The study gathered and analyzed information on individuals' awareness of smart home technology, their usage of any related products, reasons for non-usage, and opinions on product enhancement (Cheong 2024).

There were 100 respondents to the survey distributed by age as follows: 18–24 years (13%), 25–34 years (18%), 35–44 years (17%), 45–54 years (16%), 55–64 years (16%), and 65 or above (20%). In terms of gender, 55% of the participants were male, 43% were female, and 2% identified as non-binary. The sample included a diverse range of individuals, from those registered as disabled to those with chronic illnesses or suffering mild physical discomfort. Categorizing them into groups, 32% used mobility aids, 8% had visual impairment, 9% had hearing impairment, 20% experienced chronic pain, 27% had other physical and neurological disabilities, and 4% preferred not to say.

4.1 Awareness and Use of Smart Home Technology

While 72% of participants were familiar with smart home technology, only 40% reported using smart devices; 21% in South Korea, and 19% in the UK. The reasons for the 60 participants not using smart home technology were explored. They included: lack of information due to insufficient promotion (31 participants), high product and installation cost (31), benefit uncertainty (19), privacy or security concern (17), complexity of set up and use (13), lack of interest (7), and limited features (6). Despite these challenges, there was a significant interest in smart home technologies, with 88% of survey respondents (users and non-users) expressing a willingness to try new devices in the future.

4.2 Satisfaction with Smart Home Technology

The 40 participants who were users of smart home technology were presented with a list of smart device categories (e.g., medical or health management) and asked to indicate whether they felt satisfied, neutral, or dissatisfied with it. The results are shown on Fig. 1.

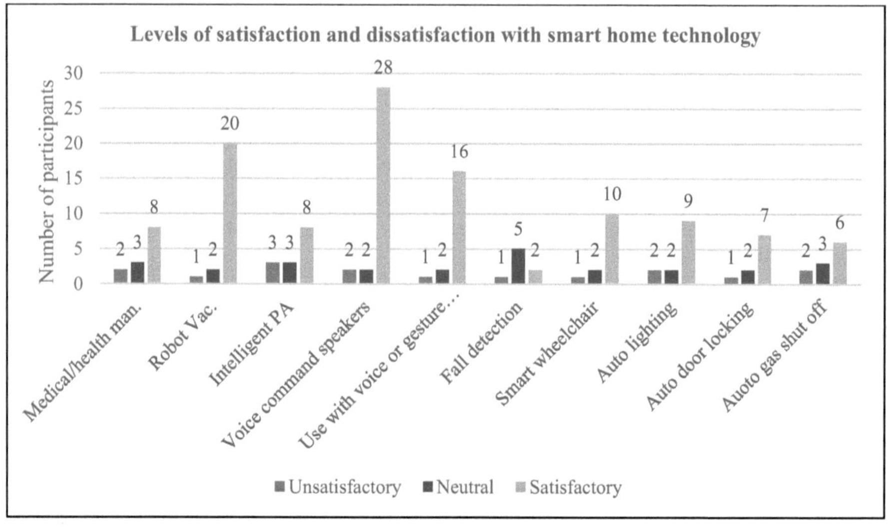

Fig. 1. Graphical representation of smart home product satisfaction (N = 100).

The devices which were most popular among the participants were: voice command smart speakers, robot vacuum cleaners, voice or gesture-controlled household appliances controlled, and automatic lighting. The chart also shows that users are mostly satisfied with the smart devices they use across nearly all the device categories, except fall detection. In terms of the percentage of users satisfied in each category, voice command products (typically smart speakers) were the highest (87.5%), followed by robot vacuum cleaners (87%), household appliances capable of voice or gesture recognition (84.2%), smart wheelchairs (76.9%), medical and health management systems (61.5%) and intelligent PA (personal assistant) systems (57.1%).

4.3 Reasons for Dissatisfaction

The reasons for dissatisfaction with smart home technology were explored with the 40 participants using it. As shown in Fig. 2, the two most frequently mentioned issues were malfunction of voice, facial, or gesture recognition, and connectivity problems with Wi-Fi or Bluetooth on smartphones. Complexity of setup and use, along with concerns about product or maintenance costs, were the third most reported problem. Other issues included reliability of device performance, energy consumption/efficiency, security and design.

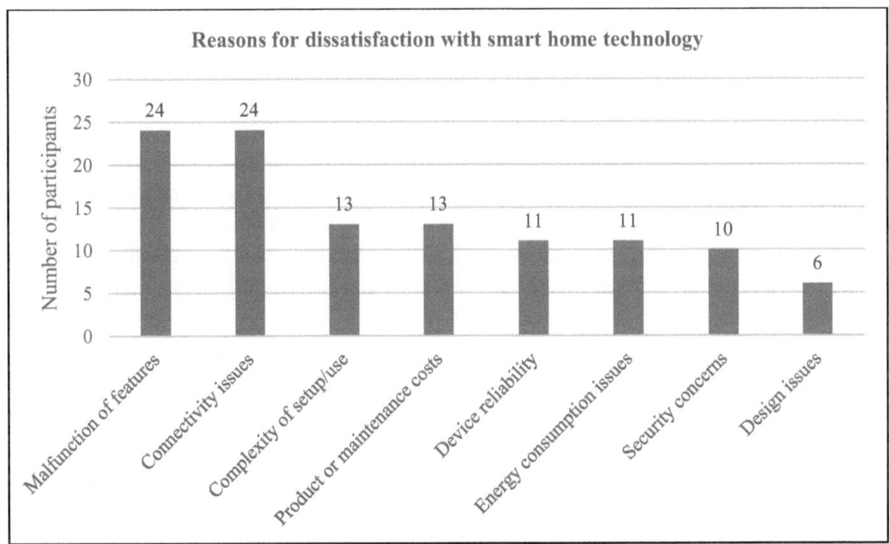

Fig. 2. Reasons for dissatisfaction with smart home technology (N = 40).

4.4 Prioritized Features Smart Home Devices and the Ideal Smart Home

All participants were asked about their priorities when selecting smart home devices. As shown in Table 2, the majority indicated that reasonable pricing and ease of use were the primary factors influencing their purchase decisions. Additionally, many respondents expressed a preference for remote control of devices via smartphones and the ability to customise devices to meet their needs. Consistent with the previous literature review, security concerns were common among the individuals, and preferences for both automation functionality and design were noted.

Table 2. Prioritized features in smart home devices.

Theme	Frequency
Cost effectiveness	68
Ease of use	65
Remote control via smartphone	53
Customizability	52
Advanced automation capabilities	38

(continued)

Table 2. (*continued*)

Theme	Frequency
Security and privacy	35
Sophisticated design	24

In a similar question, ideal features for the smart home were also explored. The most mentioned theme was remote control and automation. Convenience and efficiency was the second most frequently mentioned theme. Respondents prioritized features that simplified daily tasks and enhanced ease of use. This included functionalities such as remote control of appliances, touchless emergency lighting, and user-friendly interfaces. For example, one respondent described the convenience provided by 'helping with chores, ordering groceries online, and making my place more accessible'.

Independence and self-reliance were also highlighted. Many respondents emphasized the importance of features that enable them to manage daily tasks independently. This included technologies such as assistive robots, voice recognition systems, and devices that can be controlled without physical effort. Accessibility aids were another important consideration.

Many users envisioned smart homes equipped with devices that assist with specific physical tasks, such as opening jars or using smart wheelchairs. These features are particularly beneficial for individuals with disabilities or those experiencing age- related physical limitations.

Infrastructure and security, though mentioned less frequently, were noted as vital components of an ideal smart home. Respondent's value advanced security measures, such as enhanced locking systems and surveillance, to ensure the safety of their home. Additionally, ensuring that smart home systems are reliable, easy to program, and secure from hacking is crucial for gaining user trust.

The following Table 3 of quotes from participants with specific disabilities is informative regarding features they would like to see.

Table 3. Quotes from survey participants on design aspects of smart home technology.

Visual impairment	*"A refrigerator that automatically checks expiration dates and provides notifications through large text or voice alerts would be incredibly helpful for individuals with visual impairments."* *"It is difficult to read dates printed in small text, so having large text and high-contrast options would be beneficial."*
Hearing impairment	*"I want to try using smart home devices such as a doorbell that sends an alert to my smartphone."* *"Notifications about the status of household appliances that I have set to operate would be useful."* *"A device that can adjust the pitch and/or volume for smoke alarm, door, cooker, microwave, phone, etc."*

(*continued*)

Table 3. (*continued*)

Mobility impairment	*"I have used a profiling bed before. It was a bed where the angles of the head and foot sections could be adjusted, but the lowest point of the bed was higher than my wheelchair, making it difficult to get on and off. For wheelchair users like me, it would be much safer and more convenient if the entire bed could move up and down to adjust the height."* *"I would like to receive vocalised prompts for medication, waking up and sleeping, and therapy sessions, all controlled by voice commands."*

4.5 Customization

The importance of being able to customize smart home technology was explored. These features might include the ability to personalise the messages from, and interactions with, the system, changing the volume of spoken message or alarm sounds, and selecting simpler user interface layouts with larger or higher contrast text. Choice of controls to interact with the system could also be provided.

Generally, participants felt the need for some level of customization. The responses on this topic related to respondent's type of physical disability. Among mobility aid users and those with other physical and neurological disabilities, 18 and 15 respondents, respectively, rated customization as *very important*. People with visual and hearing impairments also marked it as *important*, with 4 and 6 respondents, respectively. Those with chronic pain and illnesses also indicated that customization is significant for them.

4.6 Follow-Up Interviews

Follow-up interviews were conducted with 4 survey participants, 2 in the UK and 2 in Korea to record their overall feelings about their use of smart home technology. Three expressed concerns about Wi-Fi reliability, security and potential risk of hacking. While two users found voice control and smartphone integration useful, they also mentioned frustrations with technical glitches, such as connectivity problems and malfunctions. Despite these challenges, the convenience and efficiency provided by smart home devices were acknowledged as significant benefits.

Participants were asked to evaluate whether smart home technology could seamlessly integrate into the daily lives of people with physical disabilities at home. The overall sentiment towards its integration into the home was generally positive.

Some other interesting issues were raised. When asked about the necessary improvements to enhance the usability and accessibility of smart home technology, participants emphasized the importance of reducing reliance on smartphones and enabling more direct interaction between users and devices. They highlighted the need to address Wi-Fi connectivity issues and simplify the user experience. Additionally, participants pointed out that cost reduction, attractive design, and effective advertising are crucial factors in increasing adoption.

The 4 interviewees unanimously agreed that training individuals to use smart home equipment is essential to prevent frustration and ensure effective use. They emphasized the value of hands-on learning opportunities, such as in-store demonstrations, especially for older users who may find modern technology challenging. Additionally, participants highlighted the need for robust support services to address issues promptly as well as the necessity for government or company led initiatives to offer continued assistance and training.

4.7   Recommendations for Improvement and Take-Up

The findings suggest that while smart home technology has the potential to greatly improve independence and convenience for those with physical discomfort, barriers hinder its broader adoption. In the Table 4 below, recommendations are proposed for designers, developers and providers, to optimize and promote smart home systems for a better user experience and greater awareness.

Table 4.   Recommendations for addressing smart home user issues identified.

Problem identified	Recommendations
Increasing adoption	Targeted advertising campaigns that showcase real-life scenarios where smart home devices simplify daily tasks and address practical issues faced at home. Provide potential customer opportunities to experience smart home devices firsthand through in-store demonstrations or exhibitions.
Cost issues	Smart home technology developers and providers should focus on modular smart home systems where users can start with basic functionalities and gradually add more components as needed (Schinle et al. 2017).
Security concerns	Users should be kept informed of their system's security status (Ansari 2024). Access should be designed to be safe and convenient using techniques such as biometrics and two-factor authentication. Users should be made aware of scams and how to identify and deal with them.
Complexity of use	Smart home system user interfaces should provide clear and concise instructions with minimal technical jargon, either through quick start guides or videos. Control panels and apps should feature intuitive layouts that prioritize essential functions and use familiar icons, thereby reducing cognitive load, learning curve and increasing interaction efficiency
Connectivity issues	User testing of setting up and connecting smart home devices should be carried out to identify problems. Simple approaches to connecting devices to the smart home network are needed. The availability of signal boosters and range extenders is recommended to enhance signal strength as well as auto-reconnect features and regular software updates (Dalvi et al. 2019).

(continued)

Table 4. (continued)

Problem identified	Recommendations
Technical failures	With beta testing and collecting target audience, developers should identify and rectify common malfunctions, such as facial and voice recognition issues as well as features users genuinely desire. Offering extended warranties and rapid response support to address stability concerns promotes user confidence and promotes smart home technology adoption
Design issues	Individuals with various physical disabilities have specific design requirements for independence and convenience. This involves making interfaces intuitive, ensuring visual displays are clear and adjustable, and incorporating voice guidance to improve accessibility. Additionally, offering a variety of input methods, such as physical buttons and touchscreens, allows users to choose the best option for their physical needs. Inclusive design should consider users' physical conditions and environments. Controls should be within easy reach; devices should be of an appropriate size and weight and feature secure grips and safe materials to ensure stability and safety.

5 Conclusions

The literature review revealed that people have concerns about smart homes such as the risk of being hacked, technical complexity, cost, usefulness and reliability. However, the popularity of smart speakers, and robot vacuum cleaners has provided a route for users to gain experience in setting up and using smart devices within their homes. As people become more experienced with smart devices, and add more elements to their system, their in it confidence increases. For people with disabilities who may have come to depend on carers, smart technology can be psychologically beneficial, increasing their feelings of independence and self-determination.

The smart kitchen survey showed that there was strong interest in technical innovations, particularly devices providing additional security and hazard alerts. There was similar interest in technology that improved comfort or convenience, provided they were not too futuristic and could see them to fitting into their routines.

The survey of people with disabilities and discomfort showed that their experience with smart home products was generally positive, showing that they can enhance independence, convenience, and safety. However technical problems such as the complexity of set-up, malfunction of voice, facial, or gesture recognition and connectivity problems were causes of dissatisfaction, so a strategy is needed from the smart home industry to deal with these issues and provide satisfactory customer support to maintain confidence and growth of the industry.

Among those not using these technologies, the gap between awareness and their adoption seemed to be a lack of information about smart home devices and their benefits, where to purchase them, the cost of the products, as well as installation, security and privacy concerns. Interestingly as people learn about the potential capabilities of smart technology to support a task, e.g., being able to recognize when items in a fridge are passing their 'consume by' dates, there seems to be more willingness to adopt it.

Smart homes can benefit many people. As people live longer and want to maintain their independence, the need for supportive technologies will grow, making this a critical area for future innovation. However, the success of the technology to genuinely enhance people's lives will depend on our ability to listen to and fulfil the diverse needs of its users.

Acknowledgements. This paper draws upon the work conducted by Hyejoo Cheong (co-author) for her Ergonomics Master's project, entitled 'Enhancing Quality of Life through Smart Home Technology for Individuals with Physical Discomfort: Insights from the UK and South Korea', which was completed at Loughborough University in 2024.

It also includes work conducted within the Transitions in Kitchen Living (TiKL) project (2007–2010) – part of the UK New Dynamics of Aging (NDA) Programme funded by five UK Research Councils. The project partners were Loughborough University and the Open University.

References

Bradbury, R.: The Martian Chronicles. Doubleday, New York (1950)

Evans, G., Realtor, U.: The Jetson's predicted house technology (2024). https://www.youtube.com/watch?v=ibj1g1mUtAc. Accessed 31 Jan 2025

Cortesi, D.: The first home computer. Volunt. Inf. Exchange **5**(8) (2015). https://s3.amazonaws.com/s3data.computerhistory.org/chmedu/VIE_05_008.pdf. Accessed 31 Jan 2025

Callaham, J.: A look back at Microsoft's 1999 smart home: what it got right and what it got wrong (2023). https://www.neowin.net/news/a-look-back-at-microsofts-1999-smart-home-what-it-got-right-and-what-it-got-wrong/. Accessed 31 Jan 2025

Liu, C., Lv, Q., Zhao, M.: Research on interaction design of smart home products based on the Internet of Things technology. In: International Seminar on Computer Science and Engineering Technology (SCSET), New York, pp. 220–225. Institute of Art & Design Qingdao University of Technology, Qingdao, April 2023. https://doi.org/10.1109/scset58950.2023.00057

Ukpanah, I.: Smart home statistics: key insights and trends. Green Match. https://www.greenmatch.co.uk/blog/smart-home-statistics. Accessed 06 Feb 2025

Marikyan, D., Papagiannidis, S., Alamanos, E.: A systematic review of the smart home literature: a user perspective. Technol. Forecast. Soc. Chang. **138**, 139–154 (2019). https://doi.org/10.1016/j.techfore.2018.08.015

Greeng, C., Roesner, F.: Who's in control? Interactions in multi-user smart homes. In: CHI 2019, 4–9 May 2019, Glasgow, Scotland, UK, paper 268 (2019). https://doi.org/10.1145/3290605.3300498

Alam, M.R., Reaz, M.B.I., Ali, M.A.M.: A review of smart homes—past, present, and future. IEEE Trans. Syst. Man Cybern. Part C Appl. Rev. **42**(6) (2012). https://doi.org/10.1109/TSMCC.2012.2189204

Nascimento, D.R., Fettermann, D.C.: The acceptance of smart home technologies: a literature review of benefits and barriers perceived by users. Contemp. Manag. Res. **19**(2), 107–129 (2023). https://doi.org/10.7903/cmr.22539

Pal, D., Funilkul, S., Vanijj, V., Papasratorn, B.: Analyzing the elderly users' adoption of smart-home services. IEEE Access **6**, 51238–51252 (2018). https://doi.org/10.1109/ACCESS.2018.2869599

Zhou, C., Qian, Y., Kaner, J.: A study on smart home use intention of elderly consumers based on technology acceptance models. PLoS ONE **19**(3), e0300574 (2024). https://doi.org/10.1371/-journal.pone.0300574

Wilson, C., Hargreaves, T., Hauxwell-Baldwin, R.: Smart homes and their users: a systematic analysis and key challenges. Pers. Ubiquit. Comput. **19**, pp. 463–476 (2015). https://doi.org/10.1007/s00779-014-0813-0

Hammi, B., Zeadally, S., Khatoun, R., Nebhen, J.: Survey on smart homes: vulnerabilities, risks, and countermeasures. Comput. Secur. **117** (2022). https://doi.org/10.1016/j.cose.2022.102677

Reolink, Top 7 frequent issues with your smart home: causes & solutions. https://reolink.com/blog/smart-home-frequent-issues. Accessed 31 Jan 2025

Paetz, A.G., Dütschke, E., Fichtner, W.: Smart homes as a means to sustainable energy consumption: a study of consumer perceptions. J. Consum. Policy **35**(1), 23–41 (2012)

Kim, J., Kim, E., Lee, J.: A study on housing and welfare support for persons with disabilities. Disabil. Soc. Welf. **2**(4), 75–107 (2011)

Sohn, R., Lim, M., Lim, S., Kim, J., Kim, J.: The design and usability testing of a smart home for the people with severe disability. Construction of a QoL Industrial Technology-Based Support Center, 10036459, pp. 767–769 (2012)

Alexandr, K.O., Archana, S., Aman, M., Rajiv, R., Bhagat, S., Sahithi, Y.: User satisfaction and technology adoption in smart homes: a user experience test. In: BIO Web of Conferences, 86, Phagwara, October 2023. 4th International Conference on Recent Trends in Biomedical Sciences, RTBS 2023 (2023). https://doi.org/10.1051/bioconf/20248601087

Sims, R.E., et al.: Older people's experiences of their kitchens: dishes and wishes. In: Anderson, M. (ed.) Contemporary Ergonomics and Human Factors 2011, Proceedings of Ergonomics & Human Factors, Stoke Rochford, UK, 12–14 April 2011, pp. 387–393. Taylor & Francis Group, London (2011)

Maguire, M., et al.: Kitchen living in later life: exploring ergonomic problems, coping strategies and design solutions. Int. J. Des. **8**(1), 73–91 (2014)

Maguire, M., et al.: A study of user needs for the 'Techno Kitchen'. In: Stephanidis, C. (ed.) HCI International 2011 – Posters' Extended Abstracts, HCI 2011. CCIS, Part II, vol. 174, pp. 66–71. Springer, Berlin, Heidelberg (2011). https://doi.org/10.1007/978-3-642-22095-1_14

Cheong, H.: Enhancing quality of life through smart home technology for individuals with physical discomfort: insights from the UK and South Korea. MSc Project Report, School of Design and Creative Arts, Loughborough, UK, August 2024

Schinle, M., Schneider, J., Blocher, T., Zimmermann, J., Chiriac, S., Stork, W.: A modular approach for smart home system architectures based on Android applications. In: 5th IEEE International Conference on Mobile Cloud Computing, Services, and Engineering, vol. 5, pp. 153–156 (2017). https://doi.org/10.1109/mobilecloud.2017.20

Ansari, A.M., Nazir, M., Mustafa, K.: Smart homes app vulnerabilities, threats, and solutions: a systematic literature review. J. Netw. Syst. Manag. **32**(29) (2024). https://doi.org/10.1007/s10922-024-09803-1

Dalvi, O.S., Ahirwar, S., Mandviwala, B., Rai, N.: Improving mobile signal reception strength using network booster. Int. J. Sci. Res. Dev. **7**(2), 213–218 (2019)

Agent-Based Simulation of Forest Fire Spread with NetLogo

Ricardo Pires[1]([✉]), Pedro Torres[1], Nuno A. Valente[1,2][iD],
E. J. Solteiro Pires[1,2][iD], Arsénio Reis[1,2][iD], P. B. de Moura Oliveira[1,2][iD],
and João Barroso[1,2][iD]

[1] Escola de Ciências e Tecnologia, Universidade de Trás-os-Montes e Alto Douro,
Vila Real 5000–811, Portugal
{al74023, al74144}@alunos.utad.pt, epires@utad.pt, ars@utad.pt,
oliveira@utad.pt, jbarroso@utad.pt
{al74023,al74144}@alunos.utad.pt, nuno.valente@inesctec.pt,
{epires,ars,oliveira,jbarroso}@utad.pt
{al74023,al74144}@alunos.utad.pt, nuno.valente@inesctec.pt,
{epires,ars,oliveira,jbarroso}@utad.pt
[2] INESC TEC - Instituto de Engenharia de Sistemas e Computadores, Tecnologia e
Ciência, Porto, Portugal

Abstract. Forest fires represent a significant and growing threat to natural ecosystems and human settlements, with their unpredictable behavior and capacity for rapid expansion over time, creating substantial challenges for effective prevention, control, and mitigation. This paper presents the development of a forest fire simulator designed to model and predict fire spread under varying environmental conditions. Such a simulator must consider how fire spreads in different locations and climate conditions, showing the final shape of the fire in a given period of time. Using the NetLogo agent-based modeling platform, a simulated forest environment was created in which trees function as autonomous agents interacting with one another and the environment. Identifying and understanding the risk factors that increase the likelihood of a fire occurring, as well as those that contribute to its spread and intensity, is essential for the development of an accurate forest fire simulator. Such a simulator can integrate the complex interactions among these variables to produce dynamic visualizations of fire progression, allowing users to evaluate different scenarios and make informed decisions for preventing, controlling and fighting forest fires. By incorporating key factors—such as vegetation density, temperature, humidity, topography, and wind direction—the system calculates the probability of fire propagation and generates visual representations of fire behavior over time. This tool allows users to forecast fire behavior and assess response strategies proactively, thereby improving the accuracy and efficiency of firefighting efforts. In addition, the simulator yields significant social benefits, especially for older adults residing in fire-prone areas, by supporting early warning systems, enabling prompt evacuations, and mitigating their susceptibility to fire-related risks through enhanced preparedness and coordinated response measures.

© The Author(s), under exclusive license to Springer Nature Switzerland AG 2026
M. Antona and C. Stephanidis (Eds.): HCII 2025, LNCS 16335, pp. 212–224, 2026.
https://doi.org/10.1007/978-3-032-12781-5_14

Keywords: Forest fires · Risk factors · Fire simulations

1   Introduction

A forest fire is a destructive and uncontrolled event characterized by the presence of flames, intense heat, release of smoke and the ability to spread rapidly, causing significant damage to objects, structures and, most importantly, human life. Unlike other natural disasters, fires are not limited to a specific period of time and, if not properly controlled, have a tendency to develop over time [4].

The forest fires are influenced by several conditions or elements, usually called by risk factors, that increase the likelihood of a forest fire occurring or that contribute to its spread and intensity. These factors can include natural elements such as a dry climate, high temperatures, low air humidity and strong winds, which create favorable conditions for the rapid spread of fire. Additionally, the presence of flammable fuels such as dry vegetation, dense shrubs, dense forests, and accumulated materials increases the risk of forest fires. Human factors also play a significant role as risk factors in forest fires, including negligent or intentional activities such as improperly extinguished fires and improper handling of flammable equipment or materials. Additionally, lack of awareness and education about fire prevention and safety can contribute to increased risk. Another important risk factor is the topography of the terrain, which can affect the speed of propagation and the difficulty of access to fight the forest fire. Steep areas, narrow canyons or remote locations can make it difficult for firefighters to respond and apply effective control strategies. Identifying and understanding these risk factors is essential for preventing and fighting forest fires, allowing the implementation of preventive measures and the adoption of appropriate fire-fighting strategies.

This paper addresses the development of a simulator designed to predict fire spread across various scenarios, taking into account multiple risk factors. By modeling how a fire is likely to evolve from a specific point of origin, the simulator aims to enhance decision-making processes and enable more effective firefighting strategies. Such a tool holds significant potential for improving ignition risk control, optimizing resource allocation, and minimizing the environmental and social impacts of forest fires. By visualizing the projected shape and extent of a fire over time, it can provide valuable insights for both emergency response teams and long-term planning efforts, ultimately contributing to better protection of natural ecosystems and vulnerable communities.

2   Literature Review

A review of existing fire simulation tools and related research was conducted and presented in this section. The reviewed literature highlights a range of modeling approaches, each offering unique capabilities in simulating fire spread and aiding fire management tools.

Morales et al. (2014) argue that the incorporation of simulation tools into fire prevention systems can significantly enhance operational efficiency. For instance, the Bogotá Fire Department (UAECOBB) could benefit from a simulator capable of predicting the fire's trajectory based on geographic and meteorological inputs. Such a system would assist in designing effective response strategies and resource allocation plans by displaying the projected fire perimeter over time [6].

Alessandri et al. (2021) emphasize the critical need for predictive modeling tools, given the growing threat of forest fires to human populations and protected natural areas. The authors highlight the value of full-physics models, which offer high accuracy by simulating the intricate dynamics of fire propagation taking into account many of the phenomena involved in fire propagation, together with their mutual interactions. These models consider local and regional climate conditions, terrain features, and fuel characteristics, and are also capable of modeling secondary effects such as smoke production and atmospheric dispersion [1].

Denham et al. (2022) note that forest fires are increasing in frequency and severity worldwide, posing considerable environmental and ecological risks. The causes of forest fires vary, with the vast majority (approximately 95%) linked to human activities such as land speculation, negligence, and uncontrolled burning [2].

In the initial stages of development, the forest ecosystems exhibit characteristics similar to shrublands, marked by elevated flammability. As the forests mature, their susceptibility to fire generally declines, attributed to the development of a closed canopy and the vertical stratification that separates the understory from surface fuels. The mechanisms governing ignition are highly variable and depend on fuel type, including distinctions between live and dead biomass, organic and inorganic components, as well as fine versus coarse materials, and the moisture content of those fuels. While fuel load plays a critical role in sustaining fire propagation, it is essential to categorize vegetation types based on their influence on fire dynamics. Additionally, previous weather conditions significantly affect fuel moisture and thus influence fire behavior, underscoring the importance of short-term climatic patterns in wildfire risk assessments.

During an active forest fire, precipitation can suppress and potentially extinguish the advancing fire front, whereas wind acts as a key driver of fire behavior by supplying oxygen to combustion processes, enhancing the horizontal spread of flames, and dispersing smoke, which may expedite the drying of nearby fine fuels [7,9]. Topographical features also play a significant role in fire dynamics; in uneven terrain, fire tends to propagate more rapidly upslope and more slowly downslope, primarily due to the effects of convective heat transfer and buoyancy-driven airflow [2,8].

2.1   Forest Fire Simulators

Morales (2014) presents a forest fire simulator structured in two distinct phases: data processing and simulation. In the first phase, input data, such as environmental and fire-related parameters, are classified into numerical attributes that relate propagation speeds to specific characteristics. The second phase involves the use of these attributes to simulate the fire's spread from a point of origin, predicting propagation speed under different conditions [6].

FARSITE is another widely used fire simulation system, based on physical and mathematical modeling. It incorporates factors such as topography, weather, fuel type, and fire behavior to simulate forest fire progression over time and space. Its robust modeling capabilities enable the assessment of complex interactions between these variables. Additionally, FARSITE offers advanced features such as smoke production and dispersion modeling, facilitating evaluations of environmental and health impacts. Its user-friendly interface allows users to define fire scenarios and visualize the results, supporting informed decision-making in forest fire management [3].

BEHAVE is a fire modeling system that combines a variety of models and equations to predict fire behavior across various environmental scenarios. It takes into account parameters such as fuel type, humidity, wind speed, topography and terrain characteristics to calculate key metrics like rate of fire spread, flame length and fireline intensity. The simulator also offers capabilities to estimate the time needed to control and suppress the fire, aiding in strategic planning and decision-making during forest fire fighting efforts. With its user-friendly interface and advanced modeling capabilities, BEHAVE is a valuable tool for professionals involved in forest fire management and control [5].

3   Development

The goal of developing the forest simulator is to create a powerful and accurate tool for modeling and simulating the behavior of forest fires. Its primary purpose is to predict the spread of forest fire in different scenarios by incorporating critical risk factors such as vegetation type and density, climatic variables (e.g., temperature, humidity, and wind), and topographical features. Through the simulation of forest fire behavior, the tool seeks to improve the understanding of forest fire spread patterns, intensity, rate of expansion, and other key parameters essential for effective forest fire management. By simulating fire behavior, the simulator aims to help understand fire spread patterns, fire intensity, growth rate, and other parameters crucial to an effective forest fire response. With a robust forest simulator, it is possible to analyze and predict the evolution of the forest fire, allowing the adoption of prevention strategies, combat planning, and efficient resource allocation, contributing to the protection of ecosystems, human life, and infrastructure within forested areas.

3.1   Materials and Methods

The software used to design the simulator was NetLogo, which is an agent-based modeling and simulation platform widely used in scientific and educational research. This platform offers a user-friendly and flexible interface for creating computational models that involve the interaction between individual agents in a simulated environment (Fig. 1). Its agent-based approach allows for the modeling of complex phenomena such as animal behavior, population dynamics, socioeconomic systems, and even ecosystems. With the NetLogo simulator, users can visualize and explore the dynamics of the model in real time, test different scenarios and hypotheses, and analyze the results obtained.

A simulated forest environment was developed, where the agents, represented by trees, are autonomous objects capable of interacting with the different elements of the environment. Patches are the individual cells of the plane that represent vegetation. The fire starts on a tree in a random position, interacts with the other elements in the scene, and the fire starts to spread.

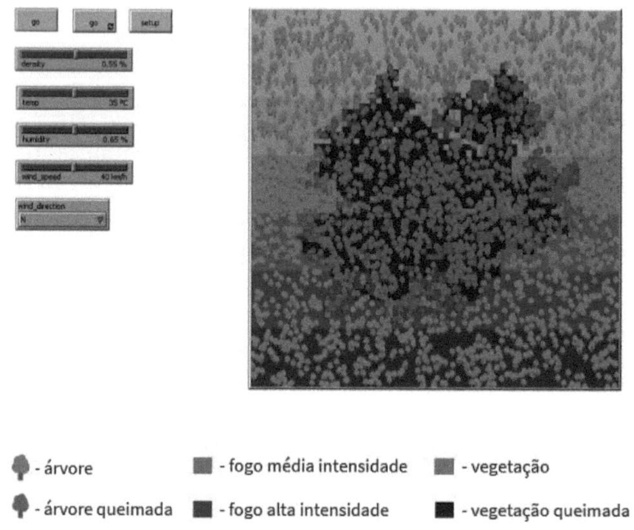

Fig. 1. Graphical Environment of the Simulator.

Once a tree agent ignites, it can transmit the fire to adjacent agents or to the patch it occupies. In turn, a burning patch can ignite the fire to the neighboring patch or to the agent that is in its position, as long as its not already on fire. To carry out this propagation, a model was used to calculate the probability of fire propagation, taking into account the risk factors involved in the simulation.

A generic fire propagation model was used to determine the probability of fire transmission. Although simplified for this study, the model aligns with risk factors commonly cited in existing literature. This modeling approach serves to simulate and predict the forest fire spread, incorporating variables such as fuel type, meteorological conditions, topography, and environmental moisture. These parameters enable the estimation of fire progression rate, affected area size, and flame intensity, thus offering valuable insights for fire behavior analysis.

Risk factors in the simulation are categorized into two types: general and individual. All risk factors are represented via user-adjustable sliders, with realistic minimum and maximum values (Fig. 2a-2d). Wind direction, due to its categorical nature, is controlled through a combobox offering eight directional options: North, Northeast, East, Southeast, South, Southwest, West, and Northwest (Fig. 2e). General risk factors uniformly influence all agents and patches, and include tree density, ambient temperature, and humidity. Individual risk factors, which dynamically affect the fire propagation probability based on specific patch characteristics, are calculated during the simulation runtime. These include wind direction—contingent upon patch positioning—and slope, which is derived from patch elevation.

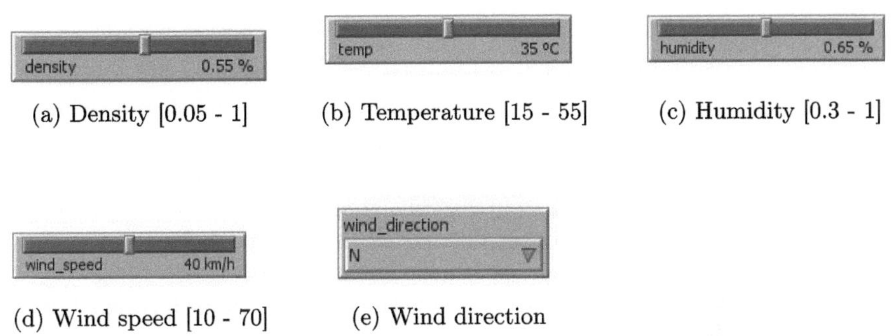

(a) Density [0.05 - 1]   (b) Temperature [15 - 55]   (c) Humidity [0.3 - 1]

(d) Wind speed [10 - 70]   (e) Wind direction

Fig. 2. Interface controls: sliders for density, temperature, humidity, wind speed, and a combo box for wind direction.

At the beginning of the simulation, the probability of forest fire spread was calculated using the general risk factors. This probability was determined according to Eq. 1, which combines the weighted influence of each factor:

$$P = w1 * T + w2 * (1 - H) + w3 * D \tag{1}$$

- P: Probability of forest fires propagation;
- T: Temperature;
- H: Humidity;
- D: Density;
- w: Coefficients.

The coefficient values for the general risk factors were determined through iterative simulations calibrated for a mild forest environment. The selected coefficients are: 0.4 for density, 0.6 for temperature, 0.8 for humidity, and 0.4 for wind speed.

The influence of individual risk factors on the computation of spread probability was incorporated within the simulation process, as these factors are contingent upon the unique attributes of each patch. Consequently, the probability must be calculated separately for each patch. For the slope variable, an initial elevation value was randomly assigned to each patch in a manner that established a general northward incline in the terrain—meaning that southern patches

were lower in elevation compared to northern ones. The slope-related probability
was then derived using the Eq. 2.

$$P = P - (|dh|) \tag{2}$$

- P: Probability of forest fire propagation;
- dh: Height difference.

If $dh > 0$:
$\quad P = P - 0.0005$
If $dh < 0$:
$\quad P = P + 0.001$

The probability of fire spread is inversely related to the distance between
patches: the greater the distance, the lower the likelihood of spread, and conversely, shorter distances are associated with higher probabilities. Furthermore,
fire is more likely to spread to patches situated at higher elevations than to
those at lower elevations, resulting in a faster uphill propagation compared to
downhill.

To compute the probability associated with wind direction, the angle between
the spatial positions of the patches is first determined and then compared to the
prevailing wind direction. This procedure yields the Eq. 3.

$$P = P + cos(|wd - a|) * w4 * ws \tag{3}$$

- P: Probability of forest fire propagation;
- wd: Wind direction;
- a: Angle formed by the Patches;
- $w4$: Wind speed coefficient;
- ws: Wind speed.

If $x2 - x1 = 0$ and $y2 >= 0$
$\quad a = 90$
If $x2 - x1 = 0$ and $y2 <= 0$
$\quad a = 270$
$\quad a = arctan(y2 - y1/x2 - x1)$

In this equation, the term $cos(|wd - a|)$ yields a value ranging from -1 to 1,
depending on the angular difference between the wind direction and the relative
angle between patches. A difference of 0° indicates that the patch lies directly
in the direction of the wind, resulting in a value of 1, whereas a difference of
180° implies that the patch is positioned directly opposite to the wind direction,
yielding a value of -1. Consequently, the probability of fire spread is higher for
patches aligned with the wind direction and lower for those situated against it.

4   Simulations

To test whether the simulator is faithful to reality, several simulations were carried out with constant risk factors, varying only one factor at a time using five different values for each, except for the wind direction which was tested for all possibilities. In addition, other constant factors were kept to perform better data collection and analysis, for example, the same type of vegetation with constant positions, the same origin of fire and the same slope were used. To obtain the graphs shown below (Figs. 3–13), 10 simulations were carried out for the variable risk factor and at the end the average of all the results was calculated.

These graphs represent the percentage of area burned and the peak of the fire, that is, the total amount of vegetation and trees burning simultaneously during the fire time measured in ticks.

By analyzing the graphs, we can conclude that the risk factors are acting as intended and that there are risk factors with more influence on the spread of the fire than others. For example density (Fig. 3) has a more prominent effect than wind speed (Fig. 6). We also found that increased humidity has a negative effect on the spread of fire, which is true (Fig. 4).

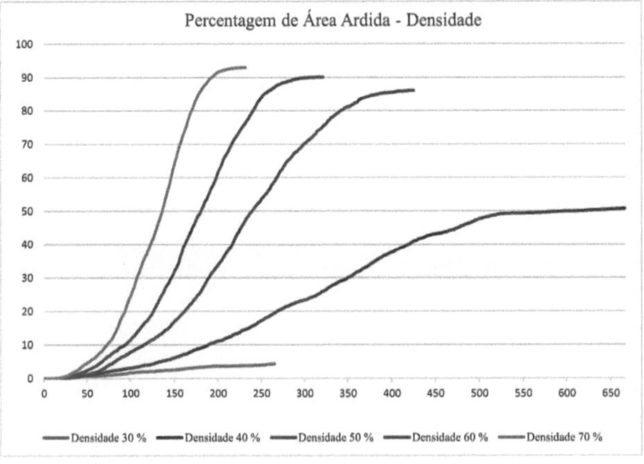

Fig. 3. Burnt percentage - Density.

The fire peak graphs show that the risk factors are acting as intended and that there are risk factors with more influence on the spread of the fire than others. For example, density (Fig. 8) has a more prominent effect than wind speed (Fig. 11), since the fire peaks faster. Also, increased humidity has a negative effect on the spread of fire, which is true (Fig. 9).

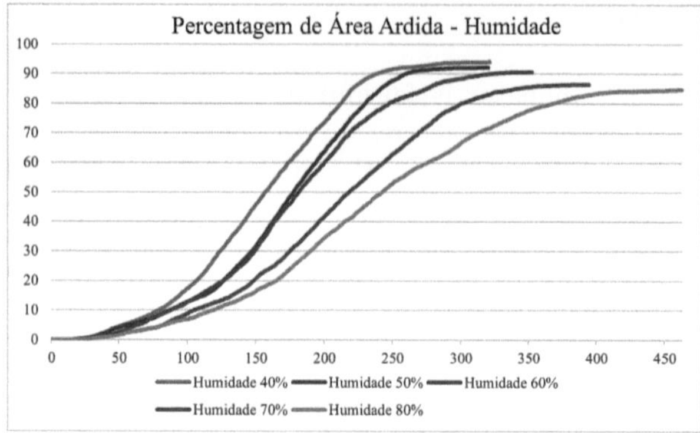

Fig. 4. Burnt percentage - Humidity.

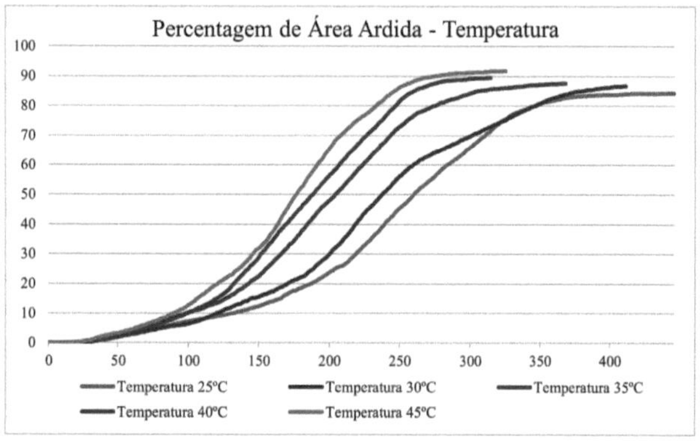

Fig. 5. Burnt percentage - Temperature.

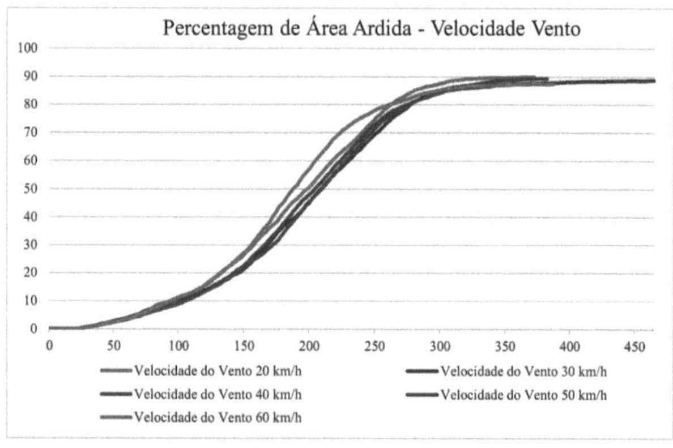

Fig. 6. Burnt percentage - Wind speed.

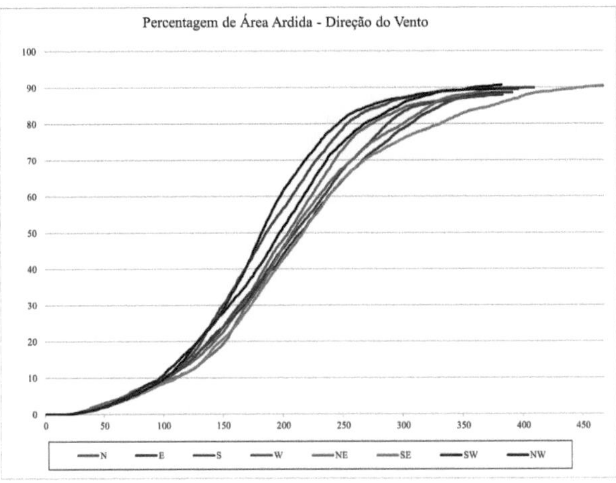

Fig. 7. Burnt percentage - Wind direction.

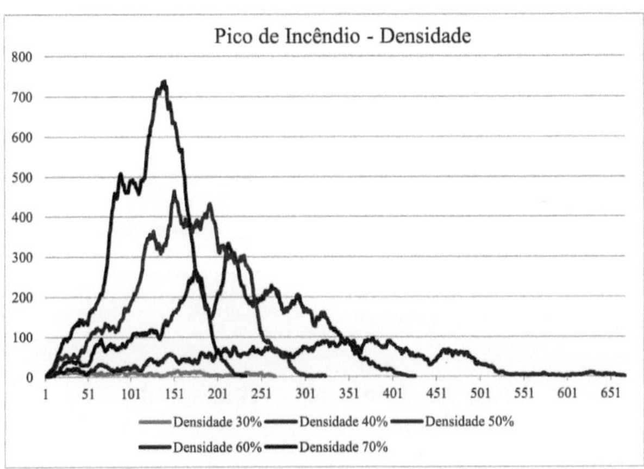

Fig. 8. Fire peak - Density.

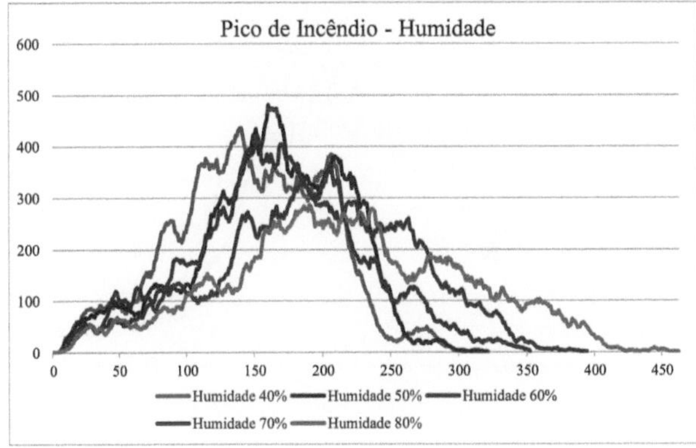

Fig. 9. Fire peak - Humidity.

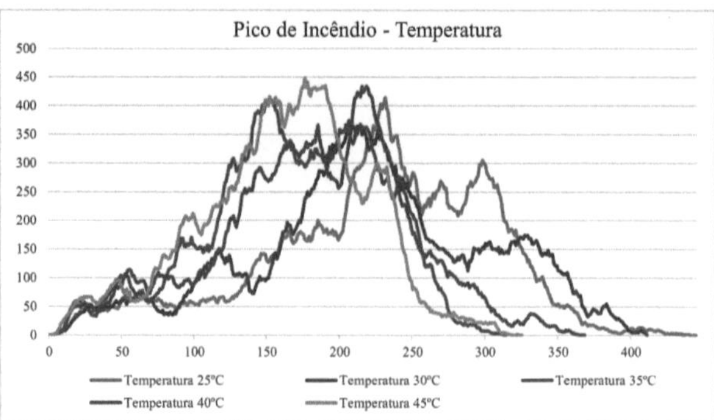

Fig. 10. Fire peak - Temperature.

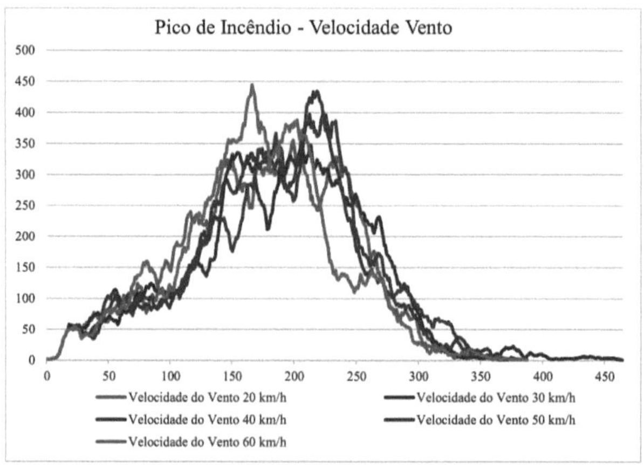

Fig. 11. Fire peak - Wind speed.

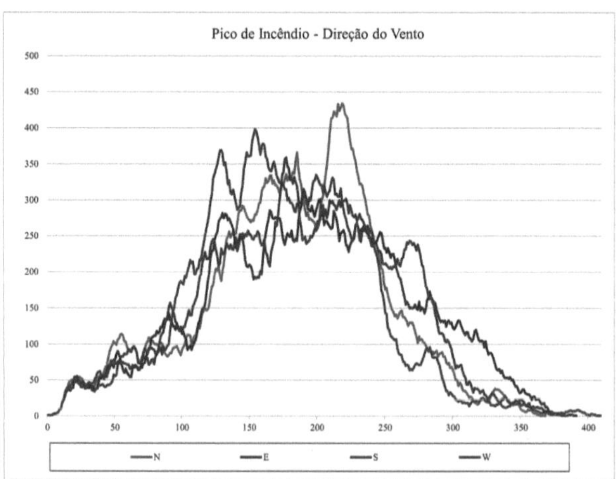

Fig. 12. Fire peak - Wind direction.

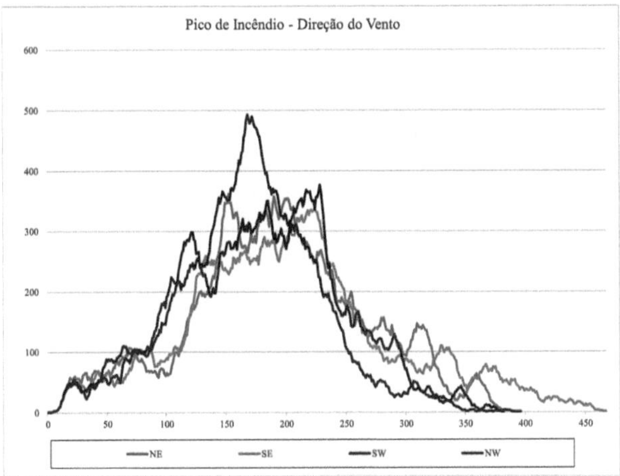

Fig. 13. Fire peak - Wind direction.

5   Conclusions and Future Work

This study focused on the development of a forest fire simulator, an essential tool for predicting and analyzing forest fire behavior. Given the severe threat forest fires pose to both natural ecosystems and human settlements, the need for effective prevention, control, and mitigation strategies is paramount. The simulator developed in this work aims to model fire spread under varying environmental scenarios by integrating multiple risk factors.

A review of established simulators, including the Morales simulator, FARSITE, and BEHAVE, provided valuable insights into existing modeling techniques used to simulate forest fire behaviour. These tools incorporate elements such as topography, climate, fuel types, and fire behavior to simulate fire dynamics across spatial and temporal scales. Additionally, they offer functionalities like smoke estimation and dispersion modeling, which are critical for assessing environmental and public health impacts.

A forest fire simulator was developed using the NetLogo software. The simulator creates a simulated forest environment, where trees are represented by agents that interact with the elements of the environment. Fire starts in one tree and spreads to neighboring trees and adjacent areas. A model was used to calculate the probability of fire spreading, considering factors such as vegetation type, density, weather conditions and topography.

The simulator serves as a decision-support tool, enabling better-informed strategies for fire prevention, suppression, and resource deployment. It contributes to the protection of ecosystems, human lives, and infrastructure by enhancing forest fire management capabilities. Nevertheless, it is acknowledged that the simulator represents a simplified abstraction of real-world conditions. The reliability of its predictions depends on the accuracy and granularity of input data and the fidelity of the underlying models. Ongoing refinement and integration of updated information are essential to enhance its precision and applicability.

The development of a forest fire simulator represents a significant advancement in forest fire research and management, enabling the formulation of data-driven responses and supports the broader goal of environmental conservation and community resilience. Research in this field is crucial for addressing the complex challenges related to forest fires, aiming to protect ecosystems and ensure a sustainable future.

Acknowledgement. This work was financed by national funds through the Portuguese Foundation for Science and Technology – FCT, under the Project "DBoidS - Digital twin Boids fire prevention System" Ref. PTDC/CCI-COM/2416/2021.

References

1. Alessandri, A., Bagnerini, P., Gaggero, M., Mantelli, L.: Parameter estimation of fire propagation models using level set methods. Appl. Math. Model. **92**, 731–747 (2021)
2. Denham, M.M., Waidelich, S., Laneri, K.: Visualization and modeling of forest fire propagation in patagonia. Environ. Model. Softw. **158**, 105526 (2022)
3. Glasa, J., Weisenpacher, P., Halada, L.: Analysis of forest fire behaviour by advanced computer fire simulators. Commun.-Sci. Lett. Univ. Zilina **13**(2), 26–31 (2011)
4. Hefeeda, M., Bagheri, M.: Wireless sensor networks for early detection of forest fires. In: 2007 IEEE International Conference on Mobile Adhoc and Sensor Systems, pp. 1–6. IEEE (2007)
5. Heinsch, F.A., Andrews, P.L.: BehavePlus fire modeling system, version 5.0: design and features. US Department of Agriculture, Forest Service, Rocky Mountain Research Station (2010)
6. Morales, G.A., Morales, R.S., Valencia, C.F., Akhavan-Tabatabaei, R.: A forest fire propagation simulator for bogotá. In: Proceedings of the Winter Simulation Conference 2014, pp. 1505–1515. IEEE (2014)
7. Rothermel, R.C.: A mathematical model for predicting fire spread in wildland fuels, vol. 115. Intermountain Forest & Range Experiment Station, Forest Service, US (1972)
8. Tiribelli, F., Morales, J.M., Gowda, J.H., Mermoz, M., Kitzberger, T.: Non-additive effects of alternative stable states on landscape flammability in nw patagonia: fire history and simulation modelling evidence. Int. J. Wildland Fire **28**(2), 149–159 (2019)
9. Wagner, C.v., Pickett, T.: Equations and fortran program for the canadian forest fire weather index system (1985)

Investigating Brain Activity in a Mixed Visual State of Simultaneous Foveal and Peripheral Vision

Akihiro Sugiura[1]([⊠]), Yuta Umeda[1], Saki Hayakawa[1], Yuna Takagi[1], Masahiro Suzuki[1], Masami Niwa[1], Kunihiko Tanaka[1], and Hiroki Takada[2]

[1] Gifu University of Medical Science, Seki, Gifu 5013822, Japan
asugiura@u-gifu-ms.ac.jp
[2] Fukui University, Fukui, Fukui 9108507, Japan

Abstract. This study examined the neural mechanisms involved in mixed vision, where both foveal and peripheral visual inputs are processed at the same time. Functional magnetic resonance imaging (fMRI) was used to compare brain activity under three conditions: foveal vision, peripheral vision, and mixed vision. Data analysis was performed using statistical parametric mapping with family-wise error correction. Mixed vision led to broader and stronger activation in brain regions related to visual processing, attentional control, and visuomotor integration. These areas included the superior parietal lobule, precentral gyrus, lingual gyrus, and occipital white matter. The findings indicate that mixed vision activates a unique and coordinated neural network. This contributes to our understanding of real-world visual perception and may inform research on attention-related disorders.

Keywords: Mixed vision · Functional MRI (fMRI) · Visual attention · Superior parietal lobule · Visuomotor integration

1 Introduction

Vision is one of the most fundamental sensory modalities that supports human perception and cognition. It enables the integration of external information to guide decision-making and behavioral responses. Visual input is initially captured by the retina and transmitted via the optic nerve to the lateral geniculate nucleus (LGN), before being processed in the primary visual cortex (V1) and subsequently in higher-order visual areas [1]. Within this visual system, two functionally distinct subsystems—foveal and peripheral vision—are processed via separate, specialized neural pathways.

Foveal vision processes high-resolution input from the central portion of the retina (the fovea), which is densely populated with cone photoreceptors. This region is essential for tasks requiring visual precision, such as object recognition, reading, and facial identification. Its neural signals are transmitted from V1 through the ventral visual pathway toward temporal lobe structures, including area V4 and the inferotemporal cortex, which are essential for processing shape and form.

© The Author(s), under exclusive license to Springer Nature Switzerland AG 2026
M. Antona and C. Stephanidis (Eds.): HCII 2025, LNCS 16335, pp. 225–234, 2026.
https://doi.org/10.1007/978-3-032-12781-5_15

In contrast, peripheral vision processes stimuli occurring outside the foveal field via rod photoreceptors, which are more sensitive to low light, motion, and spatial cues. These signals primarily travel through the dorsal visual pathway and project to the parietal cortex, supporting motion perception, spatial localization, and rapid attentional shifts. Peripheral vision, therefore, plays a key role in detecting environmental changes and facilitating reflexive attention.

Despite their functional differences, foveal and peripheral vision are typically utilized concurrently, contributing to a seamless and integrated visual experience. However, the underlying neural mechanisms that support their integration remain poorly understood. Specifically, it is unclear how the brain coordinates these two systems when both are active simultaneously, and the cognitive demands imposed by this integration.

Recent studies using functional magnetic resonance imaging (fMRI) have suggested that, beyond the visual cortex, areas in the parietal and frontal lobes may be involved in integrating visual input across the visual field [2–4]. Nevertheless, the detailed neural architecture of this integration—especially under mixed vision conditions combining foveal and peripheral stimuli—remains largely uncharacterized. To address this gap, the present study employed fMRI to investigate brain activity during simultaneous foveal and peripheral visual processing.

2   Methods

2.1   fMRI Data Acquisition and Imaging Parameters

A total of 14 healthy adult participants (5 females, 9 males; born between 2000 and 2003) took part in the study. All participants had normal or corrected-to-normal vision and no history of neurological or psychiatric disorders. The study protocol was approved by the Research Ethics Committee of Gifu University of Medical Science (approval number: 2022–9) and was conducted in accordance with institutional and national ethical guidelines. Written informed consent was obtained from all participants prior to participation.

fMRI data were acquired using an ECHELON Smart 1.5T MRI scanner (Fujifilm Medical, Japan). Functional images were obtained using a gradient-echo echo-planar imaging (GRE-EPI) sequence optimized for blood oxygenation level-dependent (BOLD) contrast [5]. The imaging parameters were as follows: repetition time (TR), 4000 ms; echo time (TE), 40 ms; slice thickness, 3.8 mm; and field of view (FOV), 224 mm. Structural T1-weighted images were also acquired to provide anatomical references and support spatial normalization.

To ensure high-quality imaging, all participants underwent a pre-scan calibration to optimize signal uniformity. Head motion was minimized using foam padding and a secure head coil. During the scans, participants were instructed to remain as still as possible and to maintain visual fixation as instructed by the task requirements.

2.2   Principle of fMRI, BOLD Signal, and Neurovascular Coupling

fMRI detects changes in brain activity by measuring fluctuations in blood oxygenation levels, reflected in the BOLD signal. The BOLD signal arises from neurovascular coupling (NVC), a tightly regulated physiological mechanism by which local neuronal activity modulates regional cerebral blood flow (CBF), cerebral blood volume (CBV), and the cerebral metabolic rate of oxygen consumption ($CMRO_2$). Increased neuronal activity elevates metabolic demand, triggering a cascade of vascular responses, including the vasodilation of nearby arterioles and capillaries. This results in a localized increase in oxygenated hemoglobin and a corresponding reduction in deoxygenated hemoglobin concentration.

The resulting change in the ratio of oxygenated to deoxygenated hemoglobin alters the magnetic susceptibility of blood. Because deoxygenated hemoglobin is paramagnetic, it disturbs local magnetic field homogeneity. Consequently, areas with increased neural activity exhibit an elevated T2*-weighted signal, allowing fMRI to indirectly detect and spatially map brain activation through BOLD contrast.

Neurovascular coupling involves complex interactions among neurons, astrocytes, endothelial cells, and vascular smooth muscle cells [6]. Astrocytes serve as key mediators, translating synaptic activity into chemical signals—such as nitric oxide, prostaglandins, and arachidonic acid derivatives—that regulate vascular tone. These mechanisms ensure that regions of increased neural demand receive a timely and localized supply of oxygen and nutrients.

Importantly, NVC exhibits both spatial and temporal specificity. Spatial resolution can reach the scale of cortical columns (on the order of millimeters), while the temporal dynamics evolve over several seconds due to delays inherent in the hemodynamic response.

However, variability in neurovascular efficiency across brain regions and between individuals may affect the sensitivity and interpretability of the BOLD signal. Furthermore, the temporal resolution of fMRI is constrained by the sluggish nature of the hemodynamic response. In this study, the repetition time (TR) was set to 4000 ms, providing a temporal resolution of approximately 4 s. While this is adequate for detecting slow hemodynamic fluctuations, it may be insufficient to capture brief or rapidly occurring neural events.

2.3 Experimental Design and Visual Stimuli

Participants viewed visual stimuli presented on a screen via a mirror attached to the MRI head coil. Figure 1 illustrates an overview of the experimental setup. Participants lay in a supine position inside the MRI scanner and observed the stimuli reflected in the mirror. The visual stimuli were rear-projected onto a screen positioned at the foot end of the scanner bore, enabling clear and stable presentation without requiring head movement.

The experiment consisted of three distinct visual conditions designed to isolate foveal vision, peripheral vision, and their simultaneous processing in a mixed visual state. In the foveal vision condition, participants were instructed to fixate on a centrally presented fixation point while ignoring surrounding stimuli. In the peripheral vision condition, participants attended to stimuli appearing in the periphery while avoiding direct fixation on any central object. In the mixed vision condition, a fixation point was superimposed on a peripheral stimulus, requiring participants to simultaneously process both foveal and peripheral visual information.

To maintain a controlled experimental environment, all visual stimuli were matched across conditions in terms of luminance, contrast, and spatial frequency. Figure 2 shows representative examples of the stimuli used in each condition. Each display consisted of multiple spherical objects oscillating in a sinusoidal back-and-forth motion at 0.25 Hz along both the horizontal and vertical axes. The content and behavior of the stimuli, along with participant instructions, were standardized as follows:

- Foveal vision condition: A single fixation point was presented at the center of the screen, oscillating sinusoidally at 0.25 Hz in both the horizontal and vertical directions. Participants were instructed to maintain fixation on this point.
- Peripheral vision condition: Multiple spherical stimuli were displayed in the peripheral field, all oscillating at 0.25 Hz in both directions. Participants were instructed to attend to these stimuli without looking at the center.
- Mixed vision condition: A yellow fixation point was superimposed on one of the peripheral stimuli. Both the fixation point and the associated stimulus oscillated synchronously at 0.25 Hz. Participants were instructed to track the moving fixation point with their eyes, thereby requiring the simultaneous processing of foveal and peripheral visual inputs.

The experiment employed a block design, alternating between task and rest periods. Each task block lasted 64 s, followed by a 32-s rest interval. This cycle was repeated across three sets for each of the three visual conditions. Stimulus presentation was synchronized with the MRI scanner to ensure precise temporal alignment between the onset of visual input and the acquisition of neuroimaging data. Figure 3 depicts the block design protocol used in this study.

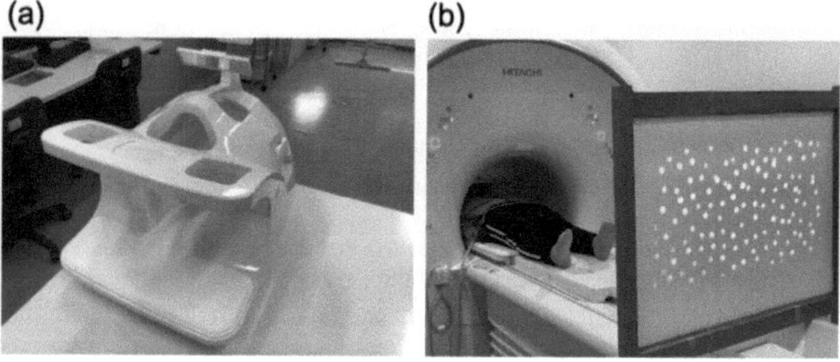

Fig. 1. Experimental setup for visual stimulus presentation during fMRI scanning. (a) MRI head coil equipped with a mirror for stimulus viewing. (b) Participant lying supine inside the scanner, observing rear-projected stimuli reflected in the mirror. The projection screen is positioned at the foot of the bore, enabling stable visual presentation without head movement.

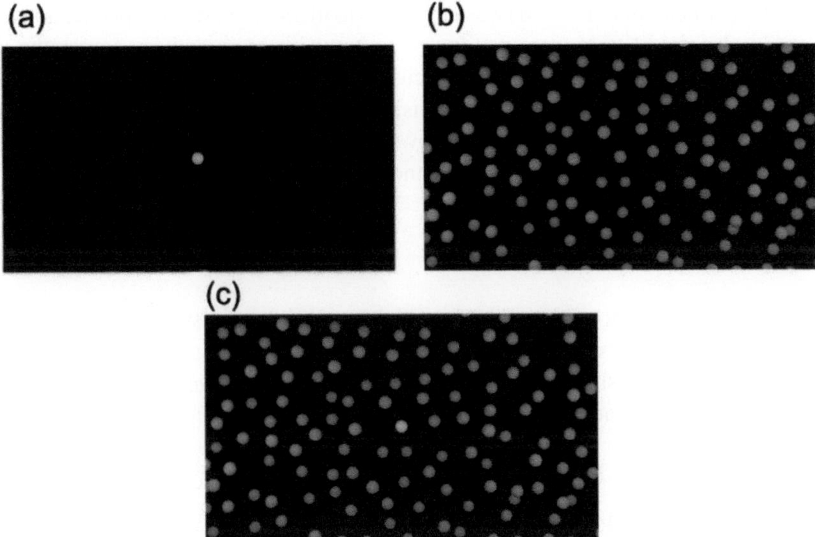

Fig. 2. Examples of visual stimuli presented under the three experimental conditions. (a) Foveal vision condition: A central fixation point oscillates at 0.25 Hz in both horizontal and vertical directions. Participants maintain fixation on this point. (b) Peripheral vision condition: Multiple peripheral stimuli oscillate at 0.25 Hz. Participants attend to these stimuli without fixating centrally. (c) Mixed vision condition: A yellow fixation point is overlaid on one peripheral stimulus, with both oscillating synchronously at 0.25 Hz. Participants track the fixation point, requiring simultaneous processing of central and peripheral input.

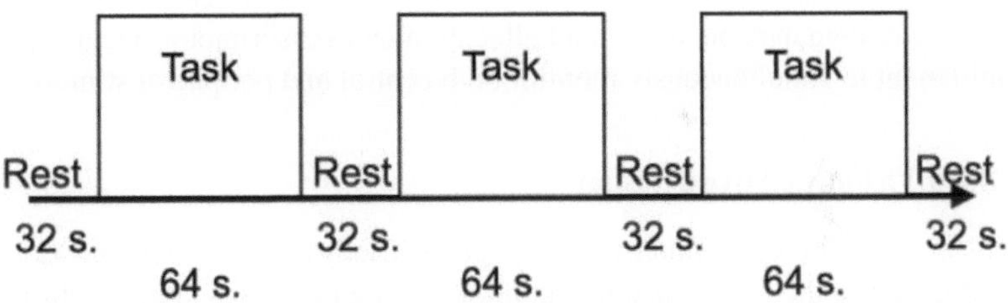

Fig. 3. The experiment employed a block design alternating between task and rest periods. Each task block lasted for 64 s and was followed by a 32-s rest period. This cycle was repeated three times per visual condition.

2.4 Data Preprocessing and Analysis

Functional imaging data were preprocessed and analyzed using Statistical Parametric Mapping (SPM12). Standard preprocessing steps included motion correction, spatial realignment, normalization to the Montreal Neurological Institute (MNI) [7] space, and spatial smoothing using a Gaussian kernel to enhance signal-to-noise ratio. Head motion artifacts were monitored, and any excessive movements exceeding predefined thresholds were corrected or excluded from analysis.

A general linear model (GLM) was employed to identify condition-specific activation patterns, and paired t-tests were conducted to compare brain activity across the three experimental conditions. The analysis focused on detecting significant differences in neural activation associated with mixed vision relative to single vision conditions. To control for multiple comparisons, family-wise error (FWE) correction was applied at the cluster level, ensuring statistical robustness in the results.

3 Results

This study used fMRI to examine brain activity under three visual conditions: foveal, peripheral, and mixed vision. Statistical analysis was conducted using a FWE correction with a cluster-size threshold of 20. Mixed vision produced significantly broader activation in regions associated with visual processing, attentional control, and visuomotor integration.

3.1 Mixed Vision vs. Peripheral Vision

Figure 4 illustrates brain regions that showed significantly greater BOLD activation during the mixed vision condition compared to the peripheral vision condition. The colored areas represent clusters in which neural responses were significantly stronger under the mixed vision condition. Specifically, mixed vision resulted in significantly increased BOLD signals in the left precentral gyrus (cluster size = 31), left superior parietal lobule (SPL) (cluster size = 55), and left postcentral gyrus (cluster size = 25). These areas are associated with the frontal eye field, the dorsal attention network, and the somatosensory cortex, respectively. These findings suggest that mixed vision imposes greater demands on attentional allocation and sensorimotor integration due to the requirement to simultaneously monitor both central and peripheral stimuli.

3.2 Mixed Vision vs. Foveal Vision

Figure 5 shows brain regions that exhibited greater activation in the mixed vision condition compared to the foveal vision condition. Colored overlays indicate clusters with significantly enhanced BOLD responses during mixed vision. Specifically, mixed vision induced stronger activation in the left occipital white matter (cluster size = 57), bilateral lingual gyri (combined cluster size = 180), and right occipital white matter (cluster size = 23). These areas are involved in early-stage visual processing (visual areas V1 and V2) and the integration of visual information across regions. The broader spatial extent of visual input during mixed vision appears to engage a larger portion of the visual cortex and requires more intensive interregional communication.

3.3 Foveal Vision vs. Mixed Vision

Figure 6 presents brain regions that exhibited greater activation during the foveal vision condition compared to the mixed vision condition. Colored clusters indicate voxels with significantly stronger BOLD responses under foveal vision. Specifically, the left middle occipital gyrus (cluster size = 25) and the right fusiform gyrus (cluster size = 26) showed reliably greater activation in the foveal condition. The middle occipital gyrus is implicated in the analysis of detailed spatial features, while the fusiform gyrus plays a central role in high-resolution object recognition. These results indicate that narrowly focused attention in the foveal condition leads to increased activation in specialized visual processing regions. In contrast, the inclusion of peripheral input in the mixed condition may diffuse attentional resources, thereby reducing activation in these regions.

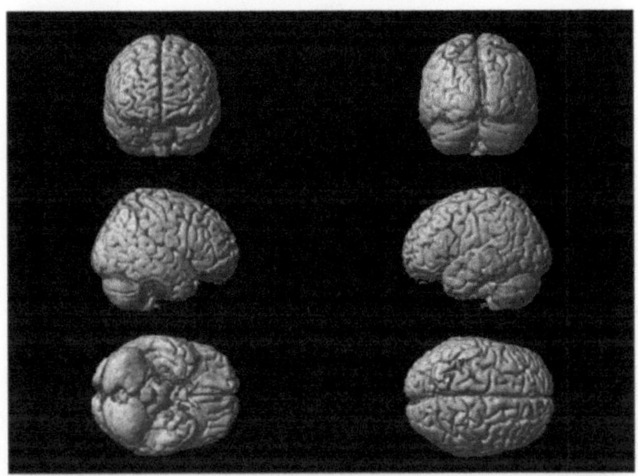

Fig. 4. Significant brain activation in mixed vision compared to peripheral vision. (FWE-corrected, cluster size ≥ 20).

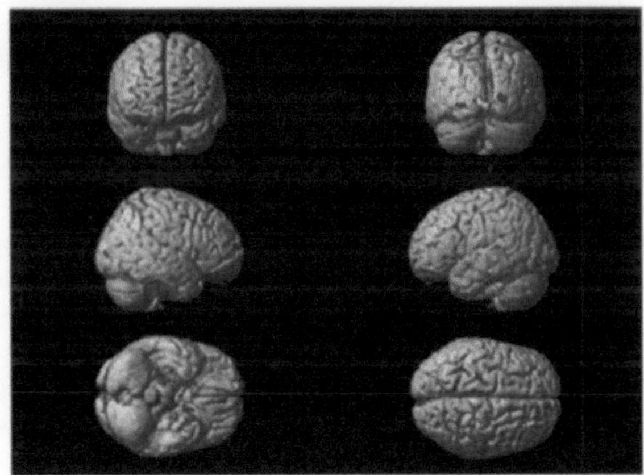

Fig. 5. Regions with greater activation in mixed vision than foveal vision. (FWE-corrected, cluster size ≥ 20).

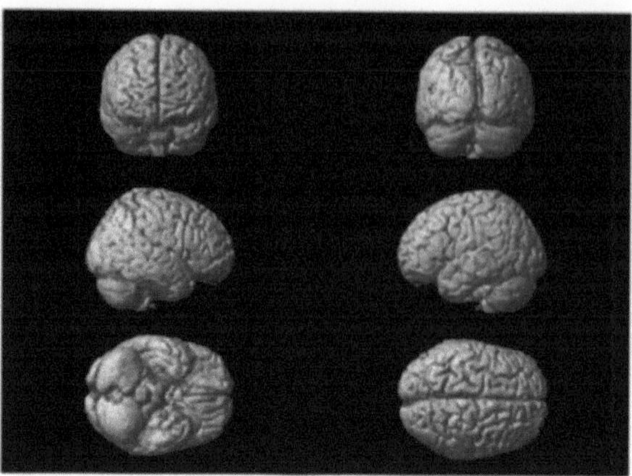

Fig. 6. Brain regions exhibiting significantly greater activation during foveal vision compared to mixed vision. (FWE-corrected, cluster size $\geq$ 20).

4   Discussion

This study demonstrated that mixed vision—the simultaneous engagement of foveal and peripheral visual fields—elicits broader and more intense neural activation compared to either foveal or peripheral vision alone. In the comparison between mixed and peripheral vision, significant activation was observed in the left precentral gyrus, superior parietal lobule (SPL), and postcentral gyrus. These regions are well-established components of the visuomotor coordination, spatial attention, and somatosensory processing networks [7, 8]. In particular, the SPL plays a central role in the dorsal attention network, enabling the flexible allocation of attention across the visual field. The left precentral gyrus likely corresponds to the frontal eye field, which is critically involved in voluntary eye movement planning and attentional shifts [9].

In the contrast between mixed and foveal vision, stronger activation was observed in the bilateral lingual gyri and occipital white matter during the mixed condition. These regions are involved in early-stage visual processing, including activity in areas such as V1 and V2 [10]. The findings suggest that the simultaneous processing of central and peripheral input requires broader cortical engagement and enhanced interregional communication. Activation in occipital white matter likely reflects increased connectivity demands to coordinate distinct streams of visual information.

Conversely, greater activation in the left middle occipital gyrus and right fusiform gyrus was observed during the foveal vision condition compared to mixed vision. These regions are crucial for fine-grained spatial analysis and high-resolution object recognition, respectively. Their heightened activation under foveal-only conditions likely reflects the benefit of concentrated attentional focus. In contrast, mixed vision introduces attentional diffusion, which may reduce the intensity of activation in these specialized processing areas.

Collectively, these findings indicate that mixed vision imposes a distinct cognitive load, requiring the co-activation of attentional control, sensory integration, and motor planning systems. This is consistent with prior fMRI research showing that increased visual attention load is associated with expanded activation in frontal and parietal regions, reflecting elevated cognitive demands [11, 12]. Importantly, the observed activation patterns under mixed vision do not merely reflect the additive effects of foveal and peripheral processing. Instead, they suggest the recruitment of a synergistic neural network capable of integrating multiple visual streams in parallel.

These results underscore the complexity of real-world visual perception, where the brain must dynamically coordinate both central and peripheral inputs. Understanding how the brain manages this integration may have implications for the design of attention-sensitive technologies, as well as for clinical populations with visuospatial deficits.

It should be noted that BOLD signals in white matter must be interpreted with caution due to lower vascular density and greater susceptibility to partial-volume effects. The responses observed in white matter in this study may therefore reflect signal contributions from adjacent gray matter or increased interregional connectivity demands.

5 Conclusion

This study investigated the neural mechanisms underlying mixed vision—the simultaneous processing of foveal and peripheral visual input—using functional magnetic resonance imaging (fMRI). The results showed that mixed vision elicited broader and more intense brain activation compared to either foveal or peripheral vision alone, particularly in regions involved in visual processing, attentional control, and sensorimotor integration.

A key finding is that mixed vision does not simply reflect the additive activity of foveal and peripheral systems. Instead, it engages a distinct and synergistic neural network responsible for integrating information across the entire visual field. This network includes the superior parietal lobule, precentral gyrus, lingual gyrus, and occipital white matter, and suggests that managing visual attention across central and peripheral inputs imposes substantial cognitive demands.

Understanding the functional organization of mixed vision provides valuable insights into how the human brain supports complex, real-world visual behavior. Future research should explore how these integrative mechanisms adapt to dynamic environments and assess their relevance in clinical populations with deficits in spatial attention or visual integration.

Acknowledgments. This work was supported by JSPS KAKENHI Grant Number 22K12710.

Disclosure of Interests. The authors have no competing interests to declare that are relevant to the content of this article.

References

1. Wandell, B.A., Dumoulin, S.O., Brewer, A.A.: Visual field maps in human cortex. Neuron **56**, 366–383 (2007). https://doi.org/10.1016/j.neuron.2007.10.012

2. Shafritz, K.M., Gore, J.C., Marois, R.: The role of the parietal cortex in visual feature binding. Proc. Natl. Acad. Sci. U.S.A. **99**, 10917–10922 (2002). https://doi.org/10.1073/pnas.152694799

3. Jovicich, J., Peters, R.J., Koch, C., Braun, J., Chang, L., Ernst, T.: Brain areas specific for attentional load in a motion-tracking task. J. Cogn. Neurosci. **13**, 1048–1058 (2001). https://doi.org/10.1162/089892901753294347

4. Kim, Y.-J., Tsai, J.J., Ojemann, J., Verghese, P.: Attention to multiple objects facilitates their integration in prefrontal and parietal cortex. J. Neurosci. **37**, 4942–4953 (2017). https://doi.org/10.1523/JNEUROSCI.2370-16.2017

5. Ogawa, S., Lee, T.M., Nayak, A.S., Glynn, P.: Oxygenation-sensitive contrast in magnetic resonance image of rodent brain at high magnetic fields. Magn. Reson. Med. **14**, 68–78 (1990). https://doi.org/10.1002/mrm.1910140108

6. Hosford, P.S., Gourine, A.V.: What is the key mediator of the neurovascular coupling response? Neurosci. Biobehav. Rev. **96**, 174–181 (2019). https://doi.org/10.1016/j.neubiorev.2018.11.011

7. Evans, A.C., Collins, D.L., Milner, B.: An MRI-based stereotactic atlas from 250 young normal subjects. Soc. Neurosci. Abstracts **18**, 408–492 (1992)

8. Wojciulik, E., Kanwisher, N.: The generality of parietal involvement in visual attention. Neuron **23**, 747–764 (1999). https://doi.org/10.1016/s0896-6273(01)80033-7

9. Kelley, T.A., Serences, J.T., Giesbrecht, B., Yantis, S.: Cortical mechanisms for shifting and holding visuospatial attention. Cereb. Cortex **18**, 114–125 (2008). https://doi.org/10.1093/cercor/bhm036

10. Jin, Z., et al.: Structural and functional MRI evidence for significant contribution of precentral gyrus to flexible oculomotor control: evidence from the antisaccade task. Brain Struct. Funct. **227**, 2623–2632 (2022). https://doi.org/10.1007/s00429-022-02557-z

11. Benedek, M., Jauk, E., Beaty, R.E., Fink, A., Koschutnig, K., Neubauer, A.C.: Brain mechanisms associated with internally directed attention and self-generated thought. Sci. Rep. **6**, 22959 (2016). https://doi.org/10.1038/srep22959

12. Tomasi, D., Chang, L., Caparelli, E.C., Ernst, T.: Different activation patterns for working memory load and visual attention load. Brain Res. **1132**, 158–165 (2007). https://doi.org/10.1016/j.brainres.2006.11.030

Surrogate Analysis of EEG Signals for Early Detection of Mild Cognitive Impairment and Dementia

Kuwon Sumi[1], Kakeru Amano[1], Masumi Takada[2]($\boxtimes$), and Hiroki Takada[1] (iD)

[1] University of Fukui, 3-9-1 Bunkyo, Fukui 910-8507, Fukui, Japan
[2] Chubu Gakuin University, 2-1 Kirigaoka, Seki City, Gifu 501-3993, Japan
takada-masumi@chubu-gu.ac.jp

Abstract. This study investigates the application of surrogate data analysis to electroencephalogram (EEG) signals for the early detection of mild cognitive impairment (MCI) and dementia. We employed the Fourier shuffle (FS) surrogate method and the Wayland algorithm to analyze EEG data from young and elderly participants during rest and while performing cognitive function tests. Our results indicate significant differences in the nonlinearity and complexity of EEG signals between age groups and cognitive states, suggesting potential biomarkers for early detection of cognitive decline. The findings provide insights into the changes in brain activity associated with aging and cognitive impairment, which may contribute to improved diagnostic and rehabilitation strategies for MCI and dementia.

Keywords: Electroencephalographic (EEG) · Surrogate data

1 Introduction

Early detection of mild cognitive impairment (MCI) and dementia is essential for timely intervention. Epidemiological meta analyses estimate that over 50 million people worldwide were living with dementia in 2019, with the prevalence projected to triple by 2050 [1–3]. National demographic projections for Japan likewise indicate a rapidly ageing population, with the proportion of those aged 65 + rising from 29% in 2020 to an estimated 38% by 2050 [4].

Electroencephalography (EEG) offers a noninvasive, cost effective means of monitoring brain electrical activity and has been widely used in clinical neurophysiology [5]. However, conventional linear spectral analyses may overlook complex, nonlinear neural dynamics. To address this, surrogate data methodology generates artificial time series that conform to specific null hypotheses—e.g., temporally uncorrelated noise or linear stochastic processes—and statistically contrasts them with original recordings [6]. Improved surrogate techniques, such as amplitude-adjusted or iterative schemes, enhance the rigor of nonlinearity testing [7].

The Fourier shuffle (FS) method reconstructs time series data by randomizing the Fourier phase while preserving the original power spectrum [6]. Based on Takens'

© The Author(s), under exclusive license to Springer Nature Switzerland AG 2026

M. Antona and C. Stephanidis (Eds.): HCII 2025, LNCS 16335, pp. 235–243, 2026.
https://doi.org/10.1007/978-3-032-12781-5_16

embedding method [9], attractors are reconstructed from the time series data, and the Wayland algorithm [10] is applied to estimate translation error between trajectories, thereby quantifying the determinism of the mathematical model underlying each series. In this study, we compared the determinism of models describing the original data with those describing phase randomized surrogate data. The translation error estimated using the Double-Wayland algorithm [11] is highly sensitive to signal to noise ratio conditions and is expected to reflect underlying physiological complexity [12].

Prior applications of surrogate analysis to EEG include assessments of sleep dynamics [8], neonatal burst suppression [13], and normal-aging EEG dynamic [14], as well as studies of EEG complexity in Alzheimer's disease [15]. Sugai et al. (2024) demonstrated the physiological effects of pen usage and the applicability of surrogate-based translation error metrics to cognitive load during handwriting tasks [16].

This study is a secondary analysis based on Kuon Sumi's master's thesis [17]. We applied FS surrogates and the Wayland algorithm to EEG recorded during the Hasegawa Dementia Scale-Revised (HDS-R) cognitive screening tests. We focused on two metrics:

1. Nonlinearity testing via the FS surrogate method to detect deviations from linear stochastic models.
2. Determinism estimation through the Wayland algorithm, computing translation errors for original versus surrogate EEG time series.

By comparing these metrics between young and elderly participants, and between resting and task conditions, we aimed to identify biomarkers indicative of early cognitive decline.

2 Methods

This study was approved by the Research Ethics Committee for Studies Involving Human Subjects of the Faculty of Engineering, University of Fukui (approval number: H2022001).

2.1 Participants and Data Acquisition

The study included 28 healthy participants (6 males, 22 females) aged 19–85 years (mean $\pm$ SD: 46.3 $\pm$ 27.4 years). EEG data were recorded using a two-electrode EEG telemetry device NS-CRE-KN-A01–1 (BioSearch) with the reference electrode attached to the right earlobe (Fig. 1). The experiment protocol consisted of three phases: 3 min with eyes open (Rest-O), 3 min with eyes closed (Rest-C), and performance of the HDS-R screening test (Table 1).

2.2 EEG Preprocessing

The recorded EEG data were preprocessed using a bandpass filter with a frequency range of 1–49 Hz to remove artifacts and noise while retaining the relevant frequency bands for cognitive function analysis (Fig. 2).

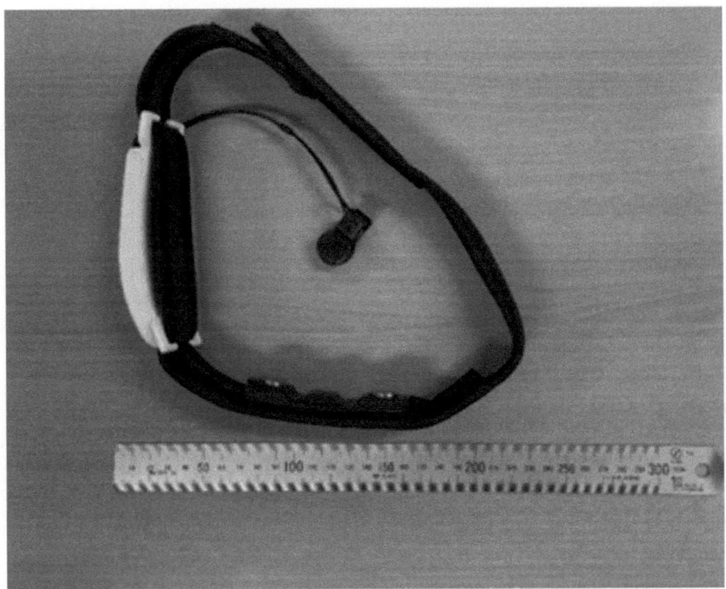

Fig. 1. Wireless EEG device.

Table 1. Experimental protocol.

Order	
1	3 min with eyes open (Rest-O)
2	3 min with eyes closed (Rest-C)
3	HDS-R screening test

2.3 Fourier Shuffle Surrogate Method

The FS surrogate method was employed to test for nonlinearity in the EEG signals. This method generates surrogate data by randomizing the phases of the Fourier transform of the original time series while preserving its power spectrum. The process can be summarized as follows:

1. Perform Fourier transform on the original EEG time series (Fig. 2a).
2. Randomize the phases of the Fourier coefficients while keeping their magnitudes constant.
3. Perform an inverse Fourier transform to obtain the surrogate time series.

   This procedure was repeated to generate multiple surrogate datasets for each original EEG signal (Fig. 2b).

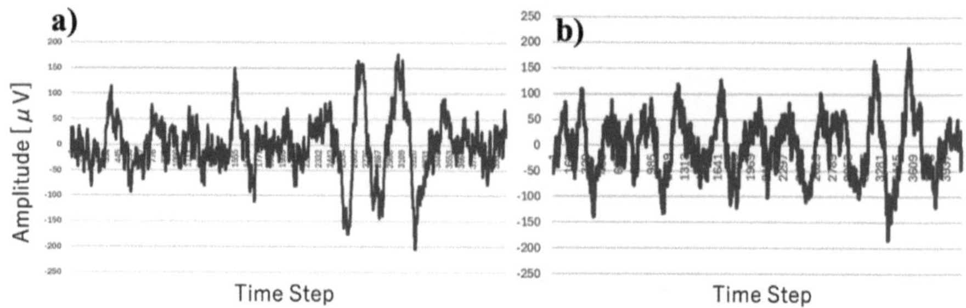

Fig. 2. Typical examples of EEG graphs. (a) Time series data, and (b) Surrogate time series.

2.4 Statistical Analysis

To compare the results between age groups and cognitive states, we performed statistical tests on the calculated translation errors. A t-test was used with a significance level of 0.05 to determine whether there were significant differences between the original EEG signals and their surrogate counterparts, as well as between the young and elderly participants during rest and HDS-R test performance.

3 Results

3.1 HDS-R Test Performance

The HDS-R test results showed a distribution of scores among the participants, with some variation between the young and elderly groups (Fig. 3). This provided a baseline for cognitive performance to compare with the EEG analysis results.

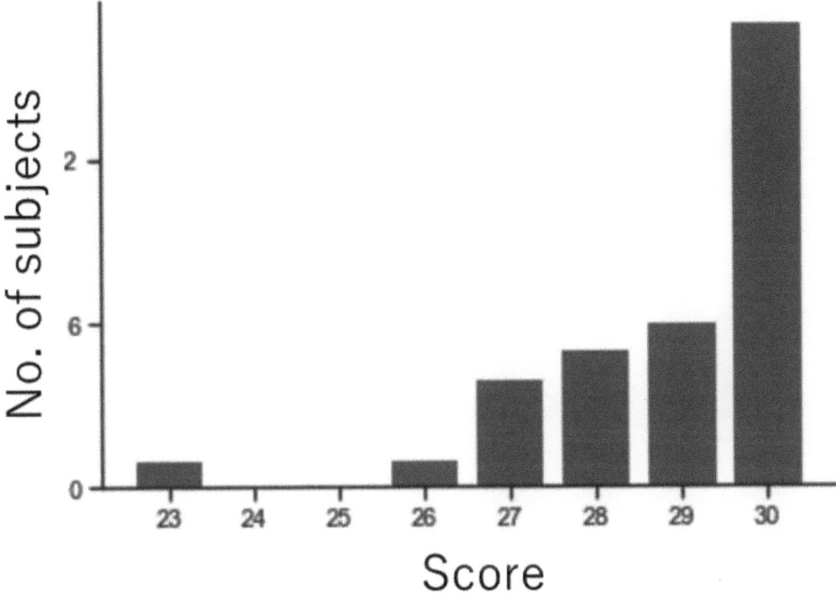

Fig. 3. Distribution of the HDS-R test scores.

3.2 Degree of Nonlinearity

The degree of nonlinearity (DEG) was affected differently for various frequency bands and brain regions. Notably, we observed significant differences between the young and elderly participants in the right hemisphere during cognitive tasks, particularly in the high-frequency bands (18–30, 41–50, 70–85, and 86–100 Hz).

3.3 Surrogate Analysis Results

The surrogate analysis revealed several key findings:

1. Translation error comparison:

- In all cases, elderly participants showed higher translation errors compared with young participants (Fig. 4).
- This suggests increased complexity in the EEG signals of elderly individuals during both the resting state and cognitive task performance.

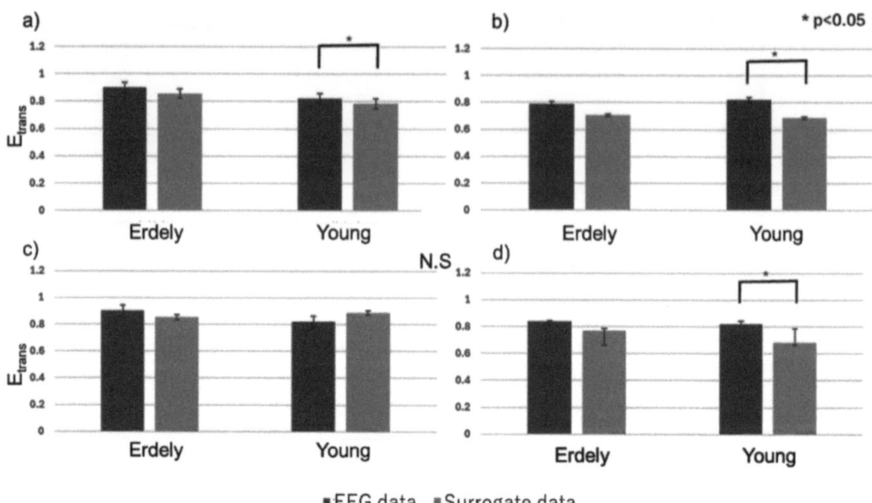

Fig. 4. Surrogate analysis results for (a) Rest with eyes open at Fp1, b) HDS-R at Fp1, c) Rest with eyes open at Fp2, and (d) HDS-R at Fp2.

2. Nonlinearity detection:

For young participants, significant differences between original and surrogate data were observed in the left brain with eyes open (Rest-O) and in both hemispheres during the HDS-R test (Figs. 4a and 4b).

- This indicates the presence of nonlinear dynamics in the EEG signals of young participants, particularly during cognitive task performance.

3. Age-related differences:

- Elderly participants did not show significant nonlinearity in their EEG signals, as evidenced by the lack of difference between original and surrogate data (Fig. 4).
- This suggests a potential loss of complex nonlinear dynamics in the brain activity of elderly individuals, which may be associated with cognitive decline.

4 Discussion

The results of our surrogate-data analysis provide several insights into the nonlinear dynamics of EEG signals during cognitive tasks, particularly in the context of age-related changes.

4.1 Increased Complexity in Elderly EEG Signals

Translation errors computed via the Wayland test were consistently higher in elderly participants during both the rest and task phases. This suggests greater temporal unpredictability and increased stochastic neural dynamics, in line with the concept of reduced physiological complexity in ageing described by Goldberger et al. [12] and corroborated by Yamaguchi's surrogate data findings in older adults [14].

4.2 Nonlinearity in Young Participants' EEG

In young participants, surrogate testing frequently rejected the null hypothesis of linearity during cognitive engagement. This indicates preserved nonlinear structure and deterministic properties. Similar observations have been reported in sleep-EEG studies [8] and neonatal analyses [13].

4.3 Loss of Nonlinearity in Elderly Participants

Despite higher translation errors, elderly EEG signals did not significantly differ from phase randomized surrogates, implying that complexity arises from randomness rather than deterministic chaos. This aligns with findings of diminished EEG nonlinearity in older adults [14] and in Alzheimer's patients [15].

4.4 Implications for Cognitive Assessment

Our dual metric approach—combining nonlinearity testing and translation error estimation—offers a richer profile of brain dynamics than spectral analysis alone. These metrics not only differentiate age groups but also respond to cognitive load within individuals. Moreover, Sugai et al. (2024) demonstrated the practical applicability of these surrogate measures by analyzing the physiological effects of pen usage during handwriting tasks [16].

4.5 Limitations and Future Directions

This study had several limitations:

- Surrogate methods: Comparing FS surrogates with amplitude-adjusted or iterative techniques would strengthen robustness [7].
- Machine learning integration: Translation error and nonlinearity features may serve as inputs for classifiers to predict MCI or distinguish dementia subtypes [18].

Future research should focus on:

- Developing standardized protocols for EEG-based cognitive assessment using surrogate analysis techniques.
- Investigating the relationship between EEG nonlinearity and specific cognitive domains or subtypes of dementia.
- Exploring the potential of machine learning algorithms to classify cognitive status based on surrogate analysis features [18].

Validating these surrogate-based markers across larger, longitudinal cohorts and diverse clinical populations will facilitate translating our findings into practical screening tools.

5 Conclusion

This study demonstrates the potential of using surrogate data analysis techniques, specifically the FS method and Wayland algorithm, in characterizing EEG dynamics associated with aging and cognitive function. The observed differences in complexity and nonlinearity between the young and elderly participants, as well as between the resting state and cognitive task performance, suggest that these measures could serve as valuable biomarkers for early detection of cognitive decline.

The loss of nonlinearity in the EEG signals of elderly participants during cognitive tasks may indicate a reduced capacity for adaptive neural responses. This finding underscores the importance of considering nonlinear dynamics in the assessment of cognitive function and the potential development of early intervention strategies for age-related cognitive decline.

By combining traditional cognitive assessments with advanced EEG analysis techniques, we can gain a more comprehensive understanding of the neural mechanisms underlying cognitive aging and potentially improve early detection and management of mild cognitive impairment and dementia.

Acknowledgments. This work was supported by JSPS KAKENHI Grant Number 20K11295 and 23K28367.

Disclosure of Interests. The authors have no competing interests to declare that are relevant to the content of this article.

References

1. Prince, M., Ali, G.-C., Guerchet, M., Prina, A.M., Albanese, E., Wu, Y.-T., et al.: The global prevalence of dementia: a systematic review and metaanalysis. Alzheimer's Dementia **9**(1), 63–75 (2013)
2. Nichols, E., Steinmetz, J.D., Vollset, S.E., Fukutaki, K., Chalek, J., Abd-Allah, F., et al.: Global, regional, and national burden of Alzheimer's disease and other dementias, 1990–2016: a systematic analysis for the global burden of disease study 2016. Lancet Neurol. **18**(1), 88–106 (2019)
3. Alzheimer's Association. 2023 Alzheimer's disease facts and figures. Alzheimer's Dementia **19**(4), 1598–1695 (2023)
4. United Nations, Department of Economic and Social Affairs, Population Division. World Population Prospects (2022). https://population.un.org/wpp/
5. Stam, C.J.: Nonlinear dynamical analysis of EEG and MEG: review of an emerging field. Clin. Neurophysiol. **116**(10), 2266–2301 (2005)
6. Theiler, J., Eubank, S., Longtin, A., Galdrikian, B., Farmer, J.D.: Testing for nonlinearity in time series: the method of surrogate data. Physica D **58**(1–4), 77–94 (1992)
7. Schreiber, T., Schmitz, A.: Improved surrogate data for nonlinearity tests. Phys. Rev. Lett. **77**(4), 635–638 (1996)
8. Fell, J., Klaver, P., Lehnertz, K., Grünwald, T., Schaller, C., Elger, C.E., et al.: Comparison of spectral and nonlinear EEG measures for distinguishing sleep stages. Neuroimage **4**(3 Pt 1), 206–218 (1996)

9. Takens, F.: Detecting strange attractors in turbulence. In: Rand D., Young, L.-S. (eds.) Dynamical Systems and Turbulence, Warwick 1980, Lecture Notes in Mathematics, vol. 898, pp. 366–381. Springer (1981)

10. Wayland, R., Bromley, D., Pickett, D., Passamante, A.: Recognizing determinism in a time series. Phys. Rev. Lett. **70**, 530–582 (1993)

11. Takada, H., Morimoto, T., Tsunashima, H., Yamazaki, T., Hoshina, H., Miyao, M.: Applications of Double Wayland algorithm to detect anomalous signals. Forma **21**(2), 159–167 (2006)

12. Goldberger, A.L., Peng, C.K., Lipsitz, L.A.: What is physiologic complexity and how does it change with aging and disease? Neurobiol. Aging **23**(1), 23–26 (2002)

13. Mirzaei, M., Ahmadi, N., Dadmehr, N.: Surrogate data analysis of neonatal burst-suppression EEG patterns. Clin. Neurophysiol. **128**(5), 789–797 (2017)

14. Yamaguchi, Y.: Nonlinear dynamics of EEG in normal aging: a surrogate data approach. J. Clin. Neurophysiol. **23**(4), 221–227 (2006)

15. Jeong, J.: EEG dynamics in patients with Alzheimer's disease. Clin. Neurophysiol. **115**(7), 1490–1505 (2004)

16. Sugai, H., Tsukamoto, K., Takada, H., Komatsu, Y., Murakata, S., Kawasaki, T.: A study on the physiological effects of pen usage: for application of EEG measurement technology to information science education. In: Hong H., Kanaparan, G. (eds.) Computer Science and Education, Computer Science and Technology, vol. 2023 CCIS, pp. 454–465. Springer (2024). https://doi.org/10.1007/978-981-97-0730-0_40

17. Sumi, K.: Research on early detection of mild dementia using simple electroencephalography and fMRI (Master's thesis). University of Fukui, Graduate School of Engineering (2025)

18. Lotte, F., Congedo, M., Lécuyer, A., Lamarche, F., Arnaldi, B.: A review of classification algorithms for EEG-based brain–computer interfaces: a 10-year update. J. Neural Eng. **15**(3), 031005 (2018)

User-Centric Route Optimisation Models for Green Mobility Decision Support

Ana Vigário[1], Rodrigo Fernandes[1], Tiago Pinto[1,2(✉)], Arsénio Reis[1,2], Tânia Rocha[1,2], and João Barroso[1,2]

[1] University of Trás-os-Montes and Alto Douro, Vila Real, Portugal
[2] INESC-TEC, Vila Real, Portugal
`tiagopinto@utad.pt`

Abstract. Graphs are present in various fields of knowledge, representing a wide range of structures and systems, such as transportation networks, pathways, electrical circuits, among others. They are mathematical structures that model relationships between objects through vertices (points of interest) and edges, which represent possible paths between these vertices and may carry weights associated with distances, times, costs, or other relevant metrics. Graphs are widely used in the modeling and effective resolution of route optimization problems, aiming to find the best possible solution by minimizing or maximizing a specific metric. Although end users often do not interact directly with or need to understand their complexity, the benefits produced lead to positive outcomes in the user experience. In urban mobility, especially with electric vehicles, optimization enables the structuring of efficient routes, benefiting both users and the environment by reducing travel time, noise, and pollutant emissions. Recent applications include route planning for agricultural drones and autonomous vehicles, as well as the management of school and industrial transportation, consistently promoting sustainability, efficiency, and cost-effectiveness. Additionally, graphs are used in the Internet of Things, smart networks, and even in aerial systems, optimizing complex operations and enhancing safety and reliability. This paper presents a study aimed at developing a solution capable of addressing the needs of route optimization and providing effective responses to the challenges of urban mobility, considering the specific application context of electric motorbikes used in service delivery.

Keywords: Route optimization · Sustainability · Urban services · Modern mobility

1 Introduction

Graphs are mathematical structures used to model relationships between objects and are defined as collections of vertices and edges, where an edge connects two vertices [1]. They can be found in various places or situations simultaneously,

© The Author(s), under exclusive license to Springer Nature Switzerland AG 2026
M. Antona and C. Stephanidis (Eds.): HCII 2025, LNCS 16335, pp. 244–255, 2026.
https://doi.org/10.1007/978-3-032-12781-5_17

being common or accessible in many different contexts. They are used to represent a wide range of things, from physical infrastructure networks, such as road systems, electrical grids, and public transportation networks, to social networks, software networks, biological networks, and more [2] (Figs. 1, 2 and 3).

For example, a section of a road map

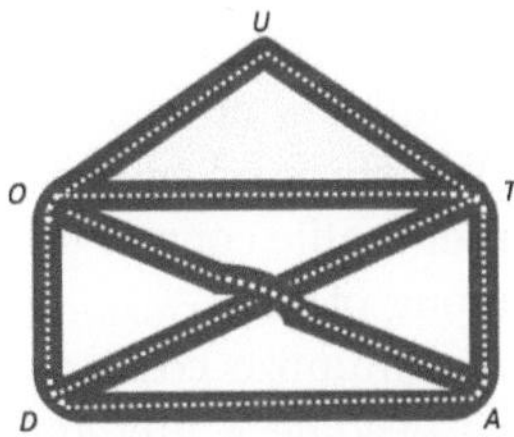

Fig. 1. Road Maps. Created by the authors.

Or the following section of connected tablets

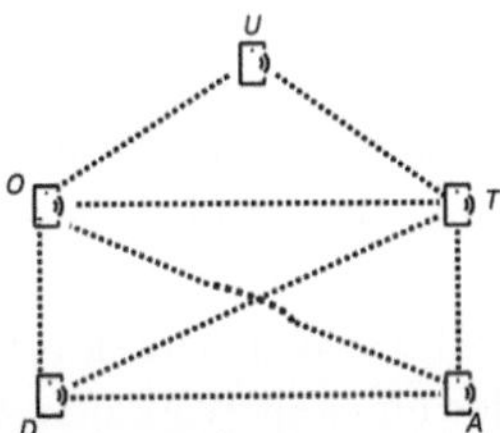

Fig. 2. Connected Tablets. Created by the authors.

Both can be represented using points and line segments

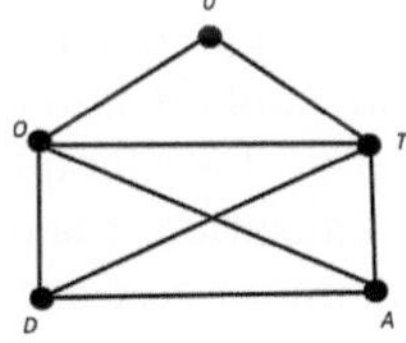

Fig. 3. Graph. Created by the authors.

Optimization algorithms and their tools are widely used to find effective solutions to the complex problems of such graphs. Algorithms that operate on graphs are essential for efficiently solving problems that have a significant impact across various domains, particularly in logistics, where they play a fundamental role in structuring distribution routes that offer benefits both for companies and their users, as well as in enhancing customer satisfaction [3].

An optimization problem seeks to find the best solution to minimize or maximize a specific metric, such as time, cost, or performance. Optimization algorithms and their mathematical tools are widely used to find an effective solution to a specific problem [4]. Route optimization and its algorithms have a significant impact in several areas. From the user's perspective, it is essential and indispensable now, because it builds a crucial tool to meet the demands with efficiency and practicability. Widely used by private and public companies, it extends to areas such as Internet traffic control [5] [6], school transportation [7], industrial noise control [8], among others.

Widely used in logistics to minimize costs or travel time between various points, route optimization has become a fundamental tool in urban contexts, where chaotic traffic and changes in road conditions make planning difficult. It benefits not only the user but also the environment by reducing travel time, noise emissions, and pollutant gas emissions. In electric vehicles, its importance is even greater, considering battery consumption and the need for recharging, promoting more sustainable operations.

In this way, route optimization is an indispensable solution for modern mobility, balancing operational efficiency and environmental preservation. Visualization makes it possible to prioritize important points, streamline the service, and reorganize operations in real time, through the dynamic presentation of information, improving decision-making, providing effective structuring of the activity, reducing travel time and costs inherent in the service.

This article presents or work towards the development of a solution capable of meeting thes needs and offer efficient responses to these challenges, considering the specific application context of electric motorbikes used to deliver urban services, developed through the **A-MoVeR** "Mobilizing Agenda for the Development of Products and Systems towards an Intelligent and Green Mobility" [9].

2   Optimized Routes

The versatility of graphs and the application of optimization algorithms are widely used by both private and public companies, spanning various fields of knowledge and industry. In logistics, for example, existing studies demonstrate the great importance of route optimization, where graphs are used to model road networks and calculate faster or more cost-effective routes, optimizing urban traffic flow and minimizing costs or travel time between multiple points. In the study"A Multiobjective Approach to the Electric Vehicle Routing Problem" [10], an approach was presented that simultaneously minimizes total travel time and the costs associated with charging electric vehicles, standing out as a practical and efficient solution for route planning in the context of green mobility.

The use of route optimization is addressed in several sectors of this area, such as last mile delivery in e-commerce, studied by Neto et al. [11], which proposed to analyze the route for product collection and subsequent delivery to end customers, with the objective of finding an optimal route, reducing the distance and time traveled, resulting in an ideal route, showing an improvement of approximately 41.69%. In Wang et al. [12], a motion planning framework was proposed for autonomous delivery vehicles in complex urban scenarios, with a focus on the last mile. In their case study, implemented in real express delivery services using JD's autonomous delivery vehicles in China, the tests totaled more than 100,000 h and 100,000 km, demonstrating high effectiveness even in congested urban environments, Optimization algorithms were used to smooth and correct trajectories, a raw trajectory profile was initially generated with decisions such as stopping, yielding, or avoiding obstacles. Optimization then refined the speed and path using algorithms that minimized travel time and enhanced comfort and safety. The proposed system significantly reduced the need for human intervention during navigation, which proves that the planned trajectory was efficient and safe.

In the area of logistics, route optimization also applies to public transport, school transport and carpooling. In a study conducted by Jang et al. [13], the optimization of public transport networks in the Republic of Korea was addressed, simultaneously considering the perspectives of users and service providers. From the user's perspective, the approach was distinguished by the use of socio-economic indicators to define traffic zones, ensuring more accessible transport for vulnerable populations, while exploring route alternatives evaluated based on metrics such as accessibility and profitability. The method demonstrated significant improvements, including a 29.7% increase in the overall route evaluation score, reflecting greater efficiency in planning and operation. For the user, optimization prioritized the reduction of travel time and increase in spatial coverage, ensuring a more efficient service adapted to needs. Additionally, the optimized routes presented less overlap, facilitating the management and use of public transport. While in Oliveira et al. [7]. the study developed mathematical models that minimized the distances traveled by school vehicles on three routes analyzed in the city of Itapiúna, Brazil, reducing operating costs and improving service efficiency. The application resulted in a reduction of up to 17.37% in the distances traveled and in the decrease of fuel consumption, generating direct savings for the municipal management.

In the collection of organic waste in homes, Libotte et al. [14] conducted a study with the objective of developing a mathematical model to minimize the distance traveled, reducing the costs involved, promoting sustainability and competitiveness in small businesses. From the company's point of view, the use of algorithms and tools from the study allowed to identify the best route, thus minimizing transport costs and time required for collections. The model created provided a 17.16% reduction in distance traveled. In collections carried out on three days of the week, making a total of fifty-four trips and traveling a total of 77.326km, the routes found by the model served all customers in two days of the week, traveling a total of 64.057Km, this corresponded to a saving of 344.994Km per year.

The route optimization also influences several areas, such as the optimization of logistic routes for temperature-sensitive items in hospital environments, in Vijaiprabhu et al. [?], focused on reducing costs, time spent and distances travelled in transport while maintaining the integrity of the product. This study resulted in a precision rate of 98.83%, surpassing traditional methods. While in Zhang et al.[?], proposes a model of guided cellular automata (GCA) to optimize navigation paths in hospitals. The study addresses the need to plan routes for patients in complex and congested environments, promoting a continuous flow and reducing waiting times in hospital areas, resulting in a viable and efficient solution.

In computer science, graph algorithms are essential in computer networks, IP networks, and even the Internet of Things. In El-Hefnawy et al. [15], a Hybrid Ant Colony Optimization (HACO) algorithm was proposed to optimize the dynamic routing problem in large-scale Software-Defined Networks (SDNs), aiming to reduce the time and space complexity associated with traditional algorithms. The algorithm achieved significant reductions in network delays, packet loss rates, and execution times. Rexford [16] explored the optimization of Internet routing protocols, particularly in IP networks, with the goal of overcoming the limitations of traditional routing protocols that did not consider traffic load in path selection. The observed benefits included reduced flow congestion, increased robustness to failures and traffic variations, reduced need for manual changes, and mitigation of instabilities caused by configuration changes. The optimization provided substantial performance and reliability gains without requiring the replacement of existing protocols.

A security protocol focused on route optimization in smart home networks with Distributed Mobility Management (DMM) was presented by Shin et al. [17]. The proposal enabled data to flow directly between the mobile device and home devices, avoiding the need to pass through multiple intermediaries (such as Mobility Gateways or unnecessary tunnels), thereby reducing round-trip time and improving responsiveness in interactions. As a result, there was lower bandwidth consumption and less processing in intermediate networks, relieving congestion and improving scalability. During handovers, the optimization maintained the session securely and seamlessly. Compared to standard protocols, the proposed protocol showed better performance and lower computational cost, proving to be more effective for mobile environments in smart home Internet of Things networks.

Recent approaches have explored the use of meta-heuristic algorithms for route optimization in IoT-assisted sensor networks, focusing on energy efficiency. For example, the **HMSFO-EARS** (Hybrid Muddy Soil Fish Optimization-based Energy Aware Routing Scheme) proposes a hybrid routing scheme for wireless sensor networks, with the aim of reducing power consumption and increasing network longevity [5]. This method uses adaptive fitness functions to select optimal routes. In a complementary way, the **ESEERP** (Enhanced Smart Energy Efficient Routing Protocol) develops an energy-efficient routing protocol, **QoS**

(Prioritizing quality of service) metrics to improve the performance of IoT integrated networks [6].

In economics and management, resource allocation problems, supply chain analysis, and production planning are addressed using graph-based optimization techniques. In supply logistics, Vasconcelos et al. [18] observed a 17.16% reduction in the route of a precision mechanics company when only one truck was used to transport materials from suppliers, which are used as raw materials. In addition to the reduction in distance traveled, it is important to consider the associated benefits of this activity, such as cost reduction, decreased carbon dioxide emissions, and the availability of vehicles for other tasks.

The application of algorithms enabled ABC (Pvt) Ltd., a fast-moving consumer goods company in Sri Lanka, to minimize transportation, warehouse, and administrative costs. In Jayarathna [19], it was proposed a route optimization, highlighting the transition from a decentralized distribution system to a centralized model. As significant results, the reduction of operating costs was verified, with a saving of 34% in total expenses. In addition, the new approach improved efficiency in resource allocation and delivery time, resulting in a more agile and reliable service, ensuring faster and cheaper distribution, increasing satisfaction, and strengthening the company's position in the market. The implementation of a mathematical model for route planning also provided greater visibility and control over logistics operations, which allowed for more informed and strategic decisions.

In the industrial sector, beyond route optimization focused on profit and productivity improvement, optimization systems can also be applied to minimize workers' exposure to high noise levels, which can lead to cardiac overload, stress, fatigue, and an increased number of accidents. The study conducted by Reis [8] demonstrated that the use of mathematical models allowed for route optimization and balancing of noise exposure doses among workers. The method reduced noise exposure by up to 67% and additionally enabled the optimized selection of noise sources to be addressed, ensuring appropriate exposure levels. For the user, the optimized routes effectively balance the workload, resulting in more efficient operations and minimizing the negative impacts of noise on workers' quality of life and performance, thus promoting a safer and more productive work environment.

In Deng et al. [20], a route optimization model was presented with the objective of helping to reduce carbon emissions in the manufacturing process. The model aimed to reduce processing time and increase carbon efficiency, considering material, energy and environmental flows. As a result, it was obtained a reduction of environmental impacts, promoting sustainability by minimizing carbon emissions during the manufacturing process. In addition, the reduction of total processing time contributes to increased productivity by providing consistent and data-driven support for process planning decisions.

In the field of agriculture, graphs are used to calculate routes, manage irrigation, among other applications. In Kethineni [21], a graph-based method was proposed to improve plant disease management in Agricultural Cyber-Physical

Systems integrated with the Internet of Agricultural Things. The study incorporated spatial analysis for detecting infection hotspots along with a Travelling Salesman Problem algorithm, optimizing both the drone's path and pesticide usage, enabling variable rate precision spraying and providing an effective and comprehensive solution for drone-based precision agriculture.

Spekken et al. [22] proposed the integration of existing route optimization methods with the aim of minimizing the time spent on turning and servicing operations in fields cultivated in straight lines. The algorithm was tested on fields of various sizes, and in small fields, optimizing the turns reduced maneuvering time by up to 50% compared to the common practice of navigating between adjacent lines. A comparison between two sprayers, in terms of servicing efficiency, showed that the algorithm can also assist in selecting the appropriate equipment based on field geometry. The study by Zhao et al. [23] addresses the optimization of pipeline layout and diameter selection in self-pressurized drip irrigation systems, focusing on the design optimization of irrigation systems in Xinjiang, China. The comparative analysis resulted in a total cost of 409,901 ¥, which is 27.5% lower than the empirical method. The number of sub-main pipes was reduced from 10 to 8, and their diameters were shortened, lowering the overall costs.

Graph algorithms play a crucial role in various aspects of aerial systems, both in commercial aviation and in unmanned aerial systems. Route optimization can be applied to air traffic management, delivering significant benefits to the user. In the study of Fang [24], solutions for optimization of helicopter routes were explored with a focus on support for spraying operations and movement between forest areas. In field experiments conducted with real helicopters, the planned route reduced redundant coverage by 17.87%, fuel consumption by 10.56% and pesticide consumption by 5.43%, while the number of manoeuvres was reduced from 51 to 40. In the context of air mission planning, Lee [25] presented the development of a **Digital Twin (DT)** integrated to systems engineering, which optimizes mission and route planning in unmanned aerial systems. The user was able to make more consistent and reliable decisions, as a basis for analysis that evaluated criteria such as time, risk and energy consumption. This approach has enabled routes to be prioritized intelligently, taking into account threat probabilities and energy efficiency, while creating a robust simulation environment to predict scenarios and optimize overall system performance. The user benefited from detailed support to reduce the impacts of human factors and obtain a higher quality in the execution of operations.

A route optimization-based equalization scheme to address the inconsistency problem in series-connected liquid metal battery (LMB) strings was studied by Cai et al. [26]. The optimization model aimed to minimize power loss during the equalization process[1]. Under static conditions, simulations showed an 88.62% increase in equalization speed and a 19.43% improvement in equalization effi-

---

[1] The process of balancing the state of charge among different cells that make up a battery pack, in order to ensure that all of them operate within the same voltage and capacity levels.

ciency, enhancing battery consistency and extending service life. In addition to the discussed applications, graphs and their algorithms are present in various fields. These approaches are especially relevant for the use of electric vehicles, where energy efficiency and sustainability are priorities. They contribute to a better understanding of route optimization, helping to reduce costs, time, and pollutant gas emissions.

3   The Interface Model

The growing need for mobility amid the heavy traffic of large cities has driven the demand for more efficient and sustainable solutions. In this context, electric motorcycles emerge as a promising alternative, offering greater operational efficiency and significantly reducing environmental impacts. In addition to contributing to the reduction of pollutant emissions and noise pollution, these vehicles have a superior dynamism in urban travel, presenting themselves as a viable option for logistics operations. With the evolution of energy storage technologies and the expansion of recharging infrastructure, the adoption of electric motorcycles tends to grow, promoting more sustainable mobility, aligned to the requirements of modern cities.

The increase in digital solutions for logistics has accompanied the evolution of mobile and connected technologies. Among the applications developed to support motorbike drivers, used in delivery and collection services, stands out the presence of essential functionalities, being route optimization one of the main ones. This feature considers factors such as transit, battery level, proximity between the delivery points and order of tasks, ensuring greater operational efficiency. For these applications, it is essential that its implementation is accompanied by safety measures for drivers, promoting a safe and intuitive user experience.

From the driver's point of view, algorithms and mathematical tools are not relevant, nor even known, but they must be robust and dynamic, able to indicate optimal routes during driving. For this reason, the frontend must be flexible and intuitive, able to adapt the display as updates, responding efficiently to unforeseen changes, such as route deviations or changes in the availability of delivery points.

The interface must be compact, useful and efficient, specially designed for electric motorcycles, simple and intuitive, versatile, able to present, in a simple and dynamic way, optimization features. The navigation interface should be designed to ensure that routes are seen as a central focus during driving. The notifications of updates cannot compromise the display of the route, but must be visually highlighted, ensuring that the changes generated by the algorithm are clearly perceived by the driver Fig. 4).

When receiving updates, the interface should respond quickly to the new route and subsequent path details. This approach contributes to a more stable driving, allowing the driver to anticipate changes of direction and make decisions with greater precision.

Thus, the applications can contribute to better mobility in large urban centers without compromising the safety of drivers and other users of public space. In

Fig. 4. Example of interface. Created by the authors.

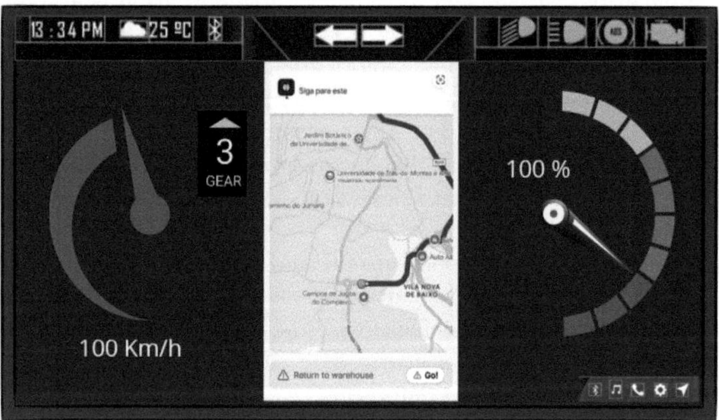

Fig. 5. Example of interface in a display of an electric motorcycle. Created by the authors.

Fig. 5), an example of how the logistics interface can be incorporated into the motorcycle display, where the navigation visualization is shown the routes of ideas found by the optimization algorithm, without compromising the display of information regarding the operation of the bike.

Route visualization makes it possible to prioritize important points, streamline the service and reorganize operations in real time, through the dynamic presentation of information, improving decision-making, providing effective structuring of the activity, reducing travel time and costs inherent to the service.

4   Conclusion

The use of algorithms and mathematical models, for the optimization of graphs present in various areas, is beyond the comprehension of most users, but is an essential tool for mobility and efficiency in various contexts. Route optimization seeks to solve, by maximizing or minimizing, factors that influence not only financial life, but also ensure greater dynamism in the service provided. By optimizing routes, whether in the area of logistics, the internet or disease prevention, it helps to reduce distances travelled, travel time, costs and environmental impacts, increasing response capacity.

In complex urban environments, where congestion is a daily challenge, these tools make it possible to create dynamic and adaptable routes, benefiting both the user and society as a whole. In the case of electric scooters, optimization becomes even more essential due to limited autonomy and the need for intelligent battery management.

Finally, integration into digital platforms and intuitive interfaces extends the use of these solutions, facilitating the user experience and offering real-time support for decision-making. Route optimization is thus an effective response to the challenges of modern mobility, promoting a balance between performance, quality of life and environmental preservation.

Acknowledgement. The study was developed under the project A-MoVeR "Mobilizing Agenda for the Development of Products and Systems towards an Intelligent and Green Mobility", operation no. 02/C05-i01.01/2022.PC646908627-00000069, approved under the terms of the call no. 02/C05-i01/2022 Mobilizing Agendas for Business Innovation, financed by European funds provided to Portugal by the Recovery and Resilience Plan (RRP), in the scope of the European Recovery and Resilience Facility (RRF), framed in the Next Generation UE, for the period from 2021 -2026

References

1. Fundamental Concepts and Basic Results. Introduction to Graph Theory, Chapter 1, pp. 1–38, https://doi.org/10.1142/13133
2. Gomes, P.F.: An introduction to network science and graph theory [Uma introdução à Ciência de Redes e Teoria de Grafos]. Brazilian J. Phys. Teach. **46**, e20240190 (2024). https://doi.org/10.1590/1806-9126-RBEF-2024-0190

3. Jawali, R.R., Ramya, S.: A study on challenges and optimization of last mile delivery and its impact on customer satisfaction. Inter. J. Multidisciplinary Res. **6**(4), 1–9 (2024). https://doi.org/10.36948/ijfmr.2024.v06i04.24486 https://doi.org/10.36948/ijfmr.2024.v06i04.24486 https://doi.org/10.36948/ijfmr.2024.v06i04.24486

4. Araujo, M.P., Lima, E.A.O.: Metrics for evaluating optimization algorithms[Métricas de avaliação de algoritmos de otimização]. Proceeding Series of the Brazilian Soc. Appli. Comput. Math. **3**1010445–10104452 (2015). https://doi.org/10.5540/03.2015.003.01.0445

5. Rizwanullah, M., Alsolai, H., Nour, M.K., Aziz, A.S.A., Eldesouki, M.I., Abdelmageed, A.A.: Hybrid muddy soil fish optimization-based energy aware routing in iot-assisted wireless sensor networks. Sustainability **15**(10), 1–15 (2023)

6. Dogra, R., Rani, S., K., ., Shafi, J., Kim, S., Ijaz, M.F.: ESEERP: enhanced smart energy efficient routing protocol for internet of things in wireless sensor nodes. Sensors **22**(16), 6109 (2022). https://doi.org/10.3390/s22166109

7. Matias, J.D.P., Oliveira, E.C., Silva Brito, E.M., Oliveira Dantas, F., Marques, C.A.N.: Optimization of school transport routes in the municipality of Itapiúna-CE[Otimização de Rotas de Transporte Escolar no Município de Itapiúna- CE]. In: Proceedings of the National Meeting on Production Engineering (ENEGEP), Brazil (2024). https://api.semanticscholar.org/CorpusID:273919758

8. Reis, D.A.S.: Optimization Procedure for Inspection Routes in Industrial Plants to Minimize Noise Dose [Procedimento de otimização de rotas de inspeção em plantas industriais visando a minimização da dose de ruído]. Ph.D. thesis, Federal University of Uberlândia, Brazil (2020)

9. "A-mover," (2022). https://www.utad.pt/gpfe/a-mover-agenda-mobilizadorapara-o-desenvolvimento-de-produtos-e-sistemas-inteligentes-demobilidade-verde/

10. Rajesh, K., Jain, E., Kotecha, P.: A Multi-Objective Approach to the Electric Vehicle Routing Problem. arXiv preprint arXiv:2208.12440 (2022).

11. Neto, J.S., Santana, J.C.O., Souza, M.V.S., Lima, A.A., Vasconcelos, C.R.: Route optimization in an e-commerce company: an application of the traveling salesman Problem[Otimização de rotas em uma empresa de e-commerce: Aplicação do problema do caixeiro viajante]. In: Proceedings of the 42nd National Meeting on Production Engineering, Foz do Iguaçu, Brazil (2022). https://doi.org/10.14488/ENEGEP2022_TN_ST_384_1900_43428

12. Wang, H., et al.: Motion planning in complex urban environments: an industrial application on autonomous last-mile delivery vehicles. J. Field Robot. **39**, 1258–1285 (2022). https://doi.org/10.1002/rob.22107

13. Jang, J., Cho, Y., Park, J.: Bus route sketching: a multimetric analysis from the user's and operator's perspectives. Sustainability **16**, 7172 (2024). https://www.mdpi.com/2071-1050/16/16/7172https://doi.org/10.3390/su16167172

14. Libotte, C.N.P., Namen, A.A., Libotte, G.B.: Route Optimization for organic waste collection in the municipality of nova friburgo-rj, brazil [otimização de rotas para coleta de resíduos orgânicos no município de Nova Friburgo-Rj, Brasil]. In: Proceedings of the National Meeting on Computational Modeling and Meeting on Materials Science and Technology (2023). https://doi.org/10.29327/1340957.26-7

15. El-Hefnawy, N., Raouf, O., Askr, H.: Dynamic routing optimization algorithm for software defined networking. Comput. Mater. Continua **70**(1), 1349–1362 (2022). https://doi.org/10.32604/cmc.2022.017787

16. Rexford, J.: Route optimization in IP networks. In: Resende, M.G.C., Pardalos, P.M. (eds) Handbook of Optimization in Telecommunications, Springer, Boston, MA (2006). https://doi.org/10.1007/978-0-387-30165-5_24

17. Shin, D., Yun, K., Kim, J., Astillo, P.V., Kim, J.-N., You, I.: A security protocol for route optimization in dmm-based smart home IoT networks. IEEE Access **7**, 142531–142550 (2019). https://doi.org/10.1109/ACCESS.2019.2943929
18. Vasconcelos, O.M., Pereira, V.M.R., Ferreira, G.S., Real, L.B.: A Proposed Tool for Route Optimization Integrated with a Mapping Service [Proposta de ferramenta para otimização de rotas integrada a um serviço de mapas]. In: Proceedings of the 4th Symposium on Engineering, Management and Innovation (SENGI), Juazeiro do Norte, Brazil (2021). https://doi.org/10.29327/sengi2021.349501
19. Jayarathna, D.G.N.D., Lanel, G.H.J., Juman, Z.A.M.S.: Industrial vehicle routing problem: a case study. J. shipp. trd. **7**, 6 (2022). https://doi.org/10.1186/s41072-022-00108-7
20. Deng, Z., Huang, L., Lv, W.Y., Shi, Y.: A high efficiency and low carbon oriented machining process route optimization model and its application. Inter. J. Precision Eng. Manufact.-Green Technol. **6**, 23–41 (2019). https://doi.org/10.1007/s40684-019-00029-0
21. Kethineni, K.K., Mohanty, S.P., Kougianos, E., Bhowmick, S., Rachakonda, L.:SprayCraft: Graph-Based Route Optimization for Variable Rate Precision Spraying. arXiv preprint arXiv:2412.12176 (2024).
22. Spekken, M., de Bruin, S.: Optimizing routes on agricultural fields minimizing maneuvering and servicing time. Precision Agricult. **14**, (2013). https://doi.org/10.1007/s11119-012-9290-5
23. Zhao, R., He, W.-Q., Lou, Z.-K., Nie, W., Ma, X.-Y.: Synchronization optimization of pipeline layout and pipe diameter selection in a self-pressurized drip irrigation network system based on the genetic algorithm. Water **11**(3), 489 (2019). https://doi.org/10.3390/w11030489
24. Fang, S., Ru, Y., Liu, Y., Hu, C., Chen, X., Liu, B.: Route planning of helicopters spraying operations in multiple forest areas. Forests **12**(12), 1658 (2021). https://doi.org/10.3390/f12121658
25. Lee, E.B.K., Van Bossuyt, D.L., Bickford, J.F.: Digital twin-enabled decision support in mission and route planning. Systems **9**(4), 82 (2021). https://doi.org/10.3390/systems9040082
26. Cai, M., Zhang, E., Lin, J., Wang, K., Jiang, K., Zhou, M.: Route optimization equalization scheme based on graph theory for liquid metal battery strings. IEEE Trans. Ind. Appl. **59**(2), 2502–2508 (2023). https://doi.org/10.1109/TIA.2022.3221383

Human-Centered Technologies for Autism and Neurodiverse Populations

Design of an Emotion-Regulating Game Interface for the Autism Spectrum Disorder Kids

Yurong Ju and Qian Ji[✉]

School of Design, Huazhong University of Science and Technology, Wuhan 430074, Hubei Province, China
`jiqian@mail.hust.edu.cn`

Abstract. Emotional volatility and difficulty in self-regulation are core characteristics of individuals with Autism Spectrum Disorder (ASD). Firstly, this study conducts color vision experiments on children with medium and high-functioning autism aged 5 to 12. Then, combined with the results of the previous experiments, a multi-sensory emotion regulation game interface based on human-computer interaction technology was designed. Through the colors and visual patterns of positive emotions, soothing music and human-computer interaction operations, an emotion soothing game of "plot narrative - visual image - color language - sound feedback - interaction mechanism" was constructed; Finally, experiments were conducted to verify the effectiveness of the emotional soothing game.

Coclusions from preliminary experiments indicate that children prefer blue, green, pink and orange hues; they tend to favor high-lightness, high-purity colors, and complementary color combinations; and they show affection for round shapes, as well as human, animal, and plant images. Based on these results, the study integrates emotional design, human-computer interaction, and five-sense therapy to build an immersive game framework with the theme of "Natural Journey" around five dimensions. Players act as travelers exploring natural scenes and complete emotional connection tasks through interactions such as clicking/long-pressing rounded animal, plant images and healing tones (blue, green, pink, orange) form a visual decompression field; dynamic natural sound effects and an adaptive music system adjust audio rhythm according to interaction frequency.

Effectiveness verification is conducted through wearable device pressure tests, user interviews, and observations. The results show that after the game, the average heart rate and stress values of the children have stabilized to a certain extent. Three follow-up tests confirm that the game scores high in innovation, effectiveness, interactivity, and usability on a five-point scale (average 4.5 points). Overall, the game provides positive emotional soothing experiences for children with autism, demonstrating value and significance for promotion.

Keywords: Autism Spectrum Disorder · Emotion-regulating games · Human-computer interaction design · Multi - Sensory therapy · Emotional interface design

© The Author(s), under exclusive license to Springer Nature Switzerland AG 2026
M. Antona and C. Stephanidis (Eds.): HCII 2025, LNCS 16335, pp. 259–275, 2026.
https://doi.org/10.1007/978-3-032-12781-5_18

1   Introduction

Autism Spectrum Disorder (ASD), a neurodevelopmental disorder, has witnessed a remarkable upward trend in diagnosis rates in China in recent years [1]. This situation has made the demand for early intervention training for children with autism increasingly urgent. Research on ASD is not only crucial for the growth and development of individuals but also has far-reaching implications for the harmony and stability of families and society. For individuals with ASD, emotion management is one of the major challenges they face. Emotional problems not only severely affect their daily lives and social interactions but may also further exacerbate their psychological stress and behavioral disorders. Therefore, research on emotional relief for ASD is of great practical significance.

Currently, the existing intervention methods for emotional relief mainly include traditional static visual intervention, psychological counseling, and drug therapy. Traditional static visual intervention can alleviate emotions in the short term, but it lacks interactivity and situational immersion, making it difficult to stimulate active participation from patients. Psychological counseling highly depends on professional personnel and is time-consuming, which hinders its large-scale promotion. Drug therapy may bring about a series of side effects, affecting the physical health of patients. The limitations of these existing intervention methods highlight the urgency of exploring new and effective ways of emotional relief.[2–4].

Intervention training based on games, with its flexibility in space and time, as well as the immersive experience and multimodal human-computer interaction characteristics endowed by digital technology [5, 6], has gradually become a research hotspot in the field of autism intervention. Emotional relief games have unique advantages. They can integrate abstract emotion regulation training into interesting game processes. Through vivid plots and rich sensory stimuli, these games can attract patients to participate actively, achieving emotional relief imperceptibly. Compared with traditional methods, they are more interesting and sustainable.

This study focuses on children with moderate to high - functioning autism aged 5–12 years, exploring the design of human-computer interaction game interfaces integrated with multisensory design. The core of emotion regulation lies in influencing emotions and stress through sensory input. As a key element of visual perception, color has a direct regulatory effect on emotions [7]. Meanwhile, the theory of multisensory integration emphasizes the collaborative role of channels such as vision, hearing, and touch, enhancing neural plasticity through cross-channel stimulation [8–10]. This provides a theoretical basis for the multimodal human-computer interaction design of game interfaces. Currently, game designs for individuals with autism mainly focus on social skills training [11–13], while research focusing on emotion regulation is relatively scarce. This study breaks through the traditional model by combining emotional design [14, 15], human-computer interaction technology, and multisensory interaction technology, constructing a framework of "plot narrative - visual image - color language - sound feedback - interaction mechanism". The aim is to create a digital human-computer interaction scene for emotion regulation that conforms to the cognitive characteristics of children with autism through dynamic visual narrative, an adaptive sound effect system, and natural interactive gestures, providing an effective and convenient emotion regulation tool for this group and offering inspiration for future research on autism games.

In conclusion, constructing digital games through emotional design, human-computer interaction, and five-sense therapy is expected to improve the emotional and stress conditions of children with autism and promote their adaptation to social norms and learning needs, which is of great significance for promoting the development of ASD research and intervention practices.

2 Related Research

2.1 Human-Computer Interaction Game Intervention

Traditional autism behavior therapy faces promotion bottlenecks due to high costs and limited accessibility, while human-computer interaction-based gamified intervention programs have demonstrated significant value in emotional relief, social skills, and self-regulation ability. Compared with traditional static visual interventions, [16] existing research has shown that multisensory interventions and digital game therapy [17] possess significant clinical value. Their core advantage lies in breaking through time and space limitations: patients can engage in emotional soothing games at any time, while providing supplementary auxiliary exercises during professional intervention intervals to effectively alleviate resource shortages. Digital platforms significantly reduce family economic burdens by decreasing reliance on special education teachers [18] and have the marginal cost advantage of large-scale replication. Digital games, with their characteristics of visualization, interactivity, and scenario-based design, contribute to educational intervention for autistic children. [19] Through vivid visual feedback and interaction mechanisms, 20 games transform rehabilitation goals into fun tasks, [21–23] improving participation compliance and providing a feasible path to compensate for the insufficient coverage of traditional therapies.

2.2 Emotional Design and Multi-Sensory Healing

Aiming at the emotional volatility and self-regulation difficulties of autism groups, [24–26] emotional design defuses stress and anxiety through safe alternative stimuli. [27] Animated characters or abstract images are used to convey social signals, avoiding tension caused by real interpersonal interactions, while non-threatening elements such as high-contrast colors and dynamic particle trajectories guide attention to key information areas [28]. Progressive cartoon expression simulation gradually cultivates emotional recognition ability, advancing from basic emotions to complex expressions in layers. Multisensory therapy further adapts to the sensory heterogeneity of autistic children, matching individual perception thresholds through modules regulating visual brightness, auditory tone, and tactile vibration intensity [29]. When users complete game tasks, cross-modal positive reinforcement mechanisms simultaneously trigger warm light effects, reward sound effects, and gentle tactile feedback, establishing a closed-loop association between behavior and positive experience. Immersive environment design constructs a low-pressure space through controllable sound fields and gradient light sources to prevent sensory overload.

The gamified framework finally integrates the above elements: the emotional interface presents social contexts to trigger user interaction, and multisensory immediate feedback strengthens cognitive reconstruction, forming a synergistic intervention cycle that reduces anxiety and enhances pleasure, gradually promoting the development of emotional self-regulation ability.

3   User Research and Preliminary Test

Informed consent was obtained from the children's guardians, and the experiment was approved by the Ethics Committee of Wuhan Tongji Hospital. The study strictly adheres to the Measures for Ethical Review of Biomedical Research Involving Humans and relevant national laws and regulations. It is an experimental study supported by the National Natural Science Foundation project declared by Professor Ji Qian, approved by the Ethical Review Committee of Tongji Medical College, Huazhong University of Science and Technology (Approval No.: [2025] IEC(A197)), with all data encrypted and stored.

3.1   Interviews and Field Surveys

Field surveys were conducted on 35 autistic children from Wuhan Xiaokuihua Rehabilitation Training Center and Changsha home-based treatment (see Fig. 2).All surveys were carried out with informed consent and voluntary participation from guardians, strictly following the Measures for Ethical Review of Biomedical Research Involving Humans and relevant national laws and regulations. Comprehensive and detailed observations were made, and interviews were conducted with rehabilitation center professionals and parents of autistic children. The rehabilitation center has licensed nurses offering rehabilitation courses and custodial services for community autistic children. Rehabilitation therapists、parents and doctors provided suggestions on the game plan (Table 1).

Table 1. Interview Results.

Questions	Parent W	Rehabilitation Therapist L	Doctor Z
Attraction Potential	Interactive links are engaging; vivid elements capture children's attention.	Multisensory design attracts children through rich sensory inputs.	Unique plot and character interactions have strong appeal potential.
Scenario Expansion Expectations	Add daily - life scenarios for real - life adaptation.	Include more nature - themed scenarios for enhanced sensory experience.	Incorporate social communication scenarios for social skill rehabilitation.

(continued)

Table 1. (*continued*)

Questions	Parent W	Rehabilitation Therapist L	Doctor Z
Multisensory Design Evaluation	Color - sound combination soothes children; elicits positive responses.	Integration of visual, auditory, and tactile feedback benefits sensory training.	Well - integrated design aligns with sensory integration therapy principles.
Interaction Difficulty Suggestions	Simplify initial tasks; increase difficulty gradually.	Define clear difficulty gradients; offer adjustable settings and prominent hints.	Tie difficulty to cognitive levels; enable adaptive adjustment.
Emotional Regulation Goal Opinion	Evidences reduced irritability; achieves emotional calming.	Aligns with rehabilitation aims; calming elements aid emotion management.	Clear and valuable; complements traditional therapy.
Strengthening Clinical Connection	Share game data with therapists for feedback - driven improvements.	Incorporate clinical assessment indicators into tasks for evaluation.	Integrate game into rehabilitation plans; track progress clinically.

3.2 Preliminary Color Vision Test

In emotional design and five-sense therapy, color vision has a significant impact on the emotions of autistic children. [30] Therefore, we conducted a 3-month preliminary color vision test to provide a basis for the color visual design of the emotional soothing game interface for autistic children. This scientific experiment explored the psychological tendencies of autistic children toward colors of different hues, lightness, saturation, and other influencing factors, aiming to enable autistic children to obtain pleasant feelings during the game and play a positive role in soothing their emotions and stress. Test 1 is to test the three elements of color: hue, purity and lightness; Test 2 is to test each combination of colors; Test 3 is to test different pattern shapes (Fig. 1).

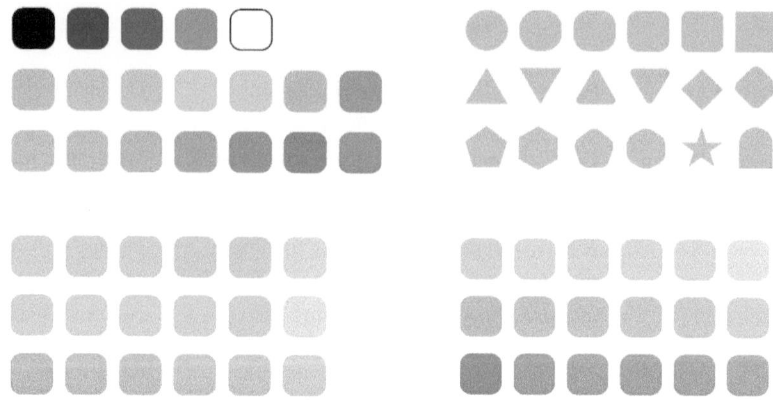

Fig. 1. Color card. From left to right and top to bottom, they are: hue color card, shape color card, purity color card, and lightness color card.

Test Subjects. This test involved 62 mild autistic children aged 5 to 12 years old from rehabilitation centers in Wuhan and Changsha, as well as those receiving home treatment. Among them, 38 were boys and 24 were girls, with an average age of 8.3 ± 2.1 years (the proportion of boys in the test subjects was higher because autistic boys account for a larger ratio). All participants had normal vision without eye diseases such as amblyopia, color blindness, or color weakness. During the test, participants were ensured to have no abnormal physiological or psychological conditions. They were required to have sufficient rest and relax reasonably within 1 h before the test to avoid fatigue or discomfort. Normal children with the same other conditions were used as the control group.

Test Settings. To avoid environmental interference with the test, the lighting conditions, indoor temperature, and indoor humidity during the test were all at normal levels. Due to the subjects being more prone to adverse reactions such as fatigue or anxiety in physical and psychological states, according to the doctor's advice, the test was set as follows: the total test time was 25 min, divided into three sub-tests. Sub-test 1 lasted 15 min, Sub-test 2 lasted 5 min, and Sub-test 3 lasted 5 min. A rest and relaxation period was given after every 5 min of testing. Children were rewarded with small items after each choice. The study obtained informed consent forms from the children's guardians, and the test has passed the ethical review of Wuhan Tongji Hospital. The study strictly follows the Measures for Ethical Review of Biomedical Research Involving Humans and relevant national laws and regulations. It is a test study supported by the National Natural Science Foundation project applied for by Professor Ji Qian, and has obtained the Ethical Review Approval Letter from the Ethics Committee of Tongji Medical College, Huazhong University of Science and Technology (Approval No.: [2025] IEC(A197)), with all data stored encrypted.

Test Design. Sub-test 1: This test produced color groups with different hues, purities, and lightness, and recorded children's choices through electronic devices.

Sub-test 2: This test produced different color matching groups and recorded children's choices through electronic devices.

Sub-test 3: This test produced different pattern and shape groups and recorded children's choices through electronic devices.

Sub-tests 1 and 3 adopted a multi-factor test design, while Sub-test 2 adopted a single-factor test design. Considering the weak thinking and expression abilities of autistic children, the test set two color cards (one group) for children to choose their preferred one, using a simple two-choice question-and-answer method. Since paper color cards had large color differences, causing significant errors in testing and data collection statistics, electronic devices were used for the test. A total of 50 groups of color cards were set. Meanwhile, to prevent selection differences caused by color matching issues (due to choosing between two colors), different color matching random combinations were set for children to choose, and repeated tests were conducted to reduce errors. The independent variables of Sub-test 1 were color hue, purity, and lightness; those of Sub-test 2 were color matching; and those of Sub-test 3 were patterns and shapes. The dependent variable for all three tests was children's choices.

In the hue test (Sub-test 1), except for hue changes, all other conditions were kept the same and suitable. The same applied to other tests.Final data were grouped and discussed according to children's age and gender.

Test Procedures. Children completed the test in the rest area under the guidance of test administrators and professionals, required to sit directly in front of the screen with their eyes approximately 60 cm away from the computer screen. The task required children to choose their favorite color from two colors presented on the electronic device. The test included 5 practice trials and 50 formal test trials. Due to children's motor and attention deficits, they mainly reported orally, and test administrators completed the selection. Finally, the children's selection rates were statistically analyzed. Pictures of the test process are shown below (Fig. 2):

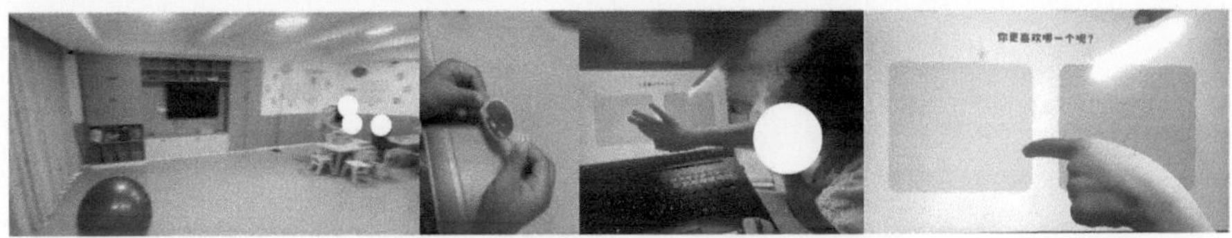

Fig. 2. Experimental environment and process. The left picture is the test environment; The picture on the right shows the test process of children choosing color cards.

Test Results and Conclusions. ① Children's gender: Boys preferred cool colors such as blue and green, while girls preferred warm colors such as orange and pink. Additionally, boys showed a stronger preference for yellow and resistance to purple, while girls preferred yellow and black and resisted red. Compared with normal children, autistic children had a higher preference for yellow and lower preferences for red and purple.

② Children's age: Within the test range (5–12 years old), age had no significant effect on color preference.

③ Hue preference: In terms of color hue preference, it was found that for 5–12-year-old autistic children, the order was: blue > green > black and brown > orange and pink > yellow > red > white > purple. Children preferred complementary color hue combinations. Literature studies have shown that [31–33] autistic children generally prefer cool tones such as blue and green over warm tones such as red and orange. Cool tones help promote balanced brain cortex activity in autistic patients, but excessive use of 5–10-degree cool colors can easily have negative impacts on children's physical and mental health, making their personalities more withdrawn. In the subsequent visual color selection for interface design, blue-green was used as the main color, followed by warm green, orange, and pink, avoiding all cool colors. Combining color psychological language, it provides a calm, stable, and vibrant psychological healing experience.

④ Lightness and purity preference: Autistic children preferred colors with higher lightness and purity. Meanwhile, autistic children may experience sensory 过敏(perceptual hypersensitivity) and irritability when seeing too bright colors. [30, 34, 35] In color adjustment and matching, colors with both high lightness and purity were selected as the main colors, supplemented by colors with medium lightness and purity, avoiding colors with too low or too high lightness and purity.

⑤ Shape and pattern preference: Autistic children preferred circular and arc shapes. They were more interested in animal patterns, followed by plant patterns and landscapes. Therefore, circular and arc shapes were chosen as the main shapes in the design, supplemented by squares with larger rounded corners. Designs were created by combining animal, plant, and landscape elements (Fig. 3).

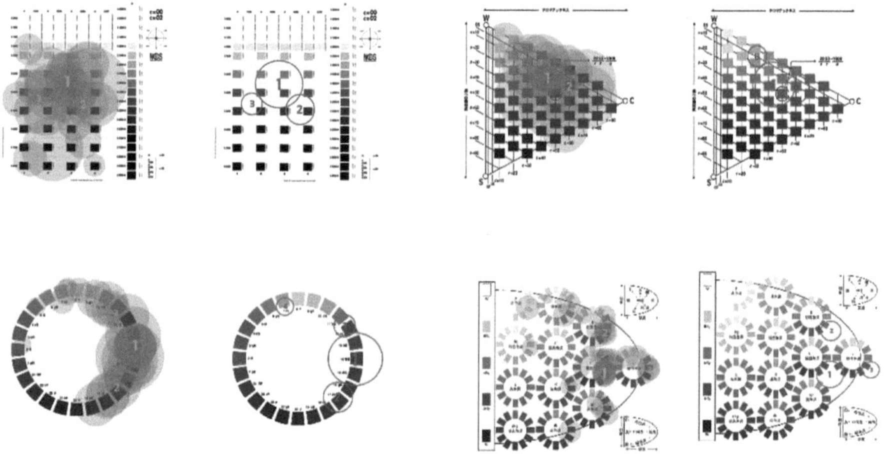

Fig. 3. Data chart. From left to right and top to bottom are the lightness data, purity data, hue data and total data in sequence.

Conclusion Summary. ① In terms of hue preference, 5–12-year-old autistic children showed: blue > green > black and brown > orange and pink > yellow > red > white > purple. ② Children preferred complementary color combinations. ③ Autistic children preferred colors with higher saturation. ④ Autistic children preferred colors with higher lightness. ⑤ Within the experimental range (5–12 years old), age had no significant effect on color preference. ⑥ Boys preferred cool colors (blue, green), while girls preferred warm colors (orange, pink). ⑦ Warm/cool and light/dark tones should be mutually adjusted to avoid depression, autism, and irritability.

Experimental Stage and Future Outlook. This study is the second stage of a long-term research project on color-assisted emotional soothing therapy for autistic children, focusing on the immediate psychological and emotional responses and preferences of autistic children to color, lasting 3 months. The long-term research on color-assisted social skills therapy for autistic children consists of three stages, with a total planned duration of two years. The first stage (3 months) mainly studies the emotions of autistic children and related factors, while the third stage will deeply investigate the long-term effects of color therapy, expected to last 14 months.

4 Game Design and Development

4.1 Game Introduction

(Figure 4)

Fig. 4. The main interface design of the game. The left picture shows the main interface design of the game, and the right picture shows the main interactive interface design of the game.

"OASIS" is specially designed for 5–12-year-old children with high-functioning autism, using game chemotherapy to soothe emotions and reduce stress in autistic children. Combining the theories of previous color vision experiments, emotional design, and human-computer interaction technology, the game allows players to obtain emotional soothing through the natural life of the protagonist and Shire and interactive games with animals and plants on the oasis, feeling nature and soothing emotions in the oasis story.

The game takes the theme of the protagonist Gwen's natural journey through the oasis puzzle, constructing an immersive game framework around five dimensions: "plot narrative-visual imagery-color language-sound feedback-interaction mechanism." Players act as Gwen, exploring different natural maps such as forests and fields, and communicating with characters and animals in the story. Players perform interactive behaviors such as clicking and long-pressing to establish emotional connections through tasks like communicating with characters, comforting small animals, and repairing ecological scenes; rounded animal and plant images with high affinity are adopted, combined with healing natural tones (blue, green, pink, orange) to form a visual decompression field; dynamic natural sound effects (stream sounds, bird songs) and an adaptive soothing music system are introduced, adjusting audio frequency and rhythm according to players' game interaction frequencies. The game takes the protagonist Gwen's journey through the oasis puzzle as its main narrative thread, and players advance through levels by reading plots, participating in dialogues, and game interactions in different story scenes. The game integrates the vision, sound, and animation of animals, plants, and the environment, guides interaction by enlarging interactive content, and provides feedback through character prompts.

The game script went through four iterations, incorporating feedback from doctors, parents, and rehabilitation therapists. The specific game script is as follows:

Act I: Oasis Wish. Evening, at home. A girl is playing with a puzzle alone (puzzle name: Oasis).

Naming: Ask players to write their names on the puzzle box to complete the protagonist's naming. (Example: Gwen)

Gwen: "Shire… Put him in the jungle over here!"

On the puzzle, there is her best friend Shire.

She looks into the distance and makes a wish to the stars, hoping to go to the oasis herself—where mountain springs murmur and paths are filled with clear songs. What attracts her most is the annual harvest festival there. When star fruits ripen, people make them into fruit pies, cakes…

Puzzle operation: Ask players to assemble the puzzle and build the "forest."

Achievement reward: Emotional record postcard - Oasis chapter

Late at night. Gwen falls into a dream. She dreams of coming to the oasis harvest festival and smelling the fragrance of star fruits…

Gwen: "Wow! What beautiful fruits!" When she opens her eyes, the oasis unfolds before her like a picture screen (Fig. 5).

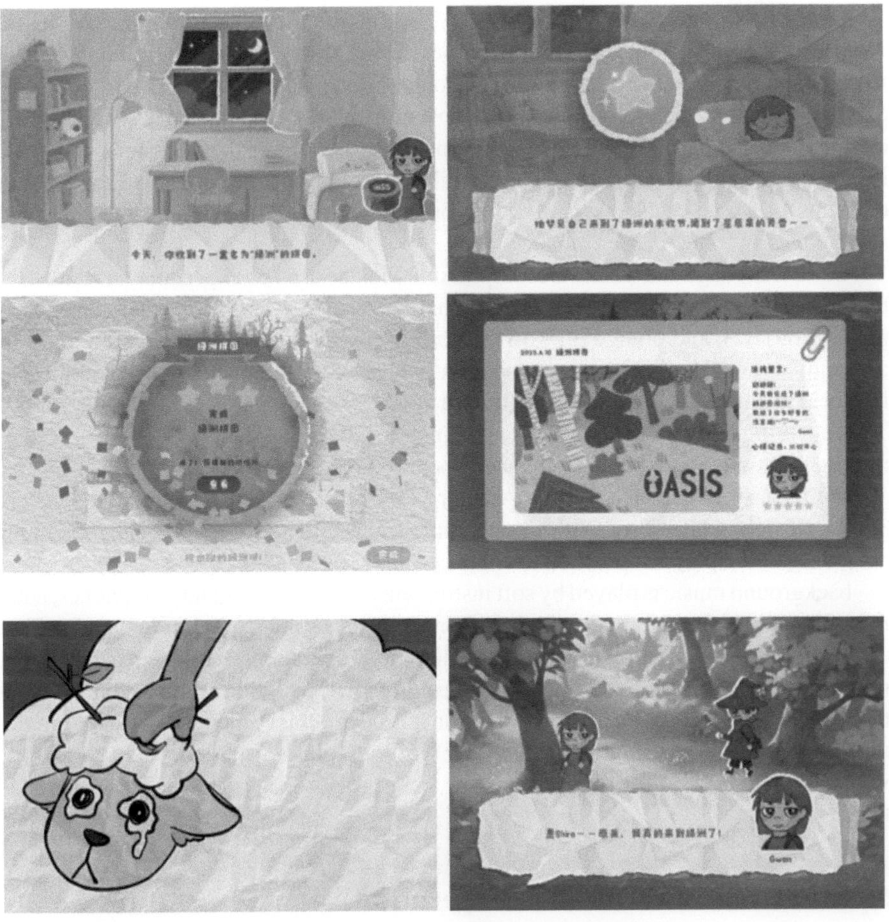

Fig. 5. The interface design of the game.

Act II: Oasis·Harvest Festival. Shire: "Hello, I'm Shire! Are you a traveler here for the harvest festival?"

Gwen thinks: It's Shire… So I really came to the oasis!

Shire: "Come over here! The star fruit pie is just out of the oven!"

Game operation: Ask players to collect star energy and pick star fruits.

Achievement reward: Emotional record postcard - Harvest Festival chapter

4.2 Game Prototype Design

Each level of the game is seamlessly connected through video clips. To achieve this, we produced detailed video scripts and supervised the animation design and production process.

After editing videos in PS, AI, and AE, we established an interactive flowchart to serve the program. The game program was written in UNITY and linked with the transitions between game levels.

Emional Narrative and Visual Imagery. The game uses "Natural Journey" as the core narrative, designing three theme scenes: home, forest, and field, guiding players to complete emotional regulation goals through linear tasks. Characters adopt rounded designs: travelers' images use soft arcs to outline body contours, paired with green clothing; animal partners use Q-version proportions, with facial expressions simplified into basic emotional symbols (such as smiles, peace), reducing cognitive load. Scene elements like trees and flowers all adopt organic forms to avoid visual pressure from sharp edges.

Color Language and Visual Decompression Field. Based on experimental results, the main color scheme uses natural color combinations of blue (#4A90E2), green (#62C462), pink (#F691B2), and orange (#F7B548): forest scenes mainly use blue-green to create a tranquil atmosphere; field scenes focus on orange-pink to convey a warm feeling. The lightness of interface elements is controlled at 60–80%, and purity is maintained at 50–70%, ensuring both visual appeal and avoiding excessive stimulation. Interactive buttons use highlight glowing effects to enhance operation recognition.

Multisensory Feedback System Auditory Design. Environmental sound effects use 3D sound field technology, with stream sounds and bird songs dynamically changing according to the player's position to enhance spatial immersion.

background music is played by soft instruments such as pianos and xylophones, automatically adjusting melody rhythm based on the player's interaction frequency (such as clicking speed, task completion time)—when rapid operations are detected, the music rhythm slows down and low-frequency white noise is added, while a light rhythm is maintained otherwise. Tactile Feedback: Vibration is used to achieve interactive touch, providing continuous micro-vibration (20−30 Hz) for long-press operations and short strong vibration (50−60 Hz) for click operations, reinforcing operational cognition through tactile signals.

5 Effectiveness Verification Experiment

5.1 Pre-Experimental Preparations

Continuing the sample framework of the previous color vision experiment, 62 children aged 5–12 with high-functioning ASD (38 males, 24 females, mean age 8.3 ± 2.1 years) were recruited from autism rehabilitation institutions in Changsha and Wuhan, all meeting the DSM-5 autism diagnostic criteria and without severe intellectual disabilities. A self-controlled before-and-after design was adopted, with all participants completing 3 game interventions (7-day intervals) to avoid grouping bias. Baseline emotional levels were assessed using the Child Anxiety Mood Disorder Screening Scale (RCADS) before the experiment to ensure sample homogeneity. After equipment setup, rehabilitation therapists invited children to participate voluntarily at the end of the game class. During the experiment, teachers provided encouragement and guidance, and parents gave support and assistance. Experimental equipment included: iPad 10th generation Wi-Fi model (10.9-inch Liquid Retina full-screen, approximately 248.6 mm long, 179.5 mm wide, 7 mm thick, 477 g weight, built-in speakers), HUAWEI WATCH GT 5 Pro wearable device, and "OASIS" game system.

In the two rounds of testing, 62 autistic children voluntarily participated in the game. Accompanied by rehabilitation therapists and parents, they sat at the game table to participate. Among them, 59 children successfully completed the game, while 3 children experienced game failure. Two encountered setbacks in the game, with problems being misunderstanding of game operation instructions (2 cases) and unwillingness to play (1 case) (Fig. 6).

Fig. 6. The left picture shows the test process of children before playing games after a 15-min gentle rest. The picture in the middle shows that children are playing in the game. The picture on the right shows the testing process after the game.

5.2 Experimental Equipment and Indicators

① Physiological Index Collection: HUAWEI WATCH GT 5 Pro wearable bracelet (sampling rate 4 Hz) was used to monitor heart rate, stress level, and pulse in real time, with heart rate and pulse serving as objective references for emotional stress levels. ② Subjective Experience Assessment: A 4-dimensional questionnaire was designed using a 5-point Likert scale (1 = very poor, 5 = very good): Innovation: "Did the game's visual design make you feel interested?" Effectiveness: "Did the game make you feel comfortable and calm?" Interactivity: "Did you like interacting with the game characters?" Usability: "How difficult was it to operate the game?" ③ Behavioral Observation: Three types of behaviors were recorded: active interaction behaviors (such as number of clicks, task completion rate); emotional regulation behaviors (such as deep breathing, facial relaxation); frequency of abnormal behaviors (such as body shaking, avoidance of gaze).

5.3 Experimental Process

Each experiment lasted 45 min, divided into three stages: Baseline period (10 min): Participants sat quietly wearing equipment and watched neutral cartoons to stabilize emotions; Intervention period (25 min): Wore a bracelet to play the "Natural Journey" game, with rehabilitation therapists recording behaviors throughout; Recovery period (10 min): Sat quietly after stopping the game and completed the subjective scale (Fig. 7).

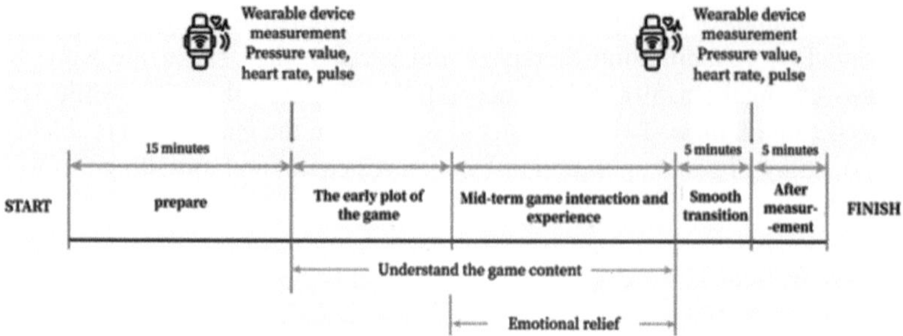

Fig. 7. Experimental flowchart.

5.4   Quantitative Result Analysis

Changes in Physiological Indicators.   Heart Rate (HR): The average heart rate during the baseline period was 109.2 ± 11.5 beats/minute, dropping to 86.3 ± 9.2 beats/minute after intervention, a decrease of 21.0% (paired t-test, t = 15.82, p<0.001, Cohen's d = 1.98), reaching a clinically significant level. Subgroup analysis showed that the heart rate decrease in boys (23.5%) was slightly higher than that in girls (18.7%), possibly related to the stronger soothing effect of cool tones on male groups ($\chi^2 = 3.89$, p = 0.048). Stress Level (EDA): The average skin conductance during the baseline period was 62.4 ± 14.7 µS, dropping to 55.2 ± 11.8 µS after intervention, with a statistically significant difference (t = 4.31, p = 0.001). Children with high-functioning autism (ADI-R social score ≤ 7 points) showed significantly faster stress relief than those with moderate-functioning autism (F = 5.72, p = 0.021), suggesting that cognitive ability may affect intervention efficiency. Pulse changes were not significant.

Subjective Scale Scores.   It is worth noting that the 8–10 age group scored significantly higher (4.81 ± 0.35) in "interactivity" than the 5–7 age group (4.23 ± 0.58), possibly related to the more mature development of social cognitive abilities in older children (F = 8.93, p < 0.001) (Table 2).

Table 2. Subjective Scale Scores

Dimension	Mean Score	Standard Deviation	95% Confidence Interval
Innovativeness	4.62	0.48	[4.51, 4.73]
Effectiveness	4.45	0.61	[4.32, 4.58]
Interactivity	4.57	0.42	[4.49, 4.65]
Usability	4.31	0.72	[4.15, 4.47]

5.5   Behavioral Observation and User Feedback

① Interaction Mode: 68% of children could independently complete tasks requiring sustained attention, such as "picking star fruits," with the average gaze duration increasing from 2.1 s in the first experiment to 4.3 s in the third (p < 0.01), consistent with the conclusion of "round shape preference" in previous color experiments. ② Emotional Regulation Behaviors: 32% of children showed spontaneous deep breathing during the game, and 25% imitated character expressions (such as smiling), while the incidence of such behaviors during the baseline period was less than 5%. ③ Abnormal Behavior Inhibition: The frequency of repetitive stereotypic movements (such as body shaking) decreased from 12.3 times/10 min during the baseline period to 4.7 times/10 min during the game (p < 0.001).

5.6 Follow-Up Tests

Three follow-up tests (once a week) were conducted within 1 month after the first experiment, finding: Emotional Regulation Sustainability: During the third follow-up, the average heart rate decrease remained at 18.6%, with no significant difference from the effect of the first intervention (t = 1.27, p = 0.21), indicating stable effectiveness. Self-Regulation Strategy Acquisition: 41% of children could use the relaxation technique of "long-pressing the screen - listening to stream sounds" in non-game scenarios, demonstrating the generalization effect of the intervention.

5.7 Discussion and Limitations

The sample did not include children with low-functioning ASD, so the scope of application needs to be inferred with caution; the lack of a blank control group makes it difficult to completely rule out the Hawthorne effect; physiological indicators only monitor the peripheral nervous system, not involving central nervous mechanisms.

5.8 Conclusion

The effectiveness verification experiment evaluated the emotional regulation efficiency and human-computer interaction user experience of the game interface. Children with high-functioning autism performed well during the game, and their emotions and stress were soothing to a certain extent after the game (average heart rate decreased from 109 to 86, average stress level decreased from 62 to 55). In the five-point scale of user interviews and observations, the game scored high in innovation, effectiveness, interactivity, and usability (average score 4.5). Through three follow-up tests over a month, it was found that the game can help improve the emotional perception and self-regulation ability of autistic children to a certain extent. Overall, the game provides positive emotional soothing experiences for autistic children, demonstrating value and significance for promotion and application.

6 Summary

This study constructs an emotional soothing game interface suitable for children with high-functioning autism through color vision experiments and multisensory interaction design. Experiments have shown that a game system integrating positive colors, natural sound effects, and intuitive interactions can effectively reduce anxiety and stress levels and soothe emotions. Future research can further expand the sample size, introduce control groups to verify long-term effects, and explore the application potential of VR/AR technology in multisensory immersion, providing more precise and personalized digital therapies for autism groups.

Our goal is to provide valuable insights and methods for designing games for autistic children through this study. By sharing observations on the behaviors and emotions of ASD children during the design process, we aim to inform the development of game solutions. The objective is to contribute to improving the design and development of games tailored for autistic children, ultimately providing them with more comfortable, convenient, and effective services and support.

Acknowledgments. This research was supported by 2025 Huazhong University of Science and Technology Self-Innovation Fund: Research on Wearable Design for Children with Autism (2025WKQN028).

Disclosure of Interests.   The authors declare that there are no competing interests or conflicts of interest relevant to the content of this article.

References

1. Xiao, S., Li, J.: Application of natural developmental behavior intervention in early intervention for autism. Adv. Psychol. Sci. 2350–2367(2023)
2. Wang, X.: Research on Online Screening Methods and Practices for Autistic Children Based on Computer Games. (2023)
3. Li, C., Bi, Q.: Application effect of parent-nurse-child interactive games in autistic children. China Health Stand. Manage. 20–23 (2024)
4. Shao, B.: The help of role-playing games for autistic preschoolers. Family Educ. World, 22–23(2023)
5. Zhang, G.: Application of human-computer interaction interface design based on digital learning in social interaction ability of autistic children. Ergonomics, 71–74 (2021)
6. Liu, Y.: A Digital Training System for Interactive Ability of Preschool Autistic Children (2021)
7. Zhang, Y.: Research on emotional intervention strategies for autistic children based on color perception. Colors, 152 (2025)
8. Chen, Y., Wang, L., Chen, Y.: Application of multisensory training combined with early intervention denver model intensive training in autistic children. J. Clin. Psychosomatic Diseases, 113–117 (2023)
9. Gao, H., Wang, L., Cao, Q.: Effect analysis of multisensory interactive therapy in 75 autistic children. Clin. Res. 63–64 (2019)
10. Sun, Y.: Research on Indoor Design of Rehabilitation Centers for Autistic Children under the Concept of Five-Sense Therapy. (2024)
11. Fang, J.: Research on Functional Game Design for Autistic Children—Taking Social Game Design Practice as an Example. Zhuangshi (Decoration), 90–94(2024)
12. Li, F.: Group Social Game Intervention for Children with Autism Spectrum Disorder. Peking University Press (2020)
13. Zeng, X., Liu, W.: Empirical research on improving social communication ability of autistic children under the "RMSO" social game intervention model. J. Yuzhang Normal Univ. 104–112 (2025)

14. Jin, Y., Shi, G.: Design practice of companion products for autistic children based on emotional design. J. Jilin Jianzhu Univ. 69–72 (2022)
15. Huo, Y.: Research on picture book design for autistic children based on emotional design. Toy World, 157–159 (2024)
16. Li, L.: Study on Visual Attention Characteristics of Autistic Children under Different Emotional Stimuli. Central China Normal University, Hubei (2020)
17. Tan, Z.: Three-dimensional analysis of the application of digital games in early intervention for autistic children. Toy World, 180–182 (2025)
18. He, Y., Wang, W.: On the positive role of games in family education of autistic children. Anhui Educ. Res. 97–98 (2021)
19. Jiang, Y., Zhu, L., Lu, X., Gao, H.: How can virtual games support education for autistic children?—a systematic literature review based on international research. Modern Distance Educ. Res. 104–112 (2022)
20. Wang, M., Zhai, H.: Somatosensory game interaction design for autistic children based on flow theory. Packaging Eng. 85–93 (2021)
21. [Author missing]: Improving Emotional Recognition Ability of Autistic Children through AR Games (2020)
22. Zhou, Z.: When Games Enter College Classrooms, What Is "Play" About?. (2020)
23. Li, W.: Research on AR Gamification Design for Emotional Ability Intervention of Autistic Children—Taking AR Emotional Pet as an Example (2023)
24. Huang, S., Li, J.: Characteristics and neural mechanisms of emotional memory in autistic children. Chin. J. Special Educ. 66–72 (2023)
25. Hu, J.: Human-Computer Interactive Assessment of Emotional Perception Ability in Autistic Children. (2024)
26. Li, D.: Intervention research on improving emotional understanding ability of autistic children through picture book teaching. Henan Educ. (Teach. Educ.), 18–19 (2025)
27. Huang, L.: Research on family art therapy space design for autistic children based on emotional design. Art Sci. Technol. 199–201 (2023)
28. Chen, Z., Zhao, Y., Zhong, Z., Xiong, R.: Research on rehabilitative indoor colors for autistic children based on NCS system. Furniture Interior Des. 128–132 (2023)
29. Liao, Y.: Influence of multisensory therapy on social and language abilities of autistic children. Chin. Sci. Technol. J. Database (Full Text Edition) Med. Health, 108–111 (2024)
30. Zhao, M., Sun, Y., Cheng, Z., Lu, X., Pan, G.: Exploration of clothing colors and graphics based on psychological characteristics of autistic children. West Leather, 97–100 (2022)
31. Liu, X., Huang, K.: Research on color usability design of educational spaces for autistic children. Archit. Cult. 259–261 (2022)
32. Zhang, M.: Research on healing clothing for autistic children based on color. Chem. Fiber Text. Technol. 147–149 (2022)
33. Wang, Y.: Research on Color Application in Improving Communication Ability of Autistic Children (2022)
34. Luo, M., Li, X., Shao, Y.: Research on toy design for autistic children based on color psychology. Popular Color, 11–13 (2022)
35. Li, X., Xiao, M., Rong, W.: Innovative strategies for life adaptation teaching of autistic children based on color therapy. Colors, 123–125 (2024)

Beyond the Avatar: Understanding Autistic Preferences in Immersive Learning Environments

Gunjan Kumari[✉][iD] and Wolfgang Broll[iD]

Virtual Worlds and Digital Games Group, Ilmenau University of Technology, Ehrenbergstraße 29, 98693 Ilmenau, Germany
`gunjan.kumari@tu-ilmenau.de`

Abstract. Immersive Learning Environments (ILEs) have shown promise in supporting learning, and in sensory, and emotional regulation in autistic individuals. However, there is a limited understanding of how different avatar characteristics influence user preferences. This study investigated the avatar preferences of autistic individuals across appearance (realistic vs. cartoon), familiarity (self, familiar, stranger), and voice type (male, female, robotic). Additionally, it examines whether preferences for autistic individuals differ between autistic individuals and autism stakeholders. A quantitative approach was employed to examine the preferences of autistic individuals for the above-mentioned avatar characteristics, in which participants ($N = 23$) completed an online survey, rating their preferences on a 7-point Likert scale. Significant overall preferences emerged for appearance ($\chi^2 = 32.89$, $p = 0.003$) and voice ($\chi^2 = 19.54$, $p < 0.001$), but not for familiarity ($\chi^2 = 5.48$, $p = 0.065$). Substantial between-group differences were found for realistic avatars (t-test, $p = 0.027$, $d = -1.08$) and familiar avatars ($p = 0.030$, $d = -1.06$). Autistic individuals preferred cartoon avatars and stranger representations, whereas stakeholders favored realistic and familiar avatars. Both groups consistently preferred human over robotic voices. The findings challenge common assumptions about autism and avatar design, revealing misalignment between autistic individuals and stakeholders. This highlights the need for user-centered approaches. The wide range of individual preferences calls for customizable, rather than one-size-fits-all, designs. The results support using universal design frameworks that allow flexible avatar personalization, promoting inclusive technology for autism education.

Keywords: Virtual reality · immersive learning environment · autism research · participatory design · co-design · inclusive design

1   Introduction

Immersive learning environments (ILEs) have emerged as powerful educational interventions, particularly for autistic individuals, offering structured, customiz-

© The Author(s), under exclusive license to Springer Nature Switzerland AG 2026
M. Antona and C. Stephanidis (Eds.): HCII 2025, LNCS 16335, pp. 276–295, 2026.
https://doi.org/10.1007/978-3-032-12781-5_19

able digital spaces that can accommodate diverse learning needs while minimizing sensory overload [21,26]. Within these virtual environments, avatars serve as critical mediating entities, a digital representations that facilitate user engagement, establish social presence, and potentially influence learning outcomes and therapeutic efficacy [4,19]. Although considerable research has investigated the technical and pedagogical dimensions of ILEs, the specific parameters of avatar design that optimize engagement and learning for autistic individuals are not adequately understood, despite their potential significance for the development of effective interventions. Autistic individuals often demonstrate distinct patterns of visual processing, social cognition, and self-representation that may influence their experiences with digital avatars [3,32]. Research in sensory processing differences suggests that autistic individuals may demonstrate atypical responses to both visual stimuli complexity and auditory characteristics, including voice pitch, intonation patterns, and synthetic versus natural speech[1,31]. The heterogeneous nature of autism suggests that avatar preferences may vary substantially within this population, potentially correlating with factors such as sensory processing patterns, social communication styles, and cognitive profiles [9].

Despite the increasing integration of ILEs into educational and therapeutic contexts for autistic individuals, several critical knowledge gaps regarding avatar preferences persist. There is a lack of systematic investigation into preferences along the realism–stylization spectrum, particularly within autistic populations. Existing studies often rely on limited avatar options or small, heterogeneous samples. Furthermore, the role of avatar familiarity, whether the avatar resembles the self, a familiar other, or a stranger, has received minimal empirical attention, despite its potential influence on user engagement and preference. The intersection of avatar appearance with identity dimensions such as ethnicity and gender remains underexplored, although these factors may hold significance for representation and inclusivity among diverse autistic users. Additionally, the impact of voice characteristics, specifically the use of natural human voices versus robotic ones, on engagement, comfort, and preference has been largely overlooked, despite well-documented differences in auditory processing and social voice perception in autism [28]. Direct comparisons between the preferences of autistic individuals and those of relevant stakeholders (e.g., caregivers, educators, and clinicians) are scarce, limiting insights into areas of alignment or divergence in design expectations.

Addressing these gaps is crucial for establishing evidence-based guidelines for design of ILEs intended for autistic users. To address these research gaps, this present study investigates the following research question (RQ) and tests the following alternative hypothesis (H_1):

RQ: What are the preferences of autistic individuals regarding avatar characteristics, specifically visual appearance, familiarity, and voice type, and do these preferences differ from those of stakeholders?

H_1: There is a statistically significant difference in avatar design preferences between autistic individuals and autism stakeholders.

To answer this research question and address the hypothesis, the study systematically varies avatar characteristics across three key dimensions, visual appearance (realistic vs. cartoon), familiarity (self-resembling, familiar other, stranger), and voice type (male, female, robotic), and compares the preferences of autistic individuals and autism stakeholders. Additionally, this study provides empirical evidence to inform user-centered avatar design practices in ILEs. These findings are intended to support the development of inclusive, engaging, and personalized virtual environments tailored to the needs of autistic users.

2   Related Work

Avatars function as advanced socio-cognitive tools that go beyond simple visuals, helping users interact with virtual environments in multiple ways [2]. Research with neurotypical populations has established that avatar characteristics significantly influence user experience across multiple psychological dimensions, including spatial presence, psychological ownership, and learning engagement [7,36]. A visual style of an avatar ranging from realistic to stylized affects key psychological responses, such as how users identify with it and whether they feel uneasy due to the uncanny valley effect [12,17]. The quality of an avatar's voice, especially whether it sounds human-like or synthetic, plays a key role in how much users accept and connect with it [20]. These factors are especially important in education, where avatar design influences psychological aspects that directly affect how people learn. Evidence indicates that avatar characteristics can modulate cognitive load [13,14], influence attention allocation, and affect emotional engagement [35]. The "Proteus effect" documented by [38] demonstrated that users' behaviors and self-perceptions are significantly influenced by avatar characteristics, with meta-analytic research confirming these effects across diverse contexts [30]. However, translation of these principles to neurodivergent populations, particularly autistic individuals, reveals significant knowledge gaps.

Autism-specific technology design has evolved from early accessibility-focused approaches toward participatory design methodologies incorporating autistic perspectives [6,25], reflecting growing recognition of designing with, rather than for, autistic users [18]. Research has documented enhanced performance on computer-based tasks compared to face-to-face interactions among autistic individuals [8], alongside preferences for clear, predictable, and structured visual representations [27]. Virtual environments have shown generally positive reception [22], though with considerable individual variation.

Limited research examining avatar preferences among autistic individuals has yielded contradictory findings. [33] reported preferences for simplified facial representations, suggesting advantages of reduced visual complexity. Conversely, [10] documented successful engagement with realistic avatars, though avatar design was not their primary focus. These contrasting findings likely reflect autism spectrum heterogeneity, methodological differences, or contextual factors. The auditory dimension presents an even more pronounced knowledge gap. While preliminary evidence for neurotypicals suggests preferences for predictable vocal patterns over naturalistic speech variations, systematic investigation comparing human versus synthetic voice characteristics remains virtually absent for autistic individuals [29]. This is a significant gap, especially in light of well-established research showing that autistic individuals have unique ways of processing auditory information.

The intersection of neurodiversity with other identity dimensions introduces additional complexity. Educational technology research highlights the importance of representational equity, demonstrating that when learners see themselves reflected in avatars or content, it can boost their engagement and success [16]. For autistic individuals from diverse backgrounds, the intersection of neurodiversity with other identity dimensions may influence avatar preferences through complex processes. Self-representation relationships may demonstrate particular intricacy due to documented differences in self-processing and bodily awareness. Theoretical frameworks suggest potential alterations in self-other boundary processing [23], while empirical research has documented distinct patterns in self-recognition among autistic individuals [34,37]. The multistakeholder nature of educational technology implementation further complicates design. Effective ILE deployment involves diverse stakeholders including parent, educators, therapists, and caregivers [39], who frequently assume crucial roles in technology selection yet may hold preferences that systematically diverge from autistic individuals' actual preferences [11].

This literature review reveals promising foundational research alongside significant knowledge gaps. While general avatar research has established multimodal design importance, and autism-specific research has documented digital intervention potential, systematic investigation of multimodal avatar preferences among autistic individuals remains limited. The present investigation addresses these gaps by systematically examining multimodal avatar preferences across visual appearance, auditory characteristics, and familiarity dimensions while directly comparing preferences between autistic individuals and stakeholders. This study aims to contribute substantially to evidence-based guidelines for inclusive ILE design, advancing both theoretical understanding and practical implementation of accessible educational technologies.

3 Methodology

This section describes our sampling strategy, details our study design to assess avatar preferences and methods used for data collection and analysis.

3.1 Sampling Strategy

This study employed purposive sampling to recruit participants who were either autistic individuals or stakeholders (e.g., family members, clinicians, educators) with relevant experiences. Purposive sampling was chosen because of the specificity of the target population and the need for informed perspectives on ILEs.

The final sample size was determined based on participant availability and eligibility rather than a predefined quota. Participants were recruited using university mailing lists, autism advocacy organizations and support networks, online communities focused on autism, and professional networks of educators and practitioners working with autistic populations. Participants were required to meet the following inclusion criteria: (1) age above 18 years; and (2) identify as either an autistic individual (with formal diagnosis or self-identified) or a stakeholder (defined as professionals, caregivers, or family members with regular interaction with autistic individuals). Exclusion criteria included the inability to comprehend the instructions provided by the researcher.

3.2   Study Design

This study employed a quantitative cross-sectional design to explore avatar preferences within an ILE. A between-groups comparative approach was adopted to assess patterns of preference between two distinct cohorts: autistic individuals and autism stakeholders. The objective was to identify both group-level differences and intra-group variability across three primary dimensions of avatar design: avatar appearance, familiarity, and voice characteristics.

- **Avatar Appearance:** Participants evaluated avatars representing two categories: realistic and cartoon. The realistic avatars were sourced from the Virtual Avatar Library for Inclusion and Diversity (VALID) [5]. Fifteen avatars were included consisting of 10 realistic avatars varying by ethnicity and gender (Asian, Black, Hispanic, Middle Eastern/North African [MENA], and White; each represented by male and female avatars). A representative example is provided in Fig. 1. Cartoon avatars were selected from openly licensed websites[1] and incorporated into the ILE.
- **Avatar Familiarity:** To investigate the influence of familiarity, participants were asked to rate their preferences for self-resembling avatars, depicting a familiar individual, or representing a stranger.
- **Avatar Voice:** Preferences were assessed for three voice types, female and male voice in human voice type, and robotic voice reflecting the most commonly implemented voice options in ILEs.

All stimuli were developed using Unity3D[2], where each avatar was embedded within a virtual classroom setting to approximate realistic educational use cases. Screenshots of these stimuli were captured and integrated into a custom-designed online questionnaire[3], allowing for remote participation and increasing accessibility beyond in-lab settings. To mitigate cognitive and sensory overload, particularly for autistic participants, design elements were presented individually within the questionnaire interface. This approach aligns with previous findings that autistic individuals can be more sensitive to visual complexity, which

---

[1] Turbo Squid https://www.turbosquid.com/ last accessed: 05.06.2025.
[2] Unity Engine https://unity.com last accessed: 15.05.2025.
[3] Unipark https://www.unipark.com/ last accessed: 16.05.2025.

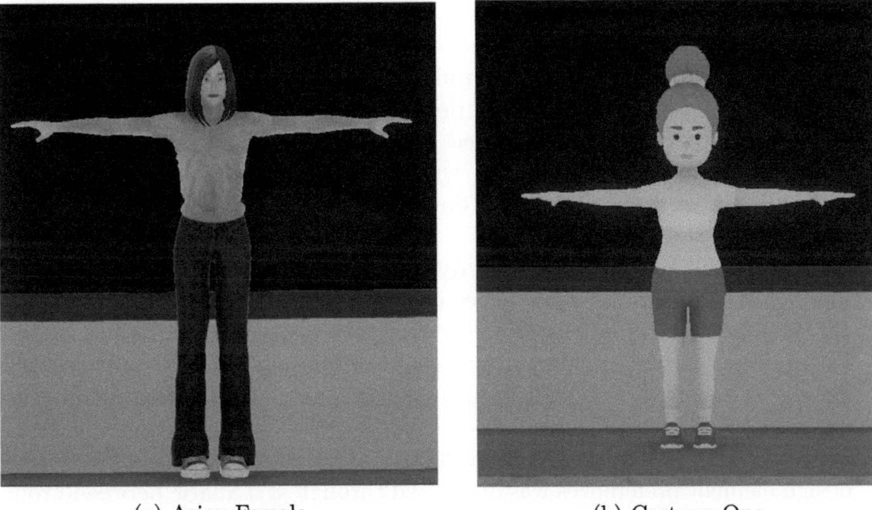

(a) Asian Female   (b) Cartoon One

Fig. 1. Examples of the Realistic and Cartoon Avatars Used in Study.

may increase cognitive fatigue and make decision-making harder [24]. Data collection was conducted through a 7-point Likert scale (1 = strongly dislike; 7 = strongly like), enabling participants to express degrees of preference with greater granularity than binary (yes/no) formats. Autistic participants rated elements according to their personal preferences, while stakeholder were instructed to rate each item based on what they believed would be preferred by autistic individuals. The selection of a Likert scale format was informed by literature suggesting that autistic individuals may experience challenges in articulating preferences or emotional responses [15], and that graded scales can offer a more nuanced means of capturing affective responses to design elements.

3.3   Data Analysis

A multi-level analytical approach was employed for data analysis, incorporating overall preference patterns, between-group comparisons, pairwise comparisons, and individual combination analysis. All statistical analyses were conducted using appropriate parametric and non-parametric tests based on data distribution characteristics and sample size considerations.

- **Descriptive Statistics:** Means, Medians, standard deviations, and 95% confidence intervals were calculated for all preference ratings across diagnostic groups and design element domains.
- **Distributional Assessment:** Shapiro-Wilk tests were systematically conducted for all preference variables within each diagnostic subgroup to determine appropriate statistical approaches for hypothesis testing. These assess-

ments ensured optimal statistical power and validity for the between-groups comparisons.

- **Within-Group Preference Analysis:** To provide context for between-groups differences, within-group preference patterns were examined using Friedman tests due to the repeated measures design and frequent violations of normality assumptions. These analyses identified which design elements were most preferred within each domain, serving as descriptive context for the hypothesis testing.
- **Hierarchical Avatar Style Analysis:** A nested analytical approach examined avatar appearance preferences at multiple levels: (1) overall preferences across all avatar types, (2) preferences within realistic avatar subcategories, (3) preferences within cartoon avatar subcategories, and (4) direct realistic versus cartoon style comparisons using participants' mean ratings across style categories.
- **Hypothesis Testing:** The hypothesis investigating group differences in design element preferences was addressed through systematic between-groups comparisons across three dimensions. Independent samples t-tests were employed for normally distributed preference variables, while Mann-Whitney U tests were used when normality assumptions were violated.
- **Effect Size Quantification:** Comprehensive effect size measures were computed to quantify the magnitude of group differences supporting or refuting the primary hypothesis: Cohen's d with 95% confidence intervals for parametric comparisons, and rank-biserial correlation (r) for non-parametric comparisons. Mean differences with 95% confidence intervals were calculated for group comparisons to provide practically interpretable effect magnitudes for design element preferences.
- **Bayesian Evidence Evaluation:** Bayesian t-tests were implemented to provide evidence for hypothesis significance testing. Bayes factors (BF_{10}) were calculated and interpreted using established conventions to quantify evidence strength for group differences in design preferences.
- **Statistical Significance:** Statistical significance was established at $\alpha = 0.05$, with appropriate corrections for multiple comparisons applied within each design element family.

3.4   Research Ethics

This study was approved by the ethics committee of our university. All participants were presented with an informed consent statement at the beginning of the survey. Consent was obtained digitally before proceeding with the rating tasks. The participants were informed of the voluntary nature of their participation. Data were anonymized at the point of collection, and no identifiable information was stored. The study adhered to ethical guidelines for research involving human participants and complied with the General Data Protection Regulation (GDPR).

4   Results

This section presents participant demographics and sample characteristics, individual avatar dimension preferences with overall patterns, between-group comparisons, and pairwise analyses for each dimension, followed by avatar combination rankings examining both theoretical optimal configurations and individual participant optimal combinations.

4.1   Demographic Data

The research sample included 23 participants from two groups: autistic individuals ($n = 16$) and autism stakeholders ($n = 7$). Gender distribution was predominantly female ($n = 15; 65.2\%$), with male participants representing 21.7% ($n = 5$) and individuals identifying with diverse gender categories accounting for 13.0% ($n = 3$).

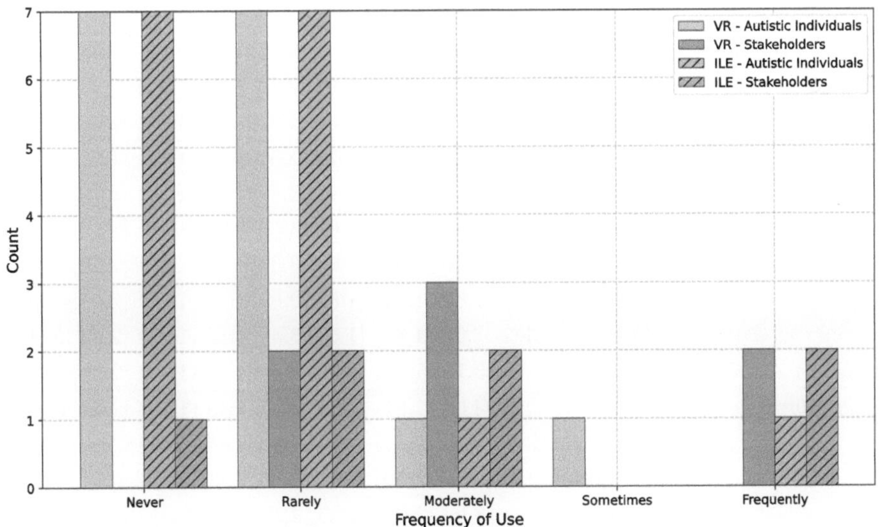

Fig. 2. Prior VR and ILE Usage Frequency for Autistic Individuals and Stakeholders

Participants were divided into younger adults (18–35 years; $n = 17$) and older adults (36–51 years; $n = 6$) with autistic individuals notably younger ($M = 29, SD = 9$) than stakeholders ($M = 39, SD = 10$). Among genders, females showed middle age range ($M = 33, SD = 9$), males the highest ($M = 37, SD = 14$), and diverse participants the youngest ($M = 21, SD = 3$). Technology familiarity varied considerably between groups. Stakeholders reported a wide range of experience with VR and ILE, with responses distributed across minimal ($n = 3$), moderate ($n = 2$), and frequent ($n = 2$) usage levels. This variation indicates heterogeneous technological backgrounds among stakeholders. In contrast, autistic participants exhibited consistently low familiarity with VR and ILEs; the majority ($n = 14; 87.5\%$) reported little to no prior experience (See Fig. 2).

4.2   Avatar Appearance Preferences

Descriptive analysis revealed notable differences in avatar appearance preferences between groups (see Table 1 for detailed statistics). For realistic avatars, autistic individuals showed consistently lower preference ratings across all demographic combinations, with an overall realistic avatar mean of $M = 2.67$ ($SD = 1.21$). Stakeholders demonstrated substantially higher preferences for realistic avatars ($M = 4.03$, $SD = 1.39$).

Table 1. Avatar Appearance Preferences by Group

Avatar Type	Avatar	Autistic Individuals	Stakeholders
Realistic Avatars	Asian Female	2.94 (1.65) [2.05, 3.83]	3.86 (2.12) [1.48, 6.23]
	Asian Male	2.44 (1.41) [1.69, 3.19]	4.29 (1.38) [2.74, 5.83]
	Black Female	3.38 (1.67) [2.48, 4.27]	3.86 (1.68) [1.96, 5.76]
	Black Male	2.31 (1.14) [1.71, 2.91]	3.43 (1.51) [1.72, 5.14]
	Hispanic Female	2.63 (1.71) [1.71, 3.54]	4.43 (1.51) [2.72, 6.14]
	Hispanic Male	2.81 (1.47) [2.03, 3.59]	3.86 (1.57) [2.06, 5.66]
	MENA Female	2.50 (1.63) [1.63, 3.37]	4.29 (1.89) [2.16, 6.41]
	MENA Male	2.00 (1.21) [1.35, 2.65]	3.71 (1.50) [2.01, 5.42]
	White Female	2.50 (1.86) [1.52, 3.48]	4.14 (1.35) [2.63, 5.66]
	White Male	3.19 (1.83) [2.22, 4.15]	4.43 (1.40) [2.86, 6.00]
Cartoon Avatars	Cartoon 1	4.06 (1.81) [3.11, 5.02]	4.43 (1.72) [2.52, 6.34]
	Cartoon 2	3.75 (1.81) [2.80, 4.70]	3.86 (1.57) [2.06, 5.66]
	Cartoon 3	2.50 (1.59) [1.66, 3.34]	2.71 (1.80) [0.71, 4.72]
	Cartoon 4	3.06 (2.08) [1.95, 4.17]	4.29 (2.14) [1.89, 6.68]
	Cartoon 5	3.13 (1.93) [2.12, 4.13]	3.57 (1.99) [1.38, 5.76]
Summary Scores	Realistic Mean	2.67 (1.21) [2.03, 3.31]	4.03 (1.39) [2.48, 5.58]
	Cartoon Mean	3.30 (1.25) [2.64, 3.96]	3.77 (1.46) [2.15, 5.40]

Autistic individuals rated cartoon avatars with a mean of $M = 3.30$ ($SD = 1.25$), while stakeholders provided slightly higher ratings ($M = 3.77, SD = 1.46$). Overall, cartoon avatars received higher preference ratings than realistic avatars across the combined sample (Fig. 3).

The Friedman test revealed strong overall differences across all avatar appearance types ($\chi^2 = 32.89$, $p = 0.003$), indicating substantial preference variability.

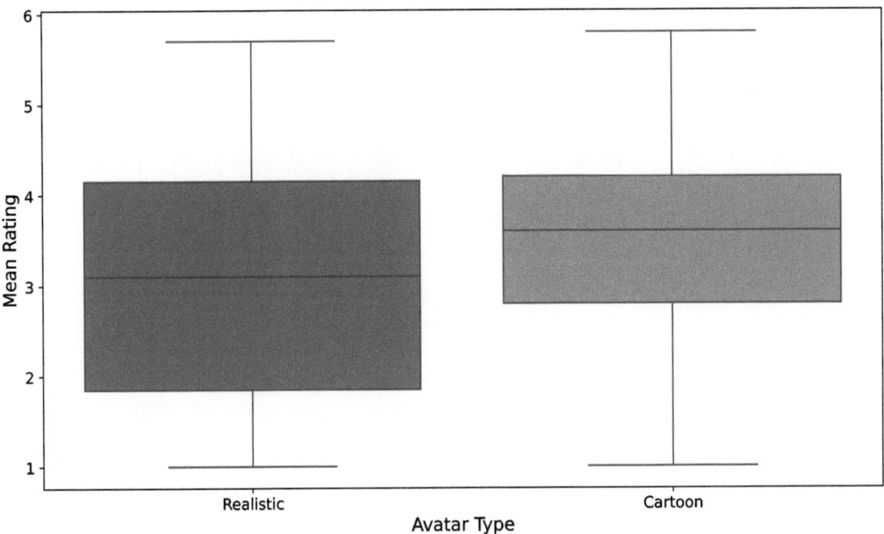

Fig. 3. Overall Comparison Between Realistic Avatars and Cartoon Avatars

Both realistic avatars ($\chi^2 = 22.59$, $p = 0.007$) and cartoon avatars ($\chi^2 = 13.40$, $p = 0.009$) showed significant internal preference differences.

Significant between-group differences emerged for realistic avatar preferences (t-test, $p = 0.027$, $d = -1.08$), with stakeholders demonstrating substantially higher preference ratings than autistic individuals.

Detailed pairwise comparisons revealed significant preferences among 27 of 105 possible avatar appearance pairs (26%). Notable significant comparisons included Asian Female vs. Black Male ($p = 0.030$), Asian Female vs. MENA Male ($p = 0.020$), Asian Female vs. Cartoon1 ($p = 0.042$), Asian Male vs. MENA Male ($p = 0.030$), and Asian Male vs. White Male ($p = 0.049$).

4.3 Avatar Familiarity Preferences

Avatar familiarity preferences revealed contrasting patterns between participant groups (see Table 2).

Autistic individuals demonstrated highest preference for stranger avatars ($M = 4.56$, $SD = 1.59$, $Mdn = 4.50$) and lowest preference for self-representation avatars ($M = 3.00$, $SD = 1.83$, $Mdn = 3.00$). Conversely, autism stakeholders showed different preferences, rating familiar avatars highest ($M = 5.71$, $SD = 1.11$, $Mdn = 6.00$), while self and stranger avatars received identical mean ratings ($M = 3.86$; $SD = 2.19$ for self, $SD = 1.35$ for stranger).

Inferential analysis indicated that familiarity preferences did not reach statistical significance overall ($\chi^2 = 5.48$, $p = 0.065$). A significant between-group difference emerged specifically for familiar avatar preferences (t-test, $p = 0.030$, $d = -1.06$), with stakeholders showing substantially higher preference ratings

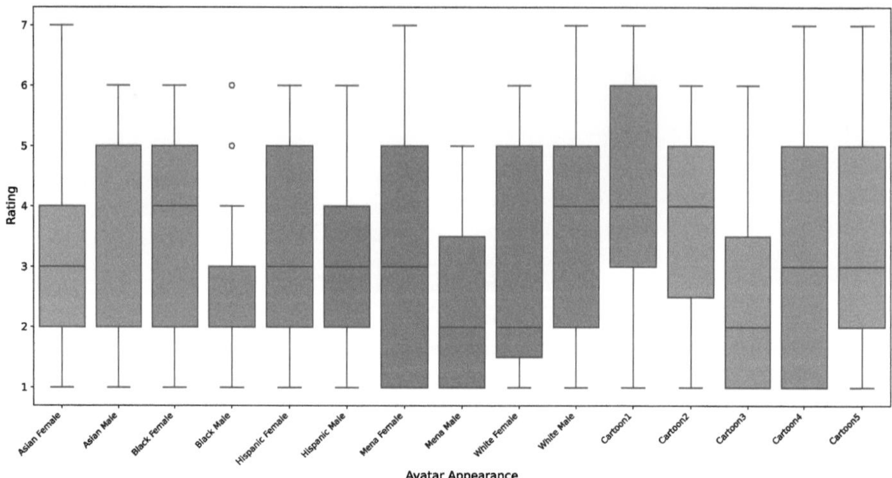

Fig. 4. Overall Avatar Appearance Distribution

Table 2. Avatar Familiarity and Voice Preferences by Group

Preference Type	Group	Mean (SD)	95% CI	Median
Self Avatar	Autistic Individuals	3.00 (1.83)	[2.03, 3.97]	3.00
	Stakeholders	3.86 (2.19)	[1.41, 6.31]	3.00
Stranger Avatar	Autistic Individuals	4.56 (1.59)	[3.72, 5.41]	4.50
	Stakeholders	3.86 (1.35)	[2.34, 5.37]	4.00
Familiar Avatar	Autistic Individuals	3.81 (2.01)	[2.74, 4.88]	3.50
	Stakeholders	5.71 (1.11)	[4.48, 6.95]	6.00
Female Voice	Autistic Individuals	4.88 (1.50)	[4.08, 5.67]	5.00
	Stakeholders	4.86 (1.95)	[2.65, 7.07]	5.00
Male Voice	Autistic Individuals	4.94 (1.06)	[4.38, 5.50]	5.00
	Stakeholders	4.86 (1.07)	[3.64, 6.08]	5.00
Robotic Voice	Autistic Individuals	2.88 (1.31)	[2.19, 3.56]	3.00
	Stakeholders	3.71 (1.60)	[1.89, 5.54]	3.00

than autistic individuals. This large effect size demonstrates a meaningful practical difference in familiar avatar acceptance. Analysis of familiarity pairwise comparisons revealed no significant differences between familiarity types, indicating that while overall group differences exist, the relative ordering of familiarity preferences does not show significant pairwise distinctions when analyzed across the combined sample.

4.4   Auditory Preferences

Voice preference analysis demonstrated strong consensus patterns across both participant groups (see Table 2). Autistic individuals rated male voices slightly higher ($M = 4.94$, $SD = 1.06$, $Mdn = 5.00$), while robotic voices received substantially lower ratings ($M = 2.88$, $SD = 1.31$, $Mdn = 3.00$). Stakeholders showed nearly equivalent preferences for male and female voices ($M = 4.86$, $SD = 1.07$ and 1.95 respectively, both $Mdn = 5.00$), with robotic voices again receiving notably lower ratings ($M = 3.71$, $SD = 1.60$, $Mdn = 3.00$).

Inferential analysis confirmed significant overall voice preferences ($\chi^2 = 19.54$, $p < 0.001$). Female voice preferences showed no group difference (t-test, $p = 0.981$, $d = 0.01$), male voice preferences were similarly equivalent between groups (t-test, $p = 0.869$, $d = 0.08$), and robotic voice preferences, while showing the largest effect size, remained non-significant (t-test, $p = 0.200$, $d = -0.60$).

Voice pairwise comparisons revealed significant differences in 2 of 3 possible voice pair combinations. Specifically, both female vs. robotic voice ($p = 0.002$, $d = 1.05$) and male vs. robotic voice ($p < 0.001$, $d = 1.36$) comparisons showed large significant differences.

4.5   Avatar Combination Analysis

Avatar preference rankings revealed distinct hierarchies across dimensions. Appearance preferences showed Cartoon1 ranking highest ($M = 4.17$), followed by Cartoon2 ($M = 3.78$) and White Male ($M = 3.57$), with MENA Male lowest ($M = 2.52$) (see Fig. 4). Familiarity preferences demonstrated near-equivalent ratings for familiar ($M = 4.39$) and stranger ($M = 4.35$) avatars, both substantially outperforming self-representation ($M = 3.26$) (see Fig. 5). Voice preferences favored male ($M = 4.91$) and female ($M = 4.87$) voices equally, with robotic voice significantly lower ($M = 3.13$) (see Fig. 6). The optimal theoretical combination ($Cartoon1 + Familiar + Malevoice$) achieved a score of 4.49, while the suboptimal combination ($MENAMale + Self + Roboticvoice$) scored 2.97. This 1.52-point difference represented 30% of the rating scale range. Analysis revealed 20 unique optimal combinations across 23 participants, with combined scores ranging from 3.00 to 7.00 ($M = 5.43, SD = 1.03$).

Three participants achieved maximum scores (7.00), while one scored minimum (3.00). Only three combinations appeared twice. Autistic individuals ($n = 16$) showed combined scores of $3.00 - 7.00$ ($M = 5.35, SD = 1.02$), with cartoon avatars selected in 50% of cases, diverse familiarity choices, and female voice preferred by 69%. Stakeholders ($n = 7$) scored $4.00 - 7.00$ ($M = 5.57, SD = 1.05$), favoring realistic avatars (71%), familiar representations (57%), and female voice (86%). Component selections across all participants included 15 different appearances, with Cartoon1 and Asian Female most frequent ($n = 4$ each). Level of familiarity showed familiar (39%), stranger (30%), and self (30%) distributions. Voice preferences strongly favored female (74%) over male (22%) and robotic (4%) options. Between-group comparison revealed no significant difference in combined preference scores ($t(21) = -0.46, p = 0.651, d = -0.21$).

Table 3. Statistical Test Results Summary

Analysis	Test Stat	p-value	Effect Size	Interpretation
Overall Preferences				
Avatar Appearance	32.89	0.003**	–	Significant overall differences
Realistic Avatars	22.59	0.007**	–	Significant internal differences
Cartoon Avatars	13.40	0.009**	–	Significant internal differences
Avatar Familiarity	5.48	0.065	–	Non-significant
Voice Preferences	19.54	<0.001***	–	Significant overall differences
Between-Group Differences				
Realistic Avatars	–	0.027*	$d = -1.08$	Large effect, stakeholders higher
Familiar Avatars	–	0.030*	$d = -1.06$	Large effect, stakeholders higher
Self Avatars U	–	0.377	$r = 0.24$	Non-significant
Stranger Avatars	–	0.319	$d = 0.46$	Non-significant
Female Voice	–	0.981	$d = 0.01$	Non-significant
Male Voice	–	0.869	$d = 0.08$	Non-significant
Robotic Voice	–	0.200	$d = -0.60$	Non-significant
Pairwise Comparisons				
Avatar Appearance	–	–	–	27/105 pairs significant (26%)
Voice Comparisons	–	–	–	2/3 pairs significant (67%)

Note. $* p < .05$, $** p < .01$, $*** p < .001$. Dashes (–) indicate values not applicable or not reported. Effect sizes are reported using Cohen's d or rank-biserial correlation r, as appropriate.

5   Discussion

The findings of this study offer significant insights into the preferences of autistic individuals and stakeholders concerning various avatar characteristics. These results hold substantial implications for the design of inclusive environments that are tailored to the needs and preferences of autistic individuals. In this section, we interpret the results and explain the limitations of this study and suggest future research directions.

5.1   Primary Findings and Hypothesis Testing

The present study examined avatar preferences across appearance, familiarity, and voice dimensions in ILEs for autistic users. Our primary hypothesis that statistically significant differences exist in avatar design preferences between autistic individuals and autism stakeholders was strongly supported across multiple avatar dimensions.

Avatar appearance demonstrated the strongest empirical effects, with significant overall differences and substantial between-group differences for realistic avatars. Autistic individuals consistently preferred cartoon avatars, while

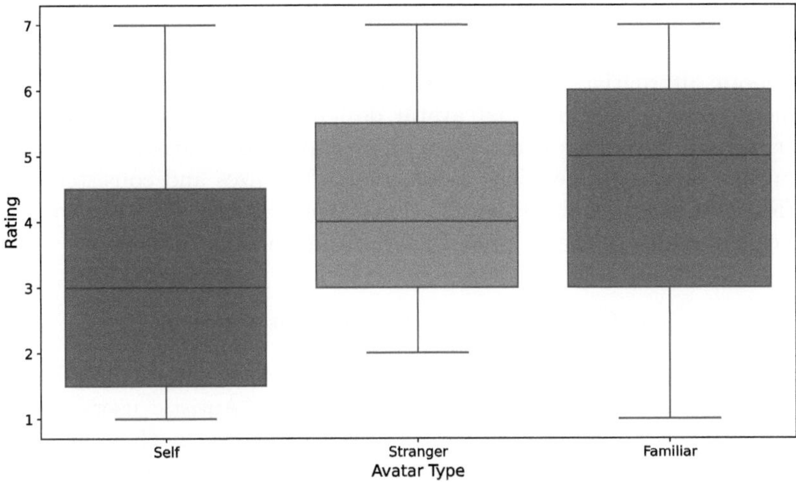

Fig. 5. Overall Avatar Familiarity Distribution

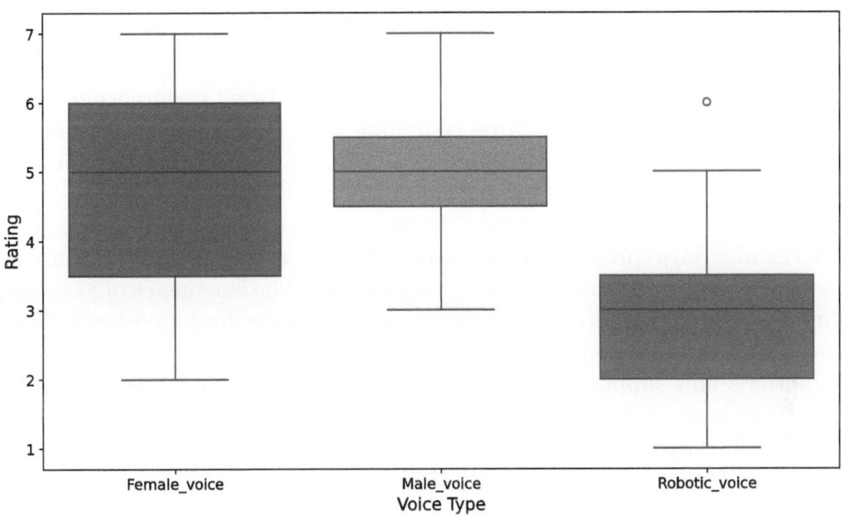

Fig. 6. Overall Voice Preference Distribution

stakeholders favored realistic representations, directly supporting our hypothesis with a large effect size indicating meaningful practical differences. Familiarity preferences revealed significant between-group differences for familiar avatars. Autistic individuals preferred stranger avatars most highly, while stakeholders strongly favored familiar avatars, providing strong evidence for our hypothesis. This pattern contradicts assumptions about autism and social familiarity, suggesting that familiar representations may increase cognitive demands for autistic users. Voice preferences showed no significant between-group differences across any voice type, representing the only dimension where our hypothesis was not supported. Both groups demonstrated equivalent preferences for human voices over robotic alternatives, indicating consensus in this design dimension.

These findings establish that avatar design decisions cannot rely on stakeholder assumptions alone and require direct input from autistic users to ensure appropriate design choices. The substantial effect sizes and consistent pattern of differences across multiple avatar dimensions confirm that diagnostic stats significantly influence avatar preference patterns in ILE contexts.

5.2   Theoretical Implications and Emergent Patterns

The preference patterns highlight key differences in how autistic individuals and stakeholders process visual and social information. Autistic users' preference for cartoon avatars supports sensory processing theories, as these avatars have simpler features and less visual detail, reducing sensory overload and cognitive effort. This suggests that simplified visuals can help communication without overwhelming users. The preference for stranger avatars challenges the idea that autistic individuals avoid social interaction. Instead, it may reflect a thoughtful strategy–interacting with strangers could offer social benefits without the emotional and cognitive demands of familiar relationships. This points to adaptive, not deficit-based, social behavior. Finally, the strong preference for human voices shows how important natural communication is. Human voices offer familiar rhythms that aid understanding, while robotic voices can make processing harder due to their unnatural sound patterns.

The systematic stakeholder-user disagreement reveals that stakeholder perspectives may misrepresent autistic user needs, reflecting neurotypical assumptions that do not generalize to autistic populations. The emergence of 87% unique optimal combinations provides strong empirical support for individual difference theories over group-based design approaches. This challenges categorical design assumptions and supports person-specific optimization strategies. The similar satisfaction levels across different combinations show that flexible designs can meet a wide range of needs. This supports customization over one-size-fits-all solutions and suggests that even well-designed group-based approaches may not work well for everyone.

5.3   Practical Implications for Inclusive Design

The findings provide clear guidance for developing inclusive ILEs that center the needs of autistic users while acknowledging the complexity that stakeholders bring to the design process. Avatar customization must prioritize user-driven over stakeholder-assumed preferences. The substantial differences between autistic users and stakeholders indicate that design decisions based solely on stakeholder input systematically misalign with actual user needs. ILE development should incorporate direct autistic user feedback and provide customizable options.

Modular avatar design architectures allowing independent selection of appearance, familiarity, and voice characteristics are essential. The 87% unique optimal combinations indicate that pre-configured packages cannot serve user needs, requiring comprehensive mixing and matching capabilities across all three dimensions. Voice selection represents a universal design opportunity with consistent cross-group preferences for human voices. ILE designers can confidently prioritize human voice options while avoiding robotic alternatives that receive consistently low ratings.

A flexible design must reflect individual differences. The wide range of pairwise differences shows that a single solution cannot work for everyone. ILEs should offer multiple choices in every design aspect to ensure comfort and engagement. Finally, designs must be tested not only for preference but also for effectiveness. While aligning with user preferences improves experience, it's important to test whether these preferences also support learning outcomes through performance-based evaluations.

5.4   Limitations and Future Directions

While this study offers valuable insights into avatar preferences among autistic individuals and stakeholders, several limitations warrant consideration to inform future research.

Firstly, the relatively small sample size may not adequately capture the full diversity of the autism spectrum. Participants could differ from the broader autistic population in terms of communication abilities, sensory sensitivities, and familiarity with technology, potentially limiting the generalizability of the findings. The methodology also presents certain constraints. Data were collected via an online questionnaire displayed on standard 2D screens rather than through VR head-mounted displays (VR-HMD). Although this approach facilitated broader participant access, it precluded an authentic representation of avatar colors and design as experienced within ILE. Moreover, the digital questionnaire format may have restricted the capacity of participants lacking prior VR or ILE experience to accurately evaluate the avatars. Additionally, the autistic participant group comprised both self-identified and clinically diagnosed individuals. While this inclusivity reflects the heterogeneity of the autistic community and supports participatory research principles, it may introduce variability in cognitive functioning and sensory sensitivities, which could influence design preferences. Finally, the study concentrated on stated preferences rather than actual usage behavior, leaving unresolved questions regarding the extent to which these preferences translate into real-world learning outcomes.

Future studies should use VR-HMD to collect the preferences on avatar design and explore whether avatars aligned with user preferences lead to measurable improvements in engagement or educational performance. While preferences are important for user-centered design, future studies must also assess performance outcomes. Only by linking avatar characteristics to learning effectiveness and user satisfaction can we fully understand the impact of multimodal customization on autistic users. Moreover, the long-term impact of preference-based design remains unknown. Longitudinal studies are needed to assess whether user preferences remain stable over time and whether preference-aligned avatars support sustained engagement and learning. Such research is critical for evaluating the long-term viability of personalized ILEs.

6   Conclusion

This study presents a comprehensive empirical analysis of avatar preferences among autistic individuals and autism stakeholders within ILEs, revealing systematic and meaningful differences with significant implications for inclusive technology design. The findings demonstrate that autistic users' preferences notably diverge from stakeholder assumptions, particularly regarding avatar appearance and social familiarity, underscoring the necessity of user-centered design approaches over proxy decision-making. The preference for cartoon avatars and stranger representations reflects adaptive strategies to manage sensory and cognitive load. Importantly, the substantial individual variability in avatar preferences highlights the inadequacy of standardized designs and supports personalized, customizable systems that accommodate diverse user needs. Consensus on voice preferences further guides universal design principles favoring human voices.

These insights emphasize the critical role of direct autistic user involvement in developing effective autism-focused technologies. This study illustrates the risks of stakeholder assumptions misaligning with actual user experiences, advocating for empirical, participatory methods in technology development. Ultimately, the results advance theoretical understanding and provide actionable guidance to create ILEs that authentically support autistic individuals' learning and social engagement.

Acknowledgment. The authors thank the autism community members who participated in this research and provided invaluable feedback on study design and interpretation.

Disclosure of Interests. The authors have no competing interests to declare that are relevant to the content of this article.

References

1. Alcántara, J.I., Weisblatt, E.J., Moore, B.C., Bolton, P.F.: Speech-in-noise perception in high-functioning individuals with autism or Asperger's syndrome. J. Child Psychol. Psychiatry **45**(6), 1107–1114 (2004). https://doi.org/10.1111/j.1469-7610.2004.t01-1-00303.x. eprint: https://onlinelibrary.wiley.com/doi/pdf/10.1111/j.1469-7610.2004.t01-1-00303.x
2. Bailenson, J.N., Blascovich, J.: Avatars. In: Encyclopedia of Human-Computer Interaction, vol. 1, pp. 64–66 (2004)

3. Brosnan, M., Johnson, H., Grawemeyer, B., Chapman, E., Antoniadou, K., Hollinworth, M.: Deficits in metacognitive monitoring in mathematics assessments in learners with autism spectrum disorder. Autism **20**(4), 463–472 (2016). https://doi.org/10.1177/1362361315589477

4. Didehbani, N., Allen, T., Kandalaft, M., Krawczyk, D., Chapman, S.: Virtual reality social cognition training for children with high functioning autism. Comput. Hum. Behav. **62**, 703–711 (2016). https://doi.org/10.1016/j.chb.2016.04.033

5. Do, T.D., Zelenty, S., Gonzalez-Franco, M., McMahan, R.P.: VALID: a perceptually validated virtual avatar library for inclusion and diversity. Front. Virtual Reality **4** (2023). https://doi.org/10.3389/frvir.2023.1248915

6. Fletcher-Watson, S., et al.: Making the future together: shaping autism research through meaningful participation. Autism **23**(4), 943–953 (2019). https://doi.org/10.1177/1362361318786721

7. Gonzalez-Franco, M., Peck, T.C.: Avatar embodiment. Towards a standardized questionnaire. Front. Roboti. AI **5** (2018). https://doi.org/10.3389/frobt.2018.00074

8. Grynszpan, O., Weiss, P.L.T., Perez-Diaz, F., Gal, E.: Innovative technology-based interventions for autism spectrum disorders: a meta-analysis. Autism **18**(4), 346–361 (2014). https://doi.org/10.1177/1362361313476767

9. Happé, F., Frith, U.: Annual research review: looking back to look forward – changes in the concept of autism and implications for future research. J. Child Psychol. Psychiatry **61**(3), 218–232 (2020), https://doi.org/10.1111/jcpp.13176. eprint: https://onlinelibrary.wiley.com/doi/pdf/10.1111/jcpp.13176

10. Kandalaft, M.R., Didehbani, N., Krawczyk, D.C., Allen, T.T., Chapman, S.B.: Virtual reality social cognition training for young adults with high-functioning autism. J. Autism Dev. Disord. **43**(1), 34–44 (2013). https://doi.org/10.1007/s10803-012-1544-6

11. Kinnear, S.H., Link, B.G., Ballan, M.S., Fischbach, R.L.: Understanding the experience of stigma for parents of children with autism spectrum disorder and the role stigma plays in families' lives. J. Autism Dev. Disord. **46**(3), 942–953 (2016). https://doi.org/10.1007/s10803-015-2637-9

12. Kätsyri, J., de Gelder, B., Takala, T.: Virtual faces evoke only a weak uncanny valley effect: an empirical investigation with controlled virtual face images. Perception **48**(10), 968–991 (2019). https://doi.org/10.1177/0301006619869134

13. Makransky, G., Lilleholt, L.: A structural equation modeling investigation of the emotional value of immersive virtual reality in education. Educ. Tech. Res. Dev. **66**(5), 1141–1164 (2018). https://doi.org/10.1007/s11423-018-9581-2

14. Makransky, G., Petersen, G.B.: The cognitive affective model of immersive learning (CAMIL): a theoretical research-based model of learning in immersive virtual reality. Educ. Psychol. Rev. **33**(3), 937–958 (2021). https://doi.org/10.1007/s10648-020-09586-2

15. Martinez, E.M.: Multiple-choice tests with correction allowed in autism: an Excel applet. J. Am. Acad. Special Educ. Prof. (2010). https://eric.ed.gov/?id=EJ1137361

16. Master, A., Cheryan, S., Meltzoff, A.N.: Computing whether she belongs: stereotypes undermine girls' interest and sense of belonging in computer science. J. Educ. Psychol. **108**(3), 424–437 (2016). American Psychological Association ERIC Number: EJ1096117. https://doi.org/10.1037/edu0000061

17. McDonnell, R., Breidt, M.: Face reality: investigating the Uncanny Valley for virtual faces. In: ACM SIGGRAPH ASIA 2010 Sketches, SA '10, pp. 1–2. Association

for Computing Machinery, New York (2010). https://doi.org/10.1145/1899950. 1899991

18. Milton, D.E.: Autistic expertise: a critical reflection on the production of knowledge in autism studies. Autism **18**(7), 794–802 (2014). https://doi.org/10.1177/1362361314525281

19. Mineo, B.A., Ziegler, W., Gill, S., Salkin, D.: Engagement with electronic screen media among students with autism spectrum disorders. J. Autism Dev. Disord. **39**(1), 172–187 (2009). https://doi.org/10.1007/s10803-008-0616-0

20. Nass, C., Brave, S.: Wired for speech: How voice activates and advances the human-computer relationship. Wired for speech: how voice activates and advances the human-computer relationship. Boston Rev., xvii, 296 (2005)

21. Newbutt, N., Schmidt, M., Riva, G., Schmidt, C.: The possibility and importance of immersive technologies during COVID-19 for autistic people. J. Enabling Technol. **14**(3), 187–199 (2020). https://doi.org/10.1108/JET-07-2020-0028

22. Newbutt, N., Sung, C., Kuo, H.J., Leahy, M.J., Lin, C.C., Tong, B.: Brief report: a pilot study of the use of a virtual reality headset in autism populations. J. Autism Dev. Disord. **46**(9), 3166–3176 (2016). https://doi.org/10.1007/s10803-016-2830-5

23. Palmer, C.J., Lawson, R.P., Hohwy, J.: Bayesian approaches to autism: towards volatility, action, and behavior. Psychol. Bull. **143**(5), 521–542 (2017). https://doi.org/10.1037/bul0000097

24. Parmar, K.R., Porter, C.S., Dickinson, C.M., Pelham, J., Baimbridge, P., Gowen, E.: Visual sensory experiences from the viewpoint of autistic adults. Front. Psychol. **12** (2021). https://doi.org/10.3389/fpsyg.2021.633037

25. Parsons, S., Nicola, Y., Judith, G., Brosnan, M.: 'Whose agenda? Who knows best? Whose voice?' Co-creating a technology research roadmap with autism stakeholders. Disabil. Soc. **35**(2), 201–234 (2020)

26. Parsons, S.: Authenticity in virtual reality for assessment and intervention in autism: a conceptual review. Educ. Res. Rev. **19**, 138–157 (2016). https://doi.org/10.1016/j.edurev.2016.08.001

27. Pennington, R.C.: Computer-assisted instruction for teaching academic skills to students with autism spectrum disorders: a review of literature. Focus Autism Other Dev. Disabil. **25**(4), 239–248 (2010). https://doi.org/10.1177/1088357610378291

28. Postarnak, S.: Voice and speech perception in autism : a systematic review. Master's thesis, February 2018. https://repositorio.ulisboa.pt/handle/10451/32759?locale=en

29. Quené, H., Port, R.: Produced speech rhythm depends on predictability of stress patterns, January 2003

30. Ratan, R., , David, B., , Benjamin J., L., , Graciano, L.: Avatar characteristics induce users' behavioral conformity with small-to-medium effect sizes: a meta-analysis of the Proteus effect. Media Psychol. **23**(5), 651–675 (2020). https://doi.org/10.1080/15213269.2019.1623698

31. Robertson, C.E., Baron-Cohen, S.: Sensory perception in autism. Nat. Rev. Neurosci. **18**(11), 671–684 (2017). https://doi.org/10.1038/nrn.2017.112

32. Schwarzkopf, S., Schilbach, L., Vogeley, K., Timmermans, B.: "Making it explicit" makes a difference: evidence for a dissociation of spontaneous and intentional level 1 perspective taking in high-functioning autism. Cognition **131**(3), 345–354 (2014). https://doi.org/10.1016/j.cognition.2014.02.003

33. Trepagnier, C.Y., Olsen, D.E., Boteler, L., Bell, C.A.: Virtual conversation partner for adults with autism. Cyberpsychol. Behav. Soc. Netw. **14**(1–2), 21–27 (2011). https://doi.org/10.1089/cyber.2009.0255
34. Uddin, L.Q.: The self in autism: an emerging view from neuroimaging. Neurocase **17**(3), 201–208 (2011)
35. Waddington, H., van der Meer, L., Carnett, A., Sigafoos, J.: Teaching a child with ASD to approach communication partners and use a speech-generating device across settings: clinic, school, and home. Can. J. Sch. Psychol. **32**(3–4), 228–243 (2017). https://doi.org/10.1177/0829573516682812
36. Wang, X., Laffey, J., Xing, W., Ma, Y., Stichter, J.: Exploring embodied social presence of youth with autism in 3D collaborative virtual learning environment: a case study. Comput. Hum. Behav. **55**, 310–321 (2016). https://doi.org/10.1016/j.chb.2015.09.006
37. Williams, D.: Theory of own mind in autism: evidence of a specific deficit in self-awareness? Autism **14**(5), 474–494 (2010). https://doi.org/10.1177/1362361310366314
38. Yee, N., Bailenson, J.: The Proteus effect: the effect of transformed self-representation on behavior. Hum. Commun. Res. **33**(3), 271–290 (2007). https://doi.org/10.1111/j.1468-2958.2007.00299.x
39. Zervogianni, V., et al.: A framework of evidence-based practice for digital support, co-developed with and for the autism community. Autism **24**(6), 1411–1422 (2020). https://doi.org/10.1177/1362361319898331

Augmented Reality Emotional Picture Book Design for Autistic Children Based on Embodied Cognition

Jiaqi Li and Qian Ji[✉]

Department of Industrial Design, School of Design of Huazhong University of Science and Technology, Wuhan, China
jiqian@mail.hust.edu.cn

Abstract. Autism Spectrum Disorder (ASD) is a neurodevelopmental disorder characterized by social communication deficits, restricted interests, and repetitive stereotyped behaviors. In recent years, the global prevalence of ASD has risen significantly, which poses substantial challenges to individuals, families, and society. Traditional interventions to enhance emotional recognition and social interaction abilities in autistic children face significant limitations. To address this gap, this study proposes an innovative visualization design method for emotional picture books, grounded in Embodied Cognition Theory and Augmented Reality (AR) technology. This approach aims to develop targeted and effective intervention tools for autistic children. The study constructed a three-layer interaction model comprising the perception, behavior, and emotion layers, creating an immersive emotional learning environment. The core contribution of this work lies in translating embodied experience design elements into a visual language of emotional picture books tailored to autistic children. This method improves emotion recognition abilities and fosters social skill development through embodied interactions. Experimental validation using the System Usability Scale (SUS) confirms high usability and user satisfaction. Behavioral observations and interviews further indicate improvements in participants' collaborative behaviors and emotion regulation. These findings demonstrate the efficacy of the design and its potential for broad application in ASD intervention.

Keywords: Embodied Cognition · Autism Spectrum Disorder · Children · Facial Expression · Augmented Reality Technology · Picture Books

1 Introduction

Autism spectrum disorder (ASD) is a highly heritable and heterogeneous neurodevelopmental disorder characterized by impaired social communication, restricted interests, and repetitive stereotyped behaviors [1]. By 2024, the global prevalence of ASD among children had reached approximately 0.77%, reflecting a continued upward trend [2]. It poses major challenges not only to individuals and families but also attracts widespread attention to the support for and intervention strategies to this group.

© The Author(s), under exclusive license to Springer Nature Switzerland AG 2026
M. Antona and C. Stephanidis (Eds.): HCII 2025, LNCS 16335, pp. 296–307, 2026.
https://doi.org/10.1007/978-3-032-12781-5_20

Autistic children exhibit significant impairments in emotion recognition and social communication [3], which substantially compromise their social adjustment and quality of life [4]. Current conventional interventions, such as static picture teaching [5] and role-playing [6], offer structured learning support, with low costs and easy implementation. However, these approaches fail to deliver dynamic multimodal feedback, limiting children's understanding of emotional dynamics in real-world social contexts. Furthermore, they demonstrate inadequate generalizability to complex, fluid social environments.

These limitations underscore the critical need for interventions incorporating interactive architectures and real-time adaptive feedback. Crucially, the constrained comprehension of abstract emotional concepts [7] by autistic children necessitates concrete, multisensory learning experiences to fortify emotional perception. Virtual environments function as dual mediators—skill-transfer bridges facilitating the application of learned competencies to real-world contexts, and behavioral mirrors revealing intrinsic response patterns during affective processing—thereby establishing an integrated framework for both intervention delivery and mechanistic observation. Specifically, Augmented Reality (AR) picture books serve as behavioral mirrors by simulating diverse emotional scenarios. These settings reveal autistic children's characteristic responses in emotion recognition and social interactions, thereby advancing mechanistic understanding for researchers. Concurrently, they provide safe virtual rehearsal spaces for repeated practice, progressively enhancing abstraction capabilities in emotional cognition.

Embodied Cognition Theory emerged in the 1980s and is an important research area in psychology. The theory emphasizes the body's foundational and inseparable role in cognitive activities. It points out that an individual's understanding of the outside world and the acquisition of experience are not solely reliant on abstract information-processing mechanisms. Instead, they are constructed and formed through the ongoing interaction between the body and the environment [8, 9].

Embodied Cognition Theory suggests that cognitive activities are influenced by the interaction between the body and the environment (see Fig. 1). It is characterized by three main features: involvement, embodiment, and environmental embeddedness [10, 11]. Embodiment refers to how individual body states and movements actively construct cognition. For instance, body movements can enhance emotional experiences. This concept also emphasizes that cognition depends on body structure and function, with the sensorimotor system providing the basis for cognition. An example of this is how facial expressions can influence emotion recognition. Environmental embeddedness indicates that cognition occurs within specific environments. Individuals interact with their environments to construct cognition. For example, in social interactions, environmental cues can influence cognitive processes. These three characteristics provide a scientific framework for emotional interventions for autistic children.

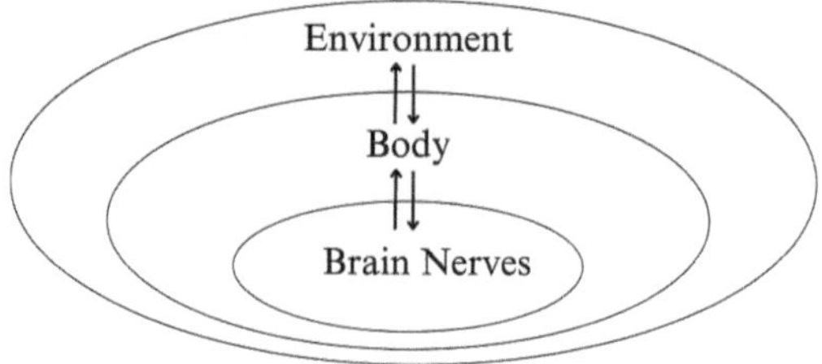

Fig. 1. Cognitive system: structural coupling of brain, body, and environment.

2 Method

The study underwent ethical review by the Tongji Medical College of Huazhong University of Science and Technology. Before the commencement of the research, the guardians of all children participating in the study signed informed consent forms to ensure the study's ethical compliance. The research adhered to the ethical principles outlined in the *Specification for the Ethical Review of Life Science and Medical Research Involving Human Participants*, including respecting the participants' right to informed consent and autonomy, as well as protecting their privacy and personal information.

2.1 Construction of Embodied Experience Design Element Model

To overcome the limitations of traditional methods, this paper constructs a three-layer interaction model (perception layer, behavior layer, and emotion layer) based on Embodied Cognition (see Fig. 2). This model informs a visual experience design approach driven by Embodied Interaction Technology. Through the specific operation of the three-layer interaction model, it provides autistic children with a multisensory and multilevel emotional learning environment.

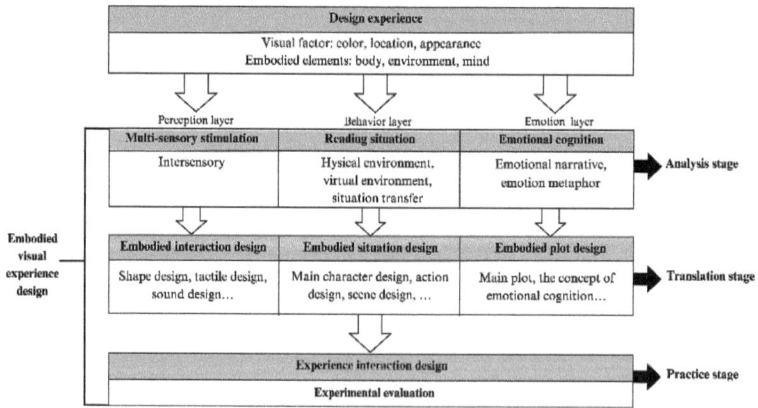

Fig. 2. AR picture book visual design model based on Embodied Cognition

The perception layer integrates multisensory stimuli—specifically visual animations, spatialized auditory cues, and haptic feedback—to prime embodied emotional processing in autistic children. The behavior layer encourages children to participate in learning through body movements. It sets up imitation tasks and action-outcome relationships. It also promotes children's sense of engagement through AR technology interactive tasks by combining real and virtual scenarios. The emotion layer helps children understand the social meaning of emotions by embedding storylines and dynamic feedback. The implementation of the model is divided into three phases: the analysis phase, the translation phase, and the practice phase. These phases progress sequentially to realize the construction of an emotional learning environment.

Considering that autistic children have weaker face recognition abilities than typically developing children, this research picture book focuses on character-centered narratives. It guides autistic children in different scenarios to experience emotional changes alongside the characters. Centered around seven basic emotions—(A) neutral, (B) happy, (C) sad, (D) fearful, (E) angry, (F) surprised, and (G) disgusted—the book utilizes a three-layer interaction model. This creates an immersive emotional learning environment and emotional metaphorical scenarios [12], helping autistic children grasp the social meaning of emotions.

2.2 Analysis of Embodied Experience Design Elements

Through literature research, competitive product research, questionnaires, and user interviews, the embodied experience of picture books is specifically analyzed and divided into three parts: body (multisensory stimulation) elements, environment (reading context) elements, and mind (emotional cognition) elements. Body elements (multisensory stimulation), i.e., the perception layer, constitute the experience for autistic children. The experience includes visual and tactile experience, music, etc. Environment elements (reading context), namely the behavior layer, pertain to the experience of the environment and relationships. The experience encompasses the image of the picture-book protagonist, actions in real-life scenarios, virtual scenarios, etc. Mind elements (emotional cognition), namely the emotion layer, are mainly composed of plots, as well as emotional and cognitive concepts (see Fig. 3).

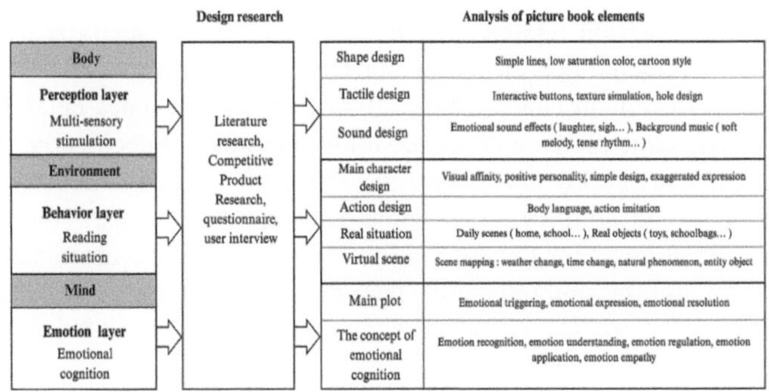

Fig. 3. Analysis of embodied experience elements.

To build an immersive emotional learning environment and enhance the ability of autistic children to recognize emotions and integrate their senses, multisensory stimulation is utilized in analyzing the perception layer. Visually, cartoon-style picture book shapes with clean lines and low-saturated colors are employed. Hand-drawn lines are added to enhance the effect, and tactile experiences, such as interactive buttons, texture simulation, and hole designs, are incorporated. Auditory elements include emotional sound effects, like laughter and sighs, as well as background music ranging from soft melodies to tense rhythms, enriching sensory stimulation. In the behavior layer of the protagonist's character design, key features are parsed. Curly hair and rounded contours with low-saturated colors are used, and facial details are simplified to form a low-sensory-load shape [13]. This design reduces visual stimulus intensity and information processing complexity, enabling autistic children to focus more intently on the emotional visual cues. Through this simplified and gentle visual presentation, children can construct emotional cognition via physical experiences and sensory interactions. This process facilitates the development of emotional understanding and social interaction skills.

2.3   Construction of Embodied Experience Design Element Model

The theory of Embodied Cognition posits that cognitive activity is a dynamic process of interaction between the embodied body and the environment. Within this framework, individuals construct conceptual representations based on bodily experiences, form imagery schemas when perceiving the external world, and develop abstract concepts through metaphorical projection, thereby attaining new insights. In the design of AR emotional picture books, the translation of embodied visual experience design elements is grounded in this theory. To realize this, it is essential to integrate physical experiences with visual elements. This approach enhances children's emotional understanding and engagement through interactive picture book content.

The Conceptual Representation Translation of " Body". Concepts are the cornerstone of cognitive activities and can be divided into concrete and abstract categories. Human perceptual-motor experiences are crucial for forming and developing abstract concepts. Individuals leverage bodily experiences to conceptualize concrete entities [14, 15]. When translating the visual experience of the "body" at the behavior layer, the focus is on transforming emotion-related body movements into imitable visual elements by integrating the aforementioned elements. For instance, guiding children to imitate the body movements of a main character in different emotional states helps them understand the body language corresponding to various emotions. Specifically, based on the captured skeletal data of body movements, the visual elements of characters' body postures are abstracted and simplified to generate corresponding "avatars" (see Fig. 4).This approach not only strengthens the correlation between body movements and emotions but also offers an intuitive and interactive learning medium for autistic children.

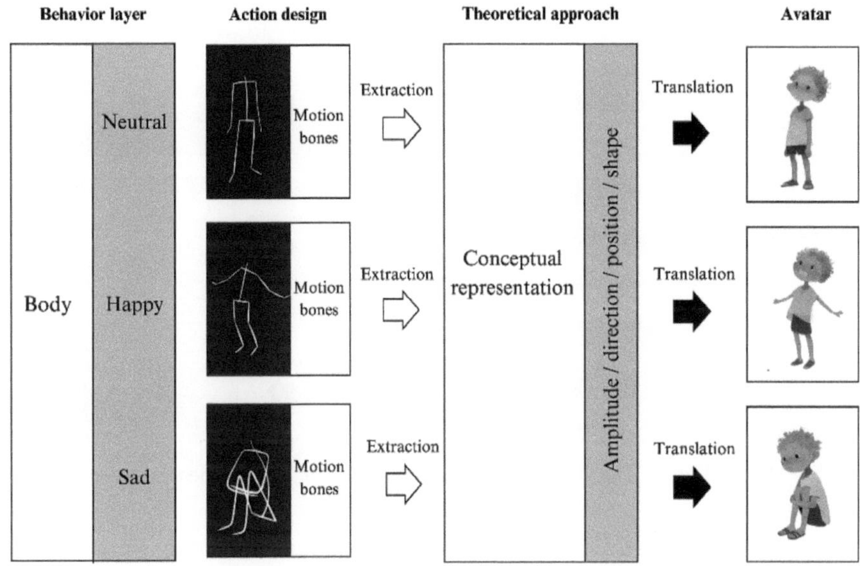

Fig. 4. The visual experience translation of "body"

Image Schema Translation of "Environment". The visual experience translation of "environment" mainly focuses on situation perception and emotion triggering. It aims to help autistic children better understand and recognize emotional changes in different situations by creating immersive scenes. In translation phase, emphasis is placed on mapping virtual scenarios. The study uses elements like weather changes, time changes, natural phenomena, and physical objects to build visual experiences closely tied to emotions. Through this "environment" —based visual experience translation, the picture book combines abstract emotional concepts with concrete scenes and objects. It creates a bridge for autistic children, helping them transfer emotional cognition between virtual and real settings. This enables them to more naturally understand and handle real-life emotional challenges. In practice, the key is a detailed mapping of virtual scenarios. The study skillfully employs various elements, including weather, day and night cycles, natural wonders, and the strategic placement of physical objects, to construct a visual experience that is inherently connected to emotional states (see Fig. 5).

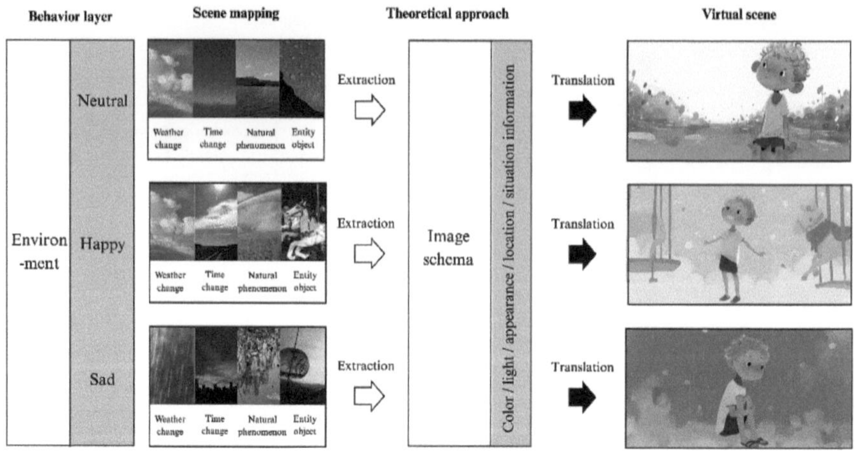

Fig. 5. The visual experience translation of "environment".

By using this innovative means of translation based on the visual experience of "environment", the picture book skillfully connects abstract and elusive emotional concepts with concrete and tangible scenes and objects. It builds a cognitive bridge connecting the virtual world and real life for autistic children. This bridge not only helps them learn and understand emotions in virtual situations but also promotes the flexible transfer of acquired emotional cognition to real life. As a result, they can better cope with real-life emotional challenges and gradually improve their emotional adaptation and coping abilities in real social situations.

Metaphorical Projection Translation of "Mind". The translation of the visual experience of "mind" focuses on the emotional cognition level. Given that emotional cognition involves internal mental processes and is non-visible, this study employs metaphorical projection techniques to translate abstract thoughts, mindsets, ideas, and concepts into concrete visual elements and plot stories (see Fig. 6). Through this translation, autistic children can visually experience these abstract concepts during the interaction. For instance, the use of colors, shapes, and dynamic changes metaphorically represents different emotional states, aiding children in identifying and understanding emotions. The storyline demonstrates the process of emotion triggering, expression, and regulation, which facilitates children's learning and application of emotion regulation strategies. This visual experience translation helps children achieve several goals: first, recognizing their own and others' emotions; second, understanding the causes and backgrounds of emotions; third, mastering effective emotion regulation methods; fourth, learning to appropriately apply emotion knowledge in different situations; and fifth, developing empathy for others' emotions. Through these specific visual presentations and interactive experiences, autistic children can develop their emotional and cognitive abilities in a more comprehensive manner.

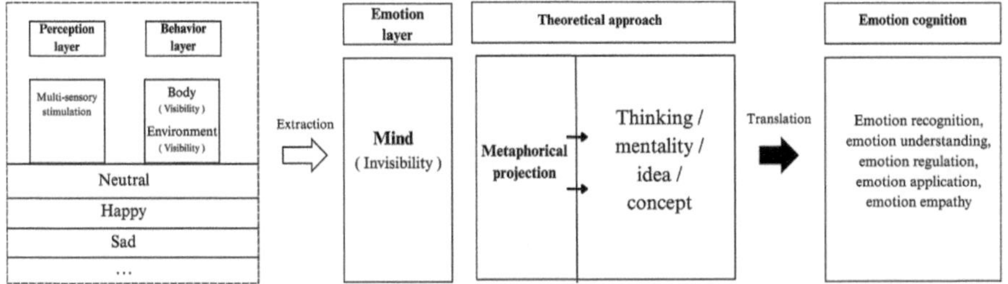

Fig. 6. The visual experience translation of "mind"

2.4   Construction of Embodied Experience Design Element Model

Based on the three-layer interaction model of the embodied cognition theory-driven emotional picture book with AR, to realize its application in emotion intervention for autistic children, the study has designed a specific process for using the picture book. This process includes four parts: story guidance, emotion expression, emotion resolution, and emotion communication. Taking the emotion of sadness as an example (see Fig. 7).

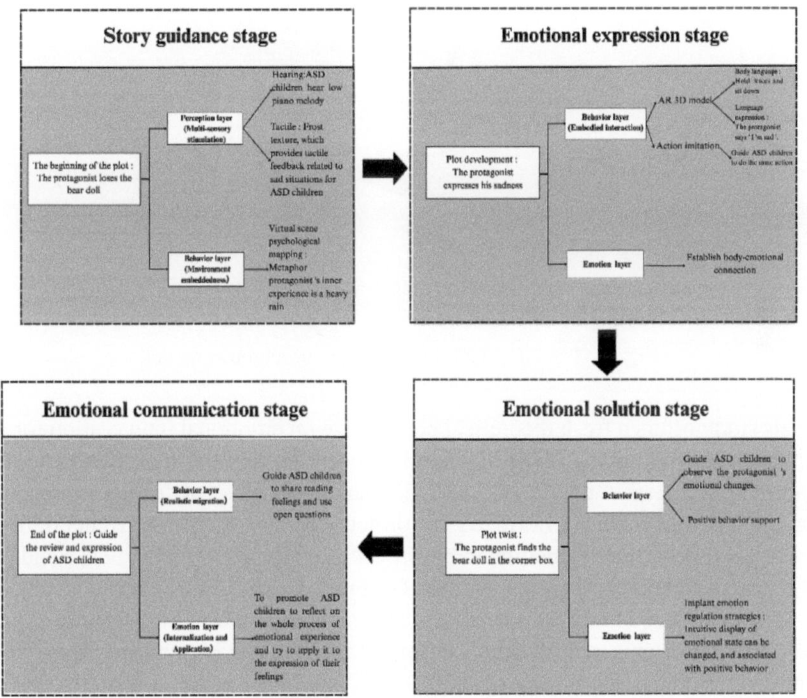

Fig. 7. Picture book usage process: an example with sadness.

Based on this process, the study further carried out experimental design and evaluation to verify the effectiveness of the picture book process in enhancing the emotion recognition ability of autistic children.

3   Result

In this study, the interaction effect of embodied experience is mainly realized with the help of AR technology. The study constructed a 3D model of the protagonist and configured corresponding action expressions for different emotional states (see Fig. 8). With the help of AR technology, the 3D protagonist could be seamlessly integrated with the real-world scene. This allows autistic children to observe in real time the subtle body changes of the protagonist under various emotions and practice imitation. This interactive approach, which integrates realistic scenes, not only enhances children's ability to identify the physiological and behavioral patterns associated with emotions but also helps them gain a deeper understanding of their own and others' emotional states.

Fig. 8. The AR effect display of the protagonist model.

This study offers a fresh theoretical perspective on emotional intervention for autistic children and validates its feasibility and efficacy through practice. Conducted at the Rehabilitation Center of the East Campus of Huazhong University of Science and Technology, the research team prioritized the protection of participants' rights during the study's design and implementation to ensure its scientific rigor and ethical standards.

For the evaluation results, the System Usability Scale (SUS) was used as the main assessment tool to quantitatively analyze the design outcomes. The questionnaire comprises 10 scoring items, scored from 1 (strongly disagree) to 5 (strongly agree), yielding a combined usability score ranging from 0 to 100, with a sample size of 20. The study results indicate that the AR illustrated book achieved an SUS score of 72.1. Referring to the SUS score classification in the literature, scores above 71.4 are rated as "GOOD," while scores above 50.9 are rated as "OK". This shows that the AR Picture Book is well-recognized by users for its ease of operation, interface friendliness, and functionality, demonstrating a significant advantage in enhancing the user's emotional experience and interaction effect. Meanwhile, this study recorded the behavioral changes of children before and after using AR picture books through behavioral observation. During the 3-week intervention (three sessions per week), researchers documented specific changes in children's social interactions, such as increased eye contact and more proactive collaborative behaviors. Additionally, interviews with guardians and healthcare professionals provided further qualitative data on children's emotional improvements. Observations revealed improvements in collaborative behavior and emotional regulation. However, due to individual differences among children, longer-term observations and feedback from diverse sources are required to confirm the effectiveness.

In summary, through analyzing the survey data on the real-experience feedback of the participants, combined with behavioral observation records, the practical effect of the innovative visual design of AR emotional picture books is verified, reflecting the feasibility and innovation of AR emotional picture book design based on Embodied Cognition Theory.

4 Discussion

The integration of Embodied Cognition Theory and AR technology has resulted in a three-layer progressive AR emotion recognition picture book design framework. This framework innovatively combines body movements with multimodal interactions, thereby realizing the embodied learning experience of emotion recognition. The study breaks from the limitations of conventional intervention methodologies in its theoretical approach. Its innovative methodology, which involves constructing hierarchical models, fosters a more robust and natural link between emotional cognition and behavior. This theoretical framework provides a more intuitive and natural basis for emotion recognition. From a technical standpoint, the system's dynamic adaptation mechanism and AR multisensory feedback, encompassing visual, auditory, and tactile components, enable real-time adjustments based on the user's unique interactive behaviors. This functionality facilitates a customized and stress-reduced immersive learning experience for autistic children, thereby enhancing their learning outcomes and engagement. In practical applications, social story narratives and scenario-based designs improve the accuracy of emotion recognition and social engagement in autistic children. This provides effective support for the emotional expression and interaction of autistic children in real-life social situations. This framework not only validates the efficacy of Embodied Cognition Theory in emotion intervention but also offers novel concepts and methodologies for the implementation of AR technology in the domain of special education.

5 Conclusion

The findings of the study demonstrate the efficacy of the method in enhancing the emotion recognition capacity of autistic children. This study innovatively integrated Embodied Cognition Theory and AR technology to propose a new emotion guidance method. This method provides a more intuitive, interactive, and immersive learning experience for autistic children. In comparison with conventional interventions, this approach overcomes its limitations and fosters a natural and engaging learning environment for autistic children. This study presents novel theoretical, technological, and practical approaches to the field, thereby transitioning research from a traditional model to a more interactive and effective one. The research will focus on further optimizing the methodology by incorporating personalization elements and artificial intelligence techniques. The aim of this incorporation is to enable more accurate real-time feedback, thereby enhancing the effectiveness of the intervention. The study will also examine the potential application of the method in the broader field of special education and conduct long-term effect-tracking studies to further enhance its effectiveness in the rehabilitation and education of autistic children. It is anticipated that these research efforts will contribute to a tangible enhancement in the quality of life for autistic children, thereby facilitating the development of their social skills and emotional well-being.

Acknowledgments. This research was supported by the 2025 Huazhong University of Science and Technology Self-Innovation Fund: Research on Wearable Design for Children with Autism(2025WKQN028)

Disclosure of Interests. The authors have no competing interests to declare that are relevant to the content of this article.

References

1. Vahia, V.N.: Diagnostic and statistical manual of mental disorders 5: a quick glance. Indian J. Psychiatry **55**(3), 220–223 (2013)
2. Issac, A., Halemani, K., Shetty, A., et al.: The global prevalence of autism spectrum disorder in children: a systematic review and meta-analysis. Osong Public Health Res. Perspect. **16**(1), 3–27 (2025)
3. Wolfe, K., Pound, S., McCammon, M.N., et al.: A systematic review of interventions to promote varied social-communication behavior in individuals with autism spectrum disorder. Behav. Modif. **43**(6), 790–818 (2019)
4. Saulnier, C.A., Klaiman, C., McQueen, E.: Adaptive behavior profiles in autism spectrum disorder. Curr. Psychiatry Rep. **24**(12), 749–756 (2022)
5. Garcia-Garcia, J.M., Penichet, V.M.R., Lozano, M.D., et al.: Using emotion recognition technologies to teach children with autism spectrum disorder how to identify and express emotions. Univ. Access Inf. Soc. **21**(4), 809–825 (2022)
6. Sepahvandi, S., Hojjatollah, H.: Investigating the effect of storytelling with role playing methods on communication and social skills of children with autism. Yafteh **21**(1) (2019)
7. Cai, R.Y., Richdale, A.L., Uljarević, M., et al.: Emotion regulation in autism spectrum disorder: where we are and where we need to go. Autism Res. **11**(7), 962–978 (2018)
8. Niedenthal, P.M., Barsalou, L.W., Winkielman, P., et al.: Embodiment in attitudes, social perception, and emotion. Pers. Soc. Psychol. Rev. **9**(3), 184–211 (2005)
9. Landau, M.J., Meier, B.P., Keefer, L.A.: A metaphor-enriched social cognition. Psychol. Bull. **136**(6), 1045–1067 (2010)
10. Varela, F., Thompson, E., Rosch, E.: Embodied Mind The Embodied Mind : Cognitive Science and Human Experience, 1st edn. MIT Press, Cambridge (1992)
11. Song, Y., Cui, J.: Embodied cognition and embodied learning design. Educ. Dev. Res **41**, 74–81 (2021)

12. Zembylas, M.: Emotion metaphors and emotional labor in science teaching. Sci. Educ. **88**(3), 301–324 (2004)
13. Yeung, M.K.: A systematic review and meta-analysis of facial emotion recognition in autism spectrum disorder: the specificity of deficits and the role of task characteristics. Neurosci. Biobehav. Rev. **133**, 104518 (2022)
14. Barsalou, L.W.: Perceptual symbol systems. Behav. Brain Sci. **22**(4), 577–660 (1999)
15. Zhang, E.T., Fang, J., Lin, W.Y., et al.: Embodied views of abstract concepts representation. Adv. Psychol. Sci. **21**(3), 429–436 (2013)

Prototyping Interfaces for Autistic People: The Role of GuideAut as Support for the ProAut Process

Áurea Melo[1]([⊠]) [iD], Diego Lopes[1] [iD], Danielle Valente[1] [iD],
Jonathas S. dos Santos[1,2] [iD], Luis Rivero[3] [iD], and Raimundo Barreto[2] [iD]

[1] Universidade Do Estado Do Amazonas (UEA), Manaus, AM, Brazil
`{asmelo,diml.eng,dvalente,jssantos}@uea.edu.br`
[2] Universidade Federal Do Amazonas (UFAM), Manaus, AM, Brazil
`rbarreto@icomp.ufam.edu.br`
[3] Universidade Federal Do Maranhão (UFMA), São Luís - MA, Brazil
`luisrivero@nca.ufma.br`

Abstract. The development of accessible interfaces for autistic people requires specialized knowledge and structured processes that are often scattered across literature. This work presents GuideAut, a web platform that provides access to the ProAut process—a structured methodology for prototyping application interfaces for autistic users. GuideAut not only offers access to the phases and activities of ProAut but also provides automated tools for generating essential Human-Computer Interaction artifacts, such as personas (PersonAut) and empathy maps (EmpathyAut), as well as a repository of collaborative recommendations. The platform was evaluated by 14 participants using the Technology Acceptance Model (TAM), showing excellent results in terms of perceived usefulness (86.7%) and ease of use (80%). The results indicate that GuideAut effectively supports interface designers and developers in creating more inclusive applications for autistic users, while also highlighting areas for improvement in user experience and mobile responsiveness.

Keywords: Human-Computer Interaction · Autism Spectrum Disorder · Interface Design · Prototyping Tools · Accessibility · Collaborative Platform

1 Introduction

The design of user interfaces for people with Autism Spectrum Disorder (ASD) presents unique challenges that require an in-depth understanding of sensory preferences, communication patterns, and interaction behaviors. Traditional design approaches often fail to consider these specificities, resulting in applications that are overwhelming, confusing, or inaccessible to this audience.

In the field of Human-Computer Interaction (HCI), there is growing recognition of the importance of inclusive design practices. However, a significant gap persists between

© The Author(s), under exclusive license to Springer Nature Switzerland AG 2026
M. Antona and C. Stephanidis (Eds.): HCII 2025, LNCS 16335, pp. 308–320, 2026.
https://doi.org/10.1007/978-3-032-12781-5_21

theoretical knowledge about autism and the availability of practical tools that systematically guide the development of accessible interfaces. Designers and developers struggle to access consolidated guidelines and structured processes focused on this context. Many projects begin with isolated actions, such as interviews with caregivers or field observations, but often lack organized methodologies that support designers and developers throughout all phases of the creation process.

To fill this gap, ProAut was proposed, a process based on Design Thinking, with specific artifacts, such as personas and empathy maps, adapted to the reality of autistic people [1]. Despite its methodological robustness, the widespread adoption of ProAut has been limited by its complexity and the absence of a mechanism that integrates its steps and tools in an accessible way. These factors highlighted the need for a digital platform that makes ProAut more accessible and provides integrated tools for generating crucial HCI artifacts.

This article presents **GuideAut**, a web platform that computerizes ProAut and expands its capabilities by offering support for building central HCI artifacts, such as PersonAut [2] and EmpathyAut [3] The platform also enables collaborative sharing and evaluation of design recommendations, promoting the dissemination of structured knowledge among professionals in the field.

By connecting user-centered design practices with the particularities of autism, GuideAut contributes to bridging the gap between theory and practice in the development of inclusive technologies. This work describes the platform's functionalities, its foundation in HCI principles, and the results of its evaluation with 14 users, demonstrating its potential as a support tool for creating more accessible interfaces for individuals with autism.

2 Background

2.1 Human-Computer Interaction and Autistic Person-Centered Design

Human-Computer Interaction is a field that seeks to understand and improve interactions between people and computational systems, having user-centered design as its central principle. This approach proposes that users' needs, limitations, and contexts should be the starting point for all design decisions [4]. However, when the target audience includes people with disabilities, such as those with ASD, applying this approach requires significant adaptations.

Individuals with autism present heterogeneous profiles, exhibiting significant variations in sensory, communication, and behavioral aspects. These specificities challenge conventional design strategies and require developers to adopt more empathetic practices based on active listening, contextualized data, and deep understanding of users. Elements such as visual overload, intense auditory stimuli, or unpredictable interfaces can significantly compromise usability for this audience.

In this scenario, autistic person-centered design emerges as a specialized branch within HCI, which seeks not only to adapt interfaces but to understand them from the experiences of those who will use them. Principles such as predictability, simplicity, consistency, and user control gain relevance, and the design process begins to incorporate specific techniques and tools to capture these needs—such as creating adapted personas, empathy maps, and iterative testing with real users or their representatives [2, 3].

Considering the complexity of this context, it becomes essential to structure processes and environments that guide development teams in applying these principles in a systematic and accessible manner, as proposed by ProAut.

2.2 Autism Spectrum Disorder and Interface Design

Autism Spectrum Disorder is characterized by persistent deficits in communication and social interaction, in addition to the presence of restricted, repetitive, and inflexible behavioral patterns [5]. These characteristics manifest from childhood and impact various areas of individuals' lives, including social, educational, and occupational aspects. According to [6], the main challenges faced by autistic people can be grouped into three axes: difficulties in social interaction, communication deficits, and restricted behavioral patterns and interests.

When designing interfaces for individuals with autism, it is essential to recognize how these cognitive and sensory traits influence digital interactions. Rather than applying conventional design rules, developers must address a distinct set of usability demands. For instance, autistic users often require environments with high levels of consistency, low sensory stimulation, and structured tasks. As [7] suggest, systems tailored for this population should prioritize predictability and reduce ambiguity in navigation and feedback.

Research in this area has identi'fied specific design considerations for autistic users, including preferences for specific color schemes, the careful use of geometric shapes and visual representations, and the need to avoid elements that may cause sensory overload [8]. These authors conducted an empirical analysis of software designed for autistic audiences. They identified significant usability deficits, indicating the need for interfaces that are more adaptable to the particularities of the autism spectrum.

2.3 Design Processes for Accessibility

Accessibility in interface design goes beyond simple compliance with technical standards—it involves understanding and meeting the real needs of people with different profiles, abilities, and contexts. In the field of HCI, this translates to adopting inherently inclusive design processes that incorporate specific guidelines from the project's initial phases.

Several models and frameworks have been proposed to guide the development of accessible interfaces, such as Universal Design [9], Inclusive Design [10], and Participatory Design [11]. These models share the premise that accessibility should be incorporated from the beginning of the design process, prioritizing active user participation and adapting solutions to different usage profiles.

In the context of ASD, this need is even more evident. Studies show that conventional requirement gathering approaches often fail to capture essential aspects of autistic people's experiences, such as sensory hypersensitivity, preference for routines, and specific visual patterns [8]. As a consequence, well-intentioned applications fail to offer truly accessible experiences. Therefore, some digital platforms have emerged to support accessibility-focused design, but most of them provide static guidelines rather than dynamic and process-oriented support. [12] developed Gaia, an open-source website that gathers web accessibility recommendations for individuals with ASD, assisting developers in creating more accessible interfaces. However, their guidelines are static and do not allow collaboration between users.

The lack of integrated tools for generating autism-specific design artifacts represents a significant gap in the current HCI toolkit. This gap motivated the development of solutions that can not only centralize existing knowledge but also facilitate the creation of new design artifacts in a systematic and collaborative manner.

Structured processes, such as ProAut, were developed precisely to fill this gap. Based on Design Thinking principles, ProAut organizes the development of interfaces for autistic people into five phases—Immersion, Analysis, Ideation, Prototyping, and Evaluation—and proposes the creation of specific artifacts, such as empathy maps and adapted personas [13]. These artifacts help design teams internalize the perspectives and needs of the target audience, promoting more adequate and autistic person-centered solutions [1].

Despite its methodological robustness, applying these processes manually can be challenging, especially for teams with little prior accessibility knowledge. This difficulty reinforces the importance of tools that automate or guide their application, expanding the reach and effectiveness of inclusive practices in HCI.

2.4 Digital Tools for Design Support

Digital tools have played a fundamental role in supporting user-centered design processes, particularly in promoting accessibility and inclusion. In the context of Human-Computer Interaction, various solutions have been developed to assist project teams in collecting, organizing, and applying data centered on the needs of users with diverse profiles, including people with cognitive disabilities or neurodivergences.

The use of platforms that structure design stages, automate artifact generation, and promote collaboration between teams has grown in recent years. Studies such as those by [14] and [15] discuss the importance of digital environments that systematize empathic data collection, improve design decision documentation, and facilitate process replicability.

These tools prove especially useful in complex contexts, such as ASD, where direct access to users may be limited and needs are highly individualized. By enabling the creation and reuse of artifacts such as empathy maps, personas, and requirement models based on specific profiles, these solutions contribute to a more grounded and efficient design.

GuideAut fits into this panorama as a platform that not only digitizes the ProAut process but also incorporates specific functionalities to support the creation of HCI artifacts aimed at the autistic population. By organizing the process into phases and allowing the sharing and evaluation of recommendations, GuideAut strengthens the practice of collaborative and neurodiversity-centered design. This approach reinforces the trend observed in conferences like HCI International, which have promoted studies focused on using digital platforms to systematize empathic and accessible design practices.

3   Methodology

The development of the GuideAut platform followed an incremental and iterative process structured in four main phases: preliminary studies, requirements and functionality definition, development, and evaluation. This methodological approach was guided by HCI principles and combined literature review, user-centered requirements engineering, user experience (UX) design, and usability evaluation to ensure the platform's effectiveness as a support tool for designing inclusive interfaces for autistic people, with a primary focus on professionals who develop these solutions.

The first phase focused on the detailed analysis of the ProAut process and on defining the resources that would be implemented in the initial version of the platform. The analysis aimed to understand the structure of ProAut, including its phases, artifacts, and guidelines, and translate this understanding into an interactive digital experience designed for developers and designers of interfaces for individuals with autism. This stage involved identifying the most strategic elements for initial inclusive design support, leading to the decision to implement the ProAut tutorial, the recommendations repository, and the interface patterns module, called DPAut [16].

Based on these inputs, we defined the platform requirements and categorized them into functional and non-functional. The MoSCoW prioritization technique [17] was applied to guide the selection of essential functionalities for the initial version. We prioritize delivering a functional core, focusing on resources that provide direct support for the practical application of ProAut while reserving collaborative functionalities and future expansions for later phases.

The development phase was conducted based on iterative cycles aligned with Design Thinking. The process included modeling the information architecture, defining interaction flows, and prototyping interfaces with a focus on navigation consistency and accessibility. The implementation used cross-platform technologies (Flutter, Firebase, and Firestore), aiming for flexibility, scalability, and compatibility with different devices.

Finally, we conducted the evaluation stage using a mixed-method approach to assess the usability and user experience of the GuideAut platform. We applied the Technology Acceptance Model (TAM) [18, 19] to gather empirical data on users' perceptions of ease of use and usefulness. In parallel, we performed a heuristic inspection based on Nielsen's usability principles. This combined strategy enabled us to collect both quantitative feedback from end-users and qualitative insights from expert analysis, providing a comprehensive understanding of the platform's effectiveness and areas for improvement.

4   GuideAut Platform

GuideAut is a web platform designed to automate the ProAut process and increase its accessibility to professionals in technology, education, and health who develop digital solutions for autistic individuals. By centralizing information, artifacts, and recommendations in a structured environment, the platform facilitates the organization and continuity of the design process, thereby overcoming the limitations observed in the manual application of ProAut.

Conceived under HCI principles, GuideAut adopts a modular architecture that aims to optimize user experience, facilitate access to content, and promote empathic and collaborative design practices. Among its main features, the following stand out: the access to ProAut phases, assisted construction of artifacts such as PersonAut and EmpathyAut (both in the integration phase), insertion and validation of design recommendations, and support for collaborative evaluation of shared guidelines. PersonAut enables the creation of autism-adapted personas based on user inputs and consolidated literature data, and EmpathyAut is responsible for generating empathy maps contextualized for autistic user experiences.

The GuideAut Platform also operates as a dynamic knowledge repository, centralizing design recommendations and best practices extracted from both academic literature and professional experiences. This is particularly relevant in a field where guidelines are still scattered across multiple sources and disciplines. The platform's library gathers validated interface design patterns—including recommendations on color schemes, navigation structures, visual hierarchies, and interaction design principles—all focused on the experience of autistic people [16]. Figure 1 presents GuideAut's main interface, highlighting the initial navigation options and access to primary resources, such as the ProAut tutorial, artifacts, the recommendations repository, and Design Patterns (DPAut).

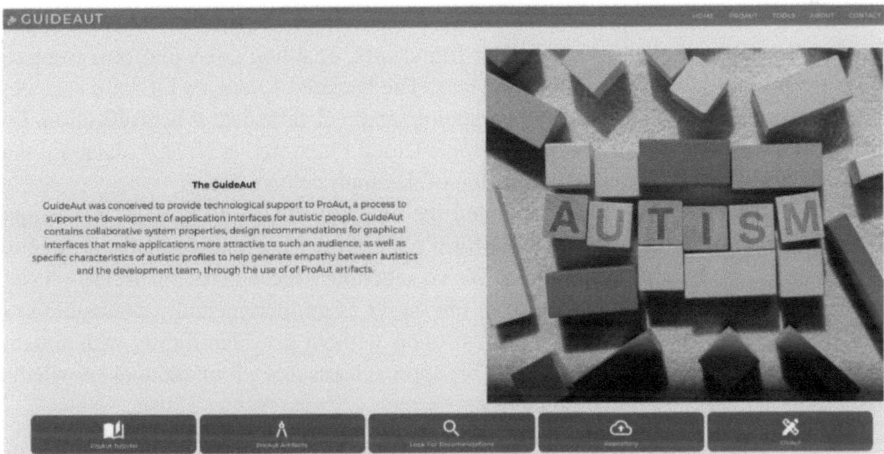

Fig. 1. GuideAut home page showing the main navigation and access to platform features.

Another central component of the platform is its collaborative environment, which allows the sharing and evaluation of recommendations based on real project experiences. Users can register new recommendations and consult and evaluate contributions from other professionals, forming a collective learning ecosystem. This space strengthens the continuous production of knowledge in neurodiversity-centered design and expands the potential for reusing successful solutions. Figure 2 presents the platform's interface for listing and classifying recommendations, illustrating how users can view, evaluate, and prioritize shared guidelines. Additional screenshots, including those of artifact creation and user management resources, will be presented in future publications. Additional screenshots, including those of artifact creation and user management resources, will be presented in future publications as we fully implement these functionalities.

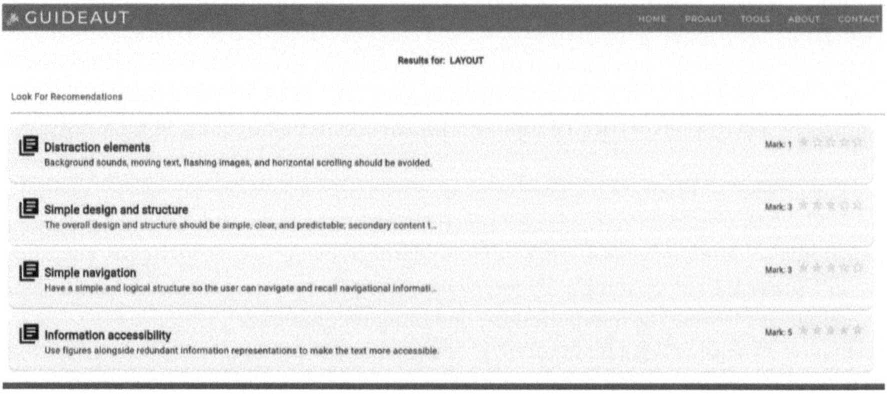

Fig. 2. Interface with the list of recommendations and their respective user comments (rating feature).

From a technical perspective, the platform uses a modern client-server architecture. We developed the client with the Flutter framework, enabling cross-platform compatibility for both browsers and mobile devices. The backend leverages Firebase services, which ensure scalability, secure authentication, and real-time data synchronization. For information storage, the system uses Google Cloud Firestore—a NoSQL database that offers flexibility and efficient organization of the application's data.

Although we've already implemented the empathy tools—PersonAut and EmpathyAut—integrating them into the platform's main interface and formally evaluating them with users remains incomplete. We've scheduled these tasks for future phases. Therefore, we designed GuideAut from the outset as an incrementally extensible system, initially focusing on enabling professionals without prior familiarity with autism-specific methodologies to use ProAut. This approach ensures a foundational knowledge base, usability, and structured processes.

We must note that our team hasn't yet evaluated the platform with individuals who are autistic. Although we designed GuideAut primarily for design and development professionals, we acknowledge that autistic users may occasionally use the platform—especially for self-representation or developing applications for their community. However, our research currently faces practical difficulties in recruiting enough participants from this demographic for validation.

Additionally, we emphasize that while our team initially developed GuideAut for researchers, educators, and students in academic projects, its industrial application potential continues to grow. Global ASD prevalence rates show consistent increases: recent CDC data reveals that clinicians now diagnose autism in 1 of every 31 U.S. children aged 8 years in 2022 [20]. This trend underscores the critical need for accessible, adapted technologies. Given this context, we anticipate growing industry interest in developing solutions for this demographic, which should expand GuideAut's scope into professional and commercial environments.

5 Evaluation

Our team conducted a usability evaluation of GuideAut to identify strengths and opportunities for improvement in the user experience, specifically for its target audience: designers and developers creating accessible interfaces for autistic individuals. We implemented two complementary approaches: an empirical user evaluation and a Nielsen heuristic-based inspection.

The study involved 14 participants with expertise in interface design, software development, or digital accessibility. We collected data using a Technology Acceptance Model (TAM) questionnaire, which measured perceived usefulness and ease of use. Results showed strong acceptance rates: 86.7% of participants agreed the platform effectively supports understanding and applying the ProAut process, while 80% rated it as user-friendly.

We designed the evaluation instrument around the core constructs of the TAM, encompassing four sections: participant profile, perceived ease of use, perceived usefulness, and behavioral intention to use the platform. We also included an open-ended field to capture qualitative feedback and suggestions for improvement. Participants rated each statement on a five-point Likert scale. For analytical clarity, responses later fell into two categories: favorable ("Strongly Agree" and "Agree") and non-favorable ("Neutral," "Disagree," and "Strongly Disagree"). This dichotomization strategy, widely applied in user experience research, facilitates the identification of broader patterns in user acceptance and overall perceptions.

Beyond quantitative data, we invited participants to suggest improvements. Key recommendations highlighted mobile interface responsiveness issues and the lack of visual feedback for actions such as submitting recommendations and completing forms. These insights directly guided our interface refinements, including real-time field validation and responsive screen adaptation.

Participants expressed a positive perception regarding the platform's ease of use. Eight of ten respondents described the interface as intuitive and easy to navigate. Many highlighted the ProAut tutorial as a well-organized and helpful feature for understanding the process. Despite these favorable impressions, some users pointed out usability limitations. More than half (53.3%) encountered difficulties during the registration process, mainly due to missing field validation and lack of real-time feedback. Others mentioned challenges in identifying how to submit recommendations and noted limited responsiveness on mobile devices. Figure 4 summarizes these usability observations.

The evaluation also revealed strong perceptions of usefulness. According to the data colleted, 80% of participants acknowledged that the platform delivers valuable content for designing accessible interfaces and contributes to deepening their understanding of the topic. Furthermore, 86.7% stated that GuideAut helps clarify the steps and artifacts involved in the ProAut methodology. The Recommendation Module stood out as the most well-received feature, with all respondents evaluating it positively. Specifically, 88% selected "Strongly Agree," and the remaining 12% chose "Agree," reinforcing its importance in guiding inclusive design decisions.

According to the data illustrated in Fig. 3, a total of 79% of participants indicated a clear intention to continue engaging with GuideAut in future interface design activities. This figure consolidates responses across high, moderate, and general interest levels (29%, 14%, and 36%, respectively). From a Human-Computer Interaction perspective, this behavioral intention reflects the platform's perceived alignment with users' workflows and its ability to support inclusive design tasks. The most frequently cited features contributing to this intent included the structured ProAut tutorial, the collaborative recommendation repository, advanced search capabilities, and integrated evaluation tools. These components collectively enhanced the system's perceived task relevance and supported a positive user experience across different stages of the design process.

Level of Interest in Using the GuidAut Platform

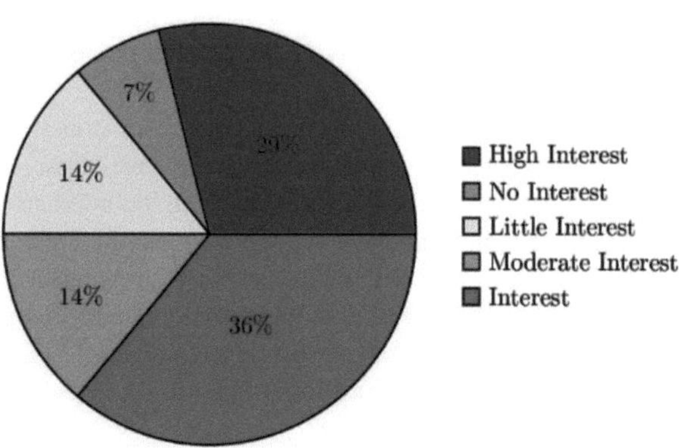

Fig. 3. Intention to use the GuideAut platform.

Participants performed a supplementary heuristic inspection using Jakob Nielsen's 10 usability principles [21]. Table 1 presents the results of this inspection.

Combining empirical evaluation and heuristic inspection yielded comprehensive insights. Users welcomed GuideAut's usability and utility while highlighting specific refinements we have completed or are currently implementing. This iterative process reinforces our commitment to accessibility and inclusive design for autistic users. Qualitative feedback highlighted key strengths, including the tutorial system, intuitive interface, logical process flow, and recommendation utility. Participants also proposed specific enhancements: making tutorials more dynamic, improving mobile responsiveness, strengthening registration validations, and expanding functionality descriptions.

Table 1. Table captions should be placed above the tables.

Heuristic	Evaluation Result
1. System status visibility	The platform displays ProAut phase progression; however, our initial version omitted visual confirmations for actions such as recommendation submissions, which we later added.
2. Match with the real world	Technical terminology (personas, empathy maps, prototyping) aligns well with the target audience's language.
3. User control freedom	While ProAut phase navigation is intuitive, evaluators recommended adding "back" options in internal interfaces, particularly the artifacts module.
4. Consistency standards	Coherent visual and interaction patterns support learnability and continuous use.
5. Error prevention	We identified mandatory field validation gaps in forms and implemented fixes in subsequent versions.
6. Recognition over recall	Self-explanatory menus and icons, along with clear phase descriptions, minimize memory load.
7. Flexibility efficiency	The platform serves novices well but currently lacks advanced features (e.g., batch editing, recommendation customization) for experts.
8. Aesthetic minimalism	Clean visuals prioritize readability, with strategic use of color and spacing that enhances the overall experience.
9. Error recovery	We are reviewing generic error messages for more precise user guidance.
10. Help documentation	Tutorials and videos are available, but we plan to expand our contextual help content.

6 Discussion

The evaluation results indicate that GuideAut effectively addresses core challenges in designing interfaces for autistic audiences. The high approval rate for perceived usefulness (86.7%) suggests that the platform provides significant practical value, bridging the gap in applying accessible, specialized methodologies for inclusive design. The 80% ease-of-use assessment reinforces that the interface maintains low frustration levels and smooth interactions.

Providing the ProAut process through the platform represents a relevant advancement by making structured prototyping models accessible—models that traditionally required prior knowledge of accessibility and autism. GuideAut's interface provides clear guidance, step-by-step resources, and integration with tools like PersonAut and EmpathyAut, enabling the practical application of HCI principles even for users with limited prior knowledge of the topic.

Our heuristic analysis, based on Nielsen's 10 principles, complemented empirical data by revealing specific areas for improvement and validating the applied design principles. We identified key strengths, including interface consistency, clear and understandable language, alignment with user mental models, and transparent visibility of system status. However, evaluators noted limitations regarding mobile responsiveness and insufficient feedback for actions like data submissions and user registration. Our improvement plan prioritizes these areas, focusing on the implementation of real-time validation and the adaptation of multi-resolution displays.

GuideAut's automated tools—PersonAut and EmpathyAut—deserve emphasis for democratizing the creation of typical HCI artifacts. Traditionally, building personas and empathy maps for autistic individuals requires deep ASD knowledge and user research experience. The platform lowers this barrier by operationalizing these artifacts through guided inputs, expanding access to user-centered practices in inclusive contexts.

Furthermore, the platform's collaborative aspect fosters a dynamic knowledge base, enabling community-driven sharing and validation of recommendations. This dimension strengthens our vision for a living, evolving repository with the potential to consolidate best practices and promote the exchange of professional experiences.

Limitations identified during the evaluation provide clear directions for future development, including optimizing mobile experiences, improving registration flows, and enhancing error messages. A critical gap remains the absence of validation with autistic users. Although developers and designers constitute the primary audience, future evaluations must incorporate autistic perspectives, especially those involved in creating solutions for their community (e.g., autistic designers/developers). This validation would strengthen results and further align the platform with diversity-centered design principles.

7 Conclusion

GuideAut represents a significant advancement in supporting HCI professionals who develop accessible interfaces for individuals on the autism spectrum. The platform bridges the gap between theoretical neurodiversity knowledge and inclusive design practices by offering an integrated solution that combines structured visualization of the ProAut process, automated tools for generating specialized artifacts, and a collaborative repository of applicable recommendations.

The evaluation results reinforce the proposal's relevance and applicability. High approval rates for perceived usefulness (86.7%) and ease of use (80%) demonstrate that GuideAut meets the target audience's expectations, delivering functionalities that are both effective and accessible. This recognition suggests that the platform concretely contributes to professional practice, especially in contexts that require sensitivity to specific needs, such as ASD.

Beyond delivering operational tools, GuideAut's primary contribution lies in establishing a collaborative, systematized paradigm for neurodiversity-centered design. By democratizing access to specialized HCI methodologies and artifacts, the platform enables professionals with diverse experience levels to consolidate a shared knowledge base. This model offers a replicable standard for other specific-need areas within HCI.

The limitations we identified during the evaluation process—such as mobile responsiveness, registration experience, and lack of direct validation with autistic individuals—clearly guide future enhancements. Our continuous feedback cycles have already demonstrated a positive impact, reinforcing the platform's potential to evolve into a reference resource within the digital accessibility-focused HCI community.

The approach's success validates the importance of specialized tools connecting academic research with professional practice. Although the platform currently serves teaching and research contexts more, growing neurodiversity awareness and rising ASD prevalence point toward expanded use in industrial and corporate environments.

As the next steps, we plan to completely integrate the PersonAut and EmpathyAut modules into the main interface, launch the 'My Projects' feature for personalized workflow management, and enhance mobile experience. Crucially, we also plan validation studies with autistic professionals—especially those developing inclusive solutions—and indirect assessments with autistic individuals who are end-users. These initiatives aim to establish GuideAut as a reference tool in inclusive design, contributing to a more accessible, participatory, and equitable digital technology ecosystem.

Acknowledgments. The authors are grateful for the support of the Amazonas State University (UEA) and the UEA Center for Research in Applied Computing and Digital Health (HealthTech) in publishing these results.

Disclosure of Interests. The authors have no competing interests to declare that are relevant to the content of this article.

References

1. Melo, A.H.D.S.: ProAut: um processo para apoiar a prototipação de interfaces de aplicações para autistas. Tese (Doutorado) – Universidade Federal do Amazonas (2021)
2. Melo, Á.H.D.S., Rivero, L., Santos, J.S.D., Barreto, R.D.S.: PersonAut: a personas model for people with autism spectrum disorder. In: 19th Brazilian Symposium on Human Factors in Computing Systems, pp. 1–6. SBC (2020)
3. Melo, Á.H.D.S., Rivero, L., Santos, J.S.D., Barreto, R.D.S.: EmpathyAut: an empathy map for people with autism. In: 19th Brazilian Symposium on Human Factors in Computing Systems, pp. 1–6. SBC (2020)
4. Norman, D.A.: The design of Everyday Things: Revised and, Expanded Basic Books, New York (2013)
5. American Psychiatric Association: Diagnostic and statistical manual of mental disorders (DSM-5®), 5th edn. American Psychiatric Association Publishing, Arlington, TX (2013)
6. Klin, A.: Autismo e síndrome de asperger: uma visão geral. Rev. Brasileira de Psiquiatria **28**(1), s3–s11. Editora Scientific (2006)
7. Parsons, S., Leonard, A., Mitchell, P.: Virtual environments for social skills training: comments from two adolescents with autistic spectrum disorder. Comput. Educ. **47**(2), 186–206. Elsevier BV (2006)
8. Sousa, F.R.M., Costa, E.A.B., Castro, T.H.C. de.: Worldtour: Software para suporte no ensino de crianças autistas. In: Simpósio Brasileiro de Informática na Educação-SBIE, vol. 23, no. 1. SBC (2012)
9. Mace, R.: Universal design in housing. Assist. Technol. **10**(1), 21–28 (1998)
10. Clarkson, P.J., et al.: Inclusive Design: Design for the Whole Population. Springer Science & Business Media, London (2013)
11. Schuler, D., Namioka, A.: Participatory Design: Principles and Practices. Lawrence Erlbaum Associates, Hillsdale, NJ (1993)
12. Britto, T.C.P., Pizzolato, E.B.: Gaia: uma proposta de um guia de recomendações de acessibilidade de interfaces web com foco em aspectos do autismo. Rev. Brasileira de Informática na Educação **26**(02), 102 (2018)
13. Melo, A., et al.: Desenvolvimento de uma aplicação educativa para o ensino derotinas diárias e quebra de rotinas a crianças Autistas. Rev. Novas Tecnologias na Educação **19**(1), 166–175 (2021)

14. Derboven, J., et al.: Participatory design and participatory research: an HCI case study with young forced migrants. ACM Trans. Comput. Hum. Interact. **21**(6), 1–39 (2014)
15. Mirza-Babaei, P., et al.: Understanding the contribution of user experience research and design to software development. In: 2018 CHI Conference on Human Factors in Computing Systems, pp. 1–12.ACM, New York (2018)
16. Gomes, D., et al.: Developing a set of design patterns specific for the design of user interfaces for autistic users. In: XX Brazilian Symposium on Human Factors in Computing Systems, pp. 1–7. (2021)
17. Clegg, D., Barker, R.: Case Method Fast-Track: a RAD Approach. Addison-Wesley, Boston (1994)
18. Davis, F.D.: A technology acceptance model for empirically testing new end-user information systems: Theory and results. Tese (Doutorado) – Massachusetts Institute of Technology (1985)
19. Venkatesh, V., Davis, F.D.: A theoretical extension of the technology acceptance model: four longitudinal field studies. Manage. Sci. INFORMS **46**(2), 186–204 (2000)
20. Shaw, K.A., Williams, S., Patrick, M.E., et al.: Prevalence and Early Identification of Autism Spectrum Disorder Among Children Aged 4 and 8 Years — Autism and Developmental Disabilities Monitoring Network, 16 Sites, United States, 2022.;74(No. SS-2):1–22. MMWR Surveill Summ (2025)
21. Nielsen, J., Molich, R.: Heuristic evaluation of user interfaces. In: SIGCHI Conference on Human Factors in Computing Systems, pp. 249–256 (1990)

Usability-Driven AAC Design: Developing "Hulo Talk' to Improve AAC Adoption for Children with Autism and Complex Communication Needs

Rahmat Raji[1,2(✉)] [iD] and Ronnautica Dixon[3]

[1] Independent Researcher, Springfield, IL 62712, USA
[2] Ashesi University, Berekuso, Ghana
[3] Independent Researcher, Springfield, IL 62712, USA

Abstract. Children with Autism Spectrum Disorder (ASD) frequently rely on Augmentative and Alternative Communication (AAC) systems. Yet, many commercial solutions are hindered by poor usability designs, especially for children with motor and cognitive impairments. This study introduces Hulo Talk, a tablet-based AAC prototype developed using a user-centered, inclusive design approach. A two-phase, mixed-methods study involving 20 children aged 4–18 first evaluated a representative AAC app, Eline Speaks, revealing high error rates and prolonged response times. Based on these findings, Hulo Talk was co-designed with caregivers and tested iteratively to address identified barriers to communication. Within-subject comparisons demonstrated that Hulo Talk significantly reduced task completion times (from 48.0 s to 20.5 s and from 14.2 s to 4.0 s, $p < 0.001$) and error rates (85% reduction, $p < 0.001$), while doubling task accuracy across user groups ($p < 0.01$). Qualitative feedback supported these improvements, citing enhanced usability and reduced cognitive load. These results confirm that accessible, user-driven design enhances AAC system performance for children with complex communication needs, reinforcing the value of inclusive methods in assistive technology development.

Keywords: Augmentative and Alternative Communication Systems · Autism Spectrum Disorder · Accessibility Design

1 Introduction

Communication is fundamental to human interaction, serving as the cornerstone for cognitive, emotional, and social development. In children, communication skills evolve from infancy through adulthood, but when this development is disrupted, it can profoundly affect social interactions and cognitive growth [1]. For children with Autism Spectrum Disorder (ASD), communication difficulties are often a primary challenge, manifesting as delayed language development, limited verbal expression, and difficulty interpreting non-verbal cues. ASD, a neurodevelopmental disorder affecting approximately 1 in 45 children, encompasses a wide range of impairments in communication, social interaction, and adaptability [8, 11].

© The Author(s), under exclusive license to Springer Nature Switzerland AG 2026
M. Antona and C. Stephanidis (Eds.): HCII 2025, LNCS 16335, pp. 321–337, 2026.
https://doi.org/10.1007/978-3-032-12781-5_22

The severity of communication impairments in individuals with ASD varies significantly. Some individuals may develop functional language skills, while others remain nonverbal throughout their lives. Additionally, many experience difficulties understanding and using nonverbal cues, such as gestures and facial expressions, which can further hinder social interactions. Research by Wodka, Mathy, and Kalb, using data from the Simon Simplex Collection, found that 40% of children aged eight (n = 1456) had not developed phrase speech or shown any signs of it by age four, highlighting the prevalence of language delays in this population [10]. This variability indicates the importance of personalized interventions tailored to each individual's unique communication profile, emphasizing the need for targeted strategies to support diverse needs.

However, traditional interventions such as speech therapy and behavior modification techniques often yield limited success, especially for non-verbal children or those with severe communication challenges. As a result, assistive technologies, particularly Augmentative and Alternative Communication (AAC) systems, have become essential in bridging communication gaps.

Recognizing the prevalence of these issues across commercial AAC systems, we first examined the usability and utility of several widely used applications, including Proloquo2Go, Avaz, TouchChat, and LAMP Words for Life in enhancing and supporting the communication needs of children with Autism. Each product was evaluated against standard usability dimensions such as interface complexity, adaptability, and ease of customization. We selected Eline Speaks as a representative application because it reflects the dominant design patterns in many commercial systems: symbol-based communication, linear navigation, and rigid categorization. Though popular in some settings, Eline Speaks embodies many key usability challenges reported in the literature, making it an appropriate benchmark for comparison.

The primary purpose of this research was to develop and evaluate Hulo Talk, our tablet-based AAC prototype designed to address these identified usability barriers through a user-centered, inclusive design approach. By incorporating accessible features tailored to diverse cognitive and motor needs, Hulo Talk aimed to reduce errors, enhance communication speed, and improve the overall user experience. We hypothesized that Hulo Talk (H1) significantly reduces the frequency of incorrect attempts compared to Eline Speaks, improving communication task accuracy for children with autism, and (H2) minimizes response times relative to Eline Speaks, enhancing the efficiency of communication processes.

This paper demonstrates that AAC systems designed with a focus on accessibility, natural environments, and user-centered principles can enhance communication capabilities for children with ASD, promoting inclusivity and reducing communication barriers. A secondary contribution is that Hulo Talk provides a roadmap for integrating usability insights into the iterative design of future assistive technologies, offering a scalable approach to addressing diverse user needs in AAC systems.

2 Related Work

This study builds upon existing research in Autism Spectrum Disorder (ASD), interface design, and augmentative and alternative communication (AAC) systems to contextualize the usability challenges and inform the development of Hulo Talk.

Prior studies have thoroughly examined the cognitive, motor, and linguistic profiles of individuals with ASD, providing foundational guidance for the creation of accessible technologies tailored to this population. However, much of the literature has focused on controlled environments or assumed uniform interaction models, resulting in persistent gaps between technological capability and real-world usability.

2.1 The Role of Visual Design in Enhancing Communication

Human-computer interaction (HCI) principles have long underpinned the design of AAC systems, especially regarding usability and visual presentation. An effective AAC interface must accommodate users' diverse cognitive and motor capabilities while ensuring interaction efficiency and readability.

Light and McNaughton [3] argue that poor usability in AAC systems exacerbates communicative barriers, particularly for users with motor or cognitive impairments. Supporting this, empirical research demonstrates that interfaces with dense layouts, excessive hierarchies, or poorly scaled elements significantly reduce communication accuracy and task completion rates [6].

Visual design strategies such as vertical layouts, visual scene displays (VSDs), and symbolic image sets have been shown to reduce cognitive processing time and enhance interaction precision [3, 7, 9]. For instance, vertical layouts are especially beneficial for younger users by minimizing eye movement and decision fatigue. At the same time, VSDs embed language in contextualized environments to facilitate conceptual learning and semantic generalization. Additionally, graphical symbol systems have been instrumental for non-verbal users by providing high-reliability, low-cognitive-load communication tools [8].

However, much of this work has been developed in clinical or lab-based environments, limiting ecological validity. Moreover, existing visual design recommendations often fail to incorporate feedback from neurodiverse users themselves. As related research suggests, integrating user-led co-design and adaptive visual frameworks may lead to better engagement and communication success.

This paper builds on these insights by embedding interface testing in classroom environments and leveraging direct user observations to iterate on visual elements such as font size, layout, and spacing. These modifications resulted in significantly improved task performance and user satisfaction, contributing new insights to the body of AAC usability research.

2.2 Attaining Communicative Competence

Communicative competence is not solely the mastery of discrete linguistic or motor skills; it encompasses integrating operational, cognitive, and social skills within authentic interaction contexts.

Light and McNaughton [4] advocate for a holistic AAC system design that supports users across a spectrum of communication demands. While early AAC systems like non-electronic communication boards established foundational interaction paradigms, contemporary tools have often replicated these outdated frameworks without leveraging the affordances of modern interaction design [3].

This gap is particularly visible in commercial AAC tools like Eline Speaks, which retain rigid menu structures and inflexible content libraries. By contrast, Gosnell's feature-matching model offers a structured way to align system selection with individual user needs, considering communication goals, sensory profiles, and motor abilities. This study applied Gosnell's framework to inform participant grouping and interface configuration, enabling a tailored evaluation of Hulo Talk's accessibility and performance.

Despite advances, many AAC systems are evaluated in artificial settings, excluding the dynamics of real-world interactions. Light and McNaughton emphasize the importance of naturalistic environments and familiar communication partners for assessing communicative success. This study was conducted in participants' classrooms with their regular teachers, capturing more authentic interaction patterns and yielding ecologically valid insights.

Furthermore, the scope of AAC design must extend beyond enabling basic speech to supporting educational, vocational, and social engagement. Research highlights that assistive technologies that fail to adapt to users' day-to-day lives risk limiting rather than empowering participation. This research addresses that risk by enabling real-time customization, supporting dynamic vocabulary growth, and allowing flexible category construction; features that proved essential to long-term engagement and adoption.

By grounding the design in cognitive, motor, and ecological realities and validating through repeated testing, this paper contributes novel strategies for aligning AAC systems with the complex, evolving needs of individuals with autism.

3 Methods

This study employed a mixed-methods approach to evaluate the usability and accessibility of our proposed tablet-based Augmentative and Alternative Communication (AAC) app, Hulo Talk, compared with a commercially available AAC system, Eline Speaks.

The research design was structured into two sequential phases, forming the foundation of a repeatable, usability-driven framework for designing assistive technologies. By combining baseline assessment with iterative co-design and validation, this study aimed to improve AAC design and articulate a scalable roadmap for aligning AAC design with real-world user needs.

3.1 Participant Recruitment and Profiles

Participants were recruited from a specialized autism therapy center known for serving a demographically and functionally diverse population of children with autism spectrum disorder (ASD). Recruitment followed a convenience sampling strategy, focusing on readily available children with prior exposure to AAC systems and whose caregivers consented to participate. The center's administration approved to conduct the study.

The study included 20 children, aged 4 to 18 years, all formally diagnosed with ASD. To ensure comprehensive coverage of functional diversity, participants were categorized into three groups based on communication and motor abilities:

1. Motor Deficits Group (n = 6): Children with significant motor impairments that affected their ability to interact with touchscreen interfaces.
2. Non-Verbal Participants (n = 8): Children with severely limited expressive language capabilities who relied heavily on tactile and visual cues.
3. Moderately Verbal Participants (n = 6): Children with some verbal communication ability and adequate motor control, who still benefited from AAC support.

This classification enabled targeted analysis of usability across diverse user needs. Secondary participants included the children's communication partners and caregivers, who provided detailed contextual insights through interviews. Ethical compliance was maintained by securing informed consent from all participants and their communication partners.

3.2 Participant Recruitment and Profiles

The study was carried out over eight weeks, comprising two major phases. Each phase consisted of one structured usability session per participant. A session was a 30-min interaction period during which a participant, with assistance from their communication partner, completed a fixed set of AAC-related communication tasks using the assigned system (Eline Speaks in Phase 1; Hulo Talk in Phase 2).

Phase 1: Baseline Usability Assessment of Eline Speaks. In this phase, participants used an iPad with the Eline Speaks application to perform structured tasks designed to simulate realistic communication scenarios. These tasks were derived from direct observation of participants' daily routines at the center, particularly around mealtimes and activity-based requests using the Picture Exchange Communication System (PECS). In addition, each session was conducted with the participants' natural communication partners present to provide support as needed and to allow observation of authentic usage patterns. This grounding in authentic use cases ensured the ecological validity of the test environment. Two types of structured tasks were administered:

- Simple Selection Tasks: Selecting a single item from the interface based on a prompt, such as: "Which one is juice?".
- Navigation Tasks: Navigating menus to locate and select items within categories, such as: "Find your snacks."

The quantitative usability metrics measured across both phases included task success rate, task completion time, error frequency, and intervention frequency. Task success rate was defined as the percentage of correct item selections. In contrast, task completion time measured the duration in seconds from the moment the prompt was given to the successful selection of the requested item. Error frequency captured the number of incorrect selection attempts made during each task. Finally, intervention frequency reflected the amount of support provided by communication partners to complete the task, including verbal prompts, modeling, and instances of physical assistance.

Phase 1: Baseline Usability Assessment of Eline Speaks. Findings from Phase 1 directly informed the design of Hulo Talk through a participatory, iterative process involving the caregivers. Initial prototypes were created through paper-based mockups, which were tested and refined using feedback loops and structured cognitive walk-throughs. These iterations followed a structured feedback loop: observe, prototype, test, and refine. The study offers a transferable model for usability-integrated development across diverse AAC contexts by embedding caregiver feedback directly into the interface design lifecycle.

Once the final prototype was developed, participants were invited to complete the same structured tasks used in Phase 1, under the same environmental conditions to ensure consistency. Each child engaged with Hulo Talk in a quiet, familiar setting with their communication partner present, as in the baseline study. The task sequence remained the same to facilitate direct within-subject comparisons. Performance was evaluated using the same metrics: accuracy, task completion time, and level of independence, defined as the number of prompts or guidance required. This repetition of structured tasks enabled the study to isolate the impact of the redesigned interface on communication outcomes.

3.3 Ethics Statement

This study was conducted in accordance with ethical standards for research involving human participants. The Ashesi University Subject Review Committee reviewed and approved the research protocol. For inquiries regarding the ethics review process, please get in touch with the Chair of the Ashesi University Human Subjects and Clinical Research Committee at dsampah@ashesi.edu.gh.

4 Results

4.1 Phase 1: Findings from the Usability Evaluation of Eline Speaks

A primary usability insight uncovered in Phase 1 was the substantial variability in participants' motor, cognitive, and linguistic communication competencies. Participants' usability barriers were categorized and analyzed across three distinct user groups:

1. Motor Deficits Group: Participants with motor impairments encountered substantial difficulty interacting with the AAC interface, Eline Speaks, primarily due to undersized touch targets and densely packed elements. Interface components fell below the WCAG-recommended minimum touch size of 44x44 pixels, contributing to frequent selection errors and extended task durations. These observations align with prior research emphasizing the need for enlarged interactive zones to support users with limited fine motor control [22]. Furthermore, inadequate spacing between interface elements compounded interaction difficulties, reinforcing the imperative for motor-accessible design considerations in AAC tools.
2. Non-Verbal Group: Hierarchical navigation structures posed significant cognitive barriers for non-verbal participants. The interface in Eline Speaks required users to navigate through multiple layers to access even basic vocabulary items (e.g., selecting "Juice" under "Snacks"), which imposed additional cognitive load and led to elevated error rates and task completion times. These findings are consistent with cognitive

load theory, highlighting the detrimental effects of complex information hierarchies, particularly for individuals with limited expressive abilities [35]. Prior work supports the efficacy of flatter, visually accessible navigation schemes in improving both efficiency and user comprehension [36].

3. Moderately Verbal Group: Although the group demonstrated relatively higher task performance and fewer errors, qualitative feedback indicated persistent dissatisfaction with the interface's structure and usability. Communication partners described the categorization and labeling as non-intuitive, and visual inspection revealed a cluttered layout with ambiguous visual cues. These issues contributed to unnecessary navigation delays, despite the users' verbal and motor capabilities. This observation affirms broader human-computer interaction principles: even higher-functioning users benefit significantly from streamlined, intuitive design frameworks [33]. As seen in Tables 1 and 2, enhancing clarity through consistent labeling, logical category grouping, and simplified user flows remains critical for this cohort.

Table 1. Evaluation of Performance Metrics Across User Groups Using Eline Speaks.

Metric	Motor Deficits	Non-Verbal	Moderately Verbal
Total Tasks	16	16	16
Total Correct Attempts	5	3	12
Total Correct Attempts	11	13	4
Average Completion Times	14.2	48.0	20.5

Table 2. Task Completion Time and Error Metrics for Eline Speaks by User Group.

Group	Avg. Time (s) $\pm$ SD	Avg. Errors (of 16)	p-value
Motor Deficits	14.2 $\pm$ 3.1	11.0	< 0.05
Non-Verbal	48.0 $\pm$ 6.5	13.0	< 0.01
Moderately Verbal	20.5 $\pm$ 4.2	4.0	NS

The analysis portrayed in both Fig. 1 and Table 1 revealed that Phase 1 resulted in substantial usability barriers in Eline Speaks, particularly for non-verbal and motor-deficit participants. Non-verbal users averaged 13 incorrect attempts out of 16 and required 48.0 ± 6.5 s per task ($p < 0.01$), largely due to hierarchical navigation complexity. Motor-deficit users recorded 11 errors and had a mean completion time of 14.2 ± 3.1 s ($p < 0.05$), underscoring the impact of dense layouts and inadequate touch spacing. Even moderately verbal participants encountered navigation inefficiencies, with an average time of 20.5 ± 4.2 s, reinforcing the need for simplified interfaces.

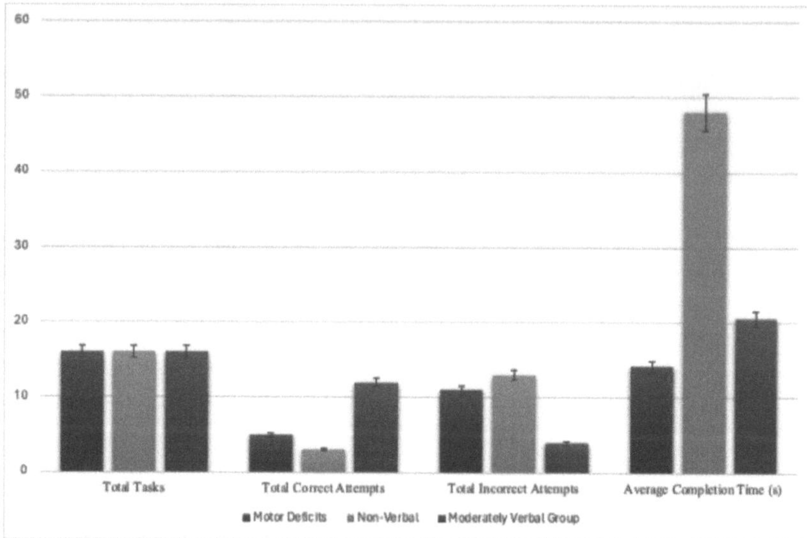

Fig. 1. Average *Task Performance by User Group Using Eline Speaks.* Clustered bar chart comparing average performance across three user groups using Eline Speaks. Data includes total tasks, correct and incorrect attempts, and average completion times. The chart highlights significant usability challenges, exceptionally prolonged task times, and higher error rates among non-verbal and motor-deficit users.

4.2   Phase 2: The Design of Hulo Talk

Building upon the usability challenges identified in Phase 1, the redesign phase focused on transforming these empirical insights into targeted interface interventions. The goal was to address specific motor, cognitive, and linguistic barriers by applying evidence-based design strategies grounded in human-computer interaction and accessibility research. The development of the Hulo Talk prototype followed a systematic, user-centered design approach. The following subsections detail the implemented design changes and their measured impact on usability and communication outcomes.

Direct-Access Grid Navigation.   To address the excessive cognitive demands imposed by the hierarchical structure in Eline Speaks, Hulo Talk implemented a direct-access grid navigation model. This system replaced multi-step category navigation with a flat information architecture, presenting all communication items simultaneously in a visual index layout. By eliminating the need for category traversal, users, especially non-verbal participants, were able to identify and select items based on visual recognition alone. This change fundamentally restructured the user interaction model from sequential navigation to immediate selection, reducing the cognitive and operational burden of communication.

Measured outcomes demonstrated substantial improvement: non-verbal users experienced a reduction in average task completion times from 48.0 s to 20.47 s, with a corresponding increase in task accuracy and independence. The shift to a flat, visually accessible interface was integral to improving user efficiency and minimizing frustration.

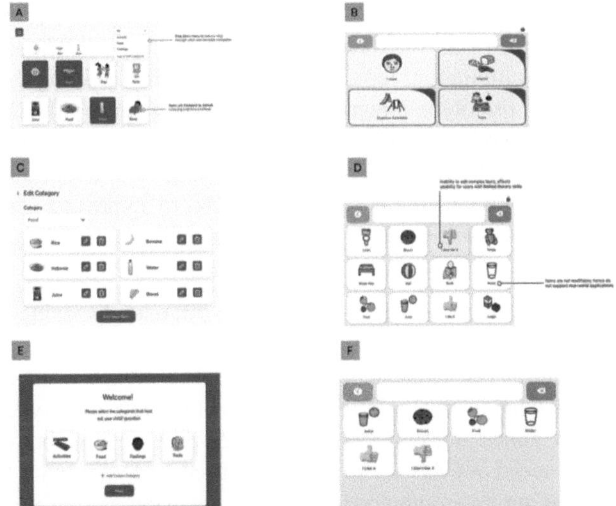

Fig. 2. Figure 2. Screenshots comparing the customization and navigation designs of Hulo Talk and Eline Speaks. In A, Hulo Talk's "Index" page displays all items in a flat grid, allowing for immediate selection and minimizing cognitive load. In contrast, B shows how Eline Speaks requires users to navigate through categories before accessing items, increasing the number of steps and time to communicate. C highlights Hulo Talk's "Edit Category" page, where users and communication partners can add, delete, or modify items, supporting flexibility and daily adaptation. D and F illustrate Eline Speaks' fixed structure, which prevents users from editing or reorganizing content, limiting its adaptability to individual needs. In E, Hulo Talk's "Landing" page prompts users to create personalized categories during setup, facilitating early customization based on user preferences.

This result supports the principle that flattening navigation hierarchies and emphasizing visual discoverability is a highly effective strategy for designing AAC systems for neurodiverse populations.

Enhanced Font Size. Enhanced font size significantly improved readability, addressing common visual processing difficulties among users with autism. The prototype employed an enlarged font size of 50 pixels, notably higher than conventional UI standards, but aligns with best practices for accessibility and cognitive support in tablet-based AAC applications. This size facilitates rapid symbol-text association and minimizes visual strain, especially for pre-literate users or those with limited visual acuity. Research has shown that large-format text (48px or larger) improves readability and processing efficiency for users with low vision or neurodiverse processing styles.

Furthermore, 50px allows content to maintain high visibility across variable lighting conditions and viewing angles, which is especially valuable in classroom or therapy settings. User testing confirmed that the increased font size reduced error rates and improved user satisfaction. This supports the recommendation that designers consistently adopt larger fonts to cater to diverse visual processing needs.

Customization and Personalization. The lack of customization observed in "Eline Speaks" significantly restricted interface flexibility and personalization. The interface review highlighted this limitation, reducing long-term utility and engagement. Consequently, the Hulo Talk prototype integrated robust editing capabilities, enabling users and their communication partners to freely add, modify, and delete categories and items. Personalization is crucial to AAC engagement and long-term adoption, as interfaces reflecting real-world communication needs are linked to improved usage rates [22]. Thus, AAC systems should inherently include customizable content features to adapt to evolving user contexts.

Increased Spacing Between Interactive Elements. Increased spacing between interactive elements specifically addressed the challenges faced by participants with motor deficits. Visual inspections of "Eline Speaks" confirmed tightly clustered icons contributing significantly to selection errors. In response, the Hulo Talk prototype implemented expanded interactive zones (48 × 48 pixels) and a 20-pixel spacing between elements. These dimensions exceed WCAG 2.1 recommendations and align with findings advocating increased spacing to accommodate reduced precision among users with motor impairments. Usability testing confirmed reduced error frequency and increased ease of interaction, strongly recommending proactive incorporation of larger interactive areas and increased spacing in design practice.

Observation of participants engaging with the Hulo Talk prototype confirmed that these targeted design modifications effectively address the significant usability limitations previously identified. Each specific adjustment, including navigation simplification, enhanced readability, customization capabilities, and increased interactive spacing, significantly improved user performance, reduced error rates by approximately 85%, and enhanced overall user satisfaction. These findings demonstrate the effectiveness of iterative, user-informed design methodologies in creating accessible and efficient AAC systems.

4.3 Phase 2: Findings from the Usability Evaluation of Eline Speaks

Once the design of Hulo Talk was completed, we began the process of conducting another usability study. This study aimed to assess whether the design adaptations implemented in Hulo Talk addressed the accessibility and usability challenges identified in the baseline system, Eline Speaks. This phase facilitated a direct and consistent comparison of the two systems by replicating the same task structure, testing conditions, and evaluation metrics. The goal was to determine whether Hulo Talk offered participants measurable improvements in user performance and communication outcomes.

Participants were once again presented with a tablet, now equipped with the working prototype, and instructed to complete tasks designed to simulate real-world communication scenarios. Performance metrics were systematically recorded and analyzed, including correct and incorrect attempts, task completion times, and error rates (Table 4).

The results shown in Table 3 showed significant improvements in the communication rates of participants across all competency groups.

1. Motor Deficits Group: While the 20% improvement in correct attempts was not statistically significant ($p = 0.34$), the zero-error performance was. This result highlights

Table 3. Summary of Usability Metrics for Hulo Talk Across User Competency Groups. Mean ± SD and 95% confidence intervals for Hulo Talk performance metrics. P-values from t-tests compare the differences with Eline Speaks. *Statistically significant at p < 0.05.

Metric	Motor Deficits	Non-Verbal	Moderately Verbal
Correct Attempts	11.2 ± 2.1 (CI: 9.4–13.0)	8.0 ± 1.2 (CI: 6.9–9.1)	14.5 ± 1.0 (CI: 13.7–15.3)
Error Rate	0.0 ± 0.0 (p = 0.005)	1.9 ± 0.9 (p = 0.002)	0.5 ± 0.7 (p = 0.06)*
Task Completion Time	4.05 ± 1.6 (CI: 3.1–5.0)	20.47 ± 5.8 (CI: 17.8–23.1)	6.8 ± 2.3 (CI: 5.2–8.4)

the system's role in removing motor barriers through design, making it a critical usability milestone. Additionally, on average, participants performed tasks 60.9 s faster, indicating reduced motor strain and improved interaction flow.

2. Non-Verbal Group: The increase in correct attempts did not reach significance (p = 0.144). However, the significant drop in errors supports Hulo Talk's effectiveness in addressing cognitive navigation challenges. Notably, some users achieved zero-error performance, improving system comprehension and reducing frustration during tasks.
3. Moderately Verbal Group: While statistical significance was not observed in correct attempt increases, qualitative reports indicated more straightforward navigation and less confusion with Hulo Talk. The interface changes were especially beneficial for high-functioning users, streamlining their interactions and minimizing delays due to menu complexity or input errors.

5   Statistical Comparison Between Hulo Talk and Eline Speaks

To validate the observed improvements in usability and performance, the study employed statistical analyses using t-tests and chi-squared tests. These tools provided a rigorous framework to evaluate whether the differences between Eline Speaks and Hulo Talk were statistically significant. The study sought to assess the efficacy of the prototype, Hulo Talk, through two primary hypotheses:

1. Hypothesis 1 (H1): The prototype reduces the number of wrong attempts compared to Eline Speaks.
2. Hypothesis 2 (H2): The prototype reduces response times compared to Eline Speaks, leading to more efficient communication.
3. Null Hypothesis (H0): The two systems have no difference in performance.

5.1   T-Test

We employed the t-test to compare mean performance metrics (e.g., right and wrong attempts) between the two systems and determine whether Hulo Talk and Eline Speaks' observed differences were statistically significant.

This study used the p-value to determine statistical significance, as shown in Sect. 4.3, Phase 2 Findings. A p-value < 0.05 indicates strong evidence that the prototype solution significantly improved participants' communication, supporting the alternative hypotheses (H1 or H2). A p-value ≥ 0.05 suggests that the observed differences might be due to chance, supporting the null hypothesis (H0).

1. Motor Deficits Group: Participants in this group showed substantial gains. The average number of correct attempts increased to 11.2 ± 2.1 out of 16 (95% CI: 9.4–13.0), while error rates dropped to 0.0 ± 0.0 ($p = 0.005$), indicating a 100% reduction from the baseline. This demonstrates complete elimination of incorrect selections. The simplified layout and expanded touch targets were particularly impactful for this group. Task completion time decreased significantly to 4.05 ± 1.6 s (95% CI: 3.1–5.0), significantly enhancing performance over the baseline average of 14.2 s.
2. Non-Verbal Group: Correct attempts improved to 8.0 ± 1.2 (95% CI: 6.9–9.1), while error rates dropped to 1.9 ± 0.9 ($p = 0.002$), an 85% reduction from the baseline. Task completion times significantly improved, decreasing from 48.0 s to 20.47 ± 5.8 s (95% CI: 17.8–23.1).
3. Moderately Verbal Group: This group experienced the highest accuracy, with correct attempts averaging 14.5 ± 1.0 (95% CI: 13.7–15.3). Error rates dropped to 0.5 ± 0.7, representing a 48.3% reduction, though not statistically significant ($p = 0.06$). Task completion time improved from 20.5 s to 6.8 ± 2.3 s (95% CI: 5.2–8.4).

5.2 Chi-Squared Test

The other statistical test used for the study was the Chi-squared test. This test assessed categorical data, specifically the frequency of response times. By comparing observed and expected frequencies, the chi-squared test evaluated whether the prototype significantly reduced the cognitive and motor effort required to use the system.

Table 4. Distribution of Task Completion Times Across Categories for Eline Speaks and Hulo Talk. A Chi-square test of independence revealed a significant difference in response time distributions between the two systems, $\chi^2(2) = 8.08$, $p = 0.0176$. Hulo Talk had faster responses, while Eline Speaks showed slower responses.

Time Category	Eline Speaks	Hulo Talk
Fast (0–10 s)	9	18
Medium (10.1–30 s)	6	7
Slow (>30)	15	5

The following is an analysis to compare the time it took for participants to complete tasks using two communication systems: Eline Speaks and Hulo Talk, across six trials per participant (totaling 30 trials for each system). Each task completion time was categorized into one of three groups: Fast ($\leq$10 s), Medium (10.1–30 s), and Slow (>30 s). The results were as follows:

- Chi-square statistic (χ^2) $= 8.08$
- Degrees of freedom (df) $= 2$

- p-value $= 0.0176$

Since the p-value is 0.0176, which is less than 0.05, there is a statistically significant difference in the distribution of task completion times between Eline Speaks and Hulo Talk. Specifically, Hulo Talk has a higher count of fast responses, while Eline Speaks shows more slow responses. These results indicate a statistically significant difference in the distribution of task completion times between Eline Speaks and Hulo Talk ($p < 0.05$).

Table 5. Statistically Significant Improvements in Usability Outcomes with Hulo Talk. Across all competency groups, Hulo Talk resulted in significantly lower task completion times, error rates, and accuracy levels compared to Eline Speaks.

Metric	Eline Speaks	Hulo Talk	% Change	p-value
Avg. Task Time (Motor Deficits)	14.2 s	4.05 s	10.15 s	<0.001
Avg. Task Time (All Groups)	48.0 s	20.47 s	27.53 s	<0.001
Avg. Task Error Rate (All Groups)	Baseline	85%	85%	<0.001
Avg. Task Accuracy (All Groups)	Baseline	50%	50%	<0.001
Avg. Time Savings Across Trials	-	14.8s	SD $= 10.57$ s	<0.001

These findings demonstrate that Hulo Talk addressed many of the challenges observed in Eline Speaks, significantly improving usability and accessibility across all user groups.

With the results in Fig. 1, paired t-tests confirmed significant improvements across all groups. Average task completion times decreased from 14.2 s to 4.05 s ($p < 0.001$) and from 48.0 s to 20.47 s ($p < 0.001$), indicating substantial enhancements in task efficiency and reduced cognitive load. Participants across all user groups demonstrated a 50% increase in correct task attempts ($p < 0.01$) and an 85% reduction in error rates ($p < 0.001$). Qualitative feedback indicated a significantly improved perception of ease of use and reduced cognitive demand, with comparative results shown in Table 5.

6 Discussion

This research highlights the critical importance of user-centered design in developing AAC systems for individuals with autism. The usability evaluation of Eline Speaks revealed significant challenges, such as cognitive strain from hierarchical navigation, inadequate touch targets, and limited personalization options. By addressing these challenges through iterative prototyping and co-design, Hulo Talk demonstrated measurable improvements in accessibility and usability.

Key design features in Hulo Talk, such as increased font sizes, simplified navigation, and customizable touch targets, effectively reduced cognitive and motor demands across all user groups. These features directly improved communication rates, reduced errors, and enhanced task efficiency.

Furthermore, the active involvement of natural communication partners, including teachers and caregivers, was pivotal in ensuring the prototype's relevance and usability in real-world contexts. This collaboration highlighted the importance of embedding AAC interventions in familiar environments to foster trust and engagement.

However, the study also revealed gaps in current AAC designs, particularly their adaptability and cultural relevance. Future research should focus on developing context-aware systems that dynamically evolve with users' needs, ensuring long-term usability and impact. Below, we expand on two pressing questions from this work: (1) What specific features most effectively enhance accessibility in AAC systems? (2) How can early intervention maximize the long-term impact of AAC systems?

6.1 What Features Truly Enhance Accessibility in AAC Systems?

The accessibility of AAC systems extends beyond usability to encompass adaptability and alignment with diverse user capabilities. This study demonstrated that simplifying navigation, increasing font sizes, and removing unnecessary hierarchical layers significantly improved performance, especially for users with motor deficits. However, accessibility is not static—it must evolve to address the changing needs of users over time.

A key avenue for enhancing accessibility lies in leveraging predictive and adaptive technologies. Machine learning models could dynamically analyze user behavior to recommend or rearrange interface elements, ensuring AAC systems remain intuitive. For example, predictive text or icon placement can reduce cognitive load and speed up communication for users with limited motor abilities. However, integrating such technologies poses challenges: How can AAC systems balance adaptability without introducing unintended complexity or reducing transparency? The solution involves participatory design processes, involving users and caregivers at every stage to ensure solutions remain contextually relevant and user-friendly.

Multimodal interaction methods also play a pivotal role in accessibility. Technologies like eye-gaze tracking, voice activation, and haptic feedback can provide alternative input methods for users with severe motor or speech impairments. While these technologies exist, their inconsistent implementation in AAC systems limits their potential. Future research should investigate how to seamlessly integrate these methods to enhance accessibility while maintaining system simplicity and usability.

6.2 What Features Truly Enhance Accessibility in AAC Systems?

Early intervention is critical to the long-term success of AAC adoption. This study found that participants with prior exposure to communication aids adapted more quickly to the prototype, demonstrating higher confidence and communication efficacy. These findings align with broader neuroplasticity research, highlighting the importance of introducing AAC systems during critical developmental periods to build foundational communication skills.

Despite the benefits, significant barriers to early intervention remain. Many families, particularly in underserved communities, face challenges such as high costs and limited awareness of AAC systems. Addressing this inequity requires open-source AAC solutions, community-driven training programs, and integration of AAC training into standard early education curricula. These initiatives could ensure that children with communication needs are identified and supported earlier, fostering equitable access to AAC technologies.

Early intervention also holds potential for addressing common comorbidities associated with autism, such as anxiety and social withdrawal. AAC systems can foster social inclusion and reduce frustration by enabling children to express themselves effectively. Future research should examine how these emotional and social benefits influence long-term outcomes for children exposed to AAC systems early in life.

7   Conclusion

This research provides strong empirical evidence that user-centered, accessibility-driven design in Augmentative and Alternative Communication (AAC) systems can improve communication outcomes for children with autism spectrum disorder (ASD). The Hulo Talk prototype, developed through iterative co-design with caregivers and grounded in the principles of human-computer interaction, significantly outperformed the commercially available Eline Speaks across all primary usability metrics. Task completion times were reduced by over 60%, error rates dropped by 85%, and task accuracy doubled, outcomes that reflect not just statistical significance, but also practical, real-world benefits.

The study's methodology, combining quantitative performance data with caregiver insights and testing in ecologically valid environments, highlights the importance of evaluating AAC systems in the contexts where they are used. Furthermore, the differentiation in outcomes across user groups (motor-deficit, non-verbal, and moderately verbal) underscores the importance of designing for functional diversity rather than a "one-size-fits-all" model.

However, several limitations must be acknowledged. First, the sample size (n = 20) and reliance on convenience sampling from a single autism therapy center may limit generalizability. Future studies should recruit more demographically and geographically diverse populations to validate findings at scale. Second, while the study used rigorous task protocols and statistical methods, longitudinal outcomes, such as long-term adoption, communication development, and emotional impact, were not assessed. These represent critical next steps for understanding the sustained value of AAC tools like Hulo Talk.

Although Hulo Talk integrated meaningful accessibility features (e.g., grid navigation, expanded touch targets, larger fonts), it did not incorporate emerging technologies such as predictive modeling, voice interaction, or multimodal input (e.g., eye-tracking, haptics). Incorporating these could further support users with more severe impairments and foster greater personalization.

In conclusion, this research contributes a validated AAC prototype and a repeatable methodological model for inclusive assistive technology design. To fully realize the potential of AAC systems as tools for autonomy, learning, and social inclusion, future development must prioritize early intervention, cultural relevance, and dynamic adaptability, elements that were partially addressed here but warrant deeper investigation. With cross-sector collaboration among educators, technologists, clinicians, and families, AAC systems can move beyond basic communication scaffolds to become powerful enablers of voice, identity, and inclusion for all.

Acknowledgments. We are so grateful for our participants and their communication partners, who were generous with their time, and the communication partners at the institute, whose insights shaped this project.

References

1. Nielsen, J.: Heuristic evaluation. In: Usability Inspection Methods, pp. 25–62. John Wiley & Sons (1994)
2. Bonvillian, D., Nelson, K.E., Rhyme, J.M.: Sign language and autism. J. Autism Dev. Disord. **11**, 125–137 (1981)
3. McNaughton, J.D.: Putting people first: Re-thinking the role of technology in augmentative and alternative communication intervention. Augment. Altern. Commun. **29**(4), 299–309 (2013). https://doi.org/10.3109/07434618.2013.848935
4. Light, J.: Designing AAC research and intervention to improve outcomes for individuals with complex communication needs. Augment. Altern. Commun. **31**(2), 85–96 (2015). https://doi.org/10.3109/07434618.2015.1036458
5. Wilkinson, K.M., Light, J.: Considerations for the composition of visual scene displays: potential contributions of information from visual and cognitive sciences. Augment. Altern. Commun. **28**, 137–147 (2012).https://doi.org/10.3109/07434618.2012.704522
6. Fager, S., Beukelman, D.R., Fried-Oobs, M., Baker, J.: Access interface strategies. Assist. Technol. **24**(1), 25–33 (2012). https://doi.org/10.1080/10400435.2011.648712
7. Drager, K., Light, J., Speltz, J., Jeffries, L.: Performance of typically developing 2½-year-olds on dynamic display AAC technologies with different system layouts and language organizations. J. Speech Lang. Hear. Res. **46**, 298–312 (2003). https://doi.org/10.1044/1092-4388
8. Wodka, E.L., Mathy, P., Kalb, L.: Predictors of phrase and fluent speech with autism and severe language delay. Pediatrics **131**(4), e1128–e1134 (2013). https://doi.org/10.1542/peds. 2012-2221
9. A. Stauffer. User interface adaptability within an augmentative communication app for children with autism spectrum disorder. Thesis, 130 (2015)
10. Lewis, C., Rieman, J.: Task-Centered User Interface Design: A Practical Introduction (1993)
11. Turner, D.: Color and autism. enduratex.blogspot.com. https://enduratex.blogspot.com/2017/04/color-and-autism.html. Accessed 14 June 2025
12. AssistiveWare. Choosing a grid size. https://www.assistiveware.com/learn-aac/choosing-a-grid-size. Accessed 14 June 2025
13. GOV.UK. Inclusive communication: Accessible formats. https://www.gov.uk/government/publications/inclusive-communication/accessible-communication-formats. Accessed 14 June 2025
14. CEUR-WS. Accessible design for users with physical or motor disabilities. https://ceur-ws.org/Vol-2524/paper16.pdf. Accessed 14 June 2025
15. The Science Brigade. HCI accessibility guidelines. https://thesciencebrigade.com/hcip/article/download/102/101/230. Accessed 14 June 2025
16. Patel, M., Huang, A.: Designing touch interfaces for accessibility: Insights and guidelines. Int. J. Hum. Comput. Interact. (2020)

17. Smith, T., Jones, R.: Spacing and accessibility in UI design. Usability J. **14**(3), 45–56 (2019)
18. Sweller, J.: Cognitive load during problem solving: effects on learning. Cogn. Sci. **12**(2), 257–285 (1988)
19. Norman, D.: The Design of Everyday Things, Revised and Expanded Edition Basic Books (2013)
20. Nielsen, J.: Heuristic evaluation. In: Usability Inspection Methods, pp. 25–62. Wiley (1994)
21. Turner, D.: Color and autism. https://enduratex.blogspot.com/2017/04/color-and-autism.html. Accessed 14 June 2025
22. Sparrow, S.S., Cicchetti, D.V., Balla, D.A.: Vineland-II: Vineland Adaptive Behavior Scales, 2nd edn. Pearson PsychCorp (2005)

An Accessible Autism Screening System for Arabic-Speaking Populations: Co-Design for Integrating Social Robots in ASD Screening

Siwar Raslan[1,2]($\boxtimes$), Leen Yarkhan[2], Rahaf Alqahtani[2], Areej Al-Wabil[1,2], Jhan Alarifi[1], and Sharifa Alghowinem[3]

[1] HCI Lab, Alfaisal University, Riyadh, Saudi Arabia
{sraslan,awabil}@alfaisal.edu
[2] Software Engineering Department, Alfaisal University, Riyadh, Saudi Arabia
{lyarkhan,ralqahtani}@alfaisal.edu
[3] Personal Robots Group, Media Lab, Massachusetts Institute of Technology (MIT), Cambridge, USA
sharifah@media.mit.edu

Abstract. This paper explores the design and development of an interactive autism screening system implemented in the Arabic language, utilizing a social robot and a tablet interface to provide early, accessible screening for Arabic-speaking children aged 4 to 8 years. Existing autism screening and diagnostic methods are often subjective, expensive, and difficult to access for many families, particularly in Arabic-speaking communities where autism resources are limited or underdeveloped. The lack of validated diagnostic tools in these communities leaves many children undiagnosed or misdiagnosed, leading to delayed interventions. Designed using the seven principles of universal design, this screening system aims to bridge that gap by incorporating principles of universal access, such as flexibility, equity, and usability. Implications for designing accessible screening systems are discussed.

Keywords: Autism Spectrum Disorder (ASD) · Human-Robot Interaction (HRI) · Inclusive Design · Early Intervention · Autism Screening Tools

1 Introduction

Autism Spectrum Disorder (ASD) is a complex neurodevelopmental condition characterized by challenges in social communication and interaction, as well as restricted and repetitive behaviors [1]. The variability in symptoms and severity among individuals with ASD has been reported as a challenge in ASD screening diagnosis [2]. Despite these difficulties, studies have shown that intervention during the foundational years of a child enhances the outcome of a child with ASD and improves the quality of life of such children [3]. However, current diagnostic practices are not always available. Most traditional methods are time-consuming and can be inaccessible since they involve prolonged observation sessions and caregiver-reported questionnaires [4]. In

© The Author(s), under exclusive license to Springer Nature Switzerland AG 2026
M. Antona and C. Stephanidis (Eds.): HCII 2025, LNCS 16335, pp. 338–354, 2026.
https://doi.org/10.1007/978-3-032-12781-5_23

Arabic-speaking communities, the screening and diagnosis of ASD have been recognized as a challenge due to limited access to culturally adapted diagnostic tools and a shortage of trained professionals. The existing tools developed for English-speaking populations are not sensitive to cultural and linguistic nuances and are, therefore, not as effective for non-English-speaking populations [5]. As a result, many children remain undiagnosed or misdiagnosed, which contributes to delays in remedial programs or interventions. Moreover, the stigma surrounding ASD in some communities can hinder early diagnosis and intervention and lead caregivers or families to be averse to professional help, which exacerbates the problem [6].

This paper describes a new approach to autism screening implemented in the Arabic language for children aged 4–8 years old. The system involves using a social robot Jibo [7] in conjunction with a tablet-based system to provide a culturally tailored and easily accessible diagnostic experience. By means of a set of localized interactive mini-games that are aligned with behaviors measured in ASD screening tools, such as joint attention, turn-taking, and decision-making, the system is designed to collect real-time behavioral data to support early diagnosis. This paper explores whether a culturally adapted, interactive autism screening system enhances ASD screening's efficiency, accessibility, and engagement in Arabic-speaking populations. We hypothesize that integrating social robotics with culturally tailored design will contribute toward improving outcomes in early ASD detection.

The system has been designed with accessibility in mind by incorporating insights from the seven principles of universal design [8]. These principles emphasize "equitable use, flexibility, efficiency, and ease of understanding, ensuring that the product, system, or service is accessible and adaptable to diverse users" [8]. These principles are considered the foundation of the system's design and determine characteristics of the software, such as customizable user interfaces, multimodal feedback, and intuitive navigation to effectively meet the needs of therapists, caregivers, and children. To address cultural and linguistic barriers in Arabic-speaking communities, the system seeks to reduce gaps in autism resources, aiming to enhance developmental outcomes for children with ASD through early intervention. A co-design focus group session was conducted to evaluate the usability and effectiveness of the system from the context of practitioners. The session's findings serve as the basis for iterative improvement and validation of the system's clinical relevance.

2 Background and Related Work

The early and accurate diagnosis of ASD is essential to facilitate timely intervention in identifying and addressing the child's specific needs to maximize their developmental potential, minimize long-term challenges, and improve their quality of life. Anecdotal evidence in Arabic-speaking communities suggests that traditionally utilized diagnostic methods are perceived as inadequate by clinicians and often do not meet the expectations and needs for accessibility and cultural relevance. Recent technological advancements, including social robotics and eye-tracking systems, have demonstrated promising approaches to address these gaps by localizing instruments and systems in the context of ASD screening in alignment with socio-cultural factors in the design and adaptation.

This section discusses existing screening methods for ASD, the role of social robotics and embodied conversational agents in interventions, and sheds light on the importance of inclusive and culturally relevant designs in screening for ASD.

2.1 Existing Autism Screening and Diagnostic Methods

Existing methods for ASD screening and diagnosis have traditionally relied on the use of the Autism Diagnostic Observation Schedule (ADOS) and the Autism Diagnostic Interview-Revised (ADI-R) tools. ADOS involves observing the child's behavior directly while performing structured tasks throughout the diagnostic session. Moreover, the ADI-R tool gathers a detailed patient history and considers the behavioral data of the patients through conducting multiple interviews with their caregivers. These methods present a robust approach to aid in the screening and diagnosing ASD. However, clinical research has highlighted two issues that hinder accessibility in underserved regions: the relatively long time to conduct these screening methods and the specialized expert training [9]. Other tools, such as the Childhood Autism Rating Scale (CARS) and the Modified Checklist for Autism in Toddlers (M-CHAT) questionnaire, are recognized as straightforward assessments that can be observed through interacting with the child during the clinical sessions and contribute toward a preliminary diagnosis [10, 11]. However, these methods have been noted to lack cultural adaptability and alignment with socio-cultural factors, especially in Arabic-speaking communities.

Emerging technologies such as AI-enabled embodied conversational agents and screening methods that utilize eye tracking have been used in ASD screening and diagnostics [e.g., 12–13]. For instance, eye-tracking systems measure the visual responsiveness of the child during the interactive sessions, which provides objective measures of visual attention in the ASD diagnosis process [12]. Under controlled conditions, it has been shown to generate sensitivity and specificity rates above 80% [13]. Additionally, robotic utilization in diagnostic procedures involves semi-autonomous systems measuring key behaviors such as joint attention and turn-taking. These innovations improve screening efficiency, yet their dependence on cultural and linguistic considerations may limit their effectiveness in culturally distinct regions. By leveraging social robotics and culturally adaptive frameworks, the proposed system's approach seeks to address the limitations of existing screening methods to ensure accessibility and cultural relevance.

2.2 Role of Social Robotics in Autism Screening and Remedial Programs

In recent years, social robots have been increasingly used for ASD diagnosis and remedial programs, offering engaging, interactive experiences for children while enabling data collection and conducting data-driven assessments. Social robots such as the NAO humanoid are frequently used to analyze behaviors such as joint attention, imitation, and turn-taking during clinical sessions [14]. These systems implement multimodal interaction capabilities, such as verbal, visual, and tactile cues, to allow for real-time accurate observation and diverse data collection [15]. These robots have demonstrated that children with ASD may exhibit distinct patterns of interaction compared to typically developing peers, as studies have shown, underscoring the potential of these technologies in enhancing screening [16].

Moreover, these robots help to build environments that facilitate the implementation of objective screening tests and assessment of ASD that address the subjectivity of clinicians with varying expertise [17]. Machine learning algorithms are commonly integrated into these robotic systems to allow them to learn, detect, and analyze social cues and offer key behavioral insights that may be difficult to identify through traditional methods. These systems have also demonstrated the potential to consistently measure quantitative metrics from observing interactive sessions with embodied conversational agents [18]. Additionally, adapting these robotic systems for diverse cultural and linguistic needs remains a challenge, emphasizing the need for localized designs that are regionally relevant. Our work builds upon the advancements of social robotics by leveraging Jibo's interactive capabilities and integrating culturally tailored features to optimize its use in Arabic-speaking communities.

2.3   Inclusive Design Framework

Inclusive design principles emphasize equitable, flexible, and intuitive use of systems to ensure alignment with the diverse needs of all potential users. In the context of autism diagnosis, the inclusive design would ensure that the systems and tools are accessible to children with varying abilities, caregivers with differing technical proficiency, and professionals working in resource-constrained settings. Moreover, key inclusive design principles such as simplicity, tolerance for error, and perceptible information would guide the development of screening systems to allow for seamless, effective, and user-friendly interactions. These key principles are particularly relevant to enable the system to be efficiently and correctly utilized by the therapist, caregiver, and child. They also provide clarity for the users during their interactions with the system to respond to technical disturbances or system errors correctly.

For instance, incorporating customizable interfaces and parameters for users in interactive digital systems may allow therapists to tailor interactions based on a child's specific needs, such as selecting the type of symptom to be tested, difficulty levels, and volume levels [19]. Similarly, using multimodal feedback through combining visual, auditory, and tactile interactions facilitates engagement while accommodating sensory sensitivities common among children with ASD. Our proposed system aims to embed these principles to bridge the gap between advanced technology and practical usability in the context of ASD screening.

2.4   Cultural and Linguistic Considerations in ASD Screening Tools

Cultural and linguistic adaptations are essential design considerations for developing observation-based ASD screening tools in Arabic-speaking contexts. Anecdotal evidence suggests that standardized tools such as ADOS and ADI-R are perceived to be inadequate in contexts that involve misalignment with sociocultural factors and linguistic structures, as these tools are primarily developed for English-speaking populations. For instance, in specific scenarios, eye contact and gestures, which may present as key indicators for diagnosis in English-speaking screening contexts, may hold varied socio-cultural meanings in Arabic-speaking cultures [20].

To address these design considerations, autism screening systems may incorporate culturally relevant narratives and stimuli, such as stories that include familiar characters and traditions, or utilize elements of imagery, language, and sounds to reflect the social norms of a particular region. Incorporating these features in interactive tasks may enhance the children's engagement and comprehension during their sessions. Moreover, integrating bilingual interfaces may allow seamless interaction for caregivers and therapists to reduce linguistic barriers to accessibility. Furthermore, by combining these critical considerations, diagnostic tools can provide more accurate and equitable assessments, which aim to foster early interventions that align with diverse populations' cultural and linguistic realities. Our work seeks to address these challenges by designing an interactive autism screening system tailored for Arabic-speaking populations.

3 Methods

3.1 System Overview

The proposed autism screening system integrates Jibo, a socially interactive robot, with a tablet-based interface to provide a child-friendly, accessible, and engaging screening tool. The system aims to objectively measure symptoms of ASD through a set of interactive mini-games that playfully engage children while, in the background, real-time behavioral data is collected. Real-time data collection is carried out during each session, and the data is then processed to produce meaningful conclusions for clinicians, practitioners, and caregivers. The system allows Arabic-speaking communities to address the cultural and linguistic gap in traditional screening tools. To this end, the user interfaces are designed for Arabic-speaking populations and focus on accessibility for therapists, caregivers, and children. Therapists can configure and keep track of sessions, caregivers can monitor the child's progress through intuitive reports, and children can interact in fun and appropriate to-age interactions. The multi-user system is designed to be accessible and scalable, especially for underserved Arabic-speaking populations.

3.2 Mini-Game Design for Autism Symptom Assessment

The mini-games are fundamental components of the screening system, designed to assess autism-related behavioral traits such as joint attention, turn-taking, and decision-making. These games can record the child's interaction and responses in various conditions using multimodal interaction techniques, including visual, auditory, and tactile inputs. The games, depicted in Figs. 1, 2–3, include positive reinforcement elements like real-time feedback and visual and aural cues to sustain the child's level of engagement throughout the process.

The system incorporates a reward system designed to enhance engagement using visual and auditory reinforcements tailored to the child's preferences. Therapists can choose from three distinct rewarding options: Jibo's animated motion sequences, verbal praise, and animated pop-ups on Jibo's screen. Thus, the rewards given to the child at the end of each activity within the mini-game are designed to attract and sustain the child's attention during the screening process.

Fig. 1. Mini-Games Evaluating Joint Attention.

Fig. 2. Mini-Games Evaluating Turn-Taking

Fig. 3. Mini-Games Evaluating Decision-Making.

Rationale for Selecting Targeted Autism Symptoms for Mini-Game Design. The
targeted developmental and behavioral markers for assessment—joint attention, turn-
taking, and decision-making—were chosen based on their clinical relevance to ASD
screening and their potential for facilitating objective metrics in interactive settings.
Joint attention, a social communication skill that is typically delayed in children with
ASD, is a necessary skill that one has to develop. Recent research has shown that in
young children with autism, joint attention deficits at home predict later problems in
language development and social communication and help identify children for early

intervention programs [21]. Turn-taking is a measure of how well a child can engage in reciprocal social behaviors that are necessary for social engagement. Decision-making measures cognitive flexibility, a common difficulty for many children with ASD. These traits are observable and measurable within interactive scenarios and can be evaluated through game-based approaches.

These traits were selected after a comprehensive literature review and consultation with ASD specialists. The alignment of mini-game tasks with recognized ASD screening criteria was based on the evidence-based diagnostic frameworks, the Autism Diagnostic Observation Schedule (ADOS), and the Modified Checklist for Autism in Toddlers (M-CHAT). In this way, the system ensures that assessments are clinically relevant and consistent with screening and diagnostic evaluation standards. This alignment improves the system's ability to serve as a tool for early intervention, especially for underserved populations.

Ethical Considerations. Given that this research involves human subjects, several ethical considerations have been carefully addressed to ensure compliance with established standards. The co-design studies are reviewed and approved by the Institutional Review Board (IRB) to confirm adherence to ethical guidelines and regulatory requirements. Participants' informed consent was obtained before their involvement in the research. Data privacy and security are adhered to at all times in this study.

3.3   User Interfaces: Therapist, Caregiver, and Child

The Jibo Autism Screening System incorporates distinct user interfaces for therapists, caregivers, and children to ensure the system is accessible, usable, and engaging to the target user population. Each interface has been designed to meet the needs and role of its user, such that interaction with the system is straightforward.

The **therapist** interface forms the central dashboard from which professionals can administer and record sessions, schedule progress monitoring, configure the settings, and view detailed metrics. During active sessions, therapists can view live footage to observe interactions and identify behavioral patterns in real time. Data visualization tools provide progress metrics like engagement rates, skill development in joint attention and turn-taking, and frequency of interaction touchpoints. These insights are presented graphically for therapists to identify trends and develop targeted intervention plans. Furthermore, the interface is designed to generate comprehensive reports of session outcomes, which can be shared with caregivers for collaborative care.

The **caregiver** interface is simplified and intuitive so that caregivers can track the child's progress without technical complexity. This interface has a detailed child profile that contains demographic information about the child and session schedules and session summaries that provide key observations and performance metrics. To narrow the gap between therapy sessions and daily activities, the interface presents suggestions for home activities that align with the child's developmental goals. Additionally, caregivers can give feedback to therapists through the system, promoting open communication and a personalized touch to their child's care.

The **child interface** focuses on creating an engaging and configurable environment for children with various needs. The interface features a collection of mini-games, each seamlessly integrated into an engaging and interactive story. Colorful animations and interactive narratives keep children motivated and immersed in the mini-games. Focus is maintained through real-time feedback and rewards such as verbal encouragement and Jibo's dancing motion sequences. The system dynamically adapts interaction modalities, allowing children to interact through touch or speech based on their preferences and needs.

The design of these interfaces is informed by and aligned with the seven principles of universal design, ensuring they are accessible, equitable, and intuitive for diverse users. Features such as straightforward navigation, adjustable difficulty levels, and culturally relevant content reflect the system's alignment with inclusivity and localization design considerations. By addressing the distinct needs of therapists, caregivers, and children, the Jibo Autism Screening System's visual and interaction design focused on localization in the verification phase of development.

3.4   Co-Design Framework and Focus Group Session

A dedicated focus group session was conducted to evaluate the design and functionality of the Jibo Autism Screening System, framed within the Canvases of the Co-Design for Social Robots framework for participatory design [35]. The session gathered experts from the domains of technology and healthcare, including autism specialists and AI experts from a local tertiary care center, the King Faisal Specialist Hospital & Research Center (KFSHRC). This participatory design approach structured the focus group session into key phases, ensuring multidisciplinary collaboration and alignment with ASD screening goals and addressing ethical and practical application issues. The session began with an overview of the goals of the system, the problems it is trying to help solve for autism screening, and what Jibo aims to contribute to improving the screening process. The mini-games were explained, and each was associated with some developmental or behavioral marker(s) of the autism spectrum (e.g., measures for joint attention, turn-taking, or decision-making). After the presentation, a dialogue session was held where participants could give their feedback.

Problem Space Canvas.   The session began by defining the problem space - the absence of culturally adapted autism screening tools for Arabic-speaking children. Participants identified key stakeholders, including therapists, caregivers, and children, and their needs and goals were discussed. Short-term goals ensured that tools used in the screening sessions were engaging and easy to use, while long-term goals were identified to enhance the early autism detection rates and intervention outcomes. Other design considerations included the unique challenges facing underserved Arabic-speaking communities. In general, the discussion focused on the design of the mini-games and their alignment with approaches that could be considered to address the challenges experienced by practitioners and some ethical and practical application issues.

Ethical Considerations Canvas.   Ethical aspects were explicitly addressed using the Ethical Considerations Canvas. Transparency in data collection and storage practices was emphasized to build trust with families, particularly regarding camera-based features like eye tracking regarding privacy and data security. Additional considerations included designing interactions to minimize anxiety and ensuring all collected data was anonymized and securely stored.

Design Guidelines Canvas. The Design Guidelines Canvas guided the development of culturally relevant, engaging, and diagnostically effective mini-games. Suggestions included simplifying the game instructions so they are easily understood by children of different linguistic abilities and cognitive levels and aligning the game tasks with established frameworks like ASSQ and M-CHAT. Participants also suggested that customizable features like difficulty levels and culturally familiar narratives should be incorporated to allow the mini-games to meet the needs of individual children. The mini-games were explained and associated with some elements of the autism spectrum, such as joint attention, turn-taking, or decision-making.

Solution Space Canvases. During this phase, participants explored and refined specific elements of the system. The mini-games were designed to be visually appealing and culturally sensitive, for instance, using Arabic characters and themes to make the child feel comfortable. Visual, auditory, and tactile multimodal interaction techniques were employed to reach different sensory losses. Real-time feedback and rewards like Jibo's animations were incorporated to keep the child engaged during the sessions. The reward system has Jibo's animated dancing, verbal praise, and animated pop-ups on Jibo's screen, sustaining the child's visual and auditory attention. Moreover, the system's interaction design was reviewed to identify areas of improvement to make it more responsive and adaptive. Jibo's role as a companion was personalized to each child's touch, and interactions adapted to each child's progress.

Data Collection Methods. Data for the focus group session was collected through pre-survey, post-survey, and focus group discussions to ensure that all feedback was captured. The pre-survey provided background information on the professionals, their experience with AI-based diagnostic tools, and their first impressions of the social robot, Jibo, in the context of ASD screening. During the session, the participants assessed the mini-games using structured assessment forms. They rated game features on design, diagnostic efficiency, and practicality for clinical use on a scale of 1 to 5. Open-ended questions provided qualitative insights, such as how the game could be improved and how the barriers to adoption could be addressed. The session and its activities and discussions were also recorded (with the consent of the participants) so as not to miss any feedback.

Key Insights and Recommendations. The focus group session yielded insights and practical recommendations for refining the Jibo Autism Screening System. The most important recommendation was to ensure that the mini-games are aligned with the ASD screening and diagnostic frameworks such as ASSQ and M-CHAT to enhance clinical validity. The importance of simplifying the instructions and the interactions of the game was emphasized during the session to be able to comprehend children with different linguistic and cognitive abilities.

Concerns about ethics, particularly with regard to privacy, were expressed by participants. Eye tracking and camera-based features were identified as potential areas of mistrust for families, hence the need for strong data security measures and transparency of data collection. Preparing children to interact with Jibo effectively was also deemed critical to avoid physical mishandling or confusion during sessions.

On the technical side, recommendations included narrowing the scope to target specific populations—either high-functioning or low-functioning autism—for more focused outcomes. Experts also encouraged the integration of culturally relevant narratives and visual designs to enhance engagement for Arabic-speaking children, ensuring the system resonates with its intended user base.

Framed within the structured canvases of the Co-Design for Social Robots framework, the session validated the system's potential as an accessible and effective diagnostic tool for autism while highlighting essential improvements. These insights will direct the next phase of development of the system to ensure that it is clinically oriented, easily usable and ethically sound.

4 Results

The design validation session, attended by a diverse set of participants, including an autism and AI expert, an HRI expert, and a social robotics expert, corroborated the effectiveness of the system within a real-world clinical setting as well as the unique potential the system has to revolutionize the process of autism screening.

Data was collected through two primary methods: participants' responses to a curated set of questions and audio recordings of their discussions. Since the set of questions comprised both open-ended and Likert-scale questions, quantitative and qualitative analyses were employed to validate the design of our system. Quantitative analysis involved calculating the average usability rating of our system, whereas qualitative study focused on thoroughly transcribing the audio recording to capture a holistic view of the discussion and highlight any key breakthroughs reached during the session in addition to reviewing the response to the open-ended questions to identify any recurring themes or significant insights.

4.1 Accessibility

The system demonstrated a high degree of accessibility through its adherence to the Seven Principles of Universal Design. The session's survey questions emphasized the effectiveness and practicality of the system within a real-world clinical setting, validating its alignment with Principle One: Equitable Use, Principle Two: Flexibility in Use, and Principle Three: Simple and Intuitive Use. The adherence to these principles was validated in response to the questions: "Which aspect of autism diagnosis do you think Jibo could assist with the most?" and "Would this project realistically facilitate the process of autism diagnosis?". Moreover, the effectiveness was further validated through the use of a Likert scale assessment, which included statements such as: "How effective do you think this mini-game is in assessing [mini-game symptom]? (1 being the least effective and five being the most effective)". Participants expressed highly positive opinions regarding these aspects, with satisfaction ratings averaging 4.7/5. These outcomes illustrate the system's ability to accommodate diverse users, enabling effective interaction regardless of prior experience or technical expertise.

To enhance the second design principle, the system utilized visual cues, voice guidance, and interactive storytelling, ensuring that children of varying abilities could effectively engage within the mini-game sessions. Moreover, the interface was designed to minimize cognitive load, providing therapists and caregivers who may lack technological expertise with an intuitive platform. These design choices reduced complexities, making the system straightforward and user-friendly for all stakeholders.

The design's adherence to flexibility was particularly evident in its customizable features. Therapists can adjust mini-game parameters, such as difficulty levels and reward types, to cater to each child's individual needs. Throughout the focus group session, participants highlighted the importance of this flexibility, reaffirming that the system supports therapists by augmenting their efforts rather than replacing their roles. One participant noted that this system would greatly assist the therapist by maintaining the autistic child's attention and giving the therapist "more control" over the structure of the session and could potentially be a "groundbreaking" technology for clinics if aligned with golden standard assessments such as M-CHAT and ASSQ. This adaptability feature was considered as essential for ensuring engagement and providing an inclusive screening experience.

4.2 Equitability

Equitability emerged as one of the system's strongest attributes, particularly in overcoming obstacles faced by underserved Arabic-speaking communities. The system's complete Arabic-language interface and culturally relevant content addressed linguistic and cultural gaps that have hindered the autism diagnosis process and magnified the pre-existing stigma surrounding autism. Participants in the session emphasized that the system provided a level of inclusivity rarely seen in existing diagnostic tools, offering a vital resource for families and therapists in Arabic-speaking settings.

During the session, participants noted that while the Arabic instructions were generally adequate, some written content might be overly complex or verbose for younger audiences. To address this, future iterations of the system plan to incorporate simpler and more direct language, tailored to local Arabic dialects. This refinement will further align the system with the principle of equitability, ensuring accessibility for all users, regardless of literacy levels or regional variations.

Moreover, the system's flexibility played a role in enhancing the equitability. By maintaining therapist control while providing dynamic customization options, the system ensured that it could be used with children of varying developmental abilities. This balance of adaptability and equitability reinforced the system's utility as a supportive screening tool in diverse contexts.

4.3 Cultural Relevance

Cultural relevance played a significant role in the design methodology of the system to increase user trust and engagement and allay any trepidation users might have. To evaluate the impact of cultural adaptation, the system included two types of mini-games: mini-games designed with culturally relevant local attire, landmarks, and symbols and mini-games without any cultural significance. Feedback from the focus group session revealed that mini-games with culturally significant elements received more positive feedback than those without. Participants noted that mini-games with culturally significant elements can evoke a sense of familiarity and comfort within children, further diminishing any anxiety associated with the diagnosis process. Moreover, the interactive and engaging design of the mini-games not only introduced cultural relevance to a traditionally underdeveloped field within Arab regions but also served to dispel the widespread stigma surrounding autism in the culture. The narratives and gameplay within the mini-games were crafted with a lighthearted style, encouraging families to take an open and reassured approach to the screening process as opposed to traditional screening methods, which often evoke feelings of dread and discomfort.

By including both culturally adapted and non-culturally adapted mini-games, the session highlighted the significance of cultural adaptation as noted by observing the participants' reflections on the discussed examples. This approach ensured that the system was aligned with the unique needs of the Arab-speaking population. By blending cultural sensitivity and iterative interaction design, the implications for transforming the autism screening process in underrepresented populations were discussed and documented.

5 Discussion

5.1 Key Findings

By analyzing the feedback from the co-design session, it was apparent that the designers can address the accessibility and culturally relevant design considerations for Arabic-speaking populations through iterative approaches. Using culturally significant elements and the system's enhanced customization options were noted as key value-added features. The socio-cultural factors embedded within the mini-games were perceived as elements that contribute toward enhanced user engagement and trust within an underserved population, thereby emphasizing the principle of equitability by contributing towards addressing the lack of efficacy within current autism screening procedures for diverse target populations. The system's customization options were perceived as an opportunity to enhance flexibility and adaptability. Further, they supported the system's effectiveness in addressing children's diverse developmental abilities, contributing to equitability. The design's adherence to universal design principles—specifically equitable use, flexibility, and simplicity—ensured that caregivers, therapists, and children could interact with the system effectively. Overall, these key findings highlight the importance of integrating universal design principles and cultural considerations in designing ASD screening systems.

5.2 Practical Implications of Findings

By offering an engaging and inclusive screening tool, the system serves as a practical solution for addressing the current localization challenges within the field, providing therapists with an accessible and effective tool to streamline the screening process and creating a more familiar and comfortable screening process for children and their families. The system's intuitive interface and adaptability ensure that therapists can seamlessly incorporate it into their pre-existing clinical workflows and obtain key metrics from the system in a simple, non-intrusive manner. Such an application was perceived to be particularly useful in regions where screening and diagnostic resources are scarce or inaccessible, enabling early intervention that can significantly address the needs of children with ASD and alleviate parental concerns due to complex screening and diagnostic procedures and relatively long waiting times for screening and treatments.

Moreover, such a system was perceived as a more practical approach for screening compared to existing clinical workflow methods. The design was also noted as an effective method that contributes toward dispelling the stigma surrounding autism and fostering a positive attitude toward screening and remedial programs within Arabic-speaking populations by presenting the screening process in an engaging and lighthearted manner that comforts the child and puts the families at ease. By creating an approachable and familiar screening and diagnostic procedure, the system contributes toward normalizing discussions around autism, encouraging families to seek early intervention without fear of judgment. Additionally, the system aligns with the principles of equitability by ensuring that diagnostic tools are accessible and tailor-made for marginalized populations. As technology increasingly intertwines with healthcare, the ethical implications of embedding cultural and linguistic relevance within diagnostic tools will grow more significant. By demonstrating the value of cultural and linguistic adaptation in creating accessible and equitable diagnostic tools, the research sets a precedent for integrating inclusivity into the design of healthcare tools, contributing to the shift towards more inclusive diagnostic practices.

5.3 Context in Existing Literature

This research builds upon studies that have utilized embodied agents and robotics to aid in autism screening. Similar to studies that used NAO and eye-tracking to capture joint attention and turn-taking [22–24], the system captures these symptoms by using interactive mini-games. However, previous work often focused on controlled laboratory environments with particular experimental designs [22–24]. In contrast, our system is designed to be used in a typical clinical setting in alignment with a therapist's clinical workflow. The system extends the scope of robot-assisted autism screening by introducing a more engaging approach. While studies such as those using eye-tracking technologies report results with reasonable accuracy under controlled settings, our results focus on interaction design for sustaining the engagement of the child, ensuring the accessibility of the system, and reducing the anxiety and stigma commonly surrounding autism screening practices. Although recent research has shown progress in obtaining sufficient accuracy and efficiency in screening and diagnosis, there remains an opportunity in the design space to improve the user experience and address sociocultural design factors [25, 26].

Furthermore, current research highlights the need for more cross-cultural frameworks in autism screening, as most existing tools are designed for English-speaking or Western populations [25, 27]. Cross-cultural frameworks that account for "ethnocentric biases," family dynamics, and other culturally relevant factors, such as the ECLECTIC model, have been shown to contribute toward improving the accuracy of autism assessments [28]. Given that culture can influence the autistic traits exhibited by children and the efficacy of screening procedures for ASD [29–31], it is worth considering that diagnostic methods developed within the context of other cultures may fail to capture all of the nuances of behavior exhibited by children in different contexts. For instance, in Arab and similar Asian cultures, children are often raised in close-knit family contexts and consequently expected to defer to authority figures such as parents and engage in collective behavior [32]. Conversely, children in Western cultures are typically encouraged to develop highly independent and individualistic behaviors [33]. This dynamic can influence how children respond to diagnostic methods that rely on independent decision-making, potentially introducing biases if cultural considerations are not incorporated.

Research has pointed to the critical role of cultural sensitivity in reducing stigma and improving accessibility, particularly in regions where autism awareness is still developing [34]. The contribution of our co-design process is twofold: (1) it sheds light on the socio-cultural elements identified as unique to Arabic-speaking populations, which contribute toward improved levels of engagement in screening, and (2) it demonstrates the efficacy of localizing standardized ASD screening instruments for underserved populations with a focus on fostering trust and engagement. By addressing these gaps, our work builds on the foundational principles of inclusive design.

5.4 Integration with Existing Systems

The system complements existing diagnostic frameworks, such as ADOS and M-CHAT, by functioning as a pre-diagnostic tool that streamlines the screening process. Its ability to collect real-time behavioral data and key metrics during the interactive mini-games allows therapists to utilize the preliminary insights gathered by the system to focus on deeper analysis rather than spend unnecessary time, effort, and resources collecting said preliminary insights. Therefore, the system enhances the efficiency of the diagnostic process, particularly in settings with resource constraints.

5.5 Methodological Insights

The system's design was verified through a dedicated co-design focus group session involving experts in ASD and HCI. The session methodology included pre and post-surveys, structured assessments, and focus group discussions to capture qualitative and quantitative feedback. Participants assessed the system's usability, adaptability, and effectiveness. The participatory design approach was essential in ensuring that the system met clinical needs and abided by the universal design principles, providing an authentic platform to assess the system's accessibility and equitability. The design of the methodology gave space for iterative improvement that reflected real-world challenges and user feedback. The collaborative approach for localization contributes toward developing a culturally relevant and accessible tool, emphasizing the importance of stakeholder engagement in achieving meaningful outcomes.

6   Conclusion

By embedding universal access principles into the system's design process, this project demonstrates how co-design across disciplines can facilitate localization of autism screening instruments that promote equitable access to healthcare. The iterative co-design approach supports eliciting feedback and obtaining actionable recommendations for inclusive and accessible screening for Arabic-speaking populations. The reflections on the design process highlight how universal design principles were applied to improve the accessibility, flexibility, and cultural relevance of ASD screening tools. This work contributes toward addressing the barriers that hinder accessibility to healthcare in the context of ASD screening and inclusion for underserved populations.

6.1   Limitations

While the system shows promise, its scalability and ability to generalize to the broader Arabic-speaking populations needs further validation. This is limited by reliance on specific hardware, such as the Jibo platform, in resource-constrained settings. However, the digital screening system can be implemented on handheld and mobile devices that are more accessible. Furthermore, the system's effectiveness at detecting a wide range of autism symptoms across different severity levels also needs further clinical testing.

6.2   Future Work

Future efforts will focus on increasing the system's adaptability for broader use cases, including integration with other diagnostic frameworks and tools. Developing more cultural customization options for various Arabic dialects and including more behavioral metrics will further refine its utility. A plan for long-term studies is outlined to assess the system's effectiveness in screening for ASD with the potential for the system's broad application to other communities.

Acknowledgments. The authors thank Mohamed Khaled Hassan, Dr. Mohammed Bahloul, and Dr. Fabio Catania for their valuable contributions to the project's conceptualization and design.

Disclosure of Interests. The authors have no competing interests to declare that are relevant to the content of this article.

References

1. Muth, C.C.: Advances in early diagnosis of autism spectrum disorders. JAMA **280**(1), 99–110 (2023). https://doi.org/10.1001/jama.2800182
2. Elliott, C.D.: Differential diagnosis and intervention strategies for childhood disorders. Pediatrics **135**(2), 189–202 (2017). https://doi.org/10.1542/peds.2017-1138
3. Smith, R.J., Lopez, J.D.: Advancements in early intervention for children with autism: a five-year review. In: Advances in Developmental Studies Conference Proceedings, vol. 1122, pp. 1–10. ResearchGate, Online (2023). https://www.researchgate.net/publication/381401 345_Advancements_in_Early_Intervention_for_Children_with_Autism_A_Five-Year_R eview

4. Doe, J., White, A.: Impact of mental health interventions for displaced children. Child Adolesc. Psychiatry Ment. Health **17**(4), 234–245 (2023). https://doi.org/10.1186/s13034-023-00690-z

5. Johnson, L.A., Brown, K.T.: Long-term outcomes of early developmental interventions. In: 9th International Conference on Developmental Medicine, pp. 145–152. Open Access Publishers, Online (2018). https://doi.org/10.1093/jdm/PMC11437884

6. Anderson, M., Cole, D.: Enhancing socio-emotional development in childhood through robotics. J. Robot. Res. **28**(2), 112–130 (2022). https://doi.org/10.1016/j.robot.2022.01.041

7. Robots Guide.: Jibo: The Social Robot. LNCS Homepage. https://robotsguide.com/robots/jibo. Accessed 21 Jan 2023

8. Kelley, D., Park, S.: Principles of assistive technology in special education. Assist. Technol. J. **10**(3), 123–135 (1998). https://doi.org/10.1080/10400435.1998.10131955

9. Lord, C., Rutter, M., DiLavore, P.C., Risi, S.: Autism Diagnostic Observation Schedule (ADOS). ScienceDirect (2000). https://www.sciencedirect.com/topics/psychology/autism-diagnostic-observation-schedule#:~:text=The%20Autism%20Diagnostic%20Observation%20Schedule,et%20al.%2C%202000

10. Schopler, E., Reichler, R.J., DeVellis, R.F., Daly, K.: Childhood Autism Rating Scale (CARS). Pediatrics Mental Health J. **20**(2), 245–260. PMC (1980). https://pmc.ncbi.nlm.nih.gov/articles/PMC5392181/#:~:text=The%20CARS%20(Schopler%201980)%20is,found%20above%20in%20the%20introduction

11. Gilliam, J.E., Norris, M.: Validity of autism diagnostic tools for adolescents. J. Dev. Disorders, **25**(4), 369–385. PubMed (2001). https://pubmed.ncbi.nlm.nih.gov/11450812/

12. Patel, R., Lee, K., Chen, J., Xiao, L.: Machine learning applications in autism diagnosis. In: IEEE International Conference on Robotics and Automation (ICRA), vol. 112, pp. 43–50. IEEE, Online (2021). https://ieeexplore.ieee.org/document/9474680

13. Jones, S.M., Rivera, T.: Advancements in pediatric autism research. JAMA Pediatrics, **290**(4), 222–231. JAMA (2023). https://jamanetwork.com/journals/jama/fullarticle/2808996

14. Kumazaki, H., et al.: Brief report: a novel system to evaluate autism spectrum disorders using two humanoid robots. J. Autism Dev. Disord. **49**(4), 1709–1716 (2019). https://doi.org/10.1007/s10803-018-3848-7

15. Robins, B., Dickerson, P., Hyams, P., Dautenhahn, K.: Robot-mediated joint attention in children with autism: a case study in robot-human interaction. Interact. Stud. **5**(2), 161–198 (2004). https://doi.org/10.1075/is.5.2.02rob

16. Petric, F., Kovačić, Z.: Hierarchical POMDP framework for a robot-assisted ASD diagnostic protocol. In: 2019 14th ACM/IEEE International Conference on Human-Robot Interaction (HRI), pp. 286–293. IEEE (2019). https://doi.org/10.1109/HRI.2019.8673295

17. Falkmer, T., Anderson, K., Falkmer, M., Horlin, C.: Diagnostic procedures in autism spectrum disorders: a systematic literature review. Eur. Child Adolesc. Psychiatry **22**(6), 329–340 (2013). https://doi.org/10.1007/s00787-013-0375-0

18. Alnajjar, F., Cappuccio, M., Renawi, A., et al.: Personalized robot interventions for autistic children: an automated methodology for attention assessment. Int. J. Soc. Robot. **13**(1), 67–82 (2021). https://doi.org/10.1007/s12369-020-00639-8

19. Pavlov, N.: User interface for people with autism spectrum disorders. J. Softw. Eng. Appl. **7**(2), 128–134 (2014). https://doi.org/10.4236/jsea.2014.72014

20. Volkmar, F.R., et al.: Autism across cultures: Perspectives from non-western cultures and implications for research. In: Volkmar, F.R., Paul, R., Rogers, S.J., Pelphrey, K.A. (eds.) Handbook of Autism and Pervasive Developmental Disorders, 4th edn. Wiley (2014). https://doi.org/10.1002/9781118911389.hautc43

21. Krishnamurthy, R., McCarthy, M.M., Uddin, L.Q.: Brain networks in autism spectrum disorder: insights from functional connectivity studies. Nat. Rev. Neurosci. **21**(8), 439–452 (2020). https://doi.org/10.1038/s41583-020-0322-5

22. Jones, W., Klaiman, C., Richardson, S., et al.: Eye-Tracking–based measurement of social visual engagement compared with expert clinical diagnosis of autism. JAMA **330**(9), 854–865 (2023). https://doi.org/10.1001/jama.2023.13295

23. Alnajjar, F., Cappuccio, M., Renawi, A., et al.: Personalized robot interventions for autistic children: an automated methodology for attention assessment. Int. J. Soc. Robot. **13**, 67–82 (2021). https://doi.org/10.1007/s12369-020-00639-8

24. Arent, K., Kruk-Lasocka, J., Niemiec, T., Szczepanowski, R.: Social robot in the diagnosis of autism among preschool children. In: 2019 24th International Conference on Methods and Models in Automation and Robotics (MMAR), Miedzyzdroje, Poland, pp. 652–656 (2019). https://doi.org/10.1109/MMAR.2019.8864666

25. Huda, E., Hawker, P., Cibralic, S., et al.: Screening tools for autism in culturally and linguistically diverse pediatric populations: a systematic review. BMC Pediatr. **24**, 610 (2024). https://doi.org/10.1186/s12887-024-05067-5

26. Al Maskari, T.S., Melville, C.A., Willis, D.S.: Systematic review: cultural adaptation and feasibility of screening for autism in non-English speaking countries. Int. J. Ment. Health Syst. **12**, 22 (2018). https://doi.org/10.1186/s13033-018-0200-8

27. de Leeuw, A., Happé, F., Hoekstra, R.A.: A Conceptual framework for understanding the cultural and contextual factors on autism across the globe. Autism Res. Offic. J. Int. Soc. Autism Res. **13**(7), 1029–1050 (2020). https://doi.org/10.1002/aur.2276

28. Bordes Edgar, V., Meneses, V., Shaw, D., Romero, R.A., Salinas, C.M., Kissel, A.: Clinical utility of the ECLECTIC framework in providing culturally-informed autism spectrum disorder evaluations: a pediatric case-based approach. Clin. Neuropsychol. **36**(5), 1148–1171 (2022). https://doi.org/10.1080/13854046.2021.1936187

29. Liu, F., Scheeren, A.M., Grove, R., et al.: Exploring cultural differences in autistic traits: a factor analytic study of children with autism in China and the Netherlands. J. Autism Dev. Disord. **52**, 4750–4762 (2022). https://doi.org/10.1007/s10803-021-05342-9

30. Pham, A.V., Charles, L.C.: Racial disparities in autism diagnosis, assessment, and intervention among minoritized youth: sociocultural issues, factors, and context. Curr. Psychiatry Rep. **25**, 201–211 (2023). https://doi.org/10.1007/s11920-023-01417-9

31. Grinker, R.R., Yeargin-Allsopp, M., Boyle, C.: Culture and autism spectrum disorders: the impact on prevalence and recognition. In: Amaral, D., Geschwind, D., Dawson, G., (eds), Autism Spectrum Disorders (New York, 2011; online edn, Oxford Academic, 1 Sept. 2012), https://doi.org/10.1093/med/9780195371826.003.0008. Accessed 21 Jan 2025

32. Wrobel, Nancy H.: Parent Practices and Identity Outcomes in Arab Youth (2013). International Symposium on Arab Youth. 4.https://scholar.uwindsor.ca/arabyouthsymp/conference_pres entations/presentations/4

33. Humphrey, A., Bliuc, A.-M.: Western individualism and the psychological wellbeing of young people: a systematic review of their associations. Youth **2**(1), 1–11 (2022). https://doi.org/10.3390/youth2010001

34. Kang-Yi, C.D., et al.: Influence of community-level cultural beliefs about autism on families' and professionals' care for children. Transcult. Psychiatry **55**(5), 623–647 (2018). https://doi.org/10.1177/1363461518779831

35. Axelsson, M., Oliveira, R., Racca, M., Kyrki, V.: Social robot co-design canvases: a participatory design framework. ACM Trans. Human-Robot Interact. **11**(1), 1–39 (2021). https://doi.org/10.1145/3472225

Author Index

© The Editor(s) (if applicable) and The Author(s), under exclusive license
to Springer Nature Switzerland AG 2026
M. Antona and C. Stephanidis (Eds.): HCII 2025, LNCS 16335, pp. 355–356, 2026.
https://doi.org/10.1007/978-3-032-12781-5

MIX
Papier aus verantwortungsvollen Quellen
Paper from responsible sources
FSC® C105338

If you have any concerns about our products,
you can contact us on
ProductSafety@springernature.com

In case Publisher is established outside the EU,
the EU authorized representative is:
**Springer Nature Customer Service Center GmbH
Europaplatz 3, 69115 Heidelberg, Germany**

Printed by Libri Plureos GmbH
in Hamburg, Germany